WINFIELD TOWNLEY SCOTT

by SCOTT DONALDSON

UNIVERSITY OF TEXAS PRESS  AUSTIN & LONDON

THIS BOOK IS PUBLISHED WITH THE ASSISTANCE OF THE

Dan Danciger Publication Fund

8 11.2
D71 P
89387
July 1974

Library of Congress Cataloging in Publication Data

Donaldson, Scott.
   Poet in America: Winfield Townley Scott.
   Bibliography: p.
   1. Scott, Winfield Townley, 1910–1968.   I. Title.
PS3537.C943Z65   811'.'2 [B]   75–38568
ISBN 0–292–76400–6

Composition and printing by The University of Texas
   Printing Division, Austin
Binding by Universal Bookbindery, Inc., San Antonio

This book is for Chase

CONTENTS

ILLUSTRATIONS

PREFACE

What I had in mind at first, shortly after hearing of Win Scott's death in April 1968, was to write a critical evaluation of his poetry. This (I must have thought) would somehow serve as a substitute for the letter never sent, the phone call unplaced, the visit to his home in Santa Fe silently contemplated before dropping off to sleep. Scott's poems had moved and shaken me, and it would have cost little to let him know that. But one resists intruding, so there was no letter or call or visit. As I learned more about him and became caught up in the fascination of discovery that motivates detectives and historians, my objective changed: I would write a life, illuminating it with Scott's poetry. Finally, it developed that his story was in many ways characteristic of the not particularly happy condition of the artist in contemporary American society. So, in writing his life, I have tried to say something, without pointing, about the American artist and the culture he uneasily inhabits.

Winfield Townley Scott was bitched by that culture, first through a middle-class, female-dominated childhood in which he was pampered, protected, and provided with enough phobic tendencies to ruin several lives, and then as the adult in whose work "most-people," to borrow Cummings's phrase, found little to value, and about whose willingness to be supported by his wife they were disposed to shake their heads. Or so it seemed to Scott himself, inescapably a creature of his time and place and hence prone to share judgments and wonderings he knew should not matter. Doubting himself, fearing he was a fraud, and lacking the ego-strength to survive the onslaughts of doubt and fear, he died their emasculated victim.

So, if it is true, as James Dickey has written, that "the only excuse for a book on an American poet is for the book to be some kind of *manifesto* as well,"[1] there is its manifesto. There, too, is one answer to the question I have heard hundreds of times, "How did you happen to do a biography of Winfield Townley Scott?" with its unstated assumption that the life of a poet, especially if less well known than T. S. Eliot or Robert Frost, hardly bears examination.

I have put down everything I know for sure about Scott, which while by no means all will have to be enough, and which for some will be a good deal more than enough. I've suppressed nothing that seems of any importance whatever. For a rationale on this point, one that Win Scott would have warmly approved, here is Augie March, on the second paragraph of his own story: "Everyone knows there is no fineness or accuracy of suppression; if you hold down one thing you hold down the adjoining." Some things, of course, one cannot know and must guess at. Scott was a complicated man, and I've had occasionally to try to solve riddles, comforted by what Emily Dickinson saw the truth of, that "The riddle we can guess/ We speedily despise."

But there has been less guesswork than one might suppose. From his fourteenth year on, Scott—or, doubtless at first, his doting female relatives—saved everything. In Brown University's collection of this lifetime of written artifacts repose scrapbooks of high school and college writings, manuscripts of his poems and essays, and the letters written to him by nearly nine hundred correspondents. Part of the man can be found there, but those unwilling to dig and scrape can turn instead to his poems. For, as Win wrote when reading page proofs of his *Collected Poems* in 1962, "my discovery in doing the job is, to put it simply, that the book is an autobiography. . . . Even the 'objective,' portrait, poems almost all come out of my life."[2]

In puzzling over the riddles, I have had the help of a great many people eager to demonstrate their feeling for Win Scott by answering queries, sending me copies of letters from him, submitting to interviews, and sometimes reading portions of this book in manuscript form. The limitations of space prevent my naming all, or

[1] James Dickey to SD, 15 December 1969.
[2] WTS to Charles H. Philbrick, 8 February 1962, Scott Collection, John Hay Library, Brown University.

even most, of these people; they know who they are, and, however mutely, I thank them.

But my debt to some, for their insight and assistance, cannot go unacknowledged. These include Ben and Betty Bagdikian, Paul and Frances Chadwick, John Ciardi, Ben C. Clough, Janet Donaldson, Thomas W. Duncan, George P. Elliott, Donald D. Eulert, Walker Gibson, Jackson George, Horace and Marya Gregory, Paul Horgan, Linnell Jones, Justin and Anne Bernays Kaplan, J. C. Levenson, Hilary and Polly Masters, Tom and Susan Scott Mayer, Frank and Christine Merchant, Norman Holmes Pearson, the late Charles H. Philbrick, James Purdy, M. L. Rosenthal, Webster Schott, Lindsay Scott, Daniel Smythe, Herbert Stern, Bradford Swan, Victor Ullman, Mrs. Elizabeth Werner, and Robert and Jeannette Wolfe.

For Scott's letters to Lee Anderson, Paul Horgan, James Purdy, and the late William Carlos Williams, I am indebted to Donald C. Gallup, supervisor of the American literature collection at Yale's Beinecke Library (and for permission to read the Scott-to-Williams correspondence, to James Laughlin); for his letters to Malcolm Cowley, a debt is owed Amy Nyholm of the Newberry Library; for those to Horace Gregory, to Jack T. Ericson of the Carnegie Library, Syracuse University; for those to Fredric Klees, to Mr. Klees and to James Govay of the Swarthmore College Library; for those to Dilys Laing, to Alexander Laing, and to Kenneth C. Cramer and Edward Connery Lathem of the Dartmouth College Libraries; for those to George P. Elliott, to Washington University Libraries, St. Louis; for letters to *Poetry*, to the University of Chicago Libraries; and for copies of applications to the John Simon Guggenheim Memorial Foundation, to Stephen Schlesinger.

Stuart C. Sherman and Mrs. Christine B. Hathaway of the John Hay Library at Brown were extraordinarily kind in opening the materials in the Scott Collection to me. But the most important and revealing documents of all were sent me by the poet's widow, Eleanor: the handwritten journal Scott kept in 1944; a typed journal from 1954, the Scotts' final year at Hampton, Connecticut; typewritten journals kept at the MacDowell Colony in 1965 and 1966, the now-published memoir of Newport called "The Owl in the Hall," and the enlightening and sometimes passionate letters exchanged by Win and Eleanor Scott. All of these materials have now been placed in the Scott Collection at Brown.

Enough cannot be said of what I owe to Mrs. Eleanor Scott. She
has revealed the most confidential communications to me. She has
written intelligent, often brilliant letters about her life with Win.
She has guided me to those who best knew and understood her late
husband. She has hospitably housed and entertained me during several visits to Santa Fe. She has read and criticized the manuscript.
Above all, she has known what most widows might choose not to
know: "that it is not ethically possible to be partially truthful."[3]

Win Scott, who loved to read biography, nonetheless observed
once that death must be a blessed state, "once the biographies and
the studies begin. Can you imagine any writer finding even one
about himself that would seem to him either accurate or fair?"[4] It
is my devout wish, what will never be known, that he might have
found this book an exception.

SCOTT DONALDSON

Lines quoted from *Collected Poems* are reprinted with permission of
The Macmillan Company from *Collected Poems* by Winfield Townley
Scott. © Copyright by Winfield Townley Scott, 1938, 1940, 1941, 1942,
1943, 1945, 1946, 1948, 1949, 1951, 1952, 1953, 1954, 1955, 1957, 1959.
Copyright renewed 1968, 1970 by Winfield Townley Scott. Copyright
renewed 1971 by Eleanor M. Scott.

Quotations from previously unpublished material and letters by William Carlos Williams © copyright 1972 by Florence H. Williams and reprinted with permission.

The following poems from the book *New and Selected Poems*, by Winfield Townley Scott, are reprinted by permission of Doubleday & Co.,
Inc.: "The Mother," copyright 1953 by Beloit Poetry Journal; "The
Ritual," copyright © 1967 by Poetry Northwest; "The Pair," copyright
© 1963 by Desert Review Press; "Variations on a Line by Carlo Bettochi," copyright © 1966 by E G & G, Inc.; "Another Return," copyright
© 1962 by Winfield Townley Scott; "Brief Encounter," copyright ©
1963 by The Little Gallery Press; "Stone-Cutter," copyright © 1967 by
Winfield Townley Scott; "Tender Star," copyright © 1967 by Prescott
College Press; random lines of poetry from "Black Bean Soup with Hot-

[3] EMS to Christine B. Hathaway, 10 February 1969.
[4] WTS, *"a dirty hand": The Literary Notebooks of Winfield Townley Scott*
(1969), p. 41.

POET IN AMERICA: WINFIELD TOWNLEY SCOTT

Note: Three names have been reduced to initials in the footnotes. WTS is Winfield Townley Scott, EM or EMS refers to Eleanor Metcalf (after her marriage, Eleanor Metcalf Scott), and SD is Scott Donaldson.

Sometimes it seems our saddest stories are biographies of 20th Century American writers, Thomas Wolfe, Hart Crane, Vachel Lindsay, Scott Fitzgerald, Edna Millay, Eugene O'Neill, probably Hemingway when we know it. Those are some of the names. And Sinclair Lewis. It would require . . . a combination of psychologist, sociologist, literary historian and critic, as well as an expert in alcoholism, to try to explain why.[1]

1. The Sad Tortoise

WINFIELD TOWNLEY SCOTT wanted to write great poetry. He wrote very good poetry. Perhaps time will show that it was great. It is too soon to tell: he died in 1968. The life of any poet deserves attention, just as his death diminishes us all. But there is another, more important reason why Scott's story should be told: what killed him as much as anything else was his conflict, as an artist, with a culture in whose system of values the artist (unless he was very, very successful in his lifetime) hardly mattered at all. Scott pas-

[1] WTS, "Our Saddest Stories are Biographies," review of *Sinclair Lewis: An American Life*, by Mark Schorer, *New Republic*, 20 November 1961, p. 18.

sionately loved his country, but in the end it helped to destroy him.
His life, like his poetry, was unmistakably, and tragically, American.

Scott published nine books of poetry and one of prose during his
lifetime. (Two posthumous books followed). His poems were widely
anthologized. He won his share of critical awards, though not the
most prestigious ones. He earned the universal respect of his fellow
poets, and the unstinting admiration of some of them. But he died
doubting his work and unable to respect himself, in a bitterness,
a sadness that could admit no remedy:

Note Left

Sex
Art
Death.
      Should I weave
      An acrostic
      Daring us both to read my three
         themes spelled out?[2]

The day of April 26, 1968, began like most others in the last few
years of his life. He slept until 10:15 A.M., ate breakfast, went to the
guest house in back of his handsome adobe home at 550 East
Alameda, Santa Fe, New Mexico, shuffled through his notes to see
if a poem would come. None did. He wrote a friendly letter to Keith
Wilson, a poet teaching at New Mexico State University, inviting
Keith and his wife, Heloise, to stay with the Scotts when they came
for a reading at St. John's College. "Do let us know whatever we can
do here to be of help," Win concluded. "Love to you all."[3] The letter
was the last of his life.

April 26 was the wedding anniversary of Win and Eleanor Scott.
Eleanor had the flu and between household chores, lying down, and
throwing up, she forgot the anniversary, while Win did not: a
reversal of the thoughtless husband, sentimental wife cliché that
might have seemed comic had it not been so ominous—and so
characteristic of the relationship between the Scotts. Win said

[2] WTS, *"a dirty hand": The Literary Notebooks of Winfield Townley Scott*
(1969), p. 158.
[3] WTS to Keith Wilson, 26 April 1968.

nothing to El about it, but scratched on his calendar, next the date, the legend "= 22."

A series of momentous events for him had occurred on the twenty-second of the month: the elopement of his grandfather and grandmother on 22 February 1886; Eleanor's birth on 22 September 1921; his visit to Edwin Arlington Robinson at the MacDowell Colony on 22 August 1929; his marriage to his first wife, Savila Harvey, on 22 May 1933; word that he had been chosen Phi Beta Kappa poet of Harvard on 22 January 1944; and that he had won the Harriet Monroe Memorial Award on 22 October 1966—to cite only a few. "I'm glad Doubleday," he wrote his publishers on 22 March 1964, "—so far anyhow—doesn't put a string of numbers after its address but sticks to New York 22. 22 is the recurring number in my life—all kinds of important days, usually lucky."[4] Eleanor's forgetting their twenty-second anniversary, he was certain, carried special significance.

In the afternoon, the Scotts' youngest child, nine-year-old Douglas, ordered roses sent home with a card, "Happy Anniversary Mom and Dad. Love Dug." Realizing then what a stupid thing she had done, Eleanor apologized. Win said nothing, instead he retreated into the silent dignity that his pipe and his tweeds and his gentleness and his overweight middle-aged body so effectively conveyed. At cocktail hour, some college boys—friends of his oldest son, Lindsay—stopped by to join Scott in his usual bout of afternoon and evening drinking; he became expansive, and Eleanor went to bed hoping that her lapse would not contribute to the deepening depression her husband's apparent serenity could no longer conceal.

It surfaced the next day at the Compound, a restaurant only a few blocks from their home where the Scotts habitually lunched. "Is the idea of being married to me all these years so dreadful that you had to forget our anniversary?" he prodded. Eleanor tried to dodge back into his good graces: what did Win want for his birthday on April 30? "I don't want much," he said, "a pair of slippers—a

[4] WTS to Anne Hutchens, 22 March 1964. The number twenty-two has borne the weight of mystery before. The Millerites expected the end of the world to occur on 22 October 1844, and Joseph Smith took the golden plates of the Book of Mormon from the earth on 22 September 1827. In numerology, "twenty-two is the number of the master . . . of the truly great man" (Richard Cavendish, *The Black Arts* [New York: Capricorn Books, 1967], pp. 53–54).

book or two—don't go to a lot of trouble." The voice was subdued, the manner self-deprecatory, almost sulky. Eleanor was uneasy. But the customary luncheon martinis (Win had two instead of three, remarked "I'm being a good boy today") worked, and his mood improved. He told the waiter they were celebrating their anniversary, and the house sent over a bottle of champagne. It was past three o'clock when they got back from lunch, and Win took the afternoon nap which had become part of his daily routine. They had a party to attend in the evening.[5]

When Win Scott awoke from his nap, the weather had turned cold and raw. Suddenly, he was convinced that the lilacs which brightened all of Santa Fe in spring would not bloom—for the second year in a row. Even the flowers, he thought despondently, were impotent. He did not want to go to the party at Tom Jameson's, but El insisted. The people at the party, she thought, might cheer Win up, and so it seemed. At the Jamesons' he was in top form. He made Lu Adler giggle, entertained others among the thirty guests with literary anecdotes, exuded charm. Fearing Win's jealousy, Eleanor was careful not to talk too long to any of the men at the party. She brought Win a plate of food, but he wouldn't eat it and kept drinking instead. At eleven, when it was time to leave, he asked Bob Saam to come with him and Eleanor for a nightcap.

At home, his geniality dissolved. Win flew into a rage at the mess Dougie and a friend had left in the living room, then could not manage to light the fire in the bedroom: "That's my life in a nutshell." He erupted in a torrent of self-hatred. He was aging, he couldn't write any more, he was no good in bed, his wife needed some one to sleep with, the kids were patently unhappy. "I'm a terrible person," he insisted. "The country is in terrible shape." Everyone would be better off with him dead.

Protesting, Eleanor at one point banged her head against the wall.

"Why are you doing that?" Win asked.

"At least it's real. At least it isn't just imaginary." He had talked death to death, she told him, until it was not real to him any longer.

"You're crazy," he said.

The tension built as Win would not be consoled or shocked back to his senses. Jeannette, the Scotts' teen-age daughter, came in with a date, and the tirade subsided momentarily. But soon the young

[5] EMS to SD, 28 October 1969.

people left, having sensed that something terrible was going on, and Win lashed once more into fury. He accused Eleanor of being unfaithful with Saam (it was not true), and returned time and again to the same refrain, "My wife and children would be better off without me."

"Name us," Eleanor insisted.

"What?"

"Name us—not 'wife and children,' but Eleanor, Jeannette, Douglas."

"That," he responded, "sounds terribly Bennington to me."

Had he talked this way to Dr. Ross (his psychiatrist in Albuquerque), Saam asked? No, and he wouldn't: "that son of a bitch doesn't know anything." All the time Win went back and forth to the kitchen for more drinks.

Neither Eleanor nor Saam remember Win's leaving the room for the last time. But then he was gone, with his pillbox and a bottle, to the guest house. At first Eleanor felt relief: the scene, repeated many times in the last years of his life, was over for one more night. She waited, as was her custom, some forty-five minutes, before going to the guest house to check the pills, remove the bottle, and cover Win up. This time, it was different. Win was unconscious, breathing with desperate irregularity. He had taken at least a dozen sleeping pills, probably more.

The doctor and the ambulance were quickly summoned. But by the time the ambulance arrived, Winfield Townley Scott had followed his broken dreams to oblivion. He was fifty-seven; his body was buried on his fifty-eighth birthday, two days later.[6]

Dr. H. Richard Landmann, Win's physician, certified that he had died at about 2:10 A.M. on 28 April 1968, of a massive circulatory collapse due to ethchlorvynol intoxication. The mixture of immense quantities of liquor with 500-milligram capsules of Placidyl had killed him. A stronger man might have survived, though, as Dr. Landmann points out, "Placidyl's action can be potentiated by alcohol and, therefore, an overdose has only a very narrow range when mixed with alcohol."[7] Whether Win Scott intended to take

[6] Interview, EMS, Santa Fe, 8 September 1969; interview, Robert Saam and Robert Kurth, Santa Fe, 7 September 1969.

[7] Death certificate, Vital Statistics section, New Mexico Health and Social Services department, 3 May 1968; H. Richard Landmann to SD, 12 March

his life can never be known, though there are certain counter-
indications. There were pills remaining in the bottle. He left no
final note. He had been asked to contribute to a Whittier issue of
the *Emerson Society Quarterly*, and to an E. A. Robinson issue of
the *Colby Library Quarterly*. Poetry journals had asked for poems.
His last book, *New and Selected Poems*, published the previous year,
was still being reviewed. He had written some twenty poems
toward the next book, and he spoke of writing better poems in his
seventies than his fifties. George Starbuck at the University of
Iowa's creative writing program had asked him "to read, to lecture
for a while, most of all to teach for a semester or a year." A similar
invitation had arrived from the University of Texas at El Paso.
Wallace Stegner at Stanford was about to write him to come for
readings.[8] He had only forty hours earlier asked the Wilsons to visit.
An upcoming lunch date with Stanley Noyes was recorded on his
calendar. But no one dies suddenly without leaving unfinished
business. Perhaps what happened on the last night of his life was
one final cry for the love and the recognition Win Scott had never
got enough of.

"A good case might be made," one review of *New and Selected
Poems* observed, "for Scott's being the most under-estimated talent
among contemporary poets." His time will come, another insisted,
"as the sheer impact of poetic novelty loses its power to shock and
intrigue, and readers are able to perceive those quieter, subtler
qualities that make Scott a fine poet indeed."[9] Never flashy, never
a coterie poet, Win Scott had to play for cumulative success, the
deferred judgment that is the only one that finally matters. It may
yet come; his reputation may grow slowly over the years. But he
did not have the patience or the strength to wait.

Winfield Townley Scott,[10] to the best of his memory, never

1970; "Placidyl (ethchlorvynol) Capsules," *Physician's Desk Reference to
Pharmaceutical Specialties and Biologicals* (Oradell, N.J.: 1969), pp. 528–529.

[8] George Starbuck to WTS, 20 December 1967, Scott Collection, John Hay
Library, Brown University; Wallace Stegner to SD, 24 January 1970.

[9] Charles A. Brady, *Buffalo Evening News*, 18 May 1968, and Chad Walsh,
Providence Sunday Journal, 19 November 1967.

[10] A word about the name. Winfield Townley Scott was no relation to the
Mexican War general, though it is often assumed otherwise. As a conversation
piece, during his first marriage, he and his wife roped off a chair as in a museum
with the placard, "The General's Chair." But as he wrote in 1959, "if I'd any

wanted to be a fireman or a forest ranger or a movie star. He discovered very young that he wanted to be a writer. At fourteen, a
sophomore in Haverhill Massachusetts High School, came the
awakening that revealed what kind of writer he must be. The year
was 1924, low clouds scudding across a mean November sky. In a
classroom, daydreaming students gazed absently out the window at
the already polluted Merrimack River. Miss R. Elaine Croston,
English teacher, stood at the front, reading "The Rime of the Ancient Mariner." She paused, looked around the room, and was
arrested by the blond boy who did more than merely pay attention,
who was with the Wedding Guest "like one that hath been stunned"
by Coleridge's revelation, who heard what was in the poem that
prose could not say, and who would never be the same again. Sitting
there transfixed, Winfield determined he would be a poet, irrevocably and not as teen-agers make such determinations—to change
their minds an hour later. Ambition sank its barb deep in the boy
that day, and it stuck until his death in 1968 the diagonal length
of the continent away from Haverhill.[11]

Young Winfield made his commitment at fourteen, and when
Charles W. Eliot, the president emeritus of Harvard, responded to
the boy's query about "how to be successful" two years later, his
advice had already been taken. "Find out as early as you can what
trade, occupation, or profession you would be most likely to enjoy
all your life," President Eliot wrote. "While you follow that calling,
read famous literature fifteen minutes a day all your life."[12] Literature was what the boy did enjoy, and he was at sixteen happily
cultivating the acquaintance of great writers in massive, five-hour
sittings, surely an advance over fifteen-minute exposures. Poets
must read to one day write.

---

sense of course I'd have thrown away the Winfield in my youth—it would have
given me a nice 2-name name *and* spared me years of explaining to apparently
disappointed people that I am not related to the famous U.S. General." As a boy,
he was Winfield; then, in high school and college, friends called him Scotty;
his first wife used Winnie; and after he was thirty years old or so almost everyone knew him as Win Scott. WTS to Robert W. Mitchner, 2 March 1959.

[11] R. Elaine Croston to WTS, 10 March 1954, Scott Collection, John Hay
Library. "My joy over the years," his former teacher wrote Scott, "has been
to know that I had a very little bit in your poetry experience those early years—
that second year in high school—how well I remember it—I can see your face
now as I read *The Rime of the Ancient Mariner.*"

[12] Charles W. Eliot to WTS, 4 June 1926, Scott Collection, John Hay Library.

For their part, the boy's parents hardly knew what to make of him. They were not readers, much less writers, and they had their pragmatic reservations. Bessie Townley Scott, his mother, could contemplate Winfield's future as a poet without blanching. As she put it, in the autograph album that was her only son's fourteenth-birthday present,

> What do I want my boy to be?
> Oft is the question asked for me. And oft I
>   ask it of myself—
> What corner, niche, or post or shelf in the
>   great hall of life would I select for him
>   to occupy?
> Statesman or writer, poet, sage or toiler for
>   a weekly wage,
> Artist or artisan, Oh what is to become his
>   future lot?
> For him I do not dare to plan.
> I only hope he'll be a man.[13]

But she hoped, too, that he would be successful: that is, rich. As Win revealed in an interview not long before he died, his family took a dubious view of his decision to be a poet. "They said I'd never make any money," Scott said. "They were right about that."[14] One great-uncle advised him, privately, not to go into anything because of the money in it and instead to do something he wanted to do, but his advice, like that of President Eliot, was startlingly at variance with the materialistic standard of value among middle-class Haverhillians, as among most middle-class Americans.

"Mrs. Turnbridge said to me this morning, 'You have the nicest house on Cedar Street' "—my Grandmother Townley talking. What was the best thing a man could accomplish? Make money. What better? Make more money. My grandfather frowned on book-buying. "What's the Public Library for?" There was art—a chromo of Sir Galahad beside his horse. There was music—Sir Harry Lauder's "Roamin' in the Gloamin' " and, for class, a record of Enrico Caruso singing "Over

---

[13] Bessie Townley Scott to WTS, 30 April 1924, Scott Collection, John Hay Library.
[14] Mary Lou Jennings, "A Poet's Voice at Santa Fe," *Albuquerque Tribune*, 18 October 1967.

There," one stanza in French. There was entertainment—records of "Uncle Josh" monologues. It was very important to appear at church Easter Sunday morning in new clothes. All ambition, all pride, all hope of respect knew only the test of possessions.

The thing to do was to get ahead, and writing poetry seemed conspicuously unlikely to accomplish the purpose, unless you became a popular versifier or slogan-maker.

"So," said an older cousin, who was prospering as an auto salesman, "I hear you want to be a poet. Will you make as much money as Eddie Guest?" At high school chapel the inspirational speaker from out of town said, "This man I'm telling you about sat down at a desk, thought a moment, and then wrote: 'Money-maker-Record-breaker-Studebaker.' And, my young friends, he walked out of that office with a check for ten thousand dollars!" Well, I thought, there's always my spare time.[15]

The Scotts lived, then, in a thoroughly middle-class environment, in the nicest house on the by-no-means "nicest" street, though their standing in the community was perhaps somewhat higher in Haverhill, because of Grandfather Townley's relative success, than it had been in Newport, where the middle class stood in awe of the splendors of the summer colony. Douglas Scott, Winfield's father, worked in *his* father's hardware store in Newport for the first ten years of Winfield's life. Worked six days a week, and on Sunday got dressed up to attend church with Bessie and the children: Winfield and his younger sister Jeannette. Still clad in their best, the family might then be treated to an afternoon drive in Grandfather Scott's car along Ocean Drive and Bellevue Avenue, where the mansions of the rich rose to be reverently admired. In 1920, at the insistence of Grandfather Townley, the Scotts moved to Haverhill. There, the gap between the rich and the merely comfortable was not nearly so wide as in Newport, but it was physically omnipresent and wide enough to make Winfield's parents devoutly hope for him that he might someday be able to span it. Winfield had higher hopes for himself, which he expressed in editorial attacks on materialism in

---

15 WTS, "Tarkington and the 1920's," *Exiles and Fabrications* (1961), pp. 103–104.

the high school newspaper. With E. A. Robinson, who was to have his greatest admiration as a model among poets, he reminded his "dear friends" that "The shame I win for singing is all mine,/The gold I miss for dreaming is all yours."[16]

If the goal of becoming a poet struck his family and friends as curiously impractical, no one could fault the vigor and single-minded dedication with which he pursued that goal. While still in high school, Winfield worked hard at the task, reading omnivorously and writing not only editorials and book reviews but poems too, and entering the poems in contests and winning his share of them, so that he could say tacitly in justification to the doubters that he would amount to something, that he did amount to something. He always wanted to please his family and the recognition helped. "It got my good middle class family a little off my neck," as he re-marked late in life, "because, after all, little Winfield was winning some prizes."[17] A trace of bitterness lay beneath the comment. Writing poetry was hard enough, but he had also learned to the last detail what it meant to be an artist in a society where commer-cial values were the prevailing measure. Unconsciously, unwill-ingly, Scott shared those values; they were part of his heritage.

The part of his heritage he could not escape, its persistent mate-rialistic streak, proved inseparable from the literary and democratic inheritance he warmly embraced. What most distinguished Win's writing from that of most of his contemporaries, in fact, was its persistent *American*ness: its sense of place, its feeling for landscape, its empathy for the commonplace and the common folk, its hero-worship of canonical American writers and its fascination with those not yet canonized, its persistent digging for roots. While still in college, Winfield Townley Scott wrote an essay in praise of Stephen Vincent Benét's *John Brown's Body* and in lament that there had been so few "American" poets: "That is what we need to be shown and to be increasingly conscious of; that in our own land and our own people there are songs to be had and poems to be made. Exactly how and when the great poet will come I do not know. That he can and must if America is to have a literature of

---

[16] Edwin Arlington Robinson, "Dear Friends," *Selected Poems*, ed. Morton Dauwen Zabel (New York: Macmillan, 1965), p. 3.
[17] Jennings, "A Poet's Voice."

its own lifeblood, I feel certain."[18] Reading between the lines: America requires its great poet, and I shall try to be that poet, keeping ever mindful of my heritage.

Win Scott felt lifelong dedication to the nation's political leaders as well as to its classical writers. Reflected in the autograph album he lovingly kept and in his letters of inquiry to such famous men as Charles W. Eliot, his worship of American heroes extended from Abraham Lincoln to Theodore Roosevelt to Woodrow Wilson, whom he saw as a tragic figure and about whom he once intended to write a play; even to Warren Gamaliel Harding, whose picture he pasted in his schoolboy briefcase; to Franklin Delano Roosevelt, whom he admired as a traitor to his upper-class background; to Adlai Stevenson and to John Kennedy, whose assassination brought Scott to depths of personal despair he tried to exorcise in an elegiac tribute.

Occasionally, this chauvinistic streak—so curious as politics and the arts became ever more international—took the unlovely form of isolationism. He went abroad but twice in his 58 years, once in 1938 and not again until 1964. His forebears had come from Scotland, but this happenstance did not ward off Anglophobia: Scotland and Ireland were not England. George P. Elliott, the distinguished writer who edited Scott's *New and Selected Poems* in 1967, finds it odd that he was "so positively indifferent to being published in England. 'I don't give a god damn what the English feel about me,' " he announced to Elliott.[19]

Some modern critics wonder if it is right or politic to read literature in terms of national origin. (Usually, they decide it is not.) The problem did not trouble Winfield Townley Scott. "Actually the necessity of nationalism in literature seems to me hardly arguable. To question it seems to me a good deal like asking, 'Should a tree have roots?' " Shakespeare put Elizabethan England into ancient Rome; Dante put Italians in hell, and it is the same with Mark Twain or Herman Melville. "It is all mankind; yes, but it keeps the special color of its age and place." But, he cautioned, nationalism in literature is not to be confused with flag-waving, or with "nation-

[18] WTS, "The Challenge to American Poetry," *The Scholastic* (3 January 1931), p. 19.
[19] Interview, George P. Elliott, New York, 3 September 1969.

lism in politics or economics, which is a very different thing, with a decidely unpleasant connotation."[20] It is simply that writers must come from some place, out of some past, and with a sense of it.

His own roots dug deep into that thin but artistically fertile topsoil of New England. Until the move to Santa Fe, when Scott was forty-four years old, he had always lived in New England, and even after the move, he continued, like Emily Dickinson, to "see— New Englandly."[21] He loved the marvelous air and the mountains and the piñon smoke on winter evenings and the lilacs blossoming in the spring and the peaches falling ripe in September of Santa Fe, but, as he told an interviewer in 1964, it still remained true that "the landscape and environment of almost anything I write is going to be New England" and "as I [get] older, I [find] myself further removed, but never separated, from New England landscape and people."[22] "Early and late," his friend and adviser Horace Gregory remarked, "[Scott] has always seemed to me a special kind of New Englander."[23]

Cheerfully enough, Scott admitted his yearning after the past. "I am an antiquarian at least in this: I like old people. I like that sense of touching at near hand extraordinary lengths into the past. I like graveyards, too."[24] Traveling, he would repair to graveyards to pay homage to Emily Dickinson, in Amherst, Massachusetts, or Willa Cather, in Jaffrey Center, New Hampshire, or Stephen Vincent Benét, in Stonington, Connecticut.

There was a special significance, for him, of headstones which began with 1869–. "That year for me is an *annus mirabilis*. Of the people who influenced my life, more were born in that year by far than in any other." Among them, especially, were Booth Tarkington, an early enthusiasm which later palled; E. A. Robinson, another early enthusiasm which lasted; Frank Lloyd Wright, the prototypical individualist; Joseph M. Coldwell, a political radical to whom Scott dedicated his poem about the Dorr Rebellion in Rhode Island, *The Sword on the Table*, and a spinster named Esther Wil-

---

[20] WTS, "Nationalism in Culture," *The Challenge of the World Crisis*, Middlebury College Cultural Conference pamphlet (1945).

[21] Poem 285, *The Poems of Emily Dickinson*, ed. Thomas H. Johnson (Cambridge, Massachusetts: Harvard, Belknap Press, 1958), I, 204.

[22] Interview in *Haverhill Gazette*, 18 June 1964.

[23] Horace Gregory to SD, 15 August 1969.

[24] WTS, "*a dirty hand*," p. 62.

bar who, "more deeply in my life than almost anyone else, . . . hovered over my whole childhood with unending love and care."[25] Close to his boyhood home in Haverhill resided the spirit of another influential antecedent, John Greenleaf Whittier. While still in college, Scott wrote a biography of Whittier. The manuscript, never published, seems now to be lost beyond finding, but the loss was not total. What he learned about Whittier boiled down to fifty-four lines of what is perhaps Scott's best poem, "Mr. Whittier." In that poem he brought the "famous, tamed, white-bearded saint with the/ Still inextinguishable dark Hebraic eyes"[26] to life in a way prose biography could hardly match.

In 1951, enabled to do so by the circumstance of his second wife's personal wealth, Scott retired as literary editor of the *Providence Journal* to pursue a full-time career as poet and man of letters. Characteristically, one of his first plans for his relative leisure was to soak himself in "the big New Englanders": Thoreau and Emerson and Dickinson and Hawthorne. "If I have any background this is it, and it behooves me, no matter how provincial I get, to know every step of it. I mean to hell—for the moment: for the moment—with Dostoevsky."[27] If these were writers grounded in locality, they still spoke to all men. "Thoreau's was an essentially poetic talent," Scott's immersion led him to conclude, "that seized with unique fierceness upon a particular locality and, in the way of such talent, proclaimed universals. . . . Even a trip to the moon will not obviate passionate thought brought back from Heywood's meadow . . . where, as Thoreau so charmingly remarked, he'd had no idea so much was going on."[28] It was the same with Dickinson: "She is obsessed with change as all her life she observes the comings and goings of flowers, birds, insects, of seasons, and of human beings and their finalities. All these in her immediate world: perhaps it is the least of Emily Dickinson's achievement, yet shouldn't we note that her *Complete Poems* belongs in its way with the supreme small-town books of American literature? However she transcends merely

---

[25] WTS, "Portrait of a Free Man," *Exiles*, p. 147.

[26] WTS, "Mr. Whittier," *New and Selected Poems* (1967), p. 52.

[27] WTS to Frank Merchant, 16 January 1961. In this letter Scott reaffirmed the intention he had expressed on leaving the *Providence Journal* in 1951 (EMS to SD, 7 September 1970).

[28] WTS, "Walden Pond in the Nuclear Age," *New York Times Magazine*, 6 May 1962, p. 84.

that, nonetheless she demonstrates yet again how the local can become the universal.''[29] Free to do so, he went back through reading—not immediately, as he'd planned, but eventually—to his origins, determined "to become as powerfully provincial as Yeats."[30]

No mean goal, but a man's reach *should* exceed his grasp, and as a way of showing how far his grasp extended, here is "Come Green Again":

> If what heals can bless
> Can what blesses heal?
> And all come green again
> That was bodied forth
> Years and years ago?
> Years before my time.
>
> Yet things I deepest learned
> Turn into memory
> As though no man's creation
> But enlarges mine;
> As though no man's existence
> But was also mine
> In its lonesomeness.
>
> Henry Thoreau bent
> In his boat on Walden Pond
> Whistling his wooden flute
> Under midnight stars
> Across the stars in the water.
>
> Hawthorne and Melville parting
> At night in Liverpool,
> Parting on a rainy corner
> For the final time,
> Something unsaid between them.
>
> Mark Twain in moonlight
> Standing in his Hartford house,
> That wounded, beautiful man,
> His hands at his white hair
> While he sang "Nobody knows
> The troubles I see but Jesus."

[29] WTS, "Afterword," to *Judge Tenderly of Me: The Poems of Emily Dickinson* (Kansas City, Missouri: Hallmark, 1968), pp. 60–61.
[30] WTS, *"a dirty hand,"* p. 137.

Then in broad daylight
The ladies of Camden drawing
Their skirts and kids aside
To avoid the dirty man
As Whitman hobbled past,
His basket on his arm
Filled with his book for sale.

Can such existences
Help but heal our hearts
Or such lonesomeness
Help but bless in us
That everlasting change
Which is our changelessness
And our humbleness?
And all come green again.

What I have learned enough
To have as air to breathe
Returns as memory
Of undiminished love:
That no man's creation
But enlarges me.
O all come green again.[31]

The poem had been made, he said, "of a combination of things: of recollections, of various tiny anecdotes in American literary history, which have stayed in my mind, and were crossed one day when I was thinking of them with a no doubt arrogant desire to write a corollary statement of John Donne's remark that 'no man's death but diminishes me.' "[32] It is those "tiny anecdotes," the quick but telling glimpses of the human beings who were Twain and Whitman and the others, that give "Come Green Again" its distinction. Scott wrote the poem in 1957, shortly after finishing "The Owl in the Hall," a long, lovely memoir of his first ten years in Newport, Rhode Island. Perhaps casting into the wells of his own memory helped fish up this poem. As he wrote in his journal, "I was obsessed and absorbed by the Newport years and content to

[31] WTS, "Come Green Again," *New and Selected Poems*, pp. 64–65.
[32] WTS, *Winfield Townley Scott Reads His Works*, Carillon YP321, Yale Series of Recorded Poets (1961).

take a vacation from poetry. Now I am itchy to make poems again, and I have done a few. One of them, 'Come Green Again,' may be good but of course I am not sure."[33]

Reassurance, for once, came in good time. As one that "may be good," Scott included the poem in his 1959 collection, *Scrimshaw*, and made certain that an advance copy went off to a man he loved in Rutherford, New Jersey, William Carlos Williams. Dr. Williams sent him the kind of letter most artists only long for:

> I got no further than the second page of *Scrimshaw* when I had to break off to write you this letter of praise for the book. The moving picture of Thoreau, Hawthorne and Whitman and Mark Twain standing in his Hartford house singing was too much for me. . . . The way you put it down gave my old heart a wrench. I entered right into the hearts of those men and their understanding of the hopelessness—and triumph—of their position facing their world. You could not have put it better using their own proper terms. A triumph of poetry, it fairly springs from the page at me. . . . I think such writing has a permanent value.[34]

John Ciardi, who had sent back "Come Green Again" from the *Saturday Review* for "revisions," turned his sheepish second thoughts into verse:

> I like that poem, Win. There's a green world
>   in it.
> Not just green acreage—any nature boy can
>   rhyme on that a dozen lines a minute: . . .
>
> .   .   .   .
>
> I mean what's green in being what a man
>   touches to leave. Say, Mark Twain at the
>   end—the green of his last thought. . . .
>
> .   .   .   .
>
> That last green, Win, after the first unrolled.
> The eighth day of the world, by a man told.[35]

A key word in "Come Green Again" is "lonesomeness," and of

---

[33] WTS, "*a dirty hand,*" p. 111.
[34] William Carlos Williams to WTS, 30 October 1959, Scott Collection, John Hay Library.
[35] John Ciardi to WTS, 17 May 1957, Scott Collection, John Hay Library.

course it is not used casually. "I would rather write 'lonesome' than 'lonely,' " Scott confided to his journal, because it has the ring of American speech. "Masefield says 'The lonely sea and the sky.' That's British poetry. 'Look down, look down that lonesome road.' That's American poetry."[36] He tried for the native intonation, for "relatively simple language; as near current spoken American as may be."[37] George P. Elliott, who has called Scott "as rock-bottom American a poet as we have had since Frost,"[38] came to that judgment partly because "his language, both the poetic and the colloquial aspects of it, is purely American."[39]

In his use of plain-spoken American diction and in his devotion to, and sense of identification with, a usable American past, Scott swam against the current of modernity. "The most obvious fact about modern poetry," as Robert Penn Warren observed in 1966, "is that it is an alienated art." Alienated first of all because it is unread: "We can trace the stages by which poetry lost its market to the novel, the newspaper, the magazine, and the movie—and later to radio and TV." Without the support of universities and foundations, it might be as true of poets as of blacksmiths that they have lost their vocation. Not only was the market lost, Warren went on, but also the mission. No longer the unacknowledged and certainly not the acknowledged legislator of mankind, the poet "couldn't even be trusted to speak the simple truth." Only the scientist could play that role, and even his judgments were suspect. Seemingly on the way to extinction, the modern poet took refuge in a self-conscious passion for style, a retreat which often led to obscurity of language and form and the accusation that he was merely talking to himself.

Another sort of alienation, according to Warren, stemmed from "the rise of industrialism, finance capitalism, and the great power states"—the development of a society so rationalized that "the sense of community and of human ties was being replaced by anonymous forces; communion seemed to be lost in the noise of communication by mass media; the historical sense disappeared into a cynical, or

[36] WTS, "a dirty hand," p. 22.
[37] "Winfield Townley Scott," University of Kansas City Review 13 (Winter 1946): 119–126.
[38] George P. Elliott to SD, 29 July 1968.
[39] Ibid., 10 August 1969.

supine, acceptance of the incoherent present."[40] Like Warren himself, however, and like Robert Lowell, Scott clung to his historical sense as an anchor amid chaos. And like Frost, Scott rarely descended to obscurity, preferring to talk to others (if they would only listen!) rather than to an ideal if limited audience of one. Does this mean that Winfield Townley Scott was that contradiction in terms: a modern unalienated poet? Not at all: he beheld the development of a programmed, technological, and materialistic society as bitterly as any modernist might wish . . . and hung on the more desperately to the eroding rock of his heritage.

If Win Scott's poetry has had less than its due so far, there are reasons enough. He was never a fashionable writer. In the thirties, he openly criticized those who attempted to mix poetry and politics: Concerned too exclusively with the problems of the here and now, he observed, they had failed to sink roots, and were "therefore, open to the charge of being, of all things, merely exotic."[41] How that judgment must have ruffled proletarian feathers!

His verse was apolitical, then, in a time of deep political upheaval. His poems were plain-spoken, in a time when deepening obscurity characterized most critically acclaimed poetry. Evading the cheap, rejecting the spectacular ("beware of glorious sunsets"), he rediscovered the wonder of the familiar at a time when the unfamiliar was the expected. He "sounded no stylish notes, never directly reflected the always changing dogma, whether social or aesthetic," and the critical colony in New York, anticipating the fashionable, tended to ignore, or to give less than due recognition to, his work.[42] What's more, he was no good at the game of literary politics, did not attend the gin-soaked soirées that bring writer and critic together, lived on the periphery of the New York circle of influence in Providence, Rhode Island, from 1931 to 1951 and beyond its periphery in Santa Fe from 1954 to 1968. Scott rarely gave readings, and after a few years of grading freshman papers at Brown and Pembroke in the thirties he virtually lost touch with the academic world which might have adopted and promoted him.

[40] Robert Penn Warren, *A Plea in Mitigation: Modern Poetry and the End of an Era* (Macon, Ga.: Wesleyan College Press, 1966).

[41] WTS, "Pianos in the Street," unpublished essay (c. 1935), Scott Collection, John Hay Library.

[42] Interview, Paul Horgan, Middletown, Connecticut, 5 December 1969.

The role of tortoise in the long competition for fame had its draw-
backs, among them a degrading envy:

Autobiography

This hare and tortoise race I've been assigned
I can hardly complain of, though it wears.
It isn't being the tortoise that I mind,
It's that there are too many hares.[43]

In a society which applied standards of production and sale and
profit to a life of art, all he could hope for was the sort of critical
acclaim occasionally lavished on his contemporaries. But the envy
and depression to which he drove himself will matter less if posterity takes the notice it should of his poetry. The historian Garrett
Mattingly, writing of the Duke of Medina Sidonia, who had the bad
luck to be placed in charge of the Spanish Armada, discounted
future judgments of the Duke's role: "Whatever he did, it was not
enough. Nor does it matter at all to the dead whether they receive
justice at the hands of succeeding generations. But to the living, to
do justice, however belatedly, should matter."[44] But the point,
questionable even for statesmen, hardly applies to artists. It is
posthumous praise they long for most of all.

The final test of a poet, Scott believed, was whether he sounded
"not quite like anybody else. If you opened a book with no names
in it, you would known damn well this one was by Robert Frost
and this one was by T. S. Eliot." It was this overtone, this stain of
personality, this slight distortion that proved the master.[45] Did he
achieve such a unique, identifiable voice? Posterity will judge, but
it is certainly true that Scott was "not an Auden poet or an Eliot
poet, not a Pound or a Williams poet."[46] He was his own man, and—
in the short term—he paid the penalty.

"He wrote superbly," Webster Schott has written of Scott, "in
the great middle of American poetry, the tradition that included
Emily Dickinson, Edwin Arlington Robinson, possibly Frost. That
could bring him high regard. It may yet bring him greatness. But

[43] WTS, "*a dirty hand*," p. 78.
[44] Garrett Mattingly, *The Armada* (Boston: Little, Brown, 1959), p. 375.
[45] Jennings, "A Poet's Voice."
[46] Webster Schott, "Winfield Townley Scott," *Fine Arts Calendar* (January
1963), pp. 53–57.

during his life . . . it could not yield what he needed above all else—
an absolute conviction of his own worth."[47] He died in depression,
but not without clinging to a hope for the future: that his poems
would work their quiet magic long after he was gone. As Schott
remarked, "I cannot imagine anyone reading these poems and remaining unmoved."[48] Let them be read: then the tortoise may have
his victory at last.

[47] Webster Schott, review of "a dirty hand," *New York Times Book Review*,
7 September 1969, p. 4.
[48] Webster Schott, review of WTS, *Collected Poems, Kansas City Star*, 2
December 1962.

So much is lost. Out of a few fragments of bone the experts can reconstruct an ancient skeleton. It is wonderful but it is only a skeleton. Yet we might go mad if no moment vanished, the load of our living would grow so great. In life as in art perhaps our salvation is the handful of seed out of which we imagine gardens.[1]

> How could you know today is today having forgotten
> Yesterday and tomorrow?[2]

2. The Newport Garden

NEWPORT, RHODE ISLAND, was Win Scott's Eden. He lived there only his first ten years, but throughout his life the sounds and the sights and, especially, the smells, for his nose remembered best, came pouring back upon him until, like D. H. Lawrence, his manhood was "cast / Down in the flood of remembrance"[3] and he was a child once more.

---

[1] WTS, "The Owl in the Hall," manuscript (1957), p. 87. Though the Newport memoir now exists in published form as part of *Alpha Omega* (1971), my references here are to the manuscript.

[2] WTS, "Memento," *New and Selected Poems* (1967), p. 70.

[3] D. H. Lawrence, "Piano," *The Norton Anthology of English Literature,* rev. ed., vol. 2 (New York: W. W. Norton, 1968), pp. 1762–1763.

His Newport childhood—the years from 1910 to 1920—hardly
qualifies as idyllic by customary standards: young Winfield grew
up in a modest two-family house, went to the school across the
street, suffered most of the emotional pangs and physical ills that
growing up visits upon the young, and minded his manners and
stayed indoors considerably more than other boys of his age. But
Winfield Townley Scott, early and late, romanticized Newport. It
was the only place in the world, he believed always and mistakenly,
where white roses grew wild.[4] Fog often closed in, but clearing
weather brought an overflow of compensations. "Nights, sometimes," as a character in Scott's verse play puts it, "The horns
sound awful lonesome. But you take/ A morning like today's, and
sure enough/ It does clear soft and sweet and kind of/ sparkling."[5]
Besides, fog never frightened young Winfield; he grew up with it,
and later welcomed fog and other kinds of shut-in weather as a
talisman of comfort and security. At fifty-five he could still conjure
up the smell of Grandmother Scott's jonnycakes and of the bread in
Phil Harrington's bakery a few blocks away.[6] The blue sea forever
pounded in his imagination. Time and again he revisited that para-
disiacal childhood in his prose and poetry.

Nostalgia for Newport set in immediately after the move to
Haverhill, in 1920, and was only compounded by the family's habit
of returning each summer during the next decade. "Why should I
go away for the summer when I'm already there?" Grandfather
Scott used to say, and, for his grandson, summer in Newport "was
merely perfect, famously perfect."[7] A poem of 5 September 1927
records Winfield's "Last Day by the Sea," before going off to college
at Brown:

> I fill my eyes with ocean,
> dazzling sun on blue,
> till it runs through and through me . . .
> For all this

---

[4] Bradford Swan to EMS, 13 May 1968, Scott Collection, John Hay Library,
Brown University.

[5] WTS, "Biography at the Open Grave," manuscript (1953), p. 2, Scott Collection, John Hay Library.

[6] WTS to Florence B. Titus, 24 February 1965.

[7] WTS, "Owl," p. 97.

> I must remember a long time;
> a long time before I come again,
> and all this sun and shining blue
> I must remember
> and keep with me.[8]

His second book of poems, *Wind the Clock*, is full of reminiscent and revelatory glimpses of childhood. And it is significant that one of his first projects after leaving the *Providence Journal* in 1951 was to write a "love letter" to Newport for the newspaper. "Mr. James once said the most beautiful combination of words in English is 'summer afternoon,'" he wrote. "And to Newport, it applies." Drive over the Mount Hope bridge from Bristol and enter an enchanted country, "softer, milder, sweeter than any of the rest of the state, perhaps as good as any on earth." So it would always be for Scott, since Newport represented the past seen through a golden veil and made more beautiful by its irrecoverability.[9]

In his forties, he decided that it was time to compose a memoir about that childhood, following the example of his idol, Mark Twain, another writer who was obsessed with his past and began, in his forties, to write movingly about it. There was no need to worry, as he wrote Dr. Williams in 1956, "about using material this way—I mean, in prose autobiography—which might be refined into poems. I've mined that past a good many times over in the other way."[10] So, late in 1956, he began work on "The Owl in the Hall," a memoir of his Newport boyhood. The following October, the job was done:

> I have unrhymed a year
> To write the book of my dead.
> I called out of their graves
> Old folk and grandparents
> And had them walk the floors
> Where forty years ago
> I looked up, seeing them walk;

[8] WTS, "Last Day by the Sea," unpublished poem (5 September 1927), Scott Collection, John Hay Library.

[9] WTS, "A Love Letter to Newport," *The Rhode Islander, Providence Sunday Journal* Magazine, 5 August 1951. pp. 8–11.

[10] WTS to William Carlos Williams, 3 June 1956, Beinecke Library, Yale University.

> Their adult talk of the world
> As though it were theirs forever.
> Opening doors with their keys,
> Their steps coming into the room,
> I have seen to it at last:
> Only their bones lie buried.[11]

Not just their bones, for Scott decided to bury the manuscript for a while. "There are just enough family skeletons in it to make me feel it cannot be published in the near future," he reflected in 1957. "Not that it is a scandalous book; such passages are very small and very few, and yet my conviction is that they are necessary to the story. And I am not sitting here impatient for anybody's death, I may add."[12] In 1965, after making some alterations, Scott started shipping the manuscript around to publishers, who found it a quiet book. (The memoir finally emerged in print in 1971, issued together with a group of late poems as *Alpha Omega*.) Certainly "The Owl in the Hall" calls back a time in the American past so slow-paced that horse-carts filled the streets, so ritualized that each day followed its own unvarying routine. But the quietness is deceptive; beneath the surface regularity of Scott's childhood lay the sources of joy and of terror.

It is axiomatic in psychiatry that the first years are the crucial ones in the formation of personality, and "The Owl in the Hall" bears out the truth of the axiom. Reading it, Eleanor Scott could "see plainly the formation of so many personality traits, some of which were to bedevil Win, seeded in these pages."[13] Most significant of all, surely, is the revelation that the boyhood of Winfield Townley Scott was one dominated to an unusual degree, even in a semimatriarchal society, by women.

The woman who gave him birth, Bessie Townley Scott, did so only after a most difficult pregnancy. "Carrying me," Scott writes, "she had been ill the whole while. . . . And she was, at the end, monstrously pregnant." Delivery was due about the middle of April, but young Winfield delayed, and when her time did come, Bessie Scott endured labor pains for forty-eight hours. The menfolk—Grand-

[11] WTS, "Owl."
[12] WTS, *"a dirty hand": The Literary Notebooks of Winfield Townley Scott* (1969), p. 110.
[13] EMS to SD, 18 November 1968.

father Townley (for Bessie, an only child, went home to her native Haverhill to give birth) and Douglas Winfied Scott, the baby's father—were of course of no use, and it was touch and go whether the big-headed baby would be born at all. The doctors "had just about resolved to save my mother's life by cutting me to pieces . . . when, suddenly, I was born. I was whole but battered. The first relative to view me, my grandmother, thought I had a harelip; and my head trickled bloody with forceps wounds. Just above my right knee was a large, strawberry-shaped, red birthmark." Winfield's father laconically recalled, many years later, that "he *was* a hard-looking chap. It was six months before he looked like a person."[14] As for the exhausted mother, "she was barely alive and it was weeks until she could walk." The birth came shortly before midnight on 30 April 1910, a *Walpurgisnacht* when witches were supposed, according to legend, to conduct their unholy Sabbath. And in the sky, "Halley's Comet streamed like the bright and wind-maddened hair of the universe," an occurrence held to signal the death hour of those born at its last appearance some seventy-five years earlier. Mark Twain, born under the comet in 1835, died under it in 1910, and Win Scott liked to maintain, superstitiously, that he was fated to die on the reappearance of Halley's Comet in 1986.

In late June of 1910 the Scotts returned to Newport to live on the ground floor of the gray clapboard two-family house on Cranston Avenue which Douglas Scott had found for his sudden family. (He and Bessie had been married less than a year when Winfield was born.) Relatives lived upstairs, and, depositing Winfield safely in the middle of a bed, the proud mother called them down for an audience. By the time she returned, the baby was gone, kidnapped. "Esther Wilbar, who lived with her mother in the house next door on Tyler Street, had spotted the arrival of the hack, had come in the back door almost as my mother came in by the front, had scooped me up in her arms and carried me home. No event in my life could be more symbolic," Scott wrote in "The Owl in the Hall." "For the next ten years (until my family moved to Haverhill) I lived as much in that house as in my own, and I was given there endless care and boundless affection, love as kind and tender as I should ever know."[15]

[14] Interview, Douglas W. Scott, Haverhill, Massachusetts, 10 July 1969.
[15] WTS, "Owl," p. 7.

Essie and Grammie Wilbar lavished upon Winfield, hard-looking though he may have been at first, the kind of love, totally unqualified and unconditional, that asked nothing more of the boy than that he come next door to visit, to be entertained, to be pampered and protected and spoiled. As he later wrote, "When we were children we got too much love,/ Grew learned to receive it not to give...[16]

In her youth Essie Wilbar had been something of a beauty. "How the delivery boys hung over the fence," when Essie was seventeen, but it fell to her lot, as to many another in those days, to stay home and care for her mother. In the year he died, Scott published a selection of Emily Dickinson's poems with an Afterword which applied as well to Essie Wilbar in the house next door: "In New England throughout the 19th and on into the 20th century there were countless spinsters who lived out their lives in their fathers' houses, who cooked and baked and gardened and did other household chores, who were seldom seen about the town and became more solitary and eccentric with the years, and wound up caring for a long-invalided parent; they accentuated the maiden aunt's life that so poignantly often gave more love than it received."[17] Essie Wilbar was just such a captive, serving out her life "as daughter, housekeeper, cook, nurse, companion, the virginity inviolate and her years so drily withering. . . . You can guess . . . what began for her when she snatched me from the bed and hurried home with me in her arms."[18] At the Wilbars' house, Winfield was treated to gingerbread and shadow games; at school, if the weather clouded, Essie hustled over with rubbers and raincoat; on weekends, Essie took him to the vaudeville to see Fatty Arbuckle and Charlie Chaplin and the acrobats and animal acts and comedians and singers on stage; when Essie went shopping, Winfield would toddle along; she walked with him when he went to secure his own, precious library card.

Where the Wilbars coddled Winfield, they would have little to do with Jeannette, his younger sister. Jeannette was born, without much difficulty, two years after her older brother, and Winfield,

[16] WTS, "Sonnet VIII," *Collected Poems: 1937–1962* (1962), p. 106.
[17] WTS, "Biography," p. 23; WTS, "Afterword," to *Judge Tenderly of Me: The Poems of Emily Dickinson* (Kansas City, Missouri: Hallmark, 1968), p. 58.
[18] WTS, "Owl," p. 18.

his nose out of joint, greeted his sibling rival by throwing cat fur at his mother. But little sister was no rival at the house next door. Jeannette still remembers timidly knocking at the Wilbars', knowing her brother, her "Brah," was inside, and receiving only silence for an answer. It was Winfield who was special for Essie and Grammie Wilbar, forty-one and seventy-four years old respectively when he was born. He was *their* child, and Jeannette could go fly a kite.[19]

The most moving and persuasive chapter in "The Owl in the Hall" is the long one entitled "The House Next Door" and detailing the boy's relationship with the Wilbars.[20] They come off the page, in fact, far more vividly than either of Winfield's parents, or anyone else in the book. A photograph from those days shows Essie, no longer beautiful, but tall, strong-jawed, capable, wearing glasses, and Grammie, white-haired, stooped, stern, a presence. Grammie, who lived into her nineties, was "an old-fashioned old lady," who took snuff, kept a yellow rag in the pocket of her dress, and cherished her hands over and over as she told stories of her youth and her heritage, with indignation how her uncle was shanghaied by the English in the War of 1812, with pathos how she, at twenty-nine, had cried in the streets when the news came of Abraham Lincoln's death. What she loved to tell, Winfield loved to hear, and at the Wilbars' he began that soaking in the past that was to characterize his life and his work. The house itself, though not so old, seemed a relic from the past; there were chamber-pots under the beds and stuffed animals in a glass case; kerosene lamps flickered at night and during the day there was hardly more light, for the blinds were drawn to protect the ladies' privacy and their rugs and furniture from fading in the sun. Ghosts hovered about the dim-lighted rooms, and Grammie's stories invoked them for young Winfield:

> One way, you could say
> A lot of things I know I know because
> She knew them; and as if I do remember
> Mornings nearly a hundred years ago,

Scott observed in 1953. "And that," he wrote, "is somehow/Strange and beautiful."[21]

[19] Interview, Mrs. Jeannette Wolfe, Los Angeles, 2 February 1970.
[20] WTS, "The House Next Door," in "Owl," pp. 16–45.
[21] WTS, "Biography," p. 35.

Though he never says it of her explicitly in "The Owl in the Hall," Winfield's mother must have relinquished her role to Essie during the boy's formative years, a development the more odd because her son was to become Bessie Scott's perpetual favorite. Of course she was busy with the housework and with Jeannette, and the Wilbars were old family friends and enormously kind. But one inevitably speculates on the psychological effect on Winfield of being brought up, if not with a feeling of neglect, at least with the knowledge that unlike others he had been adopted by a mother-surrogate. In his unpublished verse play, Scott lets a neighbor speak the thoughts unexpressed in his own memoir:

> Wasn't a thing she didn't do for you:
> Took the place of your mother, I always said.
> There's some, I'll have you know, who thought
>   it strange;
> Her fetching, carrying for a neighbor's boy
> . . . .
> Spoiled you, didn't she?

And the boy in the play, obviously Winfield himself, replies "I guess so. Anyway / She spoiled me for a lot of other people."[22]

Douglas Winfield Scott and Bessie Irving Townley, Winfield's parents, were married 9 June 1909. The mother of the groom did not attend the ceremony, since she objected to Bessie as too frail and perhaps as too fickle (she had earlier dated Douglas's cousin). In fact, for eighteen months after the marriage, Grandmother Sue Scott would not set foot in the house of her son and daughter-in-law, living nearby. She had herself eloped with William Bolger ("Red") Scott on Washington's birthday, 1886, a match opposed by her parents, who considered Red Scott wild. Later this "became a tradition with my grandmother herself: she opposed almost every marriage in her family for two generations," up to and including that of Win's sister, Jeannette, in 1936. "But by then she no longer abstained from attending the ceremony, indeed she left a sickbed to be present at my sister's wedding, and died of a heart attack in the church." In many ways, "The Owl in the Hall" records, "she had a bitterly unhappy life," the bitterness compounded by Grandfather Scott's flair for other women.

---

[22] Ibid., p. 24.

Handsome, hustling Red Scott emerges as the strongest male figure in the female-dominated memoir. He was the entrepreneur among the Scotts and helped to lift the laboring-class family into solid middle-class status. Beginning as a clerk in another store, he exerted his drive and experience to start and to keep in operation for half a century (the business went under in the 1950's) a hardware store of his own, and to employ most of his male relatives into the bargain. He was possessed of an esthetic streak and a strong sexual drive, and for a time carried on an affair with the wife of his own wife's brother He would meet her, seemingly by coincidence, at the home of Winfield's parents (a circumstance that must have intensified Sue Scott's dislike of her daughter-in-law), and Red Scott, seemingly out of courtesy, would accompany her home. Grandmother Scott adopted a stoical attitude toward this affair and others, though she knew, from sniffing his moustache for perfume and other telltale indications, what her husband was up to. When the brother involved came to her and said sadly, "Oh, Sue, I hope you never know what I know," she remained closemouthed as always. But her brother made his own eloquent, symbolic statement. "Shortly afterward he was found dead, a suicide. On the floor beside his body there was a photograph of my grandfather, torn in half." (It is but one among several suicides and murders in "The Owl in the Hall.") For Sue Scott, there was no question of divorce: " 'Why should I clear out of my own house and leave it all for some baggage to have as hers?' " She retreated instead into coldness; as if her quota of passion had been used up on the night of her elopement many years before, she lived a silent, bitter, loveless life. Once Red Scott reported to Winfield's mother, " 'I have never had a willing kiss in my own home.' "[23]

For many another bride, living in a strange town close to a disapproving mother-in-law might have led to social ostracism, but Bessie Townley Scott from Haverhill, small, blue-eyed, light-haired, cheerful, and abundantly gregarious, soon knew half of Newport. There was little about Bessie Scott, though, to indicate that she had given birth to a poet. "A slight deafness made her school days miserable, and she quit before finishing high school," where, to be sure, she had been fond of Sir Walter Scott's *The Lady*

[23] WTS, "Owl," pp. 57–64.

of the Lake and "could quote its opening lines about the stag at eve, and also the James Russell Lowell passage beginning, 'Oh, what is so rare as a day in June.' " She worked for a time as a clerk in a dry-goods store, then married, moved to Newport, and decorated the house in the customary kitschy adornments of the time.

In his parents' bedroom in Newport, Winfield recalled, "there was an engraving which from a distance seemed only a picture of a bow-tie. A closer look revealed its sweet moral. A man's face was in one end of the bow, a woman's in the other—handsome young faces in the Charles Dana Gibson manner—and in the knot between them, a smiling baby. The picture had a title: 'The Tie That Binds.' " Such ties were not much needed, however, for Douglas and Bessie Scott appear to have enjoyed that rare thing, a truly happy marriage. While he worked long hours at his father's hardware store, it fell to Mother (with, of course, the substantial assistance of the Wilbars) to care for and discipline the children. When a storm threatened she became terrified and would lock the door of the bedroom, bolt the windows, and gather her children about her to last out the blow. Oddly enough, as Jeannette observed, neither she nor Winfield inherited that fear of thunderstorms— quite the opposite, in fact, in the case of Win Scott. But her son did inherit her habit of borrowing trouble. Bessie Scott would fret constantly, anticipating future disasters. "Oh, my," she'd say, "I hope such-and-such won't happen," and if it didn't, she would be relieved only long enough to begin worrying about the next unpreventable accident. When her children misbehaved, she would send them to bed, and there were occasional bad days like the one when Jeannette opened the oven door long enough to watch, in fascination, as the cake inside fell. But for the most part she ran her home with gentleness and in good nature,[24] and her son revealed the depths of his love for her in his elegy, "Memento."

Still, his mother plays second fiddle to the Wilbars in Winfield Townley Scott's Newport memoir, and his father hardly has any part at all. Pa was the man who went off to the store in the morning, returned for his noon dinner to bring the news from downtown, and went off again in the afternoon. Douglas Scott moved and spoke with a gentle diffidence; those who remember him when he was

[24] Interview, Mrs. Jeannette Wolfe, Los Angeles, 2 February 1970. See also "Owl," pp. 3–4, 88–89, 100.

young invariably mention that he was unobtrusive, that he was a good man—a dedicated church-goer and later a deacon in the church—and that he looked younger than his years. By and large, he left the rearing of the children to Bessie and approved the results. "Sunday of course was the day Pa was home," Winfield wrote, in "The Owl in the Hall." "I saw so little of him that for some of my childhood years I resented him as though he were an intruder. Any criticism I got mostly came from him and naturally I didn't appreciate that. I felt, without resentment, that he preferred Jeannette to me. More obscurely I may have felt that he paid me very little attention." So when his father did whittle a magnificent kayak for Winfield's second-grade class, the memory stuck, vividly. Perhaps Douglas Scott had little choice in the matter, as his son suggests. "He may have felt that I was indeed the pet of my mother, the Wilbars, and my Grandmother Townley: they all adored me and in consequence perhaps he felt alienated." Yet he could recall one noon, only one, when a tense and frightening silence hung like a knife over the dinner table. Punishment of the children took mild forms—go to bed, yes, but turn over and bare your backside, no. At least that's how it seemed, in retrospect, to Win Scott. "My sister can remember Pa brandishing a hairbrush in anger and chasing me around and around the dining-room table, but I do not remember this."[25]

Violent punishment was hardly required to make Winfield behave; approval withheld would do just as well, and it *was* withheld occasionally, as when he failed, after hours on the stool, to produce the desired bowel movement.[26] Winfield was babied, and expected to be good in return: quiet, shy, dignified. As he wrote in bitter self-analysis many years later, "Alas, I suppose the difference between *Tom Sawyer* and 'The Owl in the Hall' is the difference between Tom and his brother Sid."[27] To gain approval, Winfield did act like Sid Sawyer, almost goody-goody, certainly reserved, less like a boy than his sibling. "When we were young," he wrote of Jeannette and himself, "we were pretty constantly together. She was the noisy and active one—the tomboy—and I was so quiet: visitors would say 'My! She should have been a boy!'—leaving no

25 WTS, "Owl," p. 103.
26 Interview, Lindsay Scott, Washington, D.C., 26 September 1969.
27 WTS, *"a dirty hand,"* p. 124.

doubt a psychological scar on my sensitive soul. The family doctor always said Good morning, Professor! to me—so they say."[28]

A poem called "The Difference," psychologically and biographically accurate, illustrates Winfield's reserve, his fear of the unknown, and growing awareness of his difference from others. A circus came to Newport, and Douglas Scott took his two children out to Two-Mile Corner to see the animals:

> The buffalo loomed at the far loop of the field:
> Though mildly grazing in twilight, a thunderhead
>   tethered.
> Spectators—man and two children—some others—
> Clutched tickets and kept their distance,
>   regarding the rare beast.
>
> We were—after all—suddenly there—there in
>   the same grass
> At the edge of our town: the familiar vacant
>   lot
> Usurped by the savage shape which grazed
>   inattentive:
> We grew—embarrassed, frightened—into shy
>   invaders.
>
> Staring and silent, we stood back. Though the
>   crickets rang
> And the evening star opened low over the
>   western fence
> The shadowy field was bisontine; the ground
>   shook—
> Once—with the thud of an absent-minded forefoot.
>
> The little girl said to her father "I want to
>   go see him";
> But the boy dared not: he watched them hand in
>   hand
> Go slowly within the dusk to confront—quite
>   close—
> While he stayed alone among strangers—that
>   hunching darkness.

[28] WTS to EM, 28 April 1943.

Silhouette now: the buffalo: horned ghost
Of an ancient philosopher, bearded and ominous,
Transmigrated, neither free nor dead. Nothing
    occurred
To the father and sister. They returned safe.
The three went home.

There is a measure of shame here, in the confession of a lack of daring ("But the boy dared not") while his sister Jeannette takes the risk. What most troubles Winfield, perhaps, is the *change* in his surroundings: the familiar vacant lot turned savage and frightening and foreign, the field become "bisontine," as Scott's rare pun has it.[29]

Throughout life Win Scott was to resist change—in status, in surroundings, in life style, as if staying in one place (*"Play in your own yard, kids,"* he once wrote friends who had luckily escaped death in an automobile accident) might both ensure safety and help to restore that Edenic world where once he had been loved unto repression by the women who surrounded him. In "The Owl in the Hall" he calls back rainy mornings when he would huddle in the "tiny space" between the head of his parents' bed and the wall, "back to the corner and my arms about my knees, and . . . feel safe and secure."[30] When he grew up, he could be wrenched only with difficulty from such safe corners.

Perhaps Scott's later fear of change stemmed in part from his first agonizing introduction, at four and a half, to school. "Winter was setting in when suddenly I was sent off to school. I say suddenly for the school session was already under way. . . . And I say suddenly because I don't know why my mother sent me to school before the age of five. Years later she merely said she assumed I would be kept in kindergarten yet another year following that winter and spring, but I was not." Whatever Bessie Scott's motives, the experience frightened and humiliated her son. The first day out of the nest, "my mother and one of the teachers are talking high above me, myself between them. Then my mother bends down and kisses me and goes away, and I am being led by the gray-haired old teacher into the awful room. . . . There are many other children,

29 WTS, "The Difference," *New and Selected Poems*, p. 66.
30 WTS, "Owl," p. 90.

long acclimated, older than I and all unknown to me, and I do not
look at them. I look straight ahead." What he remembered best
about that day, thirty years later, was the furnace register high in
the wall: "There I was, worse than alone; and my throat aching,
and my eyes giving me trouble—so that I had to stare and stare at
the black, grilled register high above me." Nor could he utter a
sound; when the teacher asked him a question, he could not respond. But it is important to speak, when Nature requires, and one
December day, unwilling "to be the center of attention even for
that one moment of raising one's hand," Winfield wet his pants
and was sent home (or, where he chose to go, to the Wilbars') in
his sodden shame.[31]

Certainly that first school experience presented a challenge the
boy was not yet ready to face. During the next five years of grade
school in Newport, Winfield remained at once a joy to his teachers
(in time he did learn to respond to questions: his report cards show
excellent performance in everything, but especially in conduct and
effort)[32] and a shy, frightened child to his fellow students. An early
poem, "Second Grade," sets the recess scene:

> Traman remembers the little kid in the schoolyard
> Who always stood by the drainpipe till the bell rang.
> —Why did you do that? Why did you have to
>   do that?
>
> Yet when the bell rang he was neat in the line,
> Out of step usually but first off with his cap.
> —Why were you at ease with them only in the
>   schoolroom?[33]

The boy who cowered against the drainpipe during recess was of
course Winfield himself. As he wrote Eleanor Metcalf during their
affair in 1943, "Jeannette—in Newport we lived opposite the school
—who could watch my against-the-drain-pipe immobility in the
schoolyard, frequently threatened to go forth and do battle when

---

[31] Ibid., pp. 72–74; WTS, "Bookman's Galley," *Providence Sunday Journal,*
17 September 1944, sec. 6, p. 6.

[32] Report cards from Grades 3 and 4, Cranston-Calvert School, Scott Collection, John Hay Library.

[33] WTS, "Second Grade," *Collected Poems,* pp. 10–11.

she observed my lack of response to— oh, I don't know: taunts, or challenges. I am humiliated now to think of it."[34]

The boyhood habit of withdrawing from physical conflict, of avoiding the showdown, was encouraged and applauded by the women—his mother, Essie and Grammie Wilbar, and his school-teachers—who dominated his existence. But, in the long run, it caused him to call his maleness into question. Here, for example, is another speech from his unpublished verse play, "Biography at the Open Grave," about Newport; the lines are spoken by a somewhat ill-tempered and gossipy neighbor, but they are *written* by Win Scott, and describe him as (he thought) some others must have seen him:

> Got the same light hair—same sneaky way
> Of keeping to himself. Offish, he was,
> Even at five years old, and worse at ten.
> I never considered him a manly boy.[35]

In play Winfield shied away from the difficult or the dangerous feats that boys like to test their courage against. There was, for example, the fence at Thurston Easton's grandfather's place. The rest of Winfield's companions made a game of running up slant-wise on the fence, grasping the top rail, and vaulting over onto Mr. Easton's grass. "At once," Scott recalled, "I was seized with a cold fear: I could not do it." The others dared him, jeered at his half-hearted efforts, and left, announcing that Winfield did not "amount to anything." Alone, the boy screwed up his courage and tried the fence again, awkwardly but successfully. His fear conquered, he jumped again and again until he could do it just the same as the others. And he kept jumping until Thurston Easton came out of his house to witness his accomplishment. "I guess I amount to something now. Don't I?" Winfield asked.[36] The ritual of surmounting barriers, real or imagined, is common to most cultures, and what happened to Winfield in the Eastons' yard has happened, in one form or another, to most children. But the intense emotional strug-gle—intense enough to be recollected with absolute clarity forty

---

[34] WTS to EM, 28 April 1943.
[35] WTS, "Biography," p. 11.
[36] WTS, "Owl," pp. 171–172.

years later—distinguishes the boy's experience from most such rites
of initiation. For once, he had stood up to his tormenting demons,
within and without, and won.

A number of childhood adventures are recorded in "The Owl in
the Hall," but not, surprisingly (because it produced one of Scott's
best poems), the day when Buffalo Bill came to town. The poem
will not bear excerpting:

Indian Summer—Buffalo Summer

Opened like a big new colored-picture book,
The morning took us early with the summer wind
Coming over the streets and yards from the
    harbor.

There was no game good enough for that
    morning.
By 10 o'clock my mother put on her new shirtwaist
And Aunt Essie was there in her black hat
    with the cherries.

I ran ahead of them, all the way to the
    corner
Clutching my cap pistol, ran out of the sun
And climbed a bench in the little park under
    the walnuts.

It must have been time: on the curbs all
    fathers and mothers,
Even Miss Pitman and her cane, old Mr. Kaull
    and his pipe,
Baby Shea, the big policeman, in the middle
    of Broadway.

Just then I caught my sister and pulled out
    her hair-ribbon.
O then we stood still and amazed, hearing
    far off
The sweet incredible fife, the murmur of
    coming drums.

Every now and then a cop on a motorcycle.
But at last over the dust, out of the shade
    and light,
The Indians rode before us their arrogant
    horses.

Ah I had no genuine breath for such words
   made flesh—
The brown torsos, cheekbones, streaked with
   warpaint,
The head-dresses blowing wide like unfurled
   turkeys.

Then came the squaws, then came the little
   Indians,
And cages with buffaloes, wolves, hyenas,
   coyotes,
An ancient stagecoach waddling, and then the
   scouts—

The scouts with lashed-leather gloves and
   buckskin jackets,
Bearing their rifles bravely across their
   knees,
And then just behind them an old man in an
   open carriage.

Old, old Buffalo Bill, bowing and smiling,
Lifting his hat from his long white hair,
   and riding
Right up Broadway in a little yellow-wheeled
   cart.[37]

That poem is full of wonder, and the wonder is artfully commun-
icated. Most miraculous of all is not that Buffalo Bill should have
appeared, almost ignominiously "in a little yellow-wheeled cart,"
but that he rode "Right up Broadway," the familiar, heavily traveled boundary of Winfield's young existence. Cleverly, a double point
of view is achieved. On the one hand, the boy writes in excitement
of how it was ("I ran ahead of them, all the way to the corner"),
and, on the other, the grown man who is the poet manages to suggest how transitory it all is—the exotic West, now dead, the stagecoach, now obsolete for roads that carry cops on motorcycles, and
of course Buffalo Bill himself, soon to be defunct. The event, as unfamiliar as that of the tethered buffalo grazing, does not frighten;
the glamorous past is caged to be admired and does not threaten
the familiar present. The boy worshipped the dying past, and the

[37] WTS, "Indian Summer—Buffalo Summer," *New and Selected Poems*, pp.
14–15.

man he became showed us, without telling, how it shimmered into last glow one picture-book autumn morning in Newport. Poems like "Indian Summer—Buffalo Summer" fully justified John Ciardi's 1946 declaration that he knew of "no poet in America who has written more simply and movingly of his childhood than has Scott in his sketches of early days in Newport, Rhode Island."[38]

Then the war to end all wars began, bands played and flags flew in the countless parades up and down Broadway, and with unintentional symbolism Winfield lost the Hughes button his Republican family had conferred upon him and became, at six, an ardent Wilsonian. Like all good American boys, he hated the Kaiser, named his pet cat Pershing, bought war-savings stamps, thought of the starving Belgian children (when reminded by his mother) at dinnertime, tilled a vegetable garden in the schoolyard Saturday mornings, and—best of all—joined the local boys' army, complete with a roughhewn and immobile wooden tank liberated from a boy soldier's yard, and proclaimed himself, because of his name, the General.

Winfield and his companions were part of the crusade to make the world safe for democracy. When word came, after a false alarm, that the Allies had won, the local boys' army (which had taken on Jeannette as Red Cross nurse) rejoiced in the victory. "What made it especially wonderful," Scott ironically recounted in "The Owl in the Hall," "was not just that the war was over but the relief that there would never be war again. We had done it. We had all done it; fighting in the Argonne and Belleau Woods and Chateau-Thierry, and saving stamps and peach stones, and knitting facecloths on Tyler Street."[39] Uncle Harold, his father's brother, who had fought at the Argonne, came home wounded and shaken; an ironic poem, "We'll All Feel Gay," describes his homecoming. Other veterans returned in still worse shape; one of them killed his wife and then himself. and Winfield, growing up, began to wonder, first if the glorious victory was worth the cost, and then, as the country turned against Wilson's League of Nations, to doubt whether there had been a victory at all, and finally to conclude in the 1930's that no

[38] John Ciardi, "Winfield Townley Scott," *University of Kansas City Review* 13 (Winter 1946): 120.
[39] WTS, "Owl," pp. 174–211.

war could be justified. To his death, Scott was a pacifist and inveighed against all wars, including the one in Vietnam.

The war confronted Winfield Townley Scott while he was very young, and made indelible impressions. So, too, did his early encounters with sex, which he learned to associate with shame and guilt. One night, his father came into the bedroom Winfield shared with his younger sister, covered up Jeannette, and turned to Winfield's bed, where the boy, half-asleep, lay curled up tight at the edge of the bed.

" '*Take your hands out of there!*' he said with a sudden, harsh anger; and he snatched at my arms, pulling my hands away from my crotch. He adjusted the blankets, now with my arms outside, and left me stunned, hurt, frightened, insulted. What had I done? Nothing wrong that I knew of. I knew only that I had been accused when I was innocent. For no cause I had been presented with a sense of shame. I was truly bewildered and shocked. And I can still hear his voice as he spoke that night.

"So there was an end and a beginning."[40] Winfield would never be so innocent again, and never so incurious.

His real initiation came furtively and nastily, in the dark, damp cellar of a schoolmate named Ralph. Older and stronger than Winfield, then seven or eight, Ralph prevailed upon him to follow him home from school into his empty house and then down cellar. Winfield, frightened, did not understand, and Ralph's efforts to give him an erection failed.

After a few moments he dropped me and stood up directly in front of me, almost over me. "Go ahead," he said. "Suck it." No—no—no. "Do you see that basket up there?" Ralph said. There was an old wicker basket suspended from the ceiling beams. Now I was shaking, I was so scared. "Well," said Ralph, pushing at my face, "I've got a poisonous snake in that basket. If you don't do what I say I'll let him out."

Later I felt almost sick and the terror was still so powerfully on me as I ran down Cranston Avenue that the moment I got home I blabbed the whole story to my mother. There were adult interviews, recriminations, bans on my going anywhere with Ralph, trouble for everyone. And yet it was I, not long after, who induced another boy into a privy apparently long abandoned . . . and in there, more than once, we

[40] Ibid., p. 228.

fumbled away at the half-childish, half-animal experiments, pre-orgasmic, instinctual, and nameless.[41]

What effect did that snake-in-the-basket experience have? "I am doubtful it scarred me psychologically" Scott confided to his journal in 1944 "—but I do think it brought sexual consciousness to me long before I should have had it, and that I have it to thank for the too many years of too much sexual fumbling, mostly of course with other boys." Such, however, are the experiences, he continues, "of a large majority of adolescent boys, I believe, and not at all neces-sarily vicious: after all, one large majority of us do *not* matriculate to homosexuality."[42] Just how common such experiences are is doubtful; few, certainly, are so young exposed to sex in so brutal a way. The wonder is that Scott, brought up almost exclusively by women and having begun sexual experimentation so young, did not graduate to the ranks of practicing homosexuals. His poetry sometimes indulges in fantasies about possible homosexual rela-tionships, but he far more often wrote as he lived: as a man admir-ing of and admired by women.

Still another lasting influence derived from growing up in a com-munity which also housed a Summer Colony of the very rich. It was at the home—abandoned, since fall had come—of a member of the Colony that Winfield and three of his companions suffered their first brush with the law. Broadway, only a block from the boy's house, stood at one edge of his universe; in the other direction, away from the ocean, the boy's encompassable world dead-ended at Kay Street. The houses on Kay Street did not measure up to those on *the* Avenue, Bellevue, but they were nonetheless massive compared to the Scotts' modest home. One fall afternoon, four young adventurers—Winfield, Fred Hall, Donald Manchester, and Brother Barr—decided to explore a particularly inviting yellow gingerbread house on Kay Street. In a barn to the rear of the house, behind unlocked doors, Brother Barr discovered an open touring car. One by one the boys "took turns sitting behind the wheel . . . and carrying on a continual 'Brrr-brrr-brrr' sound to simulate the motor. It was the most wonderful time. . . ." But then the police came and the boys were herded into the jingjing wagon to go to the station

41 Ibid., pp. 230–231.
42 WTS, 1944 Journal, 20 January 1944.

and eventually, as they feared, to jail. Of course they were let off with a warning to be more careful in the future, since "locked-up summer places don't do too well for playgrounds." Later the four boys reassembled and glamorized the event until each of them was sure that he at least had not been frightened. But they gave the yellow gingerbread house, with its treasured automobile in the barn, a wide berth in the future.[43]

The Summer Colony also provided the site of other adventures:

Out of Season: Newport

Always when autumn comes on and the Saturday
    morning rains
I remember hunting horsechestnuts. It is
    the best weather.
I remember a particular time, my sister and I
Setting out with the cart and a burlap bag
    toward the rich section.

It is the best weather for the rain was heavy
    at night, the wind
Chilled the dark day, spattered harbor mist
    through the town trees;
And up the street we trudged toward the Avenue
Of great lawns and chestnuts and a marvelous
    harvest.

It was something for nothing, I guess. A few
    horsechestnuts
And strings to toss them appeased my
    generation, but I
For no utilitarian reason coveted cartloads—
And there they glistened by hundreds in the
    rain-thick grass,

Bounced on the gravel walk, into the gutter
    leaves, shining
Out of their leathery husks, or half out, and
    yet more beyond
The long fence made of two iron pipes
    horizontal
Through green wooden posts carved with acorn
    tops.

[43] WTS, "Owl," pp. 149–155.

It was some minutes after I had dared crawl
    through
And had raced back and forth to the burlap
    bag which my sister
Sustained half full by strength of herself
    and the fence
I saw the rich boy and girl in the window
    laughing at us.

The house was so far across the lawn that
    maybe
They will not see my face redden, my hands'
    uncertain shame.
As if I had not been observed I pick up three
    more
And show as I leave through the rails that
    this special work

I've reason to do has been done sufficiently
    here.
"Let's go home now." And Jeannette says,
    "I'll help pull."
And we start dragging the cart very carefully
    down the street.
Anyone seeing us can see what we're doing is
    all right to do.[44]

Caught in the foolish act of carting away horsechestnuts, laughed at by the rich children, Winfield would not be shamed; at least he would not show his shame.

These two incidents—the "arrest" and the horsechestnut adventure—only begin to suggest the awe with which the boy and his family regarded the rich. Grandfather Scott was the most reverential; at his store he stocked garden supplies, and occasionally he would have dealings with the gardeners from the mansions on Bellevue or even the estates along Ocean Drive, and on Sundays he took his invariable drive in his freshly washed and polished car to behold the wonders of the Summer Colony. Once, Grandfather Scott had met Mr. Vanderbilt himself. In one of his first love letters to Eleanor Metcalf, Win Scott wrote,

[44] WTS, "Out of Season: Newport," *Collected Poems*, pp. 27–28.

. . . I think I do understand what you say of the people you've known most of your life, of what that class is like and all the rest of it. Of course, as you suppose, I know very little about them and my own reactions are not pure: I've felt in more mature years that I was marked by my Newport boyhood. Those immensely rich people there were continually referred to in my family's middleclass circles as the salt of the earth: they were the gods near whom we were privileged to live, etc., and their monstrous palaces were the object of our constant Sunday afternoon inspection—usually from afar. All this I believed implicitly. It seemed to me a wondrous dream that I might grow up and make piles of money and live in such places. Well, I got away from that long ago, god knows; but it was for a long time my habit to refer to such people with a sort of bitter hatred. Then at last I recovered from that. It no longer interests me that what I care for, mean to stand for, would only amuse them, and I am indifferent. They are not people whose approval would in any way justify me—*that*'s the point; though their disapproval might. I practice arrogance on the subject (a sign still I've not wholly forgotten them?).[45]

The chestnut-gathering child had felt a certain guilt and donned a cloak of dignity as protection against those who laughed at him. Grown up, he more consciously disdained the values of the rich Philistines whose only use for art was to be amused by it. But neither the poem nor the letter could succeed in totally exorcising the mature poet's vision of the boy and girl in the window, looking down on him with confident and scornful superiority.

By the time Winfield Townley Scott was born, what Henry James called the creation of "the palpable pile" (the Ocean Drive monstrosities) had "been going on for years to such a tune that the face of nature was now as much obliterated as possible, and the original shy sweetness as much as possible bedizened and bedevilled."[46] So it seemed to James, but not to the Scotts—they saw the gold and not the dross.

As for the Summer Colony, it observed the middle-class townspeople not at all: "The economy of Newport was of course much affected. as though the Summer Colony bestrode the rest of us like a cow; the rest of us, "in trade," sat beneath the teats. I think we were not dependent upon it to the extent we should have met

[45] WTS to EM, 14[?] April 1943.
[46] Henry James, "The Sense of Newport," *The American Scene* (New York, 1907; reissued, Bloomington, Ind.: Indiana University Press, 1968), p. 204.

disaster without it: there were enough Newporters to take in each other's washing and thus survive. Yet there was the cow, and there were we. My impression is that the cow scarcely knew we were there." And that of course made all the difference. "We were so entirely aware of the world of the rich and altogether unknown to it. . . . We were nothing to them, hardly ever looked at by them. Nor our world of little streets and hedges and picket fences, of little houses. But always we could gaze upon their sprawling world."[47] Perhaps when the Scott children gathered horsechestnuts, it was in the hope of being discovered, of for once attracting the notice of the Summer Colony. Perhaps a similar desire—not to join the very rich, but to *show* them—helped fuel Winfield's ambition to become a writer.

In the beginning there was Tom Swift and there were the Rover Boys, and Winfield noted self-consciously that the Rover Boys series had been written by Arthur M. Winfield. "(My uncommon name, after all, was a part—who can say how large a part?—of my feeling of difference.) It gave me an idea. The time would come, I decided, when I should be a writer and would write just such a wonderful series for boys." Then Essie took him to the library and he brought home *Men of Iron*, with stories about boys and pictures of knights in armor. "With *Men of Iron* I was a boy named Myles Farnsworth in the 15th Century. . . . I had entered a world of dream. And soon enough I was deep in the instinct to sustain that state: as soon as one book closed, I opened another. On and on for years and years."[48]

Acquisition of *The World Book Encyclopedia* stirred up a family crisis. An elegant lady, Mrs. K., came to call on Bessie Townley and sold her a set of the encyclopedia, for a down payment of twenty-five dollars. It so happened that there was "exactly $25 in the house, an extra $25. . . . My Grandfather Townley had sent it to us to cover train fares for an imminent Easter trip to Haverhill. But there was the accomplished lady, there was the fascinating sample book, and there were the two bright children to whom my mother would deny nothing she could help in this world." When Pa Scott came home that evening, he was quite certain that his wife had been cheated, the more so when he discovered that the receipt was signed only "Mrs. K.," no complete name to trace. Recrimina-

[47] WTS, "Owl," p. 242.
[48] Ibid., pp. 213–214.

tions ensued, and "a kind of excitement, however desperate—after all there was money involved." But Mrs. K was again discovered in the neighborhood, another twenty-five dollars came from Haverhill to finance the Easter trip, and the night the nine green and black and gold volumes arrived, the Northern Lights pulsed and swayed and Douglas Scott looked up Aurora Borealis and read about it, while Winfield and Jeannette "gathered close around and listened. . . . And there was a picture, too; all just as Mrs. K. had said."[49]

One picture in the set had a "a hypnotically sexual effect" on Winfield. "It was a full page reproduction of a painting of a gladiatorial climax. In the background the shouting Romans leaned toward the fighters with thumbs down for death. In the foreground the half-naked victor stood, sword in hand and one foot on the half-naked gladiator stretched helpless beneath him. I identified myself with the vanquished man." The boy, who was nine, began to write things. "I think I wrote a few poems of the free verse sort, and then or a little later tried to write down stories I made up in the long hours of daydreaming which, too, had begun."[50]

The best books of all came on Winfield's tenth birthday. He had asked for them for Christmas, but copies could not be found in time, and so he did not get *The Adventures of Tom Sawyer* and *The Adventures of Huckleberry Finn* until 30 April 1920, as his family was preparing to move to Haverhill. Boy and man, Win Scott loved Mark Twain, even dreamed of meeting him, and those books, one inscribed "From Pa and Ma" and the other "From Jeannette," were with him when he died, "the only books to survive from those I had as a child."[51]

Newport was the garden, and seeds planted there continued to grow. Winfield carried with him on the train to Haverhill a desire to please the womenfolk who ruled his life and would rule it still more strongly in Massachusetts; a fear of change and challenges; ambiguous and complicated attitudes toward war, sex, and the rich; a love for the past and for cool Sunday walks in graveyards; a passion for books and the fantasy world they offered; a sense of the beauty of the place he was reluctantly leaving behind; and

[49] Ibid., pp. 219–227.
[50] Ibid., p. 232.
[51] Ibid., p. 258.

above all a consciousness that he was different, that he was special, and that he must justify (by writing, perhaps) that difference.

On learning that he was moving to Haverhill, Winfield hauled his outworn tricycle out of the basement and methodically smashed it to pieces. His father was hardly more eager to leave his lifelong home in Newport: recently he had invested in a lot, and plans to build a two-story house, with separate rooms for Winfield and Jeannette, were under way; "from the lot," Scott's memoir reported, "you could smell the sea." But Grandfather Townley's health was failing, and he wanted Bessie Townley Scott, his only child, to come back to Haverhill. A job was found for Winfield's father in a shoe factory, and the matter was settled. "My Grandfather Townley was the sort of man who got his own way, and my father was not."[52]

In one sense, his son was glad enough to leave: it would spare him further confrontations with a neighbor boy named Vincent Moore, who, to settle a quarrel with Winfield that last summer in Newport, "promptly grabbed a hell of a big stick and whacked me across the head. I can still remember vividly the way some steps came up—as people always say—and hit me, and then the sidewalk. . . . It was my fault: I started the quarrel; but Vincent was, it was later decided, some sort of mental case. I could hear him say, 'There, I guess that's killed him.' " Not quite; Winfield picked himself up and ran up the back stairs to his house, his head split open and blood boiling over him and his mother too distraught at first to minister to his wounds.[53] The incident, probably, represented Win Scott's single experience with physical violence.

Leaving the Wilbars was hardest. The day before departure, Essie took Winfield for a long walk, the boy silent in the realization that this was the last of many walks. "The next morning my mother was all dressed up for the train, and Jeannette and I were all dressed up too, and my mother took us next door to the Wilbars 'just for a minute' . . . Grammie leaned forward and took me in her arms, pressing me against her soft and snuffish calico, against the aged smoothness of her face, and Essie ran from the room out into the kitchen. Then I too ran. Essie stood in the corner by the sink,

---

[52] Ibid., pp. 255–256.
[53] Ibid., pp. 260–262; also interview, Mrs. Jeannette Wolfe, Los Angeles, 2 February 1970.

her face in her hands, sobbing loudly. I made one anguished, help-less glance toward her but I kept running through the kitchen and out the back door and down the steps and away."[54] Summers, he would see the Wilbars again, and Essie wrote him notes, one of them reporting on the scandalous appearance of one of his cousins wearing knickerbockers, "from the rear she was a sight, she is as broad as a house. . . . You haven't got a pair of pants you can lend me so I can also be in style?"[55]

Then, on a visit to Newport in February 1925, he and Jeannette went to call on the Wilbars and no one answered their knocks. Win-field broke open the bathroom window and climbed through to find Essie dead on the kitchen floor, and Grammie, who had suffered a stroke but would live for another five years, fallen from her bed and unable to move. At Christmastime that year, Winfield expiated some of his grief in an editorial-poem for the Haverhill High *Chronicle*. "E.M.W.," he wrote, "was our 'second mother,' our 'first wife.' When we were very, very young, she made for us a pleasant land of stories, of princes and princesses, of dragons and little towns with colored roofs and winding streets, of sunshiny days and lavender rainy days, of cutouts and little verses." But she died, and while outside the white lilacs bloomed,

I go about the rooms and find so many things:
A piece of paper slipped into a book:
The last page read. Here I find some rings
Upon the shelf; she was going to look
For curtains to sew them on. These
        murmurings

Are all about me, and so often near
It seems she may come back to do her sewing,
Perhaps to pick this book up, lying here,
Silently to steal in without my knowing,
And so happily to startle me to fear;

It would be so like her to do just that,
Of all her daily tasks to come aware;—
Sweeping of dust of fancy or of fact,—

[54] WTS, "Owl," pp. 264–266.
[55] Esther Wilbar to WTS, 16 January 1923, Scott Collection, John Hay Library.

> I listen for her step upon the stair,
> Not yet convinced that she will not come
> back.[56]

The poem is of course sentimental, but only because words were inadequate to express the boy's loss. No one will challenge the genuineness of the emotion, the sincerity of the grief.

"I wonder how it would be with me if I had never left Newport, Rhode Island?" Win Scott speculated in *Exiles and Fabrications*. Later in the same book, writing of Thornton Wilder's *Our Town*, he unwittingly answers the question. A double point of view, Scott observed, "an intermeshing of past and present, runs throughout the play and accounts for its peculiar poignancy. It is as though the golden veil of nostalgia . . . bisects the stage down center: it glows left and right upon past and present, and the players come and go through its shimmering summer haze, now this side of it, now that; but the audience sees both sides of it."[57] Through just such a nostalgic haze, Win Scott saw his boyhood home; as a golden past against which the present necessarily suffered by comparison, as a place secure against change—for, although the horse gave way to the automobile, the gas lights to electricity, and the Yankees to the foreigners coming in from Fall River, Newport remained permanently frozen and changeless in his imagination. How would it have been with Win Scott if he had never left Newport? He never did.

[56] WTS, "The Editor Says," Haverhill High *Chronicle*, 3 December 1926, Scott Collection, John Hay Library.
[57] WTS, *Exiles and Fabrications* (1961), pp. 17, 56.

The city set northeast;
Not east enough to reach to the ocean,
Not north enough to have right of mountains.
Country where spring is sharp and late, summer
Short, the fall early, winter deep.
Home is the place that, when you grow wise
    enough.
You go away from.[1]

3. Shoetown

IN HAVERHILL, WINFIELD went through high school, enjoyed the first sweet taste of success as a writer, found heroes to worship, fell in love, encountered people and places he would later transform into some of his greatest poetry, and, accomplishment above all others, managed to please his Grandmother Townley.

Winning Aggie Townley's approval was not easy, but it was important. "A real bossy Yankee" who wore starched nightgowns,[2]

[1] WTS, "Prologue to a Portrait of an American City," unpublished poem (194?), 95 lines, Scott Collection, John Hay Library, Brown University.
[2] Interview, Roderick O'Connor, Port Republic, Maryland, 27 September 1969.

she ran her household, expanded to take in the four Scotts, as a kind
of fiefdom. From her side of the family, young Winfield derived
his only literary ancestor, the Scottish poet James Hogg; but more
directly, her influence hardened in her grandson some of those traits
of personality—insecurity, fear, a desperate desire to be approved,
the need to *earn* love—which had begun to form in Newport.

Agnes Hogg Townley was, like Winfield's Grandmother Scott,
an intensely bitter woman. But where Susan Scott retired in stoical
Yankee quiet, Grandmother Townley found ways of sharing her
misery. She had given birth to only one child, since, as she told
Winfield, "I was a frail young woman. I didn't weigh no more than
ninety pounds. Doctor didn't want me to have but the one child.
And thank goodness, I was married to a man not a beast!" Grandfather Townley did not discuss such matters with his grandson or
with others, but he was regularly absent, every Sunday when the
rest of the family went to church, visiting his mistress. Win's sister
Jeannette remembers going to the cemetery shortly after Grandfather Townley died (in the summer of 1924) and finding beautiful
red roses on his grave. Aggie Townley snatched them up and threw
them in the trash can.[3]

Grandmother Townley was occasionally possessed by an almost
uncontrollable temper, and on mornings when she had got out of
the wrong side of the bed, it was advisable not to cross her. She had
once hurled a carving knife at her still adolescent daughter Bessie.[4]

It was not much of a life for Douglas and Bessie Scott, living
under the roof of her parents and tending first to the illness of her
father and then to the far more prolonged and difficult arthritis of
her mother. At first, friends whom Douglas and Bessie, still a young
couple, had met at church would drop over to visit, while Jeannette
and Winfield perched listening and unseen on the stairs. But after
a while, when Grandmother Townley fell ill, the visits stopped, and
Winfield's parents seem to have had almost no social life. Pa Scott
was dominated by his mother-in-law; it was her home and she ruled
the roost. And Bessie Scott became a slave to her own mother, waiting on her hand and foot, responding to the brass bell that the in-

---

[3] WTS, "The Owl in the Hall," manuscript (1957), pp. 4–5, Scott Collection,
John Hay Library; interview, Mrs. Jeannette Wolfe, Los Angeles, 2 February
1970.
[4] WTS, "Owl," p. 4.

valided Aggie Townley would ring incredibly often, summoning someone to pick up a thread from the carpet or to fold the paper properly. When she was cleaning out the house in Haverhill in 1967, Jeannette found the brass bell and threw it away.[5]

Grandfather Townley, ill when his daughter brought her family to live with him in 1920, took five long, painful years to die of angina. As his health worsened, doctors and nurses hovered about, and an unnatural air of tension pervaded the house on Cedar Street. Normal childhood romping and clatter were of course taboo. Even the violin lessons which had taken Winfield as far as a passable rendering of "The Blue Bells of Scotland" were cut off. The boy himself suffered through a severe case of pneumonia in his early adolescence; the ensuing period of bedrest and curtailed activity only aggravated his tendency to withdraw into books and bedside conversations with his dying grandfather—mostly about reincarnation.[6]

Winfield was still more clearly his grandmother's favorite. She happily boasted about her "Weenfield," as she pronounced his name: he was handsome, he was obedient, he did not get into fights or come home dirty or yell like other boys, and as time went on he began to win prizes for his poems. In the autograph album Winfield received for his fourteenth birthday, she summed up her philosophy in words for her grandson to live by: "You will never be sorry for living a white life; for doing your level best; for your faith in humanity; for being kind to the poor; for looking before leaping; for hearing before judging; for being candid and frank; for thinking before speaking."[7] Eight clauses to direct a life, and three of them say— Proceed with Caution: look before you leap; hear before you judge; think before you speak. The boy learned the lesson well, and as an adult kept a tight rein on his emotions, especially the emotion of anger. Aggie Townley loved her grandson, as much as she was able, but the love was—or must have seemed to Winfield, which comes to the same thing—always conditional. If he was good, he would be loved. And if not . . . the boy did not dare to find out.

In the house on Cedar Street propriety governed behavior. At the top of the medicine chest reposed a bottle of brandy (Grand-

---

[5] Interview, Mrs. Jeannette Wolfe, 2 February 1970.
[6] EMS to SD, 13 April 1970.
[7] Agnes Townley to WTS, 30 April 1924, Scott Collection, John Hay Library.

father Townley took brandy occasionally after his first heart attack, but one bottle lasted for many, many years) and a bottle of gin (Jeannette can remember taking gin and hot water during menstruation). But no one drank for other than therapeutic reasons. Years later, when Win and Jeannette returned to Haverhill for a visit, they had each taken half a drink of Scotch when their mother asked them; "Are you drunk yet?" Not yet: both of them had, by that time, developed rather high, perhaps medically unsound, degrees of tolerance.[8]

Ties of the enduringly strong liaison of brother and sister, loosened in Newport by the Wilbars' exclusion of Jeannette, were firmly knotted in Haverhill. The Scotts had visited Haverhill before, briefly, and one summer Winfield had gone alone to stay with his grandparents in a double house (the other half occupied by a mysteriously admirable older boy named Dudley Fitts), but in 1920, when the move to Haverhill became permanent, Winfield and Jeannette knew no other children and of necessity became playmates as never before. That first winter, Jeannette remembers, they went sledding and Winfield let a little girl from the neighborhood ride on his sled. At the foot of the hill, Jeannette fought with the intruder for her impudence. "He's *my* brother."[9]

Grandfather John Townley, like Grandfather Scott, had started from humble, difficult beginnings to achieve a measure of success in the world. He was only eleven years old when his own father, who had come over from England, dropped dead in a hayfield in West Newbury, Massachusetts. Forced to leave school, he went to work in a shoe factory; soon after, his forefinger was cut off by a machine. "I try to imagine that day," his grandson wrote in "The Owl in the Hall." "The little boy. The sudden machine. Somebody running to fetch the doctor. Somebody bringing the boy home to his mother. I am stopped still, thinking of how that child kept a roof over his mother's head until she died ten years later, and of how at the other end of his life, after his death, money he had saved paid my way through college." There was no nonsense about John Townley, and Winfield stood somewhat in awe of him. "My Grandfather Townley was altogether kind and generous to me, but I can only guess that his air of independence, of concentration on busi-

[8] Interview, Mrs. Jeannette Wolfe, 2 February 1970.
[9] Ibid.

ness, struck me as a sort of severity. In business affairs he was tough and scrupulously honest. He demanded no more than he gave, but that left him to demand rigidly."

A hard worker until stricken, John Townley was up at dawn to manage the shoe factory, and he banked most of his $150 weekly salary, a princely one for Haverhill in those days. He despised shoddy work, and he was disturbed by the quickly rising wages of shoeworkers during the war. The money went to their heads. "He blamed the labor unions and the Jews. The unions had of course seen to it that wages were hiked. As for the new, Jewish element among Haverhill shoe manufacturers, it tended to specialize in a cheap shoe, and my grandfather despised that." He was a "a man who combined integrity and intolerance, generosity and strictness," and one who knew the cost of a dollar in sweat.[10] Sometimes he would toss a handful of pocket silver on the floor and watch delightedly while Winfield and Jeannette scrambled for it. Another time, Douglas Scott made plans to take Bessie to Boston for a musical show. "It would have been a most unusual event. Pa was not employed at the time and Grandfather Townley raised almighty hell: such waste, such giddiness, such irresponsibility. They did not go."[11]

In *Exiles and Fabrications*, Win Scott offers a glimpse of Haverhill in the days from 1920 to his graduation from high school in 1927:

It was a small-city boyhood with a small-town flavor, for we pretty much lived within a neighborhood. Our friends, our school, the store where groceries and meat were bought—all these were in walking distance, a few blocks this way or that. Wide open fields lay just beyond our street and not far beyond those the first low hills of New Hampshire. So it was a small-town boyhood with a country flavor too. The swimming hole, the rambles in little woods. All the adults gave up Hearts and Bridge and Poker for a while and played Mahjong. Sunday morning everybody went to church, except my Grandfather Townley. Sunday afternoon the whole family piled into the high-set Nash (gray silk shades at the rear windows and a crystal vase for flowers) and rode to Newburyport or the beaches along the short New Hampshire coast or just into the country.[12]

[10] EMS to SD, 15 February 1970; WTS, "Owl," pp. 135–138.
[11] EMS to SD, 15 February 1970.
[12] EMS, *Exiles and Fabrications* (1961), p. 102.

Winfield tramped those fields and swam naked in Merrill's Brook (there is a poem about it) with his fellows, but he was different. For one thing, he was conspicuously neat. "Somehow, as a child," he lamented to Horace Gregory in 1935, "I never had any very rough clothes and, now and then, I'd have to appear at some gang assemblage where such clothes were more or less obligatory. I'd put on my oldest blue serge suit but, no matter how shiny it was, it never looked knockabout—like the other boys' outfits. I used to be afraid that my contemporaries would think me a snob: I only looked like one, I wasn't really."[13]

Winfield's behavior, like his appearance, was circumspect. He got his exercise taking hikes through the woods, to the Whittier homestead in Amesbury, or around Lake Kenoza, but for the most part, he liked to stay home, reading, while Jeannette played football. "It was hard work to get him out of the house," his father recalled in 1969.[14] If he harbored rebellion in his breast, it stayed there. Or perhaps, as classmate John N. Dyer believes, "Winfield and I both went [to church] with the families with few of the rebellious thoughts and acts that are common today."[15] No doubt his teachers regarded him much as another classmate, Madoline Mears Granton, did. "I always had a deep respect for him," she wrote, "as he was such a gentleman, but not a 'sissy.' He was rather quiet and reserved, but he had a feeling of warmth about him. He was always immaculate. . . . He was neither mischievous nor athletic. He was inclined to be quiet, like his father."[16]

There was an aura of independence about Winfield, as if he were with the crowd but not really in it, observing what others were doing but not really part of it. "He didn't need social companionship," Jackson George, another high school friend put it. "He was perfectly happy reading or thinking."[17] But of course he did care what his peers thought of him, and since he was good at pleasing them, as well as adults, Winfield became popular. When he won prizes for poetry, his schoolmates were proud for the school and

---

[13] WTS to Horace Gregory, 9 November 1935, Syracuse University Library.
[14] Interview, Douglas W. Scott, Haverhill, Massachusetts, 10 July 1969.
[15] John N. Dyer to SD, 9 February 1970. In the 1930's, when Dyer accompanied Admiral Byrd's expedition to Antarctica, Scott wrote a poem in his honor.
[16] Madoline Mears Granton to SD, 11 February 1970.
[17] Interview, Jackson George, West Newbury, Massachusetts, 11 July 1969.

did not think him odd. Another classmate who became a poet, Daniel Smythe, provides an indication of the status Winfield enjoyed:

My first memory of Win Scott was in 1926–27 when we were in the same class in Haverhill High School, and he was editor of the *Chronicle*. I must admit I did not like him. He seemed too self-assured, too positive of his own theories of poetry, too much admired by his teachers and the administration. He was healthy, energetic, handsome—and he had ideas. And he printed his ideas. I was too shy and self-conscious to feel that I could communicate intelligently with such a person. . . . He was a big wheel in school, and I was not. We both lived on the same street in Haverhill, Cedar Street, but hardly ever spoke to each other.[18]

At church Winfield belonged to the Christian Endeavor Society of Centre Congregational Church and would walk down the Main Street hill Sunday afternoons with John Dyer, George Chase, Bob Emerson, and various sisters to attend the society's meetings. In retrospect, George Chase recalls, those were pleasant times. In his senior year, Scotty (as he was usually called in high school) was elected to a sub rosa fraternity called, oddly, the Eunuchs and made up of class leaders in athletic and academic achievement. As part of the initiation ceremony, he and Chase, blindfolded, were driven off into the country in the dead of night and left to get back home as best they could. "We sat down under trees," Chase remembers, "awaiting daylight, when I climbed high to discover signs of a road, town, etc. Eventually, we got to a small town, a telephone, and a call to his folks. His father came and got us. Mine would have none of that foolishness."[19] He belonged not only to the Eunuchs but to the officially approved Hi-Y club, and served as its secretary in his senior year. From this evidence and the reports of his classmates, it is clear that young Scott, though somewhat aloof, unathletic, and dry of wit, succeeded in earning the respect and admiration of his peers.

So others saw him. But if, as seems probable, the title character of "Finkelstein Faust," a long, unpublished poem, resembles Scott himself, that was emphatically not the way he regarded himself:

[18] Daniel Smythe to SD, "Memories of W. T. Scott," 10 January 1970.
[19] George S. Chase to SD, 4 March 1970.

> See me as I was in my youth. Try
> To put all that you know of loneliness
> And misery and self-doubt into one mess
> Of ingrown adolescence—that was I,
> All underdone but over-read.[20]

Once every two weeks, he walked to the Haverhill Public Library for a haul of books. On the way home he would start reading with the excitement of discovering for the first time books he would later treasure. The summer of his fifteenth year, for example, he began Edgar Lee Masters's *Spoon River Anthology* as he strolled along the middle-class residential streets of Haverhill; to the end he always associated a stretch of small-town-looking houses on Lawrence Street with Masters's masterpiece.[21]

Winfield's passion for reading marked him as unusual, and made him uncomfortable with his schoolmates. "If you like books and I don't," he wrote in the school newspaper, "you're a pretty queer sort of person. If you like what I don't like, there must be something the matter with you.—And that seems to be the general opinion and viewpoint of the average person, of the average student at Haverhill High School."[22] His sense of being out of place, lonely, miserable, and self-doubting had of course been accentuated by the discovery in Miss Croston's classroom in the fall of 1924 that he wanted to be a poet. The following year was a momentous one. He was not yet in love, but, as he later reflected, "what else can I surely say of 1925? . . . I have discovered it was for me a big year. By its end I was marked as a 'different' sort of boy. If there had been neighborhood and schoolroom suspicions, they were now confirmed. It was the year in which, thinking I was seated in everlasting glory, I had sat down in a trap."[23]

Winfield began to look for literary heroes to worship in *their* everlasting glory. Soon he found them. The first, a man he would admire for forty years, was Henry Beston, who came to Haverhill on 16 December 1924, to speak on "Vagabond Days in Spain" to

[20] WTS, "Finkelstein Faust," unpublished poem (1936), 14 pages, Scott Collection, John Hay Library.
[21] WTS, "Bookman's Galley," *Providence Sunday Journal*, 12 March 1950, sec. 6, p. 10.
[22] WTS, "Shoes and Sizes and Angels," Haverhill High *Chronicle*, 4 November 1926.
[23] WTS, *Exiles*, p. 94.

the Centre Congregational Church men's club, "guest tribute 50 cents." Unusually tall and prepossessing, gifted with Irish skill in talk as well as in writing, Beston was a revelation to the boy. "You must imagine my excitement," Scott said of the occasion, "for I was fourteen years old, bookish, agonizingly ambitious to Be a Writer. To this towering, overwhelming, and very kind young man (who of course, in his thirties, did not seem in the least young to me) I was scarcely able, through my awe, to whisper a word."[24] Winfield was less shy about letters, however, and soon there was a correspondence, and then there were a few meetings, and finally there began what was to be a lifelong society of joint admiration, Beston never failing to praise Scott's latest book, Scott doing whatever he could (including the writing of a stunning article) to raise Beston's *The Outermost House*, a Thoreauvian account of a solitary winter on Cape Cod, to the status of an American classic.

Henry Beston's talk had been arranged by the energetic minister of Centre Congregational, Harry Elmore Hurd, a would-be poet himself and another of Winfield's early idols. Dr. Hurd guided the boy through his confirmation as a member of the church in the spring of 1925 ("Our class meets Thursday evening at 7:45. See you there. I am delighted with your decision to give your life to the Church. I am expecting great things of you"),[25] and when he had been duly confirmed, wrote the boy urging him to go to Harvard, Hurd's alma mater. "With your ambition, your splendid family background and your clean character you are destined to accomplish great things."[26] Hurd's own career was to follow a somewhat checkered course, as he lost his parish—and his wife—in a scandal involving another woman. But Scott remained loyal to him, and he was disappointed to find, when he was to be married for the first time, that Hurd had "resigned from the ministry" and could not perform the ceremony. For young Scott, Dr. Hurd, like Beston, played the role of encourager, never finding fault, ever praising the boy's work. As early as 1932, five years before Scott was to publish his first book of poems, Hurd wrote his protégé that "I am not foolish enough to believe that I have had much to do with your success,

[24] Ibid., p. 178.
[25] Harry Elmore Hurd to WTS, 2 March 1925, Scott Collection, John Hay Library.
[26] Ibid., 15 July 1925, Scott Collection, John Hay Library.

but I like to think that I gave you some stimulation to love beauty and especially poetry. I am expecting you to go far in your literary accomplishments."[27] Hurd also introduced the boy to other artists, including the remarkable worker in stained glass, Charles J. Connick of Boston. Effervescent, gay, gentle, Connick invited the boy to visit his workshop and to attend his occasional gatherings of artists, especially of poets. Winfield, who loved Connick's magnificent stained-glass windows, responded with a laudatory rhetorical poem about them.

Through correspondence, Scotty began to collect the signatures— and on occasion the letters—of famous writers, for his autograph album. Early in 1925, the boy began to expand his autograph collection in earnest. On a summer visit to Newport he acquired from the sympathetic Mrs. Theodore Peckham her impressive list, which included the signatures of Teddy Roosevelt, Guglielmo Marconi, Woodrow Wilson, John Hay, Oliver Wendell Holmes, Jr., William Dean Howells, and a clutch of admirals who had been stationed there. On his own, astounded at how simple it was ("you simply look them up in *Who's Who* and send a stamped return envelope"), he added Rudyard Kipling, Booth Tarkington, George Arliss (on purple stationery), William Howard Taft, Dan Beard, Joseph C. Lincoln, David Grayson (pen name of Ray Stannard Baker), Edward W. Bok (his advice for success: "Thoroughness first, then speed"), Edwin Markham, William Lyon Phelps, Edna Ferber, N. C. Wyeth, and a number of Roosevelt relatives.

Presidents, admirals, and, best of all, writers began to fill his autograph album, where he noted wonderingly that there were "few really good penmen among famous people, particularly among authors."[28] In emulation, Scotty's own penmanship rapidly deteriorated to near-illegibility. His difficult handwriting developed, he confessed to Eleanor Metcalf in 1943, "of a mating of my own carelessness and my hero-worship of various authors whose penmanship, I discovered, was very vile." The chief influence was Tarkington; Scott told Frank Merchant at Brown that he got his crabbed chirography from imitating the author of *Penrod*.[29]

<hr />

[27] Ibid., 18 May 1932, Scott Collection, John Hay Library.
[28] Autograph album, Scrapbook 1, pp. 106–108, Scott Collection, John Hay Library.
[29] WTS to EM, 6 May 1943; Frank E. Merchant to SD, 7 September 1969.

A trip to Washington in the spring of 1925 brought still closer contact with a famous man. In April, perhaps as a reward for Winfield's confirmation in the church, his Grandmother Townley took her favorite grandchild to Washington, to visit his O'Connor relatives there. (In Newport, the Scotts had spent long summer days during the war visiting the O'Connors, and Winfield's special friend Rod, on Rose Island in Narragansett Bay, where Rod's father was in charge of a munitions cache.) "We left early from Boston," Winfield recalled. "We traveled by parlor car. We ate amidst glistening waiters and shining water pitchers in the dining car. We seemed to be in a green plush world safely rocking within the rainy, gray world at either side." *Safely* is the operative word here; Win Scott was later terrified by almost all modes of travel, but felt secure on trains. In Washington, there was the line at the White House where the fifteen-year-old boy shook hands, memorably, with a most forgettable President. "I can still hear the nasal repetitions of Calvin Coolidge: 'Good morning—Great pleasure—Delighted—Good morning—Great pleasure,' and so on, the thin, quick hand moving one along as one grasped it."[30]

Having firmly committed himself to become a poet, Winfield was desperately ambitious to live up to that commitment. Inspired by his heroes—Beston, Hurd, Connick, and the bearers of the names in his autograph album—he began in the fall of 1925, his junior year, to read still more widely and to write vast quantities of copy—editorials, book reviews, poems—for the new Haverhill High School paper, the *Chronicle*.

In his junior year Winfield served as associate editor of the *Chronicle*, in his senior year as editor-in-chief. In both years he wrote his share of the editorials, usually exploring one of two themes. On the one hand he invoked the need for strong personal morality and proper behavior among his schoolmates, adopting a preacherlike tone; on the other, he inveighed against the sprawling materialism, mechanization, and industrialism which the short-sighted called progress, and he spoke instead on behalf of art and beauty.

In his very first editorial, in the issue of 23 October 1925, he could not resist referring to "editorial we," but with that cuteness

[30] WTS, *Exiles*, pp. 92–93.

out of the way, Winfield cajoled his fellow students to do their best, even in subjects they were bound to fail because the subjects "in no way agreed with their particular temperament and personality." The pep talk was directed to himself as well as to his fellows: he was experiencing traumatic difficulties in math. If one must fail, he wrote, let it be "nobly." The nobility of failure! Shades of the vanquished gladiator! A pre-Christmas editorial in the same moralistic vein recommended that students adopt a "checking account" where they could deposit vices—procrastination, cheating, gambling, drinking, noisemaking—but not draw upon them. And, in the final issue of the year, Scott combined moralism with patriotism in an "au revoir" to the graduating class: "Tell yourself that you are going to be just the best man or the best woman that you know how to be. Stick to your purpose. Above all things, follow your star. . . . You are Youth. You are America. And America is the greatest country in the world." In his senior year, in another burst of piety, Winfield complained anonymously, though his teachers may have known and could hardly have failed to approve of his authorship, that there was entirely too much gum-chewing and talking on the way to and from Chapel.[31]

Scott's editorials attacking conventional progress make up a more interesting category. Ford cars, he warned, sacrificed quality to quantity and speed of production, while it was quality that counted. A sarcastic piece ending "three cheers for Henry Ford," who was apparently a special villain to young Winfield, cited gum, movies, radio, and button-pushing as the principal benefits of progress. Machines, he insisted, were not beautiful, for they made smoke. His most effective editorial on this theme, "Generation after Generation," in the February 18, 1927, *Chronicle*, indicted his elders for falling prey to false lures: "The older generation is like a great spider which has made such a huge web that he has caught himself and practically all else in it. The generation just before us has advanced as none other ever did in the line of machinery and mechanics generally. Marvelous as some aspects of this must be allowed to be, it has proved a terrible boomerang," since men in factories lose their identity as individuals. "Youth should stand up in one

31 WTS, editorials in the Haverhill High *Chronicle*: 23 October 1925, Scrapbook 1, p. 3; 4 December 1925, Scrapbook 1, p. 8; 18 June 1926, Scrapbook 1, p. 32; [?] June 1927, Scrapbook 3, p. 155, Scott Collection, John Hay Library.

great unity and smash this net. For evidently our birthright is not
freedom but a slavery to steel and money and manufactured tinsel."
Joyfully, a week later, Winfield opened a letter from the Editor's
Room of the *New York World*. "I happened to be in West Newbury
last Sunday," Walter Lippman wrote, "and was there shown your
editorial about the younger generation. I am moved to write you
and say how much I liked it, and how exceptionally well done it
seems to me. I am wondering if you plan to write professionally
when you leave school."[32]

Most pernicious of all, the modern temper exalted the practical
over the beautiful so that people ceased to look about them. The
artist, Scotty declared with Emerson, was the seer, the man who
followed the commercial road sign to "Kodak as you go." Keeping
his own eyes open, Winfield announced the coming of the late New
England spring not in terms of flowers but of "bicycles, baby-carri-
ages and roller-skates." This concept Win Scott expressed time and
again. When freshman students of his at Brown complained that
they had nothing to write themes about, he would angrily propose
that they use their eyes and their imagination. And, in an interview
in 1967, he chose the camera metaphor to delineate his concept of
the artist: "Most people most of the time don't notice things. And
I do think that the artist even though he's not always aware of it,
is like a camera with the shutter always open. Much of the time
he's not an artist. He's a human being moving around, talking, and
wasting time, but always with the incipient awareness which now
and then without warning operates for him. Click! He's seen something."[33]

How peculiar his antimaterialism must have seemed to his family
—to John Townley, who had worked since he was a boy to arrive
at a decent standard of living, to Douglas Scott, who always responded to the sight of something of his son's in print with one of
two questions: "Will you get money for that?" or "How much will

[32] WTS, editorials in the Haverhill High *Chronicle* 6 November 1925, Scrapbook 1, p. 4; 5 February 1926, Scrapbook 1, p. 16; 12 March 1926, Scrapbook
1, p. 18; 18 February 1927, Scrapbook 3, p. 49; [?] February 1927, Scrapbook
3, p. 52, Scott Collection, John Hay Library.
[33] WTS, editorials in the Haverhill High *Chronicle*: 20 November 1925,
Scrapbook 1, p. 5; 2 April 1926, Scrapbook 1, p. 20; See also Sam Larcombe,
"An Interview with Winfield Townley Scott," *Seven*, March 1967, p. 12, Scott
Collection, John Hay Library.

you get for that?" In a letter to his son in 1962, Douglas wrote: "Do you get the 'Today Show' from New York on TV? They are always introducing an author and his next book." Implication: Why not you and *your* next book? Winfield's father meant no harm, of course. It was "the response of a wholly different standard. The standard I grew up with,"[34] Scott wrote. As early as his high school years, Scotty was reacting bitterly against that standard. Later, when it would have been very much to the benefit of his reputation to give more readings and otherwise promote his work, he would indignantly tell his wife, who encouraged such exposure, that she wanted him to whore for his art.

It was on the *Chronicle*, too, that Winfield Townley Scott began his lifelong career as book reviewer. He had turned to books originally because they took him to another, fantasy world, an unreal world that became very real to him indeed. In the "Book Corner" of his high school newspaper, the boy attempted to transform himself from fantasist to critic. For the most part, his judgments were those that might have been expected of a fifteen- or sixteen-year-old boy. In the junior year "Book Corner," for example, Scotty mentioned eight authors more than three times. Most of the names were predictable. Joseph Conrad and Rudyard Kipling were on the list, and most often mentioned of all (eight times apiece) were two other distinguished tellers of adventure tales, Robert Louis Stevenson and Mark Twain. Joseph C. Lincoln (a passion of Grammie Wilbar's) and Christopher Morley were included, but so were two writers one is surprised to find there. The first was Herman Melville, only recently rescued from total obscurity, and the other Amy Lowell, imagist poet from Boston, whose work Winfield admired extravagantly in high school.

Winfield demonstrated a few innocent glimmerings of critical acumen in his column. "There is another author, Stephen Crane," he advised his readers of 20 November 1925, "who wrote a book called 'The Red Badge of Courage.' It is a book you should look up." Another recommendation suggested that "for something very original and excellent read the poems of Robert Frost. He is, certainly, a poet, and a poet quite different from any other. . . . Another poet

[34] WTS, "*a dirty hand*": *The Literary Notebooks of Winfield Townley Scott* (1969), p. 91. See also Douglas W. Scott to WTS, 29 December 1962, Scott Collection, John Hay Library.

. . . is Edwin Arlington Robinson. There is no one else quite like him; he combines a sort of old-style poetry with a bluntness and beauty peculiar to himself. Perhaps he is our greatest living poet." This, on 29 January 1926, but by 20 May 1927, the doubt had been resolved: Robinson was indeed "the greatest living poet, and one of the finest of all time." No poet, certainly, was so much to influence Scott's own work.

Ever seeking approval, the boy sent a few of his columns to Bertrand K. Hart ("Bibliotaph") at the *Providence Journal*. "I think your Book Corner has an easy stride and a good deal of spirit," Hart responded. "You are keeping in touch with the best, and it seems clear you are infected with that excellent compound of sin and sorrow which is called book-loving, from which the afflicted never recover. Go on with it, and be happily consumed; you will travel in most engaging company." Including, as it turned out, the engaging company of Bertrand K. Hart himself, under whom Scott worked from 1931 to 1941 as assistant literary editor of the *Journal*.[35]

But there was in the "Book Corner," as in the editorials and, alas, in Scott's first poems as well, an unmistakable and probably un-avoidable self-consciousness. Going back over scrapbooks full of his high school and college writing twenty-five years later, Scott was overwhelmed by "the sense that the boy and young man wrote as though writing were a way of showing off." It was the distinction, he decided, between amateurism and professionalism in any art. "If you contrast amateur acting and the successful, real thing, you can see in the amateur the essence—it is showing-off. The differ-ence in achieved (or great) acting is a showing forth. The individual creates something beyond himself, more than himself, bigger than himself. That self, unlike the amateur's, is not displayed—it is used."[36]

Winfield won his first writing award when he was twelve in the seventh grade at Walnut Square School. In the carefully preserved scrapbook, Grandmother Townley proudly noted that the award carried a cash value of three dollars for "Winfield's First Poem,"

[35] WTS, "Book Corner," Haverhill High *Chronicle*: 20 November 1925, Scrap-book 1, p. 44; 29 January 1926, Scrapbook 1, p. 54; 27 April 1926, Scrapbook 1, p. 75; 20 May 1927, Scrapbook 3, p. 135, Scott Collection, John Hay Library.
[36] WTS, *"a dirty hand,"* pp. 90, 121.

the first money the boy had ever earned. Actually, it was not a poem, but an essay on "Trees," in a citywide competition, that took the honors. In high school, still more laurels came Winfield's way. He wrote the school's best Lincoln essay in both his junior and his senior years, and *American Boy* Magazine sent him a special prize letter for a February 1926 piece on Kipling.[37] But these awards were as nothing to the success Winfield enjoyed in poetry competition. In both 1925 and 1926, he was selected as one of the "ten leading high school poets" of the nation, in the Witter Bynner Scholastic Poetry Contest, sponsored by *Scholastic* Magazine. (Dorothy Emerson of Morgantown, West Virginia, high school bested Scott both years, finishing third in 1925, when the Haverhillian was named to honorable mention, and coming in first to Scott's second in the following year.) In the 1926 *Scholastic* contest, Scott won first place in the book-review category for a tripartite review of books of poetry by Sara Teasdale, Joseph Auslander, and Amy Lowell.[38] In the spring of his junior year in high school, Winfield reached an early peak in international recognition when his poem, "Bootblack," took first prize in the competition sponsored by the similarly named English magazine, *The Scholastic*. As the awards rolled in, the school principal would proudly announce them in Chapel, and stories which appeared in local and national newspapers (*Newport News, Haverhill Gazette, Boston Globe, New York Times*) were clipped out and pasted in the scrapbook. The boy's status as a rising young poet seemed unassailable, and congratulations were extended by Connick, Orton Lowe (one of the *Scholastic* judges), a state YMCA secretary who wrote that "this is the kind of news I like to hear about Hi-Y fellows," and another high school poet from Pennsylvania who confessed that he too had been stricken with "the Ache of Beauty." Somewhat in the same vein as this last letter was the literary tribute offered "To W.T.S." by his predecessor as editor of the *Chronicle*, Raymond Fifield:

[37] Agnes Townley, "Winfield's First Poem Written at Walnut Square School, Haverhill, 1922," Scott Collection, John Hay Library; prize letter from *American Boy* February 1926, Scrapbook 2, p. 12, Scott Collection, John Hay Library; Hilda Harris to SD, 13 February 1970.
[38] "The Witter Bynner Scholastic Poetry Contest: Announcement of Awards," *Scholastic*, 20 March 1926, p. 11; "The Poetry Contest," *Scholastic*, 30 April 1927, pp. 16–17, 22.

> Delicate painter with words,
> Songster as sweet as the birds,
> Player of music of Life,
> Poet of Love and of Strife,
> Operas of beauty are thine.
> Vines of pure harmony twine
> Melodies, climb in a dear
> Ecstasy, pulsing and clear.
> Balm for my soul like a clod,
> Bringing me nearer to God.[39]

Fifield overstated the case, somewhat. For Scott's high school verse, like his prose, tended toward the *performance*, toward a showing-off rather than a showing-forth. And of course it was imitative, with Edwin Arlington Robinson and Amy Lowell the chief models.

In the *Chronicle* of 9 October 1925 appeared "An Old Ship," the first poem of Scott's to see print. Inspired by Leo Bates's illustration of the old ship in Rudyard Kipling's *Songs for Youth*, it is written in blank verse, and ends on a typical note, the romance of the past:

> The burning evening sky of distant west
> Doth cast its flame of light to dying cloth
> And gives it now a glory in the dusk,
> A glory all-remindful of the past.[40]

Nothing very remarkable here, beyond a certain power of description and the boldness to spurn rhyme in his first published poem. Winfield's early willingness to escape the conventional bounds of poetry undoubtedly derived from the remarkable, cigar-smoking Lowell. His elegy addressed to her (*"Amy Lowell Dies*, the headlines screamed") not only eschewed rhyme but adopted an irregular line length as well. Its concluding lines were much admired at Haverhill High School. Reading her poems, he wrote,

> I felt as though I had dipped my hand
> Into a garden-pool at night
> Where were reflected heaven and the stars;

[39] Congratulatory letters, Scrapbook 2, p. 58, newspaper reports, Scrapbook 2, pp. 2, 5–6, Raymond Fifield, "To W.T.S.," 30 April 1926, Scott Collection, John Hay Library.

[40] WTS, "An Old Ship," Haverhill High *Chronicle*, 9 October 1925, Scrapbook 1, p. 86, Scott Collection, John Hay Library.

> And while the cold water swam about my wrist,
> I held the stars
> And let them run
> Between my fingers![41]

Those last few lines, Dudley Fitts wrote him from Harvard, were "so much more lovely than anything in Miss Lowell's work." President A. Lawrence Lowell of the same institution, asknowledging the copy of the poem Winfield sent him, refrained from comparisons, remarking only that his sister Amy "had a marvelous poetical talent . . . and she worked with intense ferocity." In Scott's high school English class, the teacher read the poem aloud, with an approving "How wonderful!" At least one dissenter sat in that classroom. "More than forty years ago," Daniel Smythe wrote in 1970, "and I can still remember my feeling of disgust. The poetry was free verse, unrhymed, unscannable; and the figure of someone plunging his hand in a pool of water and bringing up stars was nonsensical to my way of thinking. Scott's work was just as bad as the work of Amy herself—or so I thought. I dared not express my opinion for I did not want to be cussed out by an ignorant teacher who obviously had fallen under his spell." Years later, Smythe wrote Scott about the poem, and found to his surprise that his fellow poet agreed with him. By that time, as his poem "1925–1938" shows, Scott had repudiated the Lowell influence:

> If I had to begin again
> The long diversions of my pen
> I'd hope a blesseder bestowal
> Than the style of Amy Lowell;
> Would order my first poems done
> By Ralph Waldo Emerson.[42]

He found it more difficult, however, to slough off the influence of a far greater poet, Edwin Arlington Robinson. From Robinson the boy appropriated his powerful antimaterialistic bias; from him as well Winfield borrowed the device of the character sketch con-

[41] WTS, "To Amy Lowell," Haverhill High *Chronicle*, 15 January 1926, Scrapbook 1, p. 100, Scott Collection, John Hay Library.
[42] Dudley Fitts to WTS, n.d., Scrapbook 2, p. 8, A. Lawrence Lowell to WTS. 22 March 1926, Scrapbook 1, p. 101, Scott Collection, John Hay Library; Daniel Smythe to SD, "Memories," 10 January 1970; WTS, "1925–1938," *Poetry*, 55 (December 1939): 126.

densed into a very few lines. The poem, "Penance," another prize-winner, provides an example of the first kind of borrowing. A man lies dead, so miserly in life that "The night they had buried him/ Was the first his gold had gone unfingered." Now, in greedy retaliation the worms suck his bones, flowers and grass refuse to grow above his grave,

> And all the years that tip-toed by
> He lay there silent, pondering.
> He grasped the tighter on the roots,
> Wondering.[43]

Unsubtly (one might wish that the years had passed in some other way than by tip-toeing), the poem makes its point. Another on the same theme, but still more Robinsonian for giving its central figure an odd name, is "Taine Wiggenhauser." Like Charles Ponzi, whose exploits Winfield, then only ten years old, had eagerly read about in the Boston papers, Wiggenhauser had heaped up a vast fortune and built a fabulous home, but had lost his capacity to dream in the process:

> The ways behind him all were closed
> and nothing opened up before . . .
> The fortune gained, there was no more
> of dreaming stocks and bonds and floats.

By way of contrast, Scott concocted "Richard Kane," another Robinsonian figure whose ability to dream remained unimpaired by his habit of drinking bits of broken glass with his wine.[44] These incredible figures constituted Scott's boyish models of Eben Flood and Richard Cory and Cliff Klingenhagen.

In the four years from 1925 to 1929, Scott collected, in a private, leather-bound volume named "Barbara George" (for his high school sweetheart), a total of 102 poems. There are poems about flowers, trees, paintings, music, death, melancholy, old men in the park, and Joan of Arc, but almost none about himself, or his friends, or his family, or the world he knew best. Writing, like reading, carried him off to a fantasy world. The most interesting remarks in

---

[43] WTS, "Penance," *Scholastic*, 30 April 1927, p. 16.
[44] WTS, "Taine Wiggenhauser," 23 August 1927, and "Richard Kane," 1929, in "Barbara George," Scott Collection, John Hay Library.

this juvenile outpouring of verse were recorded in the margins, where Scotty commented on when and how he had written his poems. Inspiration came often and at odd times: "written during the Geometry period at school, in a rotten mood," "said it to myself while waiting for an electric car in the evening," "written near midnight in bed, having been in Boston: hard to write," "while the folks were getting impatient, waiting outside in the car," "written to christen a desk." Scott would look at a picture and "get" a poem; alternatively, poems "started with a beguiling phrase or line." But they came wonderfully unbidden, and, in his later years, when he was blocked for extended periods, he longed for the easy production of his youth though not for the poems themselves, for Scott published in book form nothing he wrote in his high school and college years; he had not yet, as he sensibly realized, found his own voice.[45]

Scotty gave abundant proof of his ambition by entering all those contests and by striking up correspondence with established authors. Then, in the summer after graduation from high school, he decided, with youthful impracticality, that he would put together a poetry anthology for children. Yes, Robert Hillyer wrote, Scott was welcome to any of his poems for the anthology, and Hillyer went on to add a word of praise for such of the boy's poetry as he had been shown by Orton Lowe. Displaying an understandable ignorance of the realities and procedures of the publishing business, Winfield proposed his anthology to the Macmillan Company. Heavily represented were Thomas Hardy, Frost, Robinson, and Miss Lowell. In some impatience, after explaining the problems of obtaining permissions and of the need for reputation in the anthologist, Louise H. Seaman turned down the proposal in October of 1927. Little daunted, Scotty then worked up an anthology of poets long dead (to escape the permissions difficulty) and sent that off to Macmillan. No, Louise H. Seaman wrote him, "I cannot give you any criticism or encouragement. The only sensible thing is to be discouraging since there are so many anthologies in the field." Still unpersuaded, Winfield turned to the poet Joseph Auslander, who had been introduced to his work by Fred D. L. Squires (a relative of the boy's senior-class English teacher at Haverhill, Grace Squires), who re-

[45] WTS, "Barbara George," Scott Collection, John Hay Library.

ported sadly that "though I tried to interest a number of publishers in the proposition, I had no luck with it . . . it is next to impossible to get anywhere in this game unless you have already established some reputation. This is particularly true of anthologies."[46] Scott's experience with his ill-starred anthology for children was typical of his future relations with publishers; he never really came to understand that publishing is more a business than an art.

Despite his youthful accomplishments as editorialist, essayist, book reviewer, and poet, and his exemplary conduct in class, Scotty made only a fair record in high school. In English and Freehand Drawing he fluctuated in the B-plus–A-minus range, while in nearly everything else he scraped by with C's. He took the college preparatory course: four years of English, four of Latin, three of French, four of mathematics, two of history, and one of chemistry. He barely passed the chemistry, never did better than C work in Latin and French, and needed summer work to complete his math courses.

The subjects that gave his trouble were, of course, the ones he remembered. In *"a dirty hand,"* for example, he calls back the day in freshman Latin when Miss Merrill found him unable to recite and dismissed him by saying "Well—you don't know anything! Sit down!" About algebra and geometry Scotty knew no more. He attempted to make light of his deficiencies in math, as a bit of doggerel addressed to Harriet V. Evans, his junior year math teacher, demonstrates:

> Thou hatest poetry:
> That I well do know;
> But thou wilt like these lines.
> Yet thou wouldst like them more
> Were they
> That A plus B is B plus A.

Miss Evans responded with the comment that there was too much freedom in modern poetry and not enough written about "beautiful things." Is "everything covered with slime?" she inquired. But if Miss Evans could not be converted by his verse, Grace Squires

---

[46] Robert Hillyer to WTS, 9 August 1927, Louise Seaman to WTS, 12 August 1927, 10 October 1927, and 6 August 1928, Joseph Auslander to WTS, 6 August 1929, Scott Collection, John Hay Library.

certainly could. On the occasion of his seventeenth birthday, Miss
Squires and another English teacher, Lucy B. Moss, produced a defense in his behalf, styled after A. A. Milne's "James James Morrison Morrison Weatherby George Dupree":

> Winfield's
> Winfield's love for math.
> "Lost or stolen or strayed?"
> Winfield's love for math
> "Seems to have been mislaid."
> Last seen
> Wandering blissfully
> Up to 305
> Entered into the doorway—
> Will it e'er come out alive?
> Winfield
> Townley, Townley (Scott)
> We say this day of birth
> We'd rather have you a poet
> Than the best math shark on earth.

Miss Squires, as George Chase testifies, "gave Scotty *red carpet*
treatment where others of her classes were not so treated," and her
support must have cheered him. But his inability to master mathematics always rankled, and he confessed to his journal as late as
1944, after a night of wrestling unsuccessfully with an income-tax
return, that "all the humiliating—the dizzyingly humiliating—
frustration came over me that I used to feel constantly . . . in algebra
and geometry classes in school: I sweated." "We all tried to help
him in math," Jack George remembers, but Scotty had to take the
tests himself.[47] Looking at his math grades, Harvard turned him
down.

Nonetheless, Scotty did survive math, Brown accepted him, and
graduation was a happy, busy time. The yearbook picture in *The
Archive* revealed a blond, thin-faced boy, hair parted neatly on the

[47] WTS, "To H.V.E. with Due Respect," 4 December 1925, and Harriet V.
Evans to WTS, 22 January 1926, Scrapbook 1, pp. 112–113; Grace E. Squires
and Lucy B. Moss to WTS, 30 April 1927, Scott Collection, John Hay Library;
transcript of record, Haverhill High School, 10 September 1923 to 28 June 1927:
Scott's four-year average was 77.9, in the C-plus range; WTS, 1944 Journal, 14
March 1944; WTS, "*a dirty hand,*" p. 149; George S. Chase to SD, 4 March
1970.

left, wearing a bow tie, a half-smile on his sensuous mouth. As literary editor of the yearbook he probably chose the mottoes which accompany his list of accomplishments; they caution that "a good poet's made as well as born" and that "easy writing's curs'd hard reading." He wrote the class song, to the music of Beethoven's "The Heavens Resound," just as he had written a football fight song the previous fall to the tune of "Maryland, My Maryland." At the senior Chapel, Scotty presented twenty-five dollars worth of books to the school (twenty-five dollars being half of his second-place prize in the Witter Bynner *Scholastic* poetry contest), including works by David Grayson, Dallas Lore Sharp, Amy Lowell, and Will Durant, and Charles Townsend Copeland's anthology of English prose and poetry. Principal Arlington I. Clow, "responding, commended the literary talent of Winfield Scott and the splendid spirit of loyalty and cooperation of the donor of the prize during his four years in high school." At the class banquet, Scott offered two toasts —a humorous one to the *Chronicle*, which would the next year become defunct, and another, both religious and ambitious: "What we are is God's gift to us./ What we make of ourselves is our gift to God."[48]

Best of all, at graduation time Scotty was in love with Barbara George. Inside his class banquet folder is the assertion that

> Willie Baxter isn't in it
> With Winfield at this present minute.
> He can make a joke or pun
> And keep Barb giggling at his fun.

Through the last year of high school and two years of college, he dated Barbara. "We had good simple dates like walking around the park, around Kenoza Lake, sitting by the lake, and walking in the country admiring the beauty of the world," she recalled. Sometimes, they would wander to the John Greenleaf Whittier homestead, not far from the Georges' house. Scotty wrote many poems to or for her, and at Brown adopted the pseudonym "Arabab," an

---

[48] WTS, football fight song, November 1926, Scrapbook 2, p. 31; class banquet program, 27 June 1927; Scott Collection, John Hay Library; "Scholarship Fund Founded by Seniors, Class President Announces at H.H.S. Chapel," *Haverhill Evening Gazette*, 24 June 1927; "Toast to Chronicle," *Haverhill Evening Gazette*, 28 June 1927; *The Archive, 1927*, pp. 80, 96.

approximate inversion of "Barbara," for his early appearances in college publications.

Small and dark as his mother had been, as his first wife would be, Barbara looked like the sort of girl he had fallen in love with during grade school. Even in third grade, there had been a small and dark one with pigtails. But it was different at seventeen: "all the summer of his seventeenth year he watched young couples riding alone together in cars and he wished he were in love; and so that fall he was in love and that time it began with the body and before it was over he knew what a . . . girl looked like, and what she felt like and smelled like—but it was a transference of fumbling (not even final) and he did not know all these things fully . . . " The "fumbling" referred to Scotty's sexual experiments with other boys. He masturbated—himself and others, and felt guilty about it afterward. He agonized over his adolescent acne, and thought it a kind of judgment on his secret, but hardly dreadful, sins: something dirty, disgusting. "He ate tons of yeast cakes, tried every remedy in the book, and finally an old printer suggested a particularly noxious preparation which worked, more or less." Win never forgot him.[49]

Not the least of the attractions of Barbara George's house was its library, far more extensive than the Scotts' on Cedar Street. There, Scotty absorbed Kipling, Dickens, Thackeray, Stevenson—and conceived an admiration for Mrs. George, the mother of Barbara and of his *Chronicle* colleague, Jack. She had early been widowed and had brought up the children on her own; many years later, with the empathy for the old and neglected that so often characterized his poetry, Win Scott captured Mrs. George ("got her cold," son Jack put it) in a poem called "The Mother":

> Bowed down she turned but, halfway up the
>   stairs,
> Broke over—fingers, gray head, on the
>   banister.
> She cried out: "Everyone I met today
> Had someone to take care of them but me.
> Everyone wishing me a Merry Christmas,
> Then I come home to this dark and empty house.

---

[49] Class banquet program, 27 June 1927, WTS, "The Brittle Street," manuscript (11 May–28 June 1939), pp. 3, 11–12, Scott Collection, John Hay Library; EMS to SD, 13 April 1970; Barbara G. Greeley to SD, 24 February 1970.

Aren't you two children grown enough by now
To know what it's been to bring you up alone,
Earn every cent it took? And you don't give
A damn to be with me on Christmas Eve."
And we stood frightened there, seeing her cry
For the first time: deserted, shamed to be
Shamed by having not known what we did,
And seared by shame and pity then we cried
For the first time since we were children, and
She hurried down to us and put her hands
On both our shoulders and said "Oh, my dear
    boys!
What did I do wrong to hurt you so!"[50]

This poem helps to demonstrate the difference between Scott's visions of Newport and of Haverhill. Looking back on Newport, he persistently turned inward and like Narcissus found his own image in the pool of memory, whereas he rarely confronted his adolescence openly. Again and again, Scott tried to "do" those Haverhill years: novel, poem sequence, memoir. But each time he drew back, finding the subject "too embarrassing, too disgusting, too humiliating, too painful." A privately very disturbed youth hid behind the public mask of propriety—the Hi-Y boy and teacher's pet.[51]

He felt some nostalgia for Haverhill, of course, but much less than for Edenic Newport—and the nostalgia faded as time wore on. A letter to Daniel Smythe reported a walk around Kenoza in the fall of 1937, "the last good foliage weekend, I should guess. One hesitates to talk about one's feelings on such occasions, for banality is too easy. Nonetheless so real: I'd gone such a little way, alone into the road, before that extraordinary peace and happiness began to grow and go on. You are near it all the time, of course; I wonder if you feel it all the time? If you do I want to know as proof that sometime before I'm too old I must somehow get my life back where it belongs," in the countryside. The lake held a special charm for Scott, because on the hour's walk around its shore "sometimes you meet another walker—more often someone horseback riding—but seldom anyone." It was a place of peace, no autos allowed, with a "park up in the hills above the lake—just a swing and see-saw park

[50] WTS, "The Mother," *New and Selected Poems* (1967), p. 75.
[51] EMS to SD, 13 April 1970.

for kids—and a real castle: once a private estate, now abandoned to the city. A miniature Sir Walter Scott dream." In a similar mood, Scott reminisced in the *Providence Journal* of 5 June 1941 about Jack Tilton's old brick tower, whose appearance, from the train window, was "how you're sure you're getting there"; about Maggie Cline, the Haverhill native who became a great vaudeville performer and the girl friend of John L. Sullivan; about the town character, Professor Cotes, and about Gert Swasey, who had once been new-rich and ended with a house "full of stray cats up the hill and a job as cleaning woman in the railroad station."[52]

Even in these retrospective glances, however, the reminiscence was more intellectualized than in memories of Newport. Kenoza Lake had its appeal as an alternative to a city era in civilization, and it was the gentle satirist who called back Maggie Cline and Gert Swasey. Kenoza Lake with its dream castle might represent a golden past for Win Scott, but the city itself could not, because he had seen it change—and not for the better. When he traveled to Washington with his grandmother in the spring of 1925, she "supposed herself fairly well-to-do; it was later in 1925 that the ominous ruin of shoe manufacturing rumbled around us." With the ruin came the collapse of Haverhill's economy:

> Ours was the generation in our country
> Whose primer lesson, how to make a living,
> Was first of all to move somewhere else.
> The second was that if enough would move
> The rest who wouldn't might do well enough.
> Nobody did too well anywhere.

There was no one to say, Scott wrote, how it was,

> How the city had moved from the need to the
>   power,
> From power to pleasure, from noisy to quiet,
> From the river's bank to the lake shores,
> From the beginning to ending, from living to the
>   death.

Haverhill had died before his eyes; first, there had been the boom

[52] WTS to Daniel Smythe, 3 November 1937; WTS, "In Perspective: Maggie Cline's Town," *Providence Journal*, 5 June 1941; WTS to EM, 6 May 1943.

days after the war, when money was easy, and, as Scott wrote in "Shoetown,"

> . . . even
> The Armenian and Italian shoestitchers got
>   fur coats
> And the Jews were buying up Main Street
>   while the Yankees
> Moved over a block or two, I remember; and
>   the first to have
> Radios—the Irish—bought big ones on
>   installment.

But then everything began to close up, the factories shut down,

> Mr. Forrester shot himself at the Bank;
>   Benny Goldstein
> Lost his apartment houses; the stores took
>   back the Armenians'
> Rugs and furniture; the Italians moved on
>   with the shops; the
> Irish got on relief, and the Yankees voted
>   for Hoover.

Haverhill was not a place to go back to; it was a place to get away from. And whatever pull the home of his youth may have exerted on Scott in his twenties and thirties, it had lost its power by 1965, when, as he wrote Elizabeth Werner, "*How* I don't want to go back there!"[53]

Though he did not want to go back in person, Scott tried to recapture Haverhill in prose and poetry. Visiting there in 1943, he wrote Eleanor Metcalf, he was "excited by the idea—a feeling—a conception—something or other—for a long poem" that had been going "bubble, bubble" in his head for days and making him feel wonderful. "If it fades and dies, that will seem disastrous. If I *write* the thing that may be, too, because I think it will absorb that one . . . image I've ever had for that not impossible novel. Of course, it won't *be* the novel or very much like what I thought of for the novel —but it will obliterate that. And, alas,—this is the point—some-

[53] WTS, "Shoetown," *Collected Poems 1937–1962* (1962), pp. 30–32; WTS, "Prologue," pp. 2–4, WTS to Elizabeth Werner, 9 August 1965, Scott Collection, John Hay Library.

times novels sell, and the writer makes money."[54] The long poem
was never written, but a good many shorter ones about the people
of Haverhill were.

Among the people was John Greenleaf Whittier, whose nearby
homestead served as a continuous inspiration to Scott. The dusty
bones of his research for a biography of Whittier took on flesh in
what is probably Scott's greatest single poem, "Mr. Whittier." Another character transformed from dust to poetry was Mrs. Severin,
a big bulging old bore of a woman, dressed in perpetual mourning-
black, bedecked with spangles, a doily resting unsteadily atop her
false hair—deserted by her husband, ignored by her children,
avoided by her friends, talking forever, to anyone who would listen,
about her visitation from the Lord after she had attended the Meth-
odist Encampment and returned home to await His Coming, naked
on the dinning-room table. Mrs. Severin was at once pitiful and so
human as to merit the love that went into Scott's poem about her.
And there was Gert Swasey, another old, neglected, half-comic, and
touching figure, emerging from the shadow of the Boston and Maine
railroad station in Haverhill. Scott's poem about her addressed itself
to those proper women who may have given the charlady less than
the full measure of charity:

> Have you ever asked yourselves—ladies,
>   ladies—what it must have been like
> To have been Gert Swasey?
> To have a rich father,
> To run away from home
> To be a circus queen, and
> To come back a charlady?
> To come home and be old?
> Dirty and old?
>
> Few of you now can remember Gert Swasey
> When she was young—how she was young:
> What was it like do you suppose
> To drive through town as though you thumbed
>   your nose,
> Your red hair flying, and beautiful clothes?
> What was it like to want to do that
> Seventy years ago—ladies, ladies?

[54] WTS to EM, 6 May 1943.

Gert was a wild one, and when she wanted
She'd drive a pair of horses like a witch
  enchanted.
She'd drive them down from Mount Washington
As though they were fired out of a cannon;
And all the way along Merrimac,
Up Main, through Summer Street, down Mill
  and back
Till she charged up the driveway of her
  father's mansion,
Twice around where the iron stag stared,
Then as fast to the coach-house as she dared
Which was twice as fast as anybody dared;
The horses snorting and all in lather,
But there was nothing Gert would rather
Than set the whole downtown awhirl
Gasping at that Swasey girl.

I wonder how it was to be that Swasey girl
Not a Sanders nor a Dow nor a Saltonstall,
But new-rich Irish with no family at all
Save a sporting father who kept a stable.
It must have been both mad and sweet
To thunder through leaf-filled Summer Street
Disturbing the ladies at the tea table,
Disturbing the ladies in the summer house,
And all along Merrimac's shops and factories
The men's quick faces.

Then to run away—to run far away
To ride in a circus—
The colored wheels
The tights and spangles
The lights, the crowd
The wonderful horses,
The plumed, proud, wonderful horses,
The tremendous music.
To travel like a gypsy
To dress like a queen
To see all the world that she'd never seen
That was never the world where she had been.
Not a Dow nor a Sanders nor a Saltonstall
Unless they paid to get in.

And then
After thirty-five years to come home again.

Have you ever asked yourselves what it must
    have been like
To be the old charlady at the B.&M.
    railroad station?
To clean the toilets
To mop the floors
To be greasy and gray
To be poor and alone
To be Gert Swasey?
Then there is a way—easy to learn—
Of talking to yourself,
Answer yourself,
When there is no one else
Wherever you are.
There are many stray cats, a dozen—fifty—
That will stay in your house
If you will feed them,
Lock them in to keep them safe,
Whose yowling some day wakes the neighborhood
But, at last, not you.

Have you ever asked yourselves what it must
    have been like
To have been Gert Swasey?
To be a rich young nobody with red restless
    hair?
To run away from home
To be a circus queen, and
To come back,
And to be old, and to be dirty, and to be
    dead—
O ladies, ladies.[55]

So many things are said between the lines of this poem—that too-
keen consciousness of social class cripples personality; that the good
women who looked down on the Irish ("Irish," Winfield's mother
would hiss by way of explanation of bad manners) should instead
learn to look on a level and with empathy; that we must love one
another or die. And it is said with simple indirection of diction, de-

[55] WTS, "Gert Swasey," *New and Selected Poems*, pp. 55–57.

lightful humor of rhyme, and compelling depth of compassion.
"Gert Swasey" reads magnificently aloud, which is how poetry
should be read; listeners are invariably moved, which is what
poetry should do to them. "About his poetry," William Stafford
wrote after Scott's death, "I felt a very positive allegiance, particularly for the kind of poem in which he *realized* a person or character. 'Gert Swasey' is for me a touchstone for a certain kind of
direct, audaciously conversational poem. I feel sustained by such a
poem."[56] As Scott himself reflected, it is the ability to realize character, not to originate plot, which is the hard test of genius, "creating things for people to say and for people to be. Creating in a sense
life and simultaneously revelations of significance (which is more
even than God essayed). In literature as in life, action evolves from
character: not the other way around."[57]

[56] William Stafford to SD, 30 January 1970.
[57] WTS, "a dirty hand," p. 25.

4. Odd Stick at Brown

WIN SCOTT DID WELL at Brown, or rather, he *finished* well. His first two years were something else again. When the slight youth from Haverhill, with delicate features, wavy blond hair, persistent pimples, and a "somewhat dreamy, star-gazing look" arrived on the Brown campus in the fall of 1927,[2] he knew no one. As if to signal their indifference to mere freshmen from the provinces, college offices were closed on the day his parents drove him down to Providence. Even the door to his room in Hope College was locked, and Jack George, who had come along for the ride, shinnied up and climbed through a window to admit the unathletic Scott to his quarters.[3] There, for most of two years, he remained, suffering from tonsilitis and painful boils, flunking several courses, and on weekends either holing in or emerging for visits to Uncle George at the

[1] WTS, "Rory Blaine's Return," *Fantasy* 6 (1938): 15–16.
[2] William E. Wilson to SD, 28 August 1969.
[3] Interview, Jackson George, West Newbury, Massachusetts, 11 July 1969.

YMCA in Providence, to relatives in Newport, or to his family back home in Haverhill.

In later years Scott set down an anecdote about Brown president W. H. P. Faunce which aptly characterized his own case in his freshman and sophomore years:

You know, William Herbert Perry Faunce roomed in Hope as an undergraduate just above the room of another who became even a famouser man. This was—I should say in defense of my age, not fame— a good while before I lived in Hope. But in the days when I did live there, Prexy Faunce liked sometimes in chapel to reminisce about the Brown student days of the Chief Justice. "I remember," Prexy would intone in that voice of his, "I remember how voices at night would call up beneath the windows of old Hope College, 'Charlie Hughes! Charlie Hughes!' Nobody," he added slowly, "ever called up for me."[4]

Like Faunce and unlike Charles Evans Hughes, Scott in Hope College was rarely called up for.

At least one classmate and one instructor helped alleviate his loneliness, however. The classmate was Phil Kraus, son of a Providence scientist whose home, with its independent comings and goings, was a revelation to the "little bourgeois kid" from Haverhill. Win first met Phil, a taciturn boy of a scientific turn of mind, when he "strode naked out of the pond" during freshman induction weekend at Camp Yawgoog, sat down beside Scott, and inquired: "Do you have any hobbies?" When it turned out that he did (girls and books), the two boys became friends, and they would talk all evening in Scott's dormitory room, and then continue the discussion on walks around the campus. Best of all, Kraus came when needed most: "Once when I was sick and alone in my room," Scott wrote, "there was a persistent pounding—it was at night—on my door; I lay doggo; but finally a voice said It's Phil; so I got up and let him in—and there he stood, as dumb as persistent, with a pint of vanilla ice cream for me."[5] The gesture was one his mother or grandmother might have made.

With Fredric (Fritz) Klees, Win Scott established a very different kind of relationship. A young instructor, Klees taught Scott in English I for a month, at the beginning of his freshman year, and

[4] WTS to W. C. (Chet) Worthington, 14 February 1957.
[5] WTS to Ben Bagdikian, 11 December 1954.

then had him excused from the course as a gifted boy who wrote extremely well. Later in the year, Win would stop off at Klees's apartment on Benefit Street for "Oxford afternoons" of tea and talk of literature and art. When Klees left Brown for Swarthmore in the fall of Win's sophomore year, they corresponded—Klees serving now as friend, then as critic of the verse the boy sent him, again as mentor, helping him face the decisions of his young life.

Scott's visits to Klees brightened what was otherwise a depressing spring semester. He was suffering from tonsilitis, and he barely managed to make it through the academic year before going home to Haverhill to have his tonsils and adenoids removed. Placed on warning in February for flunking Greek, Scott took thirty-two absences during the spring, and flunked a second course, European History since 1900. "I studied and studied and more," he wrote Klees, but "evidently the exam wasn't passable." His only A's, freshman year, came in the two semesters of the English Literature Survey. The other grades were a smattering of B's and C's: together with the failing grades, hardly the stuff of eventual Phi Beta Kappas.[6]

Another Greek organization, however, showed an interest in Win Scott that spring semester. Apologetically, he wrote Klees in the summer of 1928, "the Lambda Chi Alpha crowd *did* talk me into it. O *that* was a marvelous sales-talk! . . . I told them (after quite a lot of that talk) that I wanted their fraternity if I could have my independence. O yes, I can have my independence! What suits my talents best is what's best for the fraternity. . . . So I'm wearing their pledge pin this summer. Et cetera. If I change my mind, all right. Et cetera."[7] By fall he *had* changed his mind, and he returned the pin. He would be independent, at whatever cost in loneliness. Klees applauded the decision, and softened the blow of the failing grade in history by recounting his own undergraduate woes: "I fear you will never be a scholar, which is precisely what I was told when I was in college, although the Dean was kind enough to add that if I were to live a thousand years I should never make a scholar. . . . But I think that I prefer to be as I am rather

[6] W. T. Scott, transcript, Brown University.
[7] WTS to Fredric Klees, 26 June 1928, Swarthmore College Library.

than to be a scholar. Scholars do not create. You, I think, will do so."[8]

On visits to Haverhill, Win continued to court Barbara George, but he seems to have discovered no girl friends at college his first year. There was a delightful letter from Dorothy Emerson, fellow winner of *Scholastic* poetry prizes: "How do you happen to write poetry? I never knew a boy who did. I wish I knew you. You must be a freak, a nice freak, a most exquisitely interesting freak. Are you?"[9] But Dorothy Emerson was in West Virginia, and they never did know one another. In a parody of Carl Sandburg, written for Brown's humor magazine, *The Brown Jug*, the freshman betrayed something of his own attitude toward romance (note the reference to "History books . . . in the dump"):

> Spring is coming. I see it. I see it in the
> ashes. I see it sprouting through a tomato
> can near my feet. My feet are sweaty, too.
> Sure sign of Spring.
> Here are pig's feet, History books, red
> flannel underwear in the dump. In the
> ashes.
> Spring is coming.
> What the hell do I care![10]

Girls were one thing and poetry another, and Win Scott continued to be idealistic in courting his muse. "We were both very romantic in our tastes in poetry, but he was even more romantic than I was," Klees recalls. "I tried to persuade him to restrain his more extravagant flights."[11] Scott was as yet unabused of the notion that poetry must depict the beautiful, and he wrote poems that year inspired by Rodin's "The Hand of God," John Singer Sargent's "Our Lady of Sorrows" and "A Spanish Woman," and Haverhill painter Sidney M. Chase's "Twilight." A better poem,

[8] Fredric Klees to WTS, 28 July 1928, Scott Collection, John Hay Library, Brown University.
[9] Dorothy Emerson to WTS, 1 December 1927, Scott Collection, John Hay Library.
[10] WTS, "Spring Is Coming Soon," *Brown Jug*, March 1928, Scrapbook 5, p. 15, Scott Collection, John Hay Library.
[11] Fredric Klees to SD, 24 July 1969.

"After Dreaming of One Dead," dealt with the death of his Grandfather Townley, viewing the world at one less artistic remove.
Indignantly, the budding poet wrote in reply to a *Boston Post* editorial proclaiming the times wrong for poetry. Read Robinson, Millay, Teasdale, Frost, Amy Lowell, and Joseph Auslander, Scott proposed, and "you will find that beauty in poetry and the highest
aspirations of the poets are as alive today . . . as in the time of Longfellow." There is no lack of poetry today, he insisted, and "lack of
appreciation for it is soon to be a thing of the past: of Longfellow
and of Boston."[12] So that he might be among those deserving of
this flood of appreciation, the boy continued to write poems for the
columns of the *Haverhill Gazette*, and took honorable mention in
the Witter Bynner undergraduate poetry contest for 1928. Then,
in March, came the beginnings of his long association with the
Providence Journal. B. K. Hart, the literary editor, asked him to
review Elizabeth Corbett's fictionalized biography, *Walt*. "Walt
Whitman is too big a man, too big a spirit, to compass in a novel,"
he told *Journal* readers, advising them to look for the poet in *Leaves
of Grass* instead. Throughout college he continued to write reviews
for the newspaper, "eventually getting paid a little bit for them."[13]
    Whether he was paid for his writing or not, it remained a serious
matter to young Scott. He listened to bad advice nearly as closely
as to the good advice which was usually forthcoming from Klees.
The summer after freshman year, Scott sent Fred D. L. Squires
some of his poetry, and back came a long letter with a set of instructions for the poetic life, prepared by a friend of Squires. The
advice boiled down to three points. (1) Learn Greek: "Such discipline is at the background of all English literary men. Keats,
Shelley, Matthew Arnold, Tennyson, and before that Milton
(Dante in Italy, too), all were passionate students and lovers of
Homer, Euripides and the other Greek writers. Greek is of more
value to a poet than any other language ancient or modern." (2)
Travel: "Spend as much time as possible tramping the country,

---

[12] WTS, letter, *Boston Post*, 12 December 1927, Scott Collection, John Hay
Library.
[13] Donald Dean Eulert, "Winfield Townley Scott: Conversations on Poets
and the Art of Poetry" (Ph.D. dissertation, University of New Mexico, January 1969), p. 19. The dissertation is especially valuable for its reproduction of
lengthy taped conversations with Scott. Actually, the first book Scott reviewed
for the *Journal* was Joseph Gaer's *The Legend Called Meryom*.

town and city irrespectively. Live with, get acquainted, know, love and work with all sorts of people. Don't go by motor, go by foot. Be a glutton for experience. Translate beauty out of and into every thing you see and meet." (3) Hold fire: "Give yourself at least ten years before you think of writing anything of permanent value, at the end of that time, burn up everything you've produced to that point and begin all over again."

Directed to a poet who had flunked Beginning Greek, who was rather more given to indoor reading than to outdoor adventuring, and who was publishing every chance he got, the letter left Win Scott reeling. "I feel his advice is *too* strict though there is much common sense beneath it . . . it all sounds more *planned* and *studied* a program than is possible. . . . As for the ten-years-from-now bonfire: I can't comment on that, because I don't know." But what if Keats had waited ten years?[14] So he wrote Klees, and back came the encouraging word that he should forget Greek and read the King James Bible, that tramping was fine for Whitman but not Blake's cup of tea, that in any case one might know life at first hand better by staying at home than by traveling. "Why do not American poets look at America?" Klees continued. "If you do travel, I do hope you won't become an expatriate."[15] Here was advice Scott could better swallow. He would travel widely in Haverhill, Newport, Providence, and in books. He would write about America. And he would study Latin in his sophomore year instead of renewing his losing battle with the "most valuable" of all languages.

Latin gave him troubles enough, but at least he got through the fall with a D, a grade he matched in his second-year French course. (Years afterward, Scott would apply to himself the Whittier quotation, "I speak only one language, and that not very well.") Mathematics was out of the question, of course, but Brown offered an alternative course, Argumentation, and Win survived that with a C in the fall and a B in the spring, despite his propensity for writing lyrics instead of logical lawyerlike briefs. In the spring he made up his history failure with a C, and at last was free to take the kind of courses (English and more English) in which he could excel. His sophomore English instructor was Cyril Harris, a man given to

---

[14] Squires's letter quoted in WTS to Fredric Klees, 1 August 1928, Swarthmore College Library.
[15] Fredric Klees to WTS, 3 August 1928, Scott Collection, John Hay Library.

pronouncing "Bully" over papers that pleased him, but who nonetheless provided Win and other students interested in writing with
close personal attention. At Harris's house, undergraduates would
read their poems for criticism; the instructor warned them against
easy cynicism and careless writing. The course "has helped me a
great deal in many ways," Scott wrote Klees in the spring, but he
also inquired in the same letter if he should consider transferring
to Swarthmore.[16]

By the end of his sophomore year, however, Scott would have
had to give up a good deal to make such a transfer. Still lonely
(weekends, he wrote Klees, were dull), still ashamed of his athletic
shortcomings (wretchedly, he struggled at compulsory handball),
still searching for a name to fit his role (he complained to Klees of a
terrible nickname, "Winnie," and of the more common one,
"Scottie"—he'd known several well-meaning dogs of that title—
and declared his preference for plain Win Scott),[17] he had nonetheless made his mark on Brown by the spring of 1929.

For one thing, Prexy Faunce had taken an interest in the sophomore from Haverhill. Scott stopped by the president's office to
get him to autograph a book, and sent a poem of his own in return.
Impressed, Faunce shuttled it along to Lindsay Todd Damon, then
chairman of the English department, and Damon dropped Win a
line: "President Faunce very kindly showed me the sonnet you
sent him. I like very much the simplicity, precision, and honest
feeling that are shown in it." Stop by, Damon encouraged Scott, and
let's talk about majoring in English.[18] Stop by Scott did, and in the
spring applied for the English honors program with Prof. William
T. Hastings. His case would require special consideration, Hastings
wrote (not many candidates for Final Honors had two F's and two
D's in their first three semesters), but with his support, the application was granted, and Scott blossomed from a mediocre student to a
remarkable one.[19]

During his sophomore year, too, Win Scott established himself
as one of the leading literary lights of the campus. He continued to

[16] WTS to Fredric Klees, 6 October 1928, Swarthmore College Library.
[17] Ibid.
[18] Lindsay Todd Damon to WTS, 5 December 1928, Scott Collection, John
Hay Library.
[19] William T. Hastings to WTS, 17 April 1929, Scott Collection, John Hay
Library.

review for the *Providence Journal* on occasion (the newspaper also printed some of his poetry) and was beginning to develop his own taste. One book he read that fall would be a lifelong enthusiasm, not least because of Scott's admiration for its author: "In the October of 1928 I sat, tenderly and uneasily propped upon pillows in an old chair, reading a book. That was in my third floor room, middle Hope College. I was a Sophomore that fall. I was 18 years old. I had boils. But the book was a wonderful and beautiful book, just published: 'The Outermost House,' by Henry Beston."[20] Beston wrote with true warmth of feeling of his winter, alone with nature, at Eastham on Cape Cod. And in his love of that book (affection would be too weak a word) Scott revealed his deeply impressionistic approach to literature. Beston was a wonderful man, he wrote of a familiar place, and his must therefore be a wonderful book—in point of fact it is. But William Faulkner, whose *The Sound and the Fury* Scott was to pan in the *Journal* the following fall, wrote of a land and in a manner foreign to Scott and was found wanting, in consequence. Faulkner, like many modernists, was guilty of a failure to communicate. Written from varying points of view, including that of the idiot Benjy, his novel "tells us nothing," Scott concluded. "In one or two cases only does his method justify itself by a certain dramatic vividness. On the whole, his novel . . . is downright tiresome. It is so much sound and fury—signifying nothing."[21] Only rarely, it should be emphasized, did Scott suffer such a blind spot as in this review, at nineteen, of Faulkner's experimental masterpiece. Not many years later, Scott renounced his error, and he was always ashamed of the stupidity he had shown in dismissing Faulkner's novel so cavalierly. Still, it is significant that his collegiate indictment of *The Sound and the Fury* was based on the issue of communication; Scott never lost his conviction that writing, to be appreciated, must be understood. Books occupied much of his time and came to have a life of their own; he took books, and their authors, personally.

Despite this impressionism, however, Scott developed over the

[20] WTS, "Bookman's Galley," *Providence Sunday Journal*, 22 May 1949, sec. 6, p. 10.
[21] WTS, review of William Faulkner's *The Sound and the Fury*, *Providence Sunday Journal*, 20 October 1929, Scrapbook 2, p. 103, Scott Collection, John Hay Library.

years a sensitive, intelligent artistic code for himself. At Brown, of course, he was still finding out what he thought about art. One such discovery came in the spring of his sophomore year when he was initiated into the prestigious Sphinx Club, a discussion group of students and faculty members. The speaker on that occasion made the point, critical to the poet's later artistic theory, that something ugly may be as much a work of art as something beautiful, so long as it stems from a particular human's creative drive. In a letter to Klees, Scott reflected on that idea approvingly, but rejected the notion that if a man makes a picture and likes it, that is art. "All of which makes Norman Rockwell an artist and Edgar Guest a poet, doesn't it? Liberal definitions seem often better when not applied."[22]

His critical skills he honed in a *Brown Literary Quarterly* essay on Amy Lowell which drew the praise of Brown professors. Scott published verse in the *Quarterly* as well, but it was in the *Brown Daily Herald* that he made his campus reputation. As a freshman he had turned out a few columns for the *Herald*, and at the beginning of his sophomore year he was named literary editor, a role in which he moved rapidly from literary chitchat to serious book reviewing to irreverent, sometimes inflammatory comment on the campus scene. In November he composed a mock-commemorative hymn in honor of Brown's upset victory over Dartmouth,[23] but, in the spring, turning to controversy, he mounted his attack on compulsory Chapel, with emphasis on the word *compulsory*. Scott's religious ardor had cooled with the ouster of Dr. Hurd from his Haverhill parish. Now he thought organized religion hypocritical: he was no more ready to give up his independence to a church than to a fraternity, and he encouraged his fellow students to join him in a strike against Chapel. "Every man on campus," he wrote in the *Herald* of 8 May 1929, "must agree not to attend Sayles Hall at nine o'clock in the morning." It is possible, he admitted, that the entire undergraduate body "may be expelled. But there are reasons for which none of us entertain the possibility of that action on the part of the administration." Ten days later, despite administration attempts to change his mind, Scott repeated his battle cry. "The time to take action on the matter is not next October, but now. And the

22 WTS to Fredric Klees, 28 May 1929, Swarthmore College Library.
23 WTS, "The Little Green Wagon," *Brown Daily Herald*, 14 November 1928, Scrapbook 2, p. 97, Scott Collection, John Hay Library.

most direct action that can be taken is on the part of the student body; and that action means Strike." But within the week he had changed his mind, perhaps under pressure, perhaps for the practical reason that the school year was drawing to a close. The time to strike, he now recommended, was on return to Brown in the fall. He suggested that, in the meantime, the Brown authorities poll students on their preferences.[24] In the fall, the struggle was joined once more, and though no general strike ensued, student sentiment clearly stood behind Scott's position; in eventual compromise, the administration cut down on the number of compulsory Chapel meetings.

Perhaps Scott's fling in campus politics was prompted by his membership in the newly formed Liberal Club. "We started the thing just a few weeks ago," he wrote Klees in late May 1929, "primarily under the inspiration of Norman Thomas. . . . I have not, personally, decided whether I am a Communist (having recently done a eulogy on Lenin) or an anarchist (having recently printed several columns against compulsory Chapel)." The role of anarchist suited Scott better; his stress on independence did not accommodate itself well, then or later, to group participation. Nonetheless, he used his column in the *Herald* to "welcome heartily the recent formation of a Liberal Club . . . not radicals, half-wits or long-haired immigrants, but those who see with both . . . eyes, listen with both . . . ears."[25]

Vice president of the Liberal Club, and fast becoming Win Scott's closest companion, was H. O. (Jeff) Werner. Both had competed for the award for the best essay on Theodore Roosevelt in April of 1929, and in that contest Scott won not only the prize but a lifelong friend. The two were startlingly different; intellectually Werner was a generalist, interested and capable in everything, whereas Scott's was a narrow-track mind concerned almost solely with literature. Jeff came from a cosmopolitan background, his mother English, his father German, both passionately American by adoption; Win from a small-town, middle-class American family. Jeff

24 WTS, "Speaking Offhand," *Brown Daily Herald*, 8 May 1929, 18 May 1929, 22 May 1929, Scrapbook 6, pp. 123, 131, 133, Scott Collection, John Hay Library.
25 WTS, "Speaking Offhand," *Brown Daily Herald*, 29 May 1929, Scrapbook 6, p. 141, Scott Collection, John Hay Library; WTS to Fredric Klees, 28 May 1929, Swarthmore College Library.

was a bridge shark, Win eschewed cards. Jeff was athletic, Win
was totally without competence in sports. Even physically, they
were opposites. A post-college picture shows the two of them on
the beach at West Barrington, Rhode Island: Werner, dark, with
well-muscled legs alongside the pale, skinny-legged Scott.[26] In a
poem, "Easy Nakedness," Win Scott presented his own version of
this contrast, to his own disadvantage. "At any rate," he wrote
Werner on completing the poem in 1939, "there must be very few
people who have been exposed down to the very phallus in poetry."[27] But the exposure is more of the poet than his friend:

> Wet-foot-printed our separate paths
> Cross into the room from morning baths
> (Traman thus of Kurt one day)
> And we towel, each a little away
> From the window where the sun floods in
> But near enough for sun on skin;
> Stay, careful of place, within the shaft.
> Your smoke escalates on the bright draught
> As the light ascends, descends.
> We are young men and old friends;
> Stripped, you are casual and I
> Am at last not reticently shy,
> You and the sun together release
> A thaw—I grow consciously at ease.
> We are different flesh, no doubt of that;
> Without affliction you favor fat
> But I cling to bone and a stomach flat
> As a boy's and very skinny arms.
> This body's not one of my major charms
> Whereas, I imagine, Marges and Megs
> Have pleasure 'round your stolid legs.
> I'm pale, of course, you ten shades browner
> Yet with a less savage fur
> Darkening toward navel and over chest.
> Your head firmer—not large for the rest;
> The sex franker and heavier,
> And one wildness: a black lozenger
> Of hairy mole on the buttock-girth.

[26] Interview, Mrs. Elizabeth Werner, Annapolis, Maryland, 27 September
1969.
[27] WTS to H. O. Werner, 6 March 1939, Scott Collection, John Hay Library.

My strawberry knee-splotch from birth
Is nothing to match that Satanic brand.
I watch your cigarette and the hand
Working it—fingers feminine,
Fine: one feature I'm stronger in.[28]

Clearly, Scott saw himself as less manly than his former college roommate whose "sex" was franker and heavier; only in the hands was he superior, because less feminine. Scott would always feel compelled to prove his own manliness.

There were other budding friendships in the sophomore spring. Jerome S. (Jerry) Anderson III, an engineering student also interested in literature, recuperated from the flu at the Scott house in Haverhill, and Win returned the visit in the summer of 1929 at the Andersons' in Stonington, Connecticut, where they "sat on a raft under the starlight . . . and over and over wound the portable phonograph for 'Star Dust.' How soft that summer night!" "Star Dust" closed the decade which had begun with "Yes, We Have No Bananas," a decade Scott had begun "in love with Warren Gamaliel Harding and ended . . . in love with (among others) Greta Garbo."[29] With Victor Ullman, who combined writing and radicalism with wrestling at Brown, Scott made a pilgrimage to Craigie house in Cambridge, where Longfellow had lived and written. The students hovered outside until a kindly disposed Longfellow descendant emerged, escorted them inside, displayed the window where R. H. Dana had scratched his name, and then took the Brown undergraduates along to see the Bolshoi Ballet.[30] That, surely, was an event to remember, but the Cambridge visit was as nothing to Scott's pilgrimage, in midsummer, to see his idol, Robinson, at the MacDowell Colony.

On 22 August 1929, having discovered that the MacDowell Colony, at Peterborough, New Hampshire, was only seventy miles from Haverhill, and having secured an appointment from Robinson, Win Scott went to see the man he considered the greatest living American poet. In a fine essay, written twenty-five years later, Scott recalled that "deep summer day full of sun and cicadas." With

[28] WTS, "Easy Nakedness," *Collected Poems: 1937–1962* (1962), pp. 17–18.
[29] Jerome S. Anderson III to SD, 19 October 1969; WTS, "Tarkington and the 1920's," *Exiles and Fabrications* (1961), p. 101.
[30] Interview, Victor Ullman, Alstead, New Hampshire, 4 December 1969.

him the nineteen-year-old brought Robinson's books to be autographed, and a "largely ecstatic essay" he had just written about the sixty-year-old bachelor, then the most eminent poet in America, for publication in the fall *Brown Literary Quarterly*. "So there I was," Scott wrote, "more nervous than ever, thin, with wavy yellow hair, pimpled face, the manuscript of my essay, and five of Robinson's books. Also, I may have been hungry, but stopping for lunch that day would have seemed to me a wild waste of life." Rollo Walter Brown, finding the young man from Haverhill wandering the Colony grounds, took him to the Veltin Studio, where Robinson was eating lunch. Casually, the poet responded to Scott's youthful questions.

"Have you any particular message for young men who want to be poets?"

Robinson chuckled: "Well, no," he said. "If you've got yourself into that trap there's nothing I or anyone else can say to get you out."

"People say a lot of things, among them that poets don't earn money."

"Well"—he looked up—if you keep at it for forty years you may have about half as much as a good carpenter."

Of course, Robinson added, there was teaching, with three months off each year, but you'd have to get some money from some other source as well, "whether you steal it or inherit it." And one last alternative: "Then there's getting married."

While they talked, Robinson alternately chewed on a sandwich and threw bits of crust and bread into the fire (even in August, Peterborough can be chilly). Finally, the Brown undergraduate began to make murmurs about his essay:

"I thought I'd simply read it to you and you might correct me if you like when it's necessary." Robinson still said nothing. I fished the manuscript from the pile of books and sat looking at him.

"Is it in print?" he asked.

"No." I waited again. He had finshed his lunch and begun smoking his Sweet Caporal.

"Go ahead," he said.

And so in a sort of naked terror I read it. As often as I dared I glanced over at the profile. Two or three times he did correct me. The essay referred to his early sonnet "On the Night of a Friend's Wedding" as "one of Robinson's few personal utterances," and at once he spoke.

"Now! Don't look for me in my poetry, because you won't find me. . . . Of course, the mood—the thought, but you won't find me. . . . In that one, to be sure, there's a little, but not much."

Soon I was quoting Robinson's statement, made in his young years, that the world is a place where people are all, like children, trying to spell God with—I said—"different" blocks. He said, "I'm not very fond of that quotation, but it is 'wrong' blocks, not 'different'—if you care to correct it."

Then: "When Clement Wood says that Robinson's message is 'that mankind has failed' "—Robinson waved a hand and exclaimed with gusto, "Oh, that's nonsense—sheer nonsense!" "—he errs," I continued. "Robinson says that mankind has failed *so far*. The very essence of the Robinsonian message is that there is somewhere a Gleam, a Light; that all the measures we have so far used . . ." and so on. I paused and asked, "Is that sheer nonsense, too?" He continued regarding the fire, then said, "Well, perhaps I've said that. I don't know."

I went on reading all the resounding rest of it. Through at last, I asked in the silence, "Have I done a bad job?"

He said, "No. I think, looking at it impersonally, you've done a very good job. . . . Of course, all those things you've said there—" but did not complete the sentence which, I presumed, would have had to comment on the flood of praise I had let loose.

I said, "I don't have to tell you—do I?—that if you autograph these books they won't be sold next week, or the next?"

He smiled, "No!" he said, and went to his desk where he signed them amidst the litter of envelopes, the fine-lined small sheets of his manuscript in progress . . . and a couple of dictionaries. A couch and the window sills were also strewn with a miscellany of papers. A long, capelike black coat hung from one wall. Robinson wandered about, gathering things into the lunch basket, and he put on a shapeless white canvas hat. He would ride up as far as the Colony Hall with me.

Behind Colony Hall he stood outside the car a moment, stooping to peer in and shake hands. He twinkled, and said, "Don't publish a book till you're thirty. Thirty's time enough." No, he hadn't been bored. "I've had a good time," he said. Lunch basket in one hand, trailing his stick with the other, he paused at the Hall door, spat, and went slowly in.

That first meeting led to others, and to a brief correspondence between the aspirant and the established poet. On one occasion

Robinson remarked that his young friend Lucius Beebe was "a high roller," and so was Isadora Duncan, who, he said, had once attempted to seduce him, unsuccessfully. He asked Scott about younger poets. "Every time I see him," Scott wrote Horace Gregory in 1933, "he solemnly inquires if there are any new developments in poetry. . . . I recall his asking me, once, what I made of Cummings: very earnestly wanted to know: he had tried, without success, to read him . . ." and declared himself an old fogey.[31] Robinson praised some of Scott's poetry and altogether gave him to feel that if he was in the trap of wanting to be a poet, he had the best of company. Finally, Win Scott came to see Robinson when he lay dying in New York Hospital, in 1935. Scott found it difficult to think of much to say; then as always he abhorred hospital rooms and their aura of decay and death. After a time, he said, "I mustn't tire you." And Robinson replied, "It's not so much a matter of your tiring me as it is of my tiring you."[32]

Robinson's influence on his young admirer, obvious at first, declined as time went on, not least because Scott consciously tried to avoid imitation and even avoided rereading Robinson in order to slough off his debt. Both poets were plainspoken, using what might be called ordinary language, but Scott's voice was neither as meditative nor as philosophical as Robinson's. As Jeff Todd Titon has observed, "That Mr. Scott could write like Mr. Robinson is amply evident in his 'Elegy for Robinson'; that he did not want to is equally evident in most of his other poems."[33]

Scott was concerned to eradicate the Robinsonian traces from his verse, primarily because he found the older man's work tremendously to his taste. (Knowing Robinson only accentuated his admiration.) In his late notebooks, he recorded going back to the fifteen hundred pages of Collected Robinson and finding that "the best things have even improved, and some unnoticed things suddenly were profound. . . . I am older: what other test is there?"[34] There, too, he declared his preference for a Robinsonian approach to lan-

[31] WTS to Horace Gregory, 21 September 1933, Syracuse University Library.
[32] WTS, "To See Robinson," Exiles, pp. 154–169.
[33] Jeff Todd Titon, "Gold from Green: The Poems of Winfield Townley Scott" ("starred paper" for the M.A. degree, University of Minnesota, Spring 1966).
[34] WTS, "a dirty hand": The Literary Notebooks of Winfield Townley Scott (1969), p. 15.

guage: "There are two kinds of poetry. One, the kind represented by Crane's line: "The seal's wide spindrift gaze toward paradise." The other represented by Robinson's: "And he was all alone there when he died." One is a magic gesture of language, the other a commentary on human life so concentrated as to give off considerable pressure. The greatest poets combine the two: Shakespeare frequently; Robinson himself now and then. If I have to choose, I choose the second: I go, in other words, for Wordsworth, for Hardy, in preference to Poe, to Rimbaud."[35]

Edwin Arlington Robinson took his place at the top of Scott's pantheon of literary heroes, where the youth worshipped him with rather more devotion, one suspects, than the retiring Robinson might have wished. After E.A.R. had died, Scott continued to build a shrine to his memory by collecting everything he could of the great man's books and letters: in 1963, when his collection of Robinson was donated to the University of New Mexico library, it was valued for income tax purposes at $2,112. The next year, Joel Townley Scott, the oldest of Win and Eleanor Scott's children, came home from class at Santa Fe High School and inquired of his father if he had "ever heard some poems called 'Richard Cory' and 'Miniver Cheevy' by a man named Robinson." Yes, his father knew the poems, and, he told a bewildered Joel, he had known Mr. Robinson, too. The boy stared at him as though he had said he had known Mr. Longfellow.[36]

From his first meeting with Robinson, Win Scott derived one of the odd, nagging superstitions that, in his agnosticism, replaced more conventional religious beliefs. The pilgrimage to Robinson was made on 22 August 1929; annually, when that date came around on the calendar, he would joyously reflect on his invasion of the MacDowell Colony. And it became Scott's conviction that momentous things would happen to him on the twenty-second.

When he returned to Brown in the fall of his junior year, Win Scott began compiling the record which led to his election to Phi Beta Kappa. Of the thirty-six credits he earned that year, thirty were in English, all A's. (In two philosophy courses he managed a B and a D). Senior year, the pattern would be the same, with all A's in the English courses which dominated his program, and a B and

[35] Ibid., p. 66.
[36] WTS to Horace Gregory, 25 May 1964, Syracuse University Library.

a C in six credits of beginning music. "You know, in literature you're asked a question and it all comes back to you," he remarked to Frank Merchant, a brilliant classmate who (with Scott) was awarded First Highest Honors in English. "Why isn't it that way with music?"[37] The obvious answer was that his ear for music was yet untrained, but by this time he had already developed his skills of comprehension and recall of books through tremendously wide reading. "Win read verse, fiction, essays, regional books, biographies of his 'heroes' (Keats, Wilson, Lenin, Teddy Roosevelt)," Merchant reports. "Like most of us, he played the game of title-title-who knows the author, and did it very well. I think he dipped into the major foreigners (Proust, maybe Mann). And read amusing and funny stuff—like Thorne Smith, whose work he introduced us to in his junior year, by getting all the Smith books from Doubleday, Page for review in the *Herald*. . . . Win really read books by the shelf, noting particular passages."[38] And he had the gift, very rare for an undergraduate, of transforming his knowledge of books into readable, interesting criticism: the kind of prose that made him a joy to the Brown English department.

Creatively as well as academically, his star contintued to rise. Over the summer he found that he had been awarded first honorable mention in the 1929 undergraduate poetry contest sponsored by the Poetry Society of America. His essay on Robinson won the Susan Colver Rosenberger award for the best piece in the *Brown Literary Quarterly*. In the spring of his junior year he was named joint winner of the Irene Glascock poetry prize for the best poetry by an undergraduate at an eastern college.

There was something of a literary tradition at Brown during Scott's undergraduate years. A burst of talent had emerged in the previous decade, from such undergraduates as Quentin Reynolds, S. J. Perelman, and Nathanael West.[39] Poetry was respected, writing encouraged. S. Foster Damon, a cousin of Lindsay Todd Damon and an effective if erratic critic of undergraduate writing, was perhaps the chief faculty encourager. An intimate of E. E. Cummings during his own undergraduate years at Harvard, an established poet himself, the author of a brilliant book on William Blake,

---

[37] Interview, Frank Merchant, Atlanta, 7 November 1969.
[38] Frank Merchant to SD, 7 December 1969.
[39] Interview, Benjamin C. Clough, Touisset, Rhode Island, 29 July 1969.

about to become the author of an Amy Lowell biography, Foster
Damon combined impeccable literary credentials with real gen-
erosity to those students he felt had talent. In April of 1930, for
example, Damon used the check provided him for delivering the
Morris Grey poetry reading at Harvard to throw a dinner at the
Boston Harvard Club. He invited Scott to come along, as well as
Merchant, W. M. Frohock, and several other Brown undergraduates.
Also in attendance were Richard Blackmur, Robert Hillyer, James
Agee (then a student at Harvard), Grant Code, and John Wheelwright, Damon's wife's brother. Heady at the distinction of the
audience, hands stuck in the side pockets of his invariable tweed
coat, Scott "read a poem full of sonorous nasals; I remember his
almost singing 'King John, King John,' " Frohock writes.[40]
     Irreverent, like most young writers, Scott and Merchant con-
ducted a minor literary feud in the pages of the *Providence Journal*
during the spring of 1930. Merchant had printed a poem about
Amy Lowell, making much of the large Bostonian's cigar smoking,
and Annie L. Laney wrote in objection. To Merchant's defense rode
Scott, who inquired rather ungallantly of the objector:

> Would you relegate Coleridge's dope to the
>   garret,
> Have Byron minus limp and Keats without claret?
> My dear, I'm afraid you're the lady who'd
>   sigh on
> A portrait of Shelley 'cause it hadn't a tie
> on.

In her own bit of doggerel, the lady responded, and Win Scott,
characteristically, concluded the controversy by smoothing her
feathers in a most tactful letter.[41]
     In a more serious vein, Scott determined that spring to write a
biography of Whittier, and he spent the summer poring over the
excellent Whittier collection in the Haverhill Public Library and
corresponding with, among others, Miss Marie V. de Nervaud,
niece of the Elizabeth Lloyd (Howell) whom Whittier once
courted. By the fall, she had written him her congratulations "on

---

[40] W. M. Frohock to SD, 21 December 1969.
[41] The controversy took place in the pages of the *Providence Journal*, May–
June 1930. See Scrapbook 2, p. 117, Scott Collection, John Hay Library.

having finished the biography," but it was to be another year before Scott considered the book in shape to send to publishers. His liking for Whittier had, in the way of biographers, grown as the research and writing proceeded. "The further I went, the less apologetic I became. . . . His personality, without sentimentalizing it, emerges as singularly fine and, in a masculine way, sweet. One can see why the ladies saw a saintly air about him!" Nonetheless, it was with some relief that he wrote Klees in November of 1931 that the book was now, finally, about ready to type.[42]

Socially, Win Scott began to blossom as he discovered the beneficient effect of liquor in breaking down his natural inhibitions. In the fall of his junior year, he was introduced to alcohol at the apartment of Miss Grace Sherwood, Rhode Island state librarian and a sister of the eminent playwright, Robert Emmet Sherwood. She served a bootleg port, and Scott, roaring drunk on wine, crashed through a plate-glass door at Liggett's drugstore. Unhurt, he soon went on to the bootleg gin and rum consumed by the congenial residents of Slater Hall.[43] Scott roomed there with Jeff Werner and Toivo Kauppi, a chemist who amused himself by throwing butcher knives into the door of their suite. He also made friends with two different groups, one basically oriented to literature, the other to politics.

In the literary group were Merchant, W. H. (Bill) Gerry, R. Wade Vliet, and C. L. (Linnell) Jones, a transfer from Colgate with a gift for humor. Jones and Merchant, in mockery of fraternities and secret organizations generally, christened a club called Stein and Spigott, to which they solemnly initiated Prohibition bartenders and fellow undergraduates. One memorable night, orange-crates blazed in the fireplace of the suite at Slater Hall while the aspiring poets talked and declaimed their own verse. Frank Merchant's elegy for Scott, "Dread Task," demonstrates the confidence he and the others had in Scott's talent:

---

[42] Marie V. de Nervaud to WTS, 23 October 1930, Scott Collection, John Hay Library; WTS to Fredric Klees, 1 November 1931, Swarthmore College Library; Ferris Greenslet to WTS, 14 February 1930, Scott Collection, John Hay Library.
[43] Frank Merchant to SD, 7 December 1969; EMS to SD, 27 October 1969.

> We write verses in and against our poetry, that
> is the poetry of others. You write, you
> wrote—I hardly know whether I gain your
> meaning
> forward or backward in time.[44]

"We," the others, were imitative; Scott found original uses for the past.

Another poem, this one a piece of doggerel addressed by Scott to Linnell Jones and "hardly anthology material," better suggests the spirit of camaraderie:

> This is no time to write a letter
> I only came to leave your sweater.
> But still it's you I have to thank
> For certain oil that met my tank.
> That is to say, because I went
> Out of my way upon your bent
> An auto nearly knocked me down
> Ass over heel, heel over crown.
> Looking around I there discerns
> His Royal Highness Garry Byrnes
> Who when my little self did see
> Ywaved a bottle (green) at me.
> To his house did invite me in
> And there 2 hours I drank his gin
> And here's three minutes gone to pot
> With best regards of
> Winfield Scott.[45]

As Jones puts it, that poem was "very much a piece of those years. There was a deal of gin drunk, and people were careless of where they left their clothes. Both poems and prose were tossed about with abandon, and every so often the Manuscript Club met for purposes of mutual admiration. Win was the godfather of the Mss., but was much too intelligent to treat it seriously. . . . Mostly, there was talk —talk and more talk. World problems were solved, the Brown faculty was torn to pieces, Amy Lowell was dissected, and everyone

[44] Frank Merchant, "Dread Task," unpublished poem (fall 1969).
[45] WTS to Linnell Jones, 1930 or 1931. Byrnes worked for the *Providence Journal.*

pretended to understand Joyce. Win was probably the only one who did, and he was the only one to admit he didn't. He puffed at his pipe, needled the rest of us in friendly fashion, and only became misty-eyed when he spoke of his goddess, Greta Garbo."[46]

Whenever anyone accumulated the wherewithal ("a nickel I didn't have," Merchant recalls, and he was not atypical), they would buy some alcohol from the bootlegger, add juniper drops, check in the chemistry lab against poisonous stuff, acquire some mix, and a party would ensue. In a *Providence Journal* column written fifteen years later, suffering through the morning after a night of reunion with Victor Ullman, Scott spoke of earlier days: "We aren't what we were when we slopped around Slater Hall. On the other hand, that alcohol and gingerale mixture we drank in those Prohibition days—well, to be honest with the younger folks, how you knew the party was over was when everybody got sick. So you felt all right next morning."[47]

Ullman, though he later became a writer, belonged to the second group of companions in Slater Hall, those more interested in politics than literature. Scott underwent a political transformation at Brown, discarding the values of his Republican, very conservative homestead for those of a Depression Liberal. He came to Brown the year Sacco and Vanzetti were martyred in Massachusetts; four years later, when he graduated, the country was about to hit bottom and ready to try anything, anyone, to bounce back again. College "made a materialist out of me, a pacifist, and some sort of Leftist or Socialist. There were those to tell me the truth about Sacco and Vanzetti. I remember, too, we ardently admired Gandhi. We would go to jail rather than to war."[48] His ideas were shaped partly by contact with Ullman and the other Jewish intellectuals—Meyer Brown and Abe Silverman—who lived across the hall his junior year. Together they frequented a speakeasy in Pawtucket—sawdust on the floor and lithographed nudes on the walls—drank beer, and talked of revolution.

Brown, an evangelical socialist, insisted on arguing with Scott in Marxist terms and in pressing propaganda pamphlets on him. They

[46] Linnell Jones to SD, 30 January 1970.
[47] WTS, "Bookman's Galley," *Providence Sunday Journal*, 23 December 1945, sec. 6, p. 6.
[48] WTS, *Exiles*, p. 144.

had little effect, for Win Scott did not know the language: he had not read Marx then, and he never would. Politics, like literature, he took personally. He was interested not so much in issues as in people; in Lenin, not Leninism. Jeff Werner fervently wanted to know about everything, Win with equal fervor wanted to know about everyone. Hence, he could make no sense of Vic Ullman and Meyer Brown's going off to jail for distributing leaflets against hunger: *they* were eating well enough.[49]

One night, however, he too made the acquaintance of the police for nonpolitical roistering:

I was out to a Pawtucket speakeasy with all my Jewish friends. . . . And we arrived back to Market Square all glowing in a thin snow-storm, all beered up. I exuberantly pushed over a couple of metal park-ing signs, and that attracted the attention of some town toughs who crossed the street to fight us, and *that* attracted the attention of the police. I don't seem to recall any real fighting: my memory of the ap-proaching fray—I'd forgotten this till this very moment, and by god it shakes my heart—is that Meyer and the others tried to persuade me to beat it: *they*'d deal with this. (Now that I have remembered that, how pregnant it seems—what a lot it must show about them, about me.) Well, I wouldn't leave, though I was scared enough. But as I say the cops rode us all up Fountain street to the Police Dept. And it must be that the aforesaid town toughs—who were innocent if anyone was in the matter—were drunker than we Brown boys—us Brown boys, I should say—for they were held, and we were merely told to march out of there and get home to the campus; which we did.[50]

So Scott wrote Eleanor Metcalf in 1943, and the instinct of his friends to protect him, as well as his long lapse of memory about that detail of the story, *does* show a lot about Win Scott. Program-med to avoid fights, as a child, he could regard such potential un-pleasantness only with terror.

A similar incident, which Scott may have blocked out of his mem-ory (he has nowhere recorded it), occurred in the winter of his junior year, when he accompanied the Brown wrestling team, Vic Ullman competing at 138 pounds, to their match with Harvard. The Brown wrestlers won, and afterward walked across the Yard singing insulting lyrics about Harvard and looking for the nearest

[49] Interview, Victor Ullman, Alstead, 4 December 1969.
[50] WTS to EM, 20 April 1943.

beer joint. Instead, they ran into the Harvard boxing team, who proceeded to clobber the Brown wrestlers before directing them to the suds. At the appearance of the belligerent boxers, Vic recalls, "Win ran like hell and observed from a safe distance," only to re-appear when the fight had quieted down. Scott was so unaccommo-dated to human conflict, in fact, that he could not argue effectively. Ullman remembers seeing Win angry only once, in college; when he got excited, his voice went into tremolo, he waved his arms, and he finally stalked away in frustration, unable to communicate his anger.[51]

In person he escaped conflicts; in print, however, he welcomed them. "Speaking Offhand," Scott's column in the *Brown Daily Herald*, once again took up the fight against compulsory Chapel junior year, though the incoming Brown President, "Gus" Barbour, warned that such dissidents as Scott "would break up the peace and faith of a University."[52] (Perhaps it is significant that Win was never suspended for his part in the Chapel revolt, while others— Ullman and Rollo Silver—were.) Hardly a flaming revolutionary (the place for reformers, he wrote, was within the system they in-tended to reform), Scott nonetheless found plenty of windmills to tilt at in his column.

The poverty of student-faculty relations, for example: ". . . there are men on the faculty of Brown University whom one has no de-sire to see and should have no desire to see in person, as it were. The immense lethargy which slumbers as dead as a dinosaur on this campus rests not entirely in the undergraduate body . . . there is a handful of men who are unapproachable by anyone but a born Rotarian." The outmoded fraternities, whose bids he had once more turned down: "On the slightest examination . . . the whole structure is seen to be flimsy and rotten. . . . I want to do whatever I desire, as long as it hurts no one else, whenever and wherever I please . . . [this freedom] I would not sacrifice for the so-called 'social posi-tion' of any fraternity." In other columns he inveighed against the idiocies of the Prohibition law and the "compulsory blanket tax" of undergraduates to support the college athletic program (an ac-companying Editor's Note absolved him from endorsement of this

[51] Interview, Victor Ullman, Alstead, 4 December 1969.
[52] Frank Merchant to WTS, 3 February 1930, Scott Collection, John Hay Library.

latter view). Like Thoreau, Win Scott would not be forced. His internal compulsions were strong enough; he needed no restrictions from other, lesser authorities.[53]

Despite his gadfly role in the "Speaking Offhand" column, Win was generally admired by the more conservative students who formed a campus majority. In his looks, in his clothes, in his manner, he did not fit the stereotype of the college radical. As Linnell Jones writes, "Win, as a college student, is a hard person to get on paper"; it would be easier if he had been crazier. "Any number of college stories come to mind, but Win doesn't enter many of them. This may be because . . . stories usually have to do with people getting into trouble, and Win was the sort who not only stayed out of trouble, but tried to keep his friends out of trouble as well. There was something of the proper Bostonian about him. He would willingly take part in a forty-eight hour poker and juniper session, but somewhere along the line he'd clean up the ash trays. Come to think of it, Win was neat and tidy not only as far as externals were concerned but intellectually as well." So Merchant and Jones and the others who "raised hell in the *Daily Herald* were considered suspicious characters, not entirely fit for human consumption," and still more suspiciously did the then silent majority regard the Marxist, radical, non-WASP intellectuals. "Win, on the other hand, seemed to be as highly regarded by the Dekes as he was by the members of Stein and Spigott. Perhaps it was his manners, his soft way of speaking, his good looks, or a sort of hazy recollection that he was highly talented. At any rate," Jones concludes, "he was generally looked up to, and probably would have been accounted even greater admiration had it not been for the unseemly crowd with which he hung out."[54]

Scott gained the admiration of several cliques largely because he wanted so much to be liked—and because he had cultivated the rare gift of listening to others. The camaraderie in Slater Hall provided opportunities for talk and more talk. If Jeff organized a bridge game, Win would puff his pipe on the sidelines and read; when it was time for conversation, he unobtrusively joined in. Occasionally,

[53] WTS, "Speaking Offhand," *Brown Daily Herald,* 17 January 1930, 25 February 1930, 28 February 1930, 18 March 1930, [?] September 1930, Scrapbook 7, pp. 61, 76, 79, 89, 113, Scott Collection, John Hay Library.
[54] Linnell Jones to SD, 30 January 1970.

to satisfy his lifetime fascination with the past, he would propose an evening walk to Swan Point cemetery, where a statuary Angel of Death stood guard over the bodies of Providence's old rich. Swan Point served a more immediate purpose for many undergraduates; it was a place to take girls and make love under a clump of full-grown evergreens.[55] And by his junior year, Win Scott had discovered girls, and vice versa.

In one of the first "Speaking Offhand" columns of his junior year, he placed his tongue firmly in cheek and proposed a system of temporary companionate marriage between Brown men and the women a few blocks away at Pembroke. If that plan should prove impracticable, Scott suggested an alternative one: coeducational fraternities. The column stirred a letter-writing response, especially from those who were unable to recognize irony. But it was straightforwardly, not ironically, that he advocated full coeducation in the last column of his junior year.[56] By that time, he had fallen in love with one girl, and made love to another.

Taboo at his home in Haverhill, sex was a subject about which Henry Beston had written him in no uncertain terms: "The essential devil of these days is an intellectualism which kills, the mind destroying the thing which is far older and more important than the mind. Aphrodite rising from the woods to take an intelligence test! Sex, of course, and nothing but."[57] Perhaps more than any other correspondent, Beston influenced Scott's thinking. He appropriated the anti-intellectual bias inherent in Beston's comment, for example, and stoutly maintained, throughout life, that he was an emotionalist, not an intellectual. Certainly sex became far more important to him than life of the mind; in fact he believed that there was a positive correlation between sexual and artistic activity, so that if his sexual energy should run low, as it did, so would—so did—his ability to create poetry.

Throughout high school and his first years in college, Win Scott had indulged in the usual heterosexual experimentation, but he remained a technical virgin at least until the spring of his junior

---

[55] Frank Merchant to SD, 7 December 1969.

[56] WTS, "Speaking Offhand," *Brown Daily Herald*, 22 October 1929, [?] 1930, Scrapbook 7, pp. 9, 141, Scott Collection, John Hay Library.

[57] Henry Beston to WTS, 15 January 1929, Scott Collection, John Hay Library.

year, when Aphrodite appeared to him in several human forms. Some Brown men had done their first lovemaking with "townies," working girls who had the reputation of being generally more complaisant than the students at Pembroke. More in humiliation than pride, Scott wrote Jeff Werner in 1932 of having renewed his acquaintance with one such "townie," a Finnish girl who talked like Garbo and insisted to Scott, over the phone, that she remembered him well. "O I'm not patting my back, my boy," Scott explained. "I know exactly why she remembers me: I'm the only Brown man who ever went out with her who preserved his shyness."[58]

He *was* shy, and he was idealistic too. He encountered a fellow idealist one winter weekend at a Northfield, Massachusetts, inn, in Florence Williams, a Mt. Holyoke student. In May, when Mt. Holyoke held the intercollegiate poetry contest, they met once more. She was transferring to Swarthmore in the fall, and he asked Klees to look her up. "The business of getting two friends together is so ticklish and generally so foolish that I shouldn't suggest it if she weren't one of the best people on earth." The Mt. Holyoke contest itself, he told Klees, was very interesting:

Never did I see a place so over-run with poets and would be poets! . . . The judges were Fannie Stearns Davis, Elizabeth Hollister Frost, and Robert Frost [no relation]. Six colleges sent representatives: Amherst, Princeton, Barnard, Mt. Holyoke, Brown, and Radcliffe. The affair was on a Friday evening; first we all dressed and had a dinner, most of which I'm sorry to say I couldn't eat for nervousness. The judges were there, some faculty, and Sharon Brown [a professor of English at Brown] who took me up. Mrs. Frost . . . is a charming woman, dressed, like some of her poems that mourn her dead husband, in black over pink, very long, so that Robert F. continually blundered on it. Mrs. Davis . . . remarked that she was born a Victorian and intended to die one; tallish, fragile-looking, dark red hair, something of a gentle crank. . . . R. F. himself wore an ordinary suit and said it wasn't fair to get a man out of his overalls, once he was in them. I noticed especially the broadness of his face and the general filled-out appearance of him altogether: a thing his portraits, so often in profile, do not indicate. The gentleness of his eyes seemed to me remarkable, and I never saw a face for so short a time that I remember so well. He was on good behavior

[58] WTS to H. O. Werner, 5 May 1932, Scott Collection, John Hay Library.

. . . and did no ranting; at dinner he was expressing a worry about death and a wish that he could feel easier about it. His hair is very white.

Among his fellow competitors, Scott especially liked the "very sharp lyrics" of Anita Young from Mt. Holyoke, and it was with her that he shared the Glascock prize awarded the co-winners. For his own presentation, the Brown junior read "One Man," a character sketch deriving from Robinson, and two love laments, one of which begins

> All things get over,
> All things mend;
> Only this fire
> Has no end.[59]

Florence Williams, sitting small and brown in the audience of girls and faculty members, was proud of her friend from Brown, and they talked long into the night. The following summer he visited her home in Pennsylvania, and he continued to see her until shortly before his marriage. Not literary, she was lively, intelligent, and, like Scott, a pacifist, though her conviction stemmed from Quaker grounds. They were seriously in love. He even brought her to Haverhill for a visit with his parents, as a possible prelude to marriage. There, after observing how possessive his mother and grandmother were of Winfield and how badly they had spoiled him, Florence demonstrated her intelligence by deciding not to marry him.[60] Like Barbara George, she was small and dark, but with shingled hair. Three months after she turned him down, in the spring of 1932, he became engaged to Savila Harvey, another small, dark girl with her hair up.

The girl in love with him junior year was Marion Doescher, a Pembroker who came from Haverhill. They had known each other since she was seventeen "the way you know some people for years— you meet them at parties, and sometimes on the street, and you always speak pleasantly and you always know them but all the while you never talk especially to them nor they to you. . . . Yet sometimes . . . you may like them very much and still, because

[59] WTS to Fredric Klees, 28 June 1930, 10 August 1930, Swarthmore College Library.
[60] Interview, EMS, Santa Fe, 6 September 1969.

you are shy, years go by and nothing happens." It was like that with
Marion Doescher, who was in many ways the opposite of Scott's
ideal woman—slender and tall and blonde. Their courtship continued through the summer following Win's junior year. Then the
liaison broke off, and she began to go out with Paul Mackesey, a
football hero. There is some evidence that Scott loved her less than
he might have, but as he grew older, she occupied his thoughts
more and more. In the spring of 1939, he started a novel, "The
Brittle Street," about their relationship. "Was he impelled to write
the girl out of his system? Or what might he be trying to recapture
and relive?" The book broke off after eighty-eight handwritten
pages when he met Marion, like himself now married, on the street
in Providence.[61]

She became in memory a symbolic representation of that girl,
young and loving, who populates so many of the poems he wrote
late in life. In 1951, he cast her in this role in "Postscript":

> I opened to where you had written my name
> On the flyleaf twenty years ago.
> Nothing else—not even from whom it came;
> As though you had known I would always know.
>
> It is winter again. In the sun new snow
> Stares blind white here as there that time.
> How foolish I should be startled, though,
> That the poems in the book haven't changed
>   a rhyme.
>
> You've changed, I suppose. Others do, and
>   I'm
> Two times as old as the twenty years.
> To discover mirrors less sublime
> Is least of griefs and which most endears.
>
> But you—but you? One knows what one fears,
> Beauty like that is not to keep;
> Yet if I imagine you now through tears
> It's the sun on snow, and the snow is not
>   deep.

[61] WTS, "The Brittle Street," manuscript (11 May–28 June 1939), 88 pages,
Scott Collection, John Hay Library.

I have seen you only when I'm asleep,
Unchanged save the unrequited vow.
I'd have more than a written name to weep
Had I loved you then as I do now.[62]

And half-a-dozen poems in *Change of Weather*, published in 1964, derive from the middle-aged Scott's memories of early, unfulfilled passions, of the opportunity forever lost, and of the girl who appears to him in dreams. "Yes, it is a real girl whom I haven't seen for thirty-five years," he told Donald Eulert in 1966. "She was lovely and I was such a fool."[63]

In his senior year Win Scott asserted his independence by moving off-campus to live with Bill Gerry at 7 Arnold Street. Jeff Werner had graduated, an English Phi Beta Kappa, and with Gerry, emotionally erratic, intellectually brilliant, artistically talented, Scott forged a strong bond of fraternal affection. Together with Wade Vliet they began a poetry magazine, *Smoke*; when Gerry moved to the West Coast they corresponded regularly until Bill's untimely death in 1947. Besides writing poetry, Gerry played piano well enough to earn occasional money at parties or speakeasies. Almost nightly he and Scott would consume a quantity of beer or, when flush, bootleg gin. No saint himself, Gerry confided to Merchant that his new roommate seemed to like the stuff too much. But no one thought of alcoholism as a danger; they all drank, and they all got sick, and Scott was less raucous (though more weak-bladdered) than most.

Certainly the liquor he consumed had no deleterious effect on Scott as a student. Cutting down on his extra curricular writing, he distinguished himself in his senior year as never before, graduating with the Hicks prize for the best grades in English. Like most other ambitious young writers on campus, he adopted Foster Damon for his mentor. In five of the six English courses he took senior year, Damon was the instructor. A brilliant storyteller, his wit occasionally tinged with malice, Damon wore his clothes until large holes appeared in the knees and elbows; he pursued curious researches into obscure literary figures and little-known spiritualists. But he had published poetry and criticism, he had connections, and at

[62] WTS, "Postscript," *Change of Weather* (1964), p. 22.
[63] D. D. Eulert, "Scott," pp. 162–163.

times his advice was helpful, as Scott wrote Klees in February of
1931:

S. Foster continues to be as crazy and as friendly as ever. He spent a
lot of time with me during last December. I went to him for advice
about publishers, in connection with the Whittier biography stunt. He
asked to look over the manuscript and went through the whole thing,
making notes. Then we read it over together, with several dozen suggestions from him, many of which I am going to try to follow. Furthermore, he dug up various pieces of material for me. I've no intention,
if it can be helped, of emerging a little Damon, but surely many of his
ideas are extremely worthwhile.[64]

Still more surely, few teachers would have taken so much time and
effort to help an undergraduate, no matter how promising. In return, however, Damon may have expected rather more loyalty than
Scott was able to provide; relations between them were strained
when Scott married, and were temporarily severed in a subsequent
altercation over editorship of *Smoke*. But the years healed the
breach, and when Win Scott sent Damon a copy of his *New and
Selected Poems*, in 1967, the distinguished scholar replied with a
note which began, "I still think of you in terms of 'When I beget
a son,' so it startles me a bit to discover that Time marches on,
birthday after birthday."[65]

Damon introduced his student to Robert Hillyer, and both of
them encouraged Scott to spread his poetic wings. Under their endorsement, he sent a batch of sonnets to Harriet Monroe at *Poetry*
in October of 1930 (they were returned).[66] On his own, however,
he landed the job which would provide him with a meager suste-
nance over most of the succeeding twenty years. Writing Klees in
February of his senior year, he spoke of the past and of his future
prospects:

B. K. Hart of the *Journal*, deciding he had too much work on his
hands, very kindly asked me if I would take over most of the running
of his Sunday Book Pages; a part-time, afternoon job, but large enough
to keep me moving a good deal of the time. Its is pleasant work, doesn't
require any great amount of brains, and, inasmuch as Hart is expecting

[64] WTS to Fredric Klees, 5 February 1931, Swarthmore College Library.
[65] S. Foster Damon to WTS, 10 November 1967.
[66] WTS to Harriet Monroe, 22 October 1930, University of Chicago Library.

to repeat his last summer's European sojourn this coming season, it will probably spread a bit to something more like full-time position and, it's likely, provide me with bread and butter for a time. I've no hopes or intention or desire to become a Literary Editor for life but—particularly because there is nothing in sight, after college, besides the attempt to write books—it all looks rather a godsend for the present moment, at any rate.

A godsend indeed in 1931, when bookish jobs for literary young men were almost nonexistent. Teaching was a possibility, he continued, and there were

> One of two things I'd like to teach, but my desire isn't strenuous enough to make me want to enter the profession. It might be very agreeable to drop in at college a half-dozen hours or so a week and do what you like with a class or two. A naive ambition, no doubt. But if ever you cause to exist that Utopian college of yours—(the one thing I seem to recollect of it is brooks with bridges over them: is that correct?)—I'd like to be somewhere about.[67]

His academic achievement was such that Lindsay Todd Damon thought Scott ought to apply for a Rhodes scholarship.[68] He wasn't really the all-around type that usually is awarded a Rhodes, however, being neither socially nor athletically inclined. He may have felt, with Klees, that he would never really make a scholar; he may have shared something of the Yankee antipathy toward the English. But, in any case, Scott never took up Damon's suggestion. With or without the scholarship, however, Win Scott graduated in glory. His parents came down for the exercises, where everyone was struck with the youthful appearance of his father. "You look more like his ancestor than his son," Foster Damon remarked to Win, and Douglas Scott did indeed outlive his son.[69] In the class poem, "Prologue," Win provided still another reason for sticking on home grounds: his love for his native soil. If he should move away, it would be with a profound sense of regret:

[67] WTS to Fredric Klees, 5 February 1931, Swarthmore College Library.
[68] Lindsay Todd Damon to WTS, 6 May 1931, 1 October 1931, Scott Collection, John Hay Library.
[69] Interview, Frank Merchant, Atlanta, 7 November 1969.

Now do I think it time to praise the earth,
The soil that is my own, New England ground,
To sing it while the life that it has given
Be yet not far from it in land newfound.

. . . .

The flavor of the ground itself is mine:
Thus do I take and stamp it for my own,
Because I feel its rivers in my blood,
And its cold, ancient hardness in my bone.

So close a part of it am I that sometime,
If, after years had turned me other ways
And I could lose remembrance, coming here,
Something would leap within me, and the
    praise

Of what was near to me as heart and flesh
Would suddenly give me halt—tremendous so,
That, being not told and seeing nothing
    marked,
All at once I should tremble—I should
    know.

. . . .

For this I know—whatever else be gone,
Whatever else be whirled off out of reach,
That here I found what may be rarely known:
The awful beauty that is silence's speech.

And I have walked within these woods and
    meadows
And watched the hills along familiar skies,
And never turned away at coming darkness
Without a deeper wonder in my eyes.[70]

It would be twenty years and more before he would leave his native land for the Southwest, and even in Santa Fe Win Scott's mental geography remained that of New England.

Brown was not Harvard, where Scott had hoped to go, but the Providence institution was remarkably tolerant of Scott's literary single-mindedness. "I used to wonder," Bradford Swan, a friend

[70] Interview, EMS, Santa Fe, 6 February 1970; WTS, "Prologue," *Providence Journal*, 2 June 1931, Scrapbook 2, p. 129, Scott Collection, John Hay Library.

and fellow worker on the *Journal*, reflected after Win's death, "at a university which had been so wise as to make Win Scott Phi Beta Kappa when he hadn't climbed the regulation ladder." (His grades, exclusive of English courses, averaged out at about C.) "He knew so much about literature—and so little about mechanics or geology or all those other practical but really worthless subjects by which men could better the lot of their fellow men. In their place he developed sensitivity and compassion and a sense of relationship and involvement which had nothing to do with social science or anthropology or the world as the scientists would describe it. He *knew* the world; he didn't need to have it dissected or described by a taxonomist; he *knew* it, *felt* it, *loved* it or *sorrowed* for it, just as his wonderfully beautiful spirit told him."[71] Many years after their graduation, Scott wrote Frank Merchant in alarm at the rumor that Brown now insisted on its applicants being "well-rounded" and "the hell . . . with the odd stick whose record is contemptible in some ways but brilliant in others . . . somebody said only Harvard and the 'small colleges' now tolerate such as (it was put to me this way) the sort of kid I was." This in 1953, but in 1964, with real delight, Scott wrote Merchant that "Brown's off the recent or current all-round type so popular with colleges and is taking the kid who's bright as hell in some things and not necessarily at all bright in others. Bravo! (We heard this the other day from a goddam rich Bircher . . . who'd removed her daughter who was happy there at Pembroke because 'Brown is full of beatniks.')"[72]

Brown treated young Winfield Scott from Haverhill with rare generosity and understanding during his undergraduate career. If the university has seen fit to award him an honorary degree, when his *Collected Poems* appeared in 1962, for example, Brown's record vis-à-vis Win Scott would have been perfect. But Brown did not, to the everlasting annoyance of Ben Clough, a delightfully witty and talented classicist, who had urged the step on university administrators—and to the disappointment of Scott, reflected in this 1964 letter to Clough: "It's curious how we literary people—quite rightly I suppose—don't think honorary degrees 'prove' anything —and feel 'superior' to them—and yet—and yet—would be enor-

---

[71] Bradford Swan to EMS, 13 May 1968.
[72] WTS to Frank Merchant, 29 April 1953, 31 March 1964.

Scott at the time of his graduation from Haverhill High School, 1927.
(*Photo by A. S. McKeen, Haverhill, Massachusetts*)

Winfield Townley Scott and his mother, 1910.
(*Smith Photo*)

Scott at his desk at the *Providence Journal* offices, c. 1950.

All the Scotts, at home, in Santa Fe. (Photo by Laura Gilpin)

mously touched by one from our *own* college. This is all silly of course."[73]

At graduation in June of 1931, however, Brown heaped its honors on Scott, and the prospect of honorary degrees hardly weighed on his mind. He had a job—one he would hold for twenty years—on the *Journal*'s book page; he had a new girl—the very pretty, very brilliant Savila Harvey who had been a 1929 graduate of Pembroke; and he had a role—that of the promising young poet—to live up to. By his professors and friends, Scott "was encouraged to think his great promise was already accomplishment by 1931—and then the whole economic world was ruling that his best kind of success could be only moderate, unless he'd play editor or teacher."[74] That was all right; he would play the game by the rules of expediency, and still fulfill his promise, writing poetry on *Journal* time, writing poetry late at night, and meanwhile reviewing books for his "bread and butter." He was actually being *paid* to read, the thing he liked best in the world to do. No matter that the compensation was small (fifteen dollars a week): the wonderful thing was that he could read and write on the job. The world was his oyster, if it was anyone's oyster in 1931.

[73] WTS to Benjamin C. Clough, 22 October 1964, Scott Collection, John Hay Library. Others, including I. J. Kapstein, also pushed for an honorary degree for Scott.

[74] Frank Merchant to SD, 7 December 1969.

Print was the Token, its page the stamped coin
Who'd counterfeit or steal for?[1]

5. Making It, Once

IF YOU HAVE TO LIVE through a depression, the time to do it is when
you're young. Like many another member of the class of 1931,
Win Scott graduated with little money and no real prospects of
acquiring more. But he *was* young, and times did not seem really
hard. At the *Providence Journal*, he had a job which paid him
fifteen dollars a week and all the books he wanted (some of them
eventually found their way to secondhand bookstores as an addi-
tional means of supporting Scott and such friends as Frank Merchant). He also had considerable responsibility. During the summer of 1931, his boss, B. K. (Bert) Hart, traveled in Europe, and
Scott put out the book page himself. When the literary editor returned, his young assistant continued to do the bulk of the work:
"Mr. Hart was boss, naturally; but after seeing what he and his
wife wanted to do in the way of reviewing, almost from the beginning, it was all left to me. In other words, my duties, as I recall,
were: to assign books to people for review; to make up weekly page,

[1] Frank Merchant, "Dread Task," unpublished elegy for Scott (fall 1969).

to proofread it; once a month to make out the list of contributors
and what money was owed them."² For ten years, he continued to
perform these tasks, normally those of the literary editor himself,
until Hart died in 1941 and Scott finally assumed the title for his
role.

For a man who loved books as Scott did, the post on the *Journal*
constituted the best of all possible stopgaps against starvation.
Emerging from his coldwater flat on Waterman Street, he would
walk to the newspaper building to find, more often than not, the
day's pile of new books to be considered for review. When Scott,
as a freshman at Brown, had first met Hart, the older man told
him, "I've got the best job in the world . . . I like books, and here I
sit while all the books there are keep pouring onto my desk."³ Four
years later, sitting at the next desk, Scott was inclined to agree.
Not only could he browse contentedly; he also had the chance to
review books by writers who particularly interested him, and who
would later take an interest in Scott's own work—men like Robert
Hillyer and Horace Gregory. Only one drawback remained, and
that one the budding author was determined to remedy: none of
the books bore his name.

Through the summer and fall of 1931, with the assistance of
S. Foster Damon, Scott worked over his Whittier biography, and in
January of 1932 took the manuscript to New York to try his luck.
As he wrote Jeff Werner,

> I kicked two or three last kicks into the Whittier, got the Introduc-
> tion—a good one, a real piece of introducing—out of S. Foster, and his
> advice to go to New York with the MS. rather than shipping it.
> So I went to New York. I went by boat last Thursday night, spent
> Friday there with Savila [Harvey] all day acting as my most excel-
> lent guide and thereby removing all the cold horrors I'd had of getting
> lost, and saw life with a great deal of joy. I rather like the city, though
> I saw so little of it. Lunch in a genuine Greenwich Village stable, saw
> Robinson in the afternoon for an hour, then Cass Canfield, President
> of Harper's, who was most cordial. I expect to hear from them in about
> two weeks.

² Donald Dean Eulert, "Winfield Townley Scott: Conversations on Poets and
the Art of Poetry" (Ph.D. dissertation, University of New Mexico, January
1969), pp. 19–20.
³ WTS, obituary for B. K. Hart, *Providence Journal*, [?] May 1941.

After a weekend visit to Florence Williams's home in Pennsylvania, Scott returned to New York Monday to explore the possibility of reviewing with Carl Van Doren. (Robinson had supplied a letter of introduction.) Van Doren advised him to visit the more prominent editors, in person, but it would be several years before Scott began to write reviews for the *New York Herald Tribune* and for some of the literary magazines.[4]

Both Canfield and Van Doren said, encouragingly, that the Whittier biography was "a good subject," but not, apparently, good enough. In May, Win wrote Werner, "the Whittier has been to (1) Harpers, (2) Knopf, (3) Macmillan and (4) Putnams. . . . Putnam's letter was mildest: several read it and found it 'interesting' but can't use it. Harpers and Knopf and Macmillan all said it is a good book but they are afraid of its financial capabilities. Macmillan said they'd 'probably' have taken it in better times . . . O well, what the hell."[5] Perhaps Scott was too young to be deeply disappointed by such rejections; surely he was too young to know that he might have continued to mail out his manuscript, which simply disappeared. But the book was far from a dead loss. For one thing, Scott had proved to himself that he *could* write a book-length manuscript. Out of his research came Scott's excellent essay on "Snowbound," reprinted in *Exiles and Fabrications*. Out of it as well came his best-known poem, "Mr. Whittier." As he told Donald Eulert, thirty-five years later,

It still interests me the way I got the "Mr. Whittier" poem. I wasn't really out of college, it was my senior year and I had already begun to work on a biography of Whittier; I thought there *should* be a new one. There hadn't been any since Victorian times or close Victorian. They were still being written by people who knew him and things like that, but there was no modern estimate of the man and his life. I tried to do it and I even finished a whole book. I don't know where it was rejected . . . but it *was* rejected, thank God and has long since been destroyed, I am sure. I was very young, really; here I was working at such a job when I was twenty-one or so, and I did my research fairly well. And I did my prose I think I would guess fairly badly. I was not

[4] WTS to H. O. Werner, 27 January 1932, Scott Collection, John Hay Library, Brown University.
[5] Ibid., 5 May 1932, Blanche W. Knopf to WTS, 15 March 1932, Scott Collection, John Hay Library. Houghton Mifflin also saw and rejected the manuscript.

in command of the situation. I was not equipped at that point in my life to write such a book very well—and that is the only way to write such a book. So, as I say, this was the very beginning of the 1930's; and somewhere in the very early 1940's, perhaps literally 1941, that poem (if it is a poem) just poured out, everything. I didn't look up anything; I even wrote some passages when there were visitors sitting in the room because I couldn't stop. I'd pick up my paper and write some more lines and it just-swist-everything I wanted to say. I am much happier to have *it* around than that benighted biography that disappeared so long ago.[6]

Here is the poem—and indeed it *is* a poem—that "just poured' out of Scott after his ten-year gestation period. Written in a long, loose line, "Mr. Whittier" follows its theme—the distinction between what is hard and what is easy—with so sound a structure as to belie its having come to Scott merely by inspiration. Best of all, his poem does what biographies only rarely succeed in doing: it brings its subject to life. For anyone who reads this poem, John Greenleaf Whittier no longer remains merely one of the nineteenth-century fireside poets, gazing dreamily from behind his bearded portrait in a deck of "Authors" cards, along with Longfellow, Lowell, and Holmes. Unlike these gentlemen, Whittier was no Boston Brahmin—quite the opposite.

Mr. Whittier

It is so much easier to forget than to have been
  Mr. Whittier.
Though of course no one now remembers him when
  he was young.
A few old ladies who were little girls next door
  in Amesbury,
Or practically next door, have reminiscences of
  pears and apples
Given them by the famous, tamed, white-bearded
  saint with the
Still inextinguishable dark Hebraic eyes; and
Of course there is the old man—and I for one am
  grateful—who

---

[6] Eulert, "Scott," pp. 149–151. Scott's poem was not printed in book form until 1948.

Recalls the seedy coat, the occasionally not so
    clean high collar,
And that like many another he read his paper by
    the hour in the privy.
Carl Schurz, finding him rained in by the stove at
    the village store,
Thought "So superior to those about him, and yet
    so like them"; and
His official biographer decided that Mr. Whittier's
    poetry was the kind
"Written first of all for the neighbors." There
    are lesser and worse.

In any case, here is a city, founded in 1630,
    present population somewhere about
55,000—has been more in boom times, and has been
    a lot less;—say,
In three hundred years has birthed a couple of
    hundred thousand people
And one poet. Not bad. And as proof of the
    title I shall only remark
It is easier to leave *Snow-Bound* and a dozen
    other items in or out of
The school curriculum than it is to have written
    them. Try it and see.

Born where the east wind brought the smell of the
    ocean from Plum Island up-river,
At a brookside haunted in the foggy dark of
    autumn nights
By six little witches in sky-blue capes—Uncle
    Moses had seen them;—
Born on a farm to the *Bible, Pilgrim's Progress*,
    a weekly paper, the Quaker meeting-house,
To hard poverty, obscure, and a few winters of
    country school;
To die—though only after there were thirteen
    for dinner, and the clock
Suddenly stopped—ancient with fame, with
    honorary degrees, and
One hundred thousand dollars all made out of
    poems,—I say

Even this was not easy, though also it is not
What I am talking about, but is really incidental
    along with
Not liking Walt Whitman and never quite affording
    marriage.

Neither, under the circumstances, could it have
    been easy, and it was important,
To stand suddenly struck with wonder of old
    legends in a young land,
To look up at last and see poetry driving a buck-
    board around the bend,
And poetry all the time in the jays screeching
    at the cats in the dooryard,
Climbing with the thrush into the August noon
    out of the boy's sight
As he dawdled barefoot through poetry among the
    welts of the goldenrod;
But nothing is hardest which treads on nobody
    else's toes.

Let us not begrudge Mr. Whittier his white beard,
    his saintliness, his other foibles;
Let us remember him when he was young, not to
    begrudge his rise
As a goddam Abolitionist hated not only in the
    South,
Hated by manufacturers, politicians, the
    neighbors, our folk, all
Who hate the outspoken radical and know a safer
    way;
Denounced by the clergy—a serious matter in that
    time; by the good men who
Rotten-egged him in New Hampshire, burned him out
    in Pennsylvania,
Jailed those who read him, and twenty years later
    immortally froze
With Webster on whom he turned his scorn of
    compromise.
It is so much easier to forget than to have been
    Mr. Whittier.

He put the names of our places into his poems
and he honored us with himself;
And is for us but not altogether, because larger
    than us.
When he was an old man, the Negroes came to him
    free to come and sang to him
"The Lord bless thee and keep thee;
The Lord make his face to shine upon thee and be
    gracious unto thee;
The Lord lift up his countenance upon thee, and
    give thee peace."
—No more begrudge their freedom than his tears.[7]

There is more than admiration in that poem. Win Scott loved
Whittier, and the love shines through. From him Scott had learned
a valuable lesson about poetry: to stick to the land and the people he
knew, and "not to fly too far above ground." Many poets two generations after Whittier, Win wrote in 1934, "who still have their
ears stopped to native sounds by the strains of a remote, if courtly,
muse, might do well to learn of [Whittier]. He created a handful
of enduring poems out of the lure of New England, rather than the
faery lore of some far East; his was the authentic goldenrod, rather
than exotic flowers transplanted from foreign lands; not the lark
and the nightingale, but the jay and the nuthatch, sing in his
verse."[8] With guidance from Whittier and from Ralph Waldo
Emerson, Scott rejected the courtly muses of Europe and chose
rather the familiar, the commonplace, and the near-at-hand.

Finding it easier to write about others than about himself, Win
Scott had barely swallowed the rejection of his Whittier biography
when he plunged ahead with another prose work still less likely to
attract enthusiasm from publishers. This time he focused on "Lord"
Timothy Dexter, an eccentric eighteenth-century Newburyport
merchant, who made a fortune in trade, and on his equally eccentric "poet laureate," Jonathan Plummer. The spring and summer
of 1932, Scott raked up broadsides written by Plummer, pored over
old newspaper clippings, consulted Harvard and the American
Antiquarian Society, and hugely enjoyed the process. J. P. Mar-

---

[7] WTS, "Mr. Whittier," *New and Selected Poems* (1967), pp. 52–54.
[8] WTS, "Poetry in American: A New Consideration of Whittier's Verse,"
New England Quarterly 7 (June 1934): 258.

quand had published a book on Dexter, but, Scott reported to Jeff Werner, he found Marquand's treatment "badly padded, careless. . . . And as for Plummer, who is the epitome of the town crank —pedler [sic], rhymster [sic], religious fanatic, and thwarted male —Marquand did very little with him . . . I'm going to try to get both gentlemen down by telling the whole story, legends and all—even about D's cooking excrement—plus the airs of their times. Late 18th century Newburyport was a grand place, with . . . ships and barks and brigs and schooners sailing out, shipbuilding going on, beautiful Georgian houses going up, men in blue coats and silver buckles, ladies in silk bonnets etc., the sea, the town witch, the whole movement of early American life there. Well, you see what it's trying to be. One of those books about odd characters, presumably with a lot of charm and whatnot."[9]

By the turn of the year he had finished the book, and he sent it off to New York, where there proved to be still less interest in Dexter-Plummer than in Whittier. "Harpers repeated the Houghton Mifflin dope on Jonathan," Scott wrote Werner in February of 1933. "It's good and it won't sell. I'm now trying to get in touch with a literary agent. . . . Let *her* get the letters; I'm sick of them."[10] The agent had no luck, either, and it remained for another agent, Alan Collins, to tell Scott a decade later that *Lord Dexter and Mr. Plummer* "is extremely well-written . . . but it is just not a book. It is more in the field of curiosa-Americana and I am afraid publishers don't see a commercial sale in that sort of thing."[11] In 1946 Scott sent the manuscript to Edna H. Greenwood, another Dexter-Plummer fan, who promised to try to get it published, or to get a film made. Eventually, she reported sadly, she lost the manuscript, and so another of Scott's early attempts to publish a book ended.

It is significant that both the Whittier biography and the Dexter-Plummer informal history concentrated on an area within fifteen miles of his family home in Haverhill, and that they looked back to the recent and distant past. Obviously, Scott was keenly conscious of his literary heritage; quite explicitly, he made the case for regionalism in literature. "It seems to me," he wrote, "that we are

---

[9] WTS to H. O. Werner, 5 May 1932, Scott Collection, John Hay Library.
[10] Ibid., 10 February 1933, Scott Collection, John Hay Library.
[11] Alan C. Collins to WTS, 20 October 1942, Scott Collection, John Hay Library.

recovering from the notion that, since these United States are an immense and sprawling wonder, any work of art must share those qualities. . . . Again and again it has been proved that literature begins as a thing of locality. Shall your Pepys become timeless—let him write of his days in London. Shall your Thoreau speak for many men in many places—let him travel and write in Concord."[12] In a roundup of New England poets published in the *New Republic* in 1935, Scott reminded the competition of their debt to New England and warned that the region might once more burst into creative flame:

> Keepsakes, testaments—
> We have given you the best:
> Pebble from Walden Pond, moss of the Manse,
> Skyrocket over Concord—or, anyway, a bit
>   of the stick,
> A cup of Ishmael's sea-brewed liquor,
> That Amherst letter unsent.
>
> Maybe we swapped:
> All these for your river raft and a leaf
>   of grass.
> And who's poorer? Who's lost anything?
> Now in a poor vanity of greedy fear
> You scorn us, old, with all your youth.
> We've sent all we have, you say,
> And to hell with us:
> We've gone thin in the chest, thick in the
>   head
> And breathe museum air.
>
> You need not despair of us,
> Though we gave you so much you think we must
>   fail now
> Better be cautious:
> There might be a bomb packed in the next
>   mail.[13]

The Whittier and Dexter-Plummer endeavors had turned out to be duds rather than bombs. Meanwhile, however, Scott was pub-

---

[12] WTS, "Literature: North–North-East," unpublished essay (1937), Scott Collection, John Hay Library.

[13] WTS, "For Certain Sectionalists," *New Republic*, 14 August 1935, p. 15.

lishing reviews regularly in the *Journal*; *Poetry*, in Chicago, as well as *Hound and Horn* and other magazines, were accepting some of his poetry. He also found a certain solidarity in companionship with the young literary hopefuls who were gathered in Providence (or who had left Providence for the town down the river, New York, but still kept closely in touch). They were all poor, none of them had yet published *the* book, and the camaraderie of college days continued. Among the company were Frank Merchant, Bill Gerry (whose marriage was breaking up), R. Wade Vliet (who would never be married), Jeff Werner (in graduate school at Harvard), and a newcomer from Holland, David Cornel DeJong, who arrived at Brown for graduate work in the fall of 1932. All of these men appear, under fictional names, in Scott's first book of poetry, *Biography for Traman*; together in the early 1930's all of them were struggling to make an impression in the literary world.

As Merchant put it in his elegy for Scott, "Print was the Token" for them all, the coin of admission, the chit which would start them on their journey to whatever limited immortality the printed word might bestow.[14] One way to get their work into print, a sovereign way, was to start their own magazine, and so, in the month before he graduated from college, Scott, together with Gerry and Vliet, had brought out the first issue of *Smoke*, a journal devoted to "poetry and occasional prose," with Foster Damon acting in an advisory capacity. *Smoke* was to remain in existence, during a stormy history appropriate to its name, for another half-dozen years, but the first issue none of the editors was ever to forget. The venture originated during a Sunday bull session, when someone casually remarked "Let's get out a magazine." So they did. Each of the young men had poems to help fill its pages, and Damon added one of his. By Thursday, the loan of a print shop had been arranged, and Scott, Gerry, and Vliet, doing the composing themselves, put in an incredible weekend of work to produce the first sixteen-page number of ninety copies. "On Friday evening, they started work at seven o'clock; at half past six on Saturday morning they stopped. . . . On Saturday afternoon they went back to work at 4:30 o'clock . . ." working through to three Sunday morning. "After brief hours of sleep, the editors went to work again at 9:30 o'clock Sunday morn-

[14] Merchant, "Dread Task."

ing, this time to labor until 8 o'clock Monday morning." At the end, Gerry recalled, "We were dirty, unshaven and pretty well played out, but we were very happy." Eight days from inception to publication: such was the lure of print, such the vigor of youth.[15]

Linnell Jones, who did not aspire to be a poet, took the magazine lightly. "I paid a dollar for a subscription to 'Smoke,' " he wrote, "and then devoted a weekend to the production of a rival publication, 'Gas', which purported to be satiric and obscene and succeeded in its second objective."[16] But Merchant and DeJong and John Wheelwright, the talented brother of Foster Damon's wife, Louise, soon became seriously involved with *Smoke*, and a hand-wrestle for control of the magazine, Damon-Wheelwright versus the young Brown graduates, followed.

Damon, of course, was a power to be reckoned with. Mentor to the bright young men on campus, possessor of a very keen if not especially orderly mind, two books of poetry to his credit and well launched on a distinguished career as writer and scholar, he was on the ground floor of all literary doings on campus. Louise Damon recalls that there were "a lot of little boys buzzing around my husband" in the early 1930's, and that it was "a lot of fun having them around for meals." Scott was regarded by both Damons as the most promising of the "little boys," and he possessed a degree of charm the others could not match. "Everybody felt his charm," according to Mrs. Damon.[17] Certainly Foster Damon was extraordinarily kind to Win Scott. Not only did he provide valuable advice and an introduction to the Whittier biography; he also saw to it that Scott was invited to all possible literary occasions. In the summer of 1932, while the Damons vacationed in Massachusetts, Scott stayed in their house in Providence, tending the cats. One memorable weekend that summer, Damon took him on a visit to the Robert Hillyers at Pomfret, Connecticut. "We had a delightful time," Win wrote Jeff Werner, "for they—and their two or three other guests— were all most pleasant; and furthermore their place is surrounded by fields and woods and they even have a very swimmable pond at the foot of their lawn. We had quite a Nudist time, by the way, and

[15] "New Magazine Launched Here," *Providence Journal*, 15[?] May 1931.
[16] Linnell Jones to SD, 30 January 1970.
[17] Interview, S. Foster Damon and Louise Damon, Annisquam, Massachusetts, 11 July 1969.

I was very much interested to find how easily natural and unexciting mixed nakedness is of a Sabbath morn."[18] The friendship between Damon and Scott began to cool when Win married Savila Harvey in May of 1933. Either Damon disapproved of the match and called Savila "shanty Irish," or Win Scott thought he did, and had. Shortly thereafter the struggle over control of *Smoke* came to a boil, and it produced differences between the two men that took long years to heal.

In addition to its internal problems, *Smoke* was having financial woes, and an angel named Susanna Valentine (Mitchell) Gammell came to the rescue. In October of 1933 she sent one hundred dollars to keep the magazine going and assured Scott by letter that "you three young men [Scott, Merchant, and DeJong, Gerry having gone to New York and Vliet to Oklahoma City] are the editors of 'Smoke.' Your hands are free . . . if I pay the piper you call the tune." That was fine with Win Scott, but not with Foster Damon, and, characteristically, faced with conflict, Scott simply retired from the field. "I'm sorry," Mrs. Gammell wrote him in November, "you've felt obliged to resign as Editor-in-Chief, but if you thought your remaining in that position would create an unbearable situation for you it seems to me you did quite right."[19] The very next issue— for December 1933—was devoted entirely to a long poem by Damon, "Seelig's Confession." That was too much for the young men who had begun *Smoke* largely as a convenient repository for their own work (though its pages were also graced by the work of Wallace Stevens, William Carlos Williams, R. P. Blackmur, Yvor Winters, J. V. Cunningham, Dudley Fitts, and Muriel Rukeyser). Two issues later Damon's name went off the masthead, leaving Susanna Valentine Mitchell as editor-in-chief and David Cornel DeJong and Frank Merchant as editors. Scott, no longer an editor, continued to contribute poems.

Apparently, the petty struggle was over, with the angel in charge, but the backbiting continued. And Scott wrote, in March of 1934, "Ah, God, Werner, the gossip I'm storing up":

[That] I was practically drugged into marriage. [That] Savila is shallow. We are unhappy, do not love each other. Savila, dumb in col-

18 WTS to H. O. Werner, 1 August 1932, Scott Collection, John Hay Library.
19 Susanna Valentine (Mitchell) Gammell to WTS, 23 October 1933 and 9 November 1933, Scott Collection, John Hay Library.

lege, met me while we were both there, got to smattering books; is sore
at Foster Damon because he kept her from being a Phi Bete; Frank and
I are more interested in each other than in women; Frank is going
mad, will commit murder or suicide probably; my father-in-law tried
to get control of Smoke, is now running down the magazine in jealous
frenzy; I am all through—write no longer, stick to hack work or do
nothing, am completely dominated by my shallow wife; I say nothing
about Smoke because I am ashamed of my part in it, of my resigning
from it—oh, and a lot more, including the "fact" that my wife is shanty-
Irish (like Frank) and therefore untrustworthy, etc. etc. etc. And who,
do you suppose, is telling this, inventing this all over the landscape?
Mr. S. Foster Damon . . . All this has come, through one or two sources,
directly from headquarters.[20]

Or so it seemed. Perhaps, though, the sources themselves were not
to be trusted. On his part, Damon consistently maintained his innocence of the charge of gossipmongering. Please, he wrote Win
Scott, *"don't believe anything* about me except what I say or do in
your presence. I think that some day you and Savila will be interested to learn what has really been going on. It is a rather pathetic
story."[21] Damon was certainly right about that: it *was* a rather
pathetic, sorrily petty, quarrel, in which pride of publication and
a worsening relationship between mentor and protégé were clearly
somehow involved.

In a long letter to Lindsay Todd Damon, 3 January 1936, Scott
once more rehearsed the charges supposedly levied against him
and Savila by Foster Damon. And in "Professor Black's Baby
Elephant," published in the Winter 1936 number of *Smoke*, Win
Scott avenged himself by comparing the professor's (Foster
Damon's) poetry to the defecations of a baby pink elephant.[22] The
animosities stirred up by this teapot tempest lasted nearly twenty
years, until Scott sent his laudatory article about John Wheelwright, partly as a peace offering, to Damon.[23]

Barely a year after graduation from Brown, Win Scott had be-

---

[20] WTS to H. O. Werner, 27 March 1934, Scott Collection, John Hay Library.
[21] S. Foster Damon to WTS, undated, Scott Collection, John Hay Library.
[22] WTS to Lindsay Todd Damon, 3 January 1936, David Cornel DeJong to
WTS, 16 March 1942, Scott Collection, John Hay Library; WTS, "Professor
Black's Baby Elephant," *Smoke* 5 (Winter 1936).
[23] S. Foster Damon to WTS, 7 August 1954, Scott Collection, John Hay
Library.

come engaged to Savila Harvey. Two years older than he, she had graduated from Pembroke in 1929 and had gone to New York to live with relatives in Brooklyn and to work in Manhattan. But Savila, who (she told friends) had set her cap for Win Scott, managed occasional visits to Providence, and her beau reciprocated with trips to New York and to Darien, Connecticut, where her mother and father lived. In April of 1932 the small, dark, vivaciously pretty Miss Harvey came to Providence, where she and Win "had a grand time" seeing their first Gilbert and Sullivan. Soon thereafter, encouraged by liquor and the enthusiastic approval of Bill Gerry, Win called her in Brooklyn and proposed marriage. Over the Fourth of July, Win and Bill took the boat to New York, and while Savila worked, Scott spent the afternoon at Minsky's burlesque show. "I figured I owed it to my cosmopolitan air to see at least one in my life," he wrote Werner, in semiapology. Actually, Scott was anything but cosmopolitan in his sexual experience, and he was soon consulting books on the subject. "Such books," he confessed, "get pretty sickening, methinks." Still, there was much to be learned; the danger was "of getting such things so firmly fixed in your educated mind that, every pass you make, you think 'Page 86, paragraph 3,' or somesuch."

Concurrent with Scott's visit to New York over Independence Day, his engagement was announced in the *Norwalk* (Connecticut) *Hour*. Both Miss Harvey and Mr. Scott, the story pointed out, were members of Phi Beta Kappa. "Miss Harvey is at present employed by a New York advertising concern, and Mr. Scott is assistant to the Sunday editor of the Providence Journal. The date for the wedding has not yet been announced." Nor indeed would it be for another nine months; engagement was one thing, marriage a more difficult one to manage on Scott's meager salary. Meanwhile, Savila journeyed up to Haverhill in August for the ritual meeting with Win's family, and Werner put them up over in Boston. For New Year's, Werner, his girl Elizabeth Ward, Win, and Savila delightedly secured Jo Gerry's apartment. "I told Jo the important thing was bunking you and Elizabeth; but Jo says, blithely, Oh I'll have two empty rooms you know; one for you and Jeff, one for Elizabeth and Savila." However, the weekend ended badly, when Scott read the wrong timetable and subjected Savila and himself to a two-hour wait in Boston. "It was terrible," he wrote Werner, but it was also characteristic. In his dreams, Scott persistently ran for trains that had just left; in his life, he consistently arrived far in advance of the scheduled time of departure. Nonetheless, Win was more and more eager to be married; the difficulty and cost of travel made his meetings with Savila frustratingly infrequent. "In 1933," he wrote Jeff, "I get married with or without money."[24]

Without, as it turned out. "Desperation is in the air," Scott wrote in February 1933. "Savila and I are thinking seriously of taking the extra risk in May, if we can amass enough cash to get us modestly through the summer, and hope the Fall will bring me, or (and) the interim will bring her, some work. After all, Werner, are we all to ossify by sitting still while the world goes steadily to ruin? (Rhetorical.)" By mid-April the matter was settled, a date set, and a first home found, "a most attractive four-room and bath flat over Roome Lane, on John Street," which rented for twenty-five dollars a month.

The wedding was small, very informal, at Central Congregational Church on Angell Street in Providence, at noon on May 22. (Another momentous twenty-second of the month.) "It's not, you understand, a Church Wedding: just in a church, and Dr. Bradford seems extremely nice about the whole thing," Win explained to Jeff. The two families came; Savila's bother James served as best man, Win's sister Jeannette as maid of honor. A picture shows the four of them, Savila dark, rather round-faced, but slim, and though unsmiling, certainly bride-pretty, looking something like Maureen O'Sullivan, Win very young and very solemn. After the ceremony, Governor Theodore Francis Green, one of the wedding guests, placed his car and chauffeur at the couple's disposal for the day. The *next* day, the bridegroom went back to work; financially, a honeymoon was out of the question.[25]

Actually, Governor Green had helped to make the wedding possible. Since shortly after graduation, Scott had been turning an extra dollar writing speeches for the governor, a practice which

[24] WTS to H. O. Werner, 5 May 1932, 1 August 1932, 15 August 1932, 18 August 1932, 27 September 1932, 14 December 1932, and 19 February 1933, Scott Collection, John Hay Library; engagement announcement, *Norwalk* (Connecticut) *Hour*, 4 July 1932.

[25] WTS to H. O. Werner, 10 February 1933 and 18 April 1933, Scott Collection, John Hay Library; Garrett D. Byrnes, "Poet Cheerfully Forecasts Death," Providence, R.I., *Evening Bulletin*, 19 March 1937.

continued when Green won election as United States senator from
Rhode Island. "We shan't be wealthy," Scott wrote Werner, "but
I think we'll manage, ok, short of a flood or some kind of plague,
such as the cholera or babies. . . . The speeches continue; irregularly,
but still they go on. At the least, I think we'll make 1200 total
(Journal plus Green) and we can pinch on that; S, of course, is job-
hunting." In retrospect, Scott found the decision "incredible . . .
when I was sure of $25 a week I got married." But at the time he
had no "sense of fear."

And then of course you got so much for your money, so you went to
the store—of course you're young, you're childless, and there are just
the two of you to look out for—and you came back having spent $1.25
and you had a bag full of groceries. Then everybody, so to speak, was
in the same spot. It was a curious era in American history and one,
in the fashion I suppose of most middle-aged people, looking back I
am now glad I lived through. If I have blotted out some of the more
worrisome aspects of it in my own life, I just don't know. In looking
back I recall buying very cheap clothes; I was slender for a long while
after I was in college, and I can remember that by going into the boy's
department of the store, I could get a cheap pair of summer trousers
that fit me and cost a little less than if I went into the men's department.[26]

As time went on, further small supplements to the family income
materialized. Win began to write movie reviews, at five dollars a
week and all the free movies he and Savila could stand. For two
years, beginning in the fall of 1934, he taught freshman English
sections part time at Pembroke and Brown. "You'll be knocked back-
wards," he wrote Werner in October of 1934, "when you hear that
no less than 28 Pembroke freshmen are in my more or less complete
charge." Scott was not particularly impressed with the quality of
Pembroke prose, nor with his prospects of improving it. "I suppose
one must be philosophical and realize that not only writing cannot
be taught, even a fair degree of literacy cannot." His students, happily, reacted differently. Stuart C. Sherman, now John Hay librarian at Brown, fondly remembers his 1935–1936 freshman composition course under the tutelage of Win Scott. Tweedy, ubiquitous

    [26] WTS to H. O. Werner, 18 April 1933, Scott Collection, John Hay Library;
Eulert, "Scott," pp. 19, 24–25.

pipe in hand, Scott perched on the edge of the desk in class. "He was the first informal teacher I ever had," Sherman recalls. "And he taught me the best lesson possible: that I didn't yet know how to write."[27] Predictably, what Scott remembered best about his teaching days was the social gaffe he committed in inadvertently squirting canned beer on a visiting dignitary, Bonamy Dobree.[28]

That moment of embarrassment, typical though it may have been of Win Scott's eternal bewilderment when confronted with even the simplest of mechanical tasks, had nothing to do with Brown's letting him go as a part-time instructor. A full-time man was hired, and part-timer Scott learned in the spring of 1936 that he would not be rehired that fall.

Casting about for a second job to make ends meet, Win Scott immediately found one as a news announcer for the radio station owned by the *Journal*. "This is my job," he wrote Horace Gregory in June of 1936:

It is six days a week, alack!, and stretches over about 7 hours a day, though I don't really work all that time. Sample: I arrive at the Journal between 6 and 6:30 a.m. and work till 8 partly writing, partly editing a mess of news; at 8 I go on the air and read it (15 minutes). Then I do as I please, plus a small amount of clerical work in the Literary Dept., till 11. Then I go to the newsroom again and work till 1: thereupon another 15 minutes on the air; then home. I'm afraid it Takes Time, but it's bread and butter and really, as for the actual work, I find it pleasant enough. Just now I keep waiting for my head to clear of it outside hours, and I can't say what effect it will have on my trying to be an author.[29]

Never, perhaps, did any position so please his family in Haverhill as their son's newscasting. Here was daily evidence, audible in Haverhill, that Winfield was getting ahead. Interspersed with warnings against overwork and colds in Bessie Scott's letters ran a series of approving exclamations about Win's radio magnificence. "You know Winfield that Ma is listening every time . . . I don't see how it [the broadcast] could be [better]. Every word is spoken

    [27] WTS to H. O. Werner, 25 October 1934, Scott Collection, John Hay Library; interview, Stuart C. Sherman, Providence, 3 June 1969.
    [28] WTS, "Bookman's Galley," *Providence Journal*, 2 February 1947, sec. 6, p. 6.
    [29] WTS to Horace Gregory, 18 June 1936, Syracuse University Library.

distinctly and your voice carries finely." The Scotts' neighbors and friends were alerted to listen as well: "Zeke heard you today. He said, 'It sounds just like Winnie. He is the one to broadcast because he can pronounce all the hard words correctly.' "[30] From 1936 to 1941 Win broadcast news, and the general public, as well as his parents, came to know his name and voice. He was good at the job, possessing "a timbre and vocabulary and cultivated tone . . . pleasantly removed from the Philistine manner of most broadcasters of the day." Occasionally, though, like all announcers, he committed a blooper. Ben Clough remembers one, when Win was reporting the day's racing results: "Win was not very hep in horse-racing but gave the results as they came in. One day a horse named Hope To Do won the first. Not knowing one Narragansett racer from another, Win told the world that the winner was "Hoppy-Toad-oh." "Oh" indeed. The track followers were heard from at once, wanting this ignoramus admonished or fired—probably they really thought he should be disembowelled in Market Square."[31]

At least the broadcasting job removed him from the pall of anonymity which hung over most *Journal* staffers. "It seems to me quite possible," he wrote in a piece bemoaning the passing of personal journalism, "that more of the population of Rhode Island know the name of the young man who broadcasts news from the *Providence Journal* than know the name of his managing editor. (The m.e. has his compensations.)"[32] Halfhearted attempts to secure teaching appointments at Bennington and Sarah Lawrence petered out, but the Scotts managed. Savila added to the meager family income by working at the Community Fund office and later at the book shop run by Ben Clough's wife, Elsie. There was money to scrape by on, to feed Timmie the cat, and even to afford an occasional trip to the dentist.

Socially, life was pleasant enough. In the Roome Lane flat, he and Savila threw weekend parties for young writers, artists, professors, and newspapermen. On such occasions, at least while prohibition continued in effect, the bootlegger would arrive in a black

[30] Bessie Townley Scott to WTS, 10 May 1936, 13 May 1936, and 20 May 1936, Scott Collection, John Hay Library.

[31] Benjamin C. Clough to SD, 24 March 1970 and 8 June 1970.

[32] WTS, "New England's Newspaper World," *Saturday Review*, 22 May 1943, pp. 19–21.

suit, a black tie, and with a chesterfield folded over his arm. The gin was inside the chesterfield; mixed with grapefruit juice, it was enthusiastically downed by everyone, and talk of books and politics continued long past midnight. "Truthfully," a latecomer to the circle, City Lansing, confesses, "I can't remember one glowing or memorable phrase from any of us. We had wonderful fun together and were quite confident that we knew more, felt more and were capable of doing more than any of the older forces in power. In short, we were much like the young of today."[33] Helen Moffitt, Frank Merchant's girl (and, later, Dave DeJong's wife), threw a 1934 Come-as-a-Thorne-Smith-character party, where Win Scott appeared as Topper himself, in black tie, dinner jacket—and undershorts. But *the* social event of the year was usually Class Night, in June, when the Scotts held open house for returning alumni. In 1934, for example, Scott reported to Werner, "the liquor flowed quite as usual and I think, in fact, we made—all by ourselves— about 29 people drunk here Friday evening, before, after and during the campus dance. You would have thought we'd made a better mousetrap—or whiskey punch, perhaps, is more exact. We are— need I add—still making up lost sleep."[34] In a poem called "Black Bean Soup with Hotdogs and Hard-Boiled Eggs," written at the MacDowell Colony in 1965, Scott looked back on that early time in Providence:

> We hauled ourselves up
> Under poverty-stricken years
> To which the title of this
> Refers—a party meal;
> Sherry added if cheap.
> When we were young,
> Often angry, rarely unhappy
> Then.[35]

Summers, the work load at the *Journal* slacked off and Win and Savila spent four days a week at a West Barrington shack adjoining one occupied by Dave DeJong. It was a short walk from Narragan-

---

[33] Elizabeth H. Lansing to SD, 9 October 1969; interview, Mrs. Jeannette Wolfe, Los Angeles, 2 February 1970.

[34] WTS to H. O. Werner, 20 June 1934, Scott Collection, John Hay Library.

[35] WTS, "Black Bean Soup with Hotdogs and Hard-Boiled Eggs," *New and Selected Poems*, pp. 135–136.

sett Bay, and Win had plenty of time for loafing. "All I've done so far," he wrote Jeff in June of 1935, "is sit in the sun and look at the sky and grass. It brings back my lost youth, my lost irresponsibility and all. I'm having a grand time."[36] The Scotts had occasional social engagements, too, with such literary lights as Robert Hillyer and Horace Gregory.

On the strength of Scott's weekend at Pomfret the previous summer, Hillyer wrote in September of 1932 calling his new novel, published by Knopf, to the young reviewer's attention. "If you like the book, you might be willing to give it a favourable word in your columns." Scott liked it, and did. The next fall, he printed still more appreciative words about Hillyer's poetry, drawing from the established poet an acknowledgment that "I am in your debt for a splendid review. Your criticism is discriminating, finely phrased, and of course, to me personally, a tremendous satisfaction." It was not long before Hillyer had an opportunity to repay the debt.

If you're not older than twenty-five, a young woman named Ann Winslow, executive secretary of the College Poetry Society of America, wrote Scott in July of 1934, please send along some poems for an anthology of recent college verse. Fine: the poems were sent, Miss Winslow liked them, but there was a hitch in the plans. Each of the young poets was to be introduced by a figure of considerable stature, and Foster Damon had not supplied the critical note of introduction to Scott's work requested by Miss Winslow. "I wish I *knew* what happened to Mr. Damon," the anthologist wrote Scott in October of 1934. "He was so nice when I wrote him before . . . Was there something in my letter to you to which he objected?" Win advised her instead to try Hillyer, who provided the necessary laudatory note.[37] Years later, Scott turned out an essay on Robert Hillyer's work, and on several occasions Hillyer favorably reviewed books of poems written by the younger man.

A similar pattern led to Scott's lifelong friendship with and respect for the distinguished poet and critic, Horace Gregory. In June of 1933 Win wrote Gregory asking for a copy of his new book to review; when the review appeared, Gregory sent back thanks: "it

[36] WTS to H. O. Werner, 25 June 1935, Scott Collection, John Hay Library.
[37] Robert Hillyer to WTS, 7 September 1932 and 28 October 1933, Ann Winslow to WTS, 22 September 1934 and 5 October 1934, Scott Collection, John Hay Library.

gave me hope that what I had written was actually being *read* by my contemporaries." In the fall, after Bill Gerry had spent an evening touting Win's work to the Gregorys, Scott went to New York to meet the man who, more than any other, was to serve both as his single most effective promoter and as his keenest and most sensitive artistic guide. It was Gregory who arranged for Win to be interviewed at Sarah Lawrence in June of 1935. ("Miss Warren thought you looked too young," Gregory explained; "and somehow you frightened the life out of Henry Ladd." Besides, Sarah Lawrence, social-science oriented, was looking for an interdisciplinary type.) Horace and his wife Marya Zaturenska vacationed with the Scotts at West Barrington for a few weeks later that summer, and the two men talked and corresponded regularly until Win's death in 1968. Gregory found Scott's early work very promising, very honest; he admired his independence, and he thought the New England strain the strongest point of Scott's work.[38]

Most important of all, Gregory was instrumental in getting Scott's first book of poetry, *Biography for Traman*, published. Only twenty-six at the time, Win must nonetheless have uttered Finally! when Covici-Friede brought out *Traman* on 19 March 1937. For he had suffered disappointments in poetry to match those in connection with the Whittier and Newburyport prose efforts. The manuscript he entered in the Yale series of younger poets, for example, was a tantalizingly near miss. "I'm sending back 'Toward Spring' with a great deal of regret," Stephen Vincent Benét wrote in January of 1934. "It was one of the best four manuscripts submitted—out of a hundred and fifty. But the Yale Press, unfortunately, has room for only one in the series. [The one was James Agee's *Permit Me Voyage*.] You've done some lovely work in the book and I'm genuinely sorry to turn it back." Ranking in the top four was little consolation to the unbooked Scott, of course, although it was only later that he learned from Benét how totally lacking in merit most of the submissions were. "First," he told Scott, "you put aside all the manuscripts with snapshots and pink-ribboned

[38] W. H. Gerry to WTS, 1 November 1933, WTS to H. O. Werner, 25 June 1935, Horace Gregory to WTS, 26 July 1933 and 26 June 1935, Scott Collection, John Hay Library; WTS to Horace Gregory, 26 June 1933, Syracuse University Library; Horace Gregory and Marya Zaturenska, *A History of American Poetry 1900–1940* (New York: Harcourt Brace, 1946), pp. 183, 494; interview, Horace and Marya Gregory, Palisades, N. Y., 5 December 1969.

swatches of the baby's hair pasted in." More encouraging was
Benét's offer to send a note to John Farrar, of Farrar and Rinehart,
about Scott's work.[39]

Another project that sank, this time in a political fiasco, was the
opera "King Philip" written to commemorate Rhode Island's tercentenary in 1935. Wassili Leps supplied the score, S. Foster Damon
the scenario, and Win Scott the libretto, but no one supplied the
money—and the opera was never performed.[40] The incident typi-
fies the view of Providence and Rhode Island held by such lover-
haters of the place as DeJong and Merchant. Merchant, especially,
has suggested that "for all he drew from them, it was Providence
and Brown—the stamp of the second-rate about them—that held
him [Scott] back from great reputation."[41] Perhaps, but Win's disappointment in the collapse of the opera was soon assuaged by word
from Harriet Monroe in Chicago that he had won the Guarantors'
Prize, presented each year for a poem or poems printed the preced-
ing year in *Poetry*. "We enclose our check for one hundred dollars,
and wish you a career equal in honor to those of some of the other
recipients of our prizes," wrote the good fairy of American poetry.
The same week, however, Miss Monroe refused to take Scott's long
"Elegy for Robinson" for her magazine, and chided him for making second-thought corrections. If you only knew what such corrections cost, she testily asserted, you poets wouldn't send us your
poems until you were through with them.[42]

Meanwhile, Scott was trying to interest publishers in "Toward
Spring," his book of poems. Gregory read it and liked it, and he
went to talk to Farrar about it, but nothing developed. He also suggested, first, that Scott drop the name "Traman" (an anagram for
art-man), as too poetic, then, later, when no substitute name occurred to Scott, that the manuscript be titled "Biography for
Traman" rather than "Toward Spring." In January of 1936,

[39] Stephen Vincent Benét to WTS, 22 January 1934, Scott Collection, John
Hay Library; WTS to Thorpe Menn, 4 December 1963.

[40] WTS to Edward McSorley, 25 February 1947, Scott Collection, John Hay
Library; "Opera is Planned for Tercentenary Program," *Providence Journal*,
11 August 1935.

[41] Frank Merchant to SD, 26 September 1969; interview, Frank Merchant,
Atlanta, 7 November 1969.

[42] Harriet Monroe to WTS, 23 October 1935, WTS to H. O. Werner, 14
November 1935, Scott Collection, John Hay Library.

Gregory took Scott to meet publisher Pascal Covici, "an extremely likeable, keen gent of middleage" who asked to see his poetry. Returning home, Win found "a letter from Simon and Schuster asking to see stuff: three days later had one from Macmillan. Extraordinary they should, independently, look me up within a few days. New in my life. But such things often come to nothing," he cautioned Werner—and himself, "so (listen to me) I'm not hoping."[43]

For once, though, his hopes were to be realized. In March, Pat Covici summoned him to New York, where he signed a contract for *Biography for Traman* and gave the new firm of Covici-Friede options on his next two books as well. Considerable work on the manuscript still remained, he wrote Jeff, "for C and Gregory (who's C's advisor in many things and who gets prime credit for this deal) want me to make the book a coherent unit . . . the 15 poems, let's say, which were never specifically written for the Traman series will be placed in positions supposed to render them integral . . . also, I think I'll need two to five new Traman poems to carry the thing through." Gregory helped guide Win through this process of revision and addition, and finally to press. On the "Day of Publication," 19 March 1937, Scott acknowledged Gregory's contribution: "It's very plain: if it weren't for you there'd be no book. And over and above that I hope you know what it means to me that you think the book is good." That last sentence Scott wrote in absolute sincerity; he would always rely on Gregory's judgment and seek his approval of whatever he published. "What you have to do," Win told an interviewer in 1952, "is find some one person whose abilities you respect, who you think really understands what you're trying to do and can tell when you've done it. In my own case that person has been Horace Gregory. . . . When he says a thing of mine is no good, I generally find that it is."[44]

If the publication of *Traman* was not accompanied by skyrockets, the book was enthusiastically received by friends and given more than usual attention by the reviewers. In comradely spirit, Roderick O'Connor, in Washington, D.C., a boyhood friend from New-

[43] Horace Gregory to WTS, 27 February 1935 and 8 June 1936, WTS to H. O. Werner, 15 February 1936, Scott Collection, John Hay Library.

[44] WTS to H. O. Werner, 18 April 1936, Scott Collection, John Hay Library; WTS to Horace Gregory, 19 March 1937, Syracuse University Library; Howard Norman, interview with WTS, in *Brunonia* 7 (March 1952): 20–24.

port, dated the girl at Brentano's lending library and persuaded her
to put the book in circulation. More touchingly a young Providence
painter named Florence Leif, who could not afford to buy a copy,
borrowed one and made a complete typescript of it. "One such gesture," Scott confided to his journal, "may not quiet me, or anybody, for a lifetime, but perhaps it should."[45] Among the reviews,
Bert Hart of the *Journal* (no judge of verse) fulsomely heralded
"the most distinguished book of poetry that has appeared in America this year," while at the other extreme Tench Tilghman blasted
it as "another case of execution falling far short of conception.
Traman and his friends . . . remain always dim figures, groping
and gibbering in a mist which the language and images, though
occasionally incisive, do little to dispel."[46]

Overall, the consensus was encouraging. Perhaps Louis Untermeyer, in a review in the *American Mercury*, best summed up the
critical judgment that here was a poet of promise who had yet to
find his own voice: "Excellent as writing, but bewildering in its
echoes; the tone, as well as the technique, is alternately that of
Aiken, Eliot, Putnam, and Robinson, sometimes a confusion of
them all. Under the shifting diction a personality begins to struggle; it will be interesting to watch it—if it emerges." William Rose
Benét, also, noted the debt to Robinson and Aiken, but, he added,
"there is plenty of originality too . . . Mr. Scott is not always lyrical
but he is already a thoroughly interesting poet."[47]

According to Scott himself, the book was intended "to do in verse
much the same sort of thing James Joyce did in prose in his "Portrait of the Artist as a Young Man.' " By that elevated standard,
Biography for Traman must be accounted a failure; only Traman
(Scott himself) comes to life with any real impact, and the others
—Darrah (Frank Merchant), Cary (Bill Gerry), Kurt (Jeff Werner), Big Dutch (David DeJong), and Little Dutch (Wade Vliet)—

---

[45] Roderick O'Connor to WTS, 27 April 1937, Scott Collection, John Hay
Library; WTS, *"a dirty hand": The Literary Notebooks of Winfield Townley
Scott* (1969), p. 103.

[46] B. K. Hart, review of *Biography for Traman*, *Providence Journal*, 21 March
1937; Tench Tilghman, review of *Biography for Traman*, *Baltimore Sun*, [?]
June 1937.

[47] Louis Untermeyer, review of *Biography for Traman*, *American Mercury*,
October 1937; William Rose Benét, "The Phoenix Nest," *Saturday Review of
Literature*, 19 June 1937, p. 16; for these and other reviews, see Scrapbook 8,
pp. 5–14, Scott Collection, John Hay Library.

serve merely as buffers against which to measure Scott's own deepening spiritual and political agnosticism.[48] The best poems, in fact,
are those which look back to childhood rather than to the immediate past in Providence and its artistic circle. Scott was not Joyce,
and he had not tried hard enough to be himself. As he wrote Hilary
Masters in 1952, "I trust I can sometime reprint 50% of it and
throw away the rest; if that's not too conservative. Too many influences: MacLeish, Robinson, Eliot, Aiken." In the *Collected
Poems* he decided to preserve rather less than half, including one,
"Truth of This Time," which he liked best because it was simplest
and, incidentally, rather prophetic.[49] In the poem, Scott made it
clear that he would worship neither science nor religion:

> Truth of this time, so proved and undefiled,
> The secret of the atom tethered, even
> The plotting of our planetary voyage
> With prophecy—you mathematical truth:
> You shall outlast us and you shall be brave
> When we are corollary to the last
> Lost undiscoverable fire at the earth's core.
>
> Yet in a ruinous twilight, even you
> Our careful calculations shall be told
> While watchers of the burning ash of the west
> Wait for the glow to cool, as once we stared;
> The young men laughing but the children all
> Wondering at you, such proud beautiful
>   answers.
> For the mythmen have you all in the end,
> Whether you speak of light or the end of light
> Or the agony of God's Son, it is all one—
> A tale for wide-eyed children who must
>   sleep.[50]

It is difficult to believe that this poem was written in 1937, long
before the development of an apocalyptic bomb.

By mid-1937, Depression clouds were receding, and Win Scott
emerged in the sunshine. He was not interested in making money;

[48] Garrett D. Byrnes, "Poet Cheerfully Forecasts Death."
[49] WTS to Hilary Masters, 8 December 1952, Scott Collection, John Hay
Library.
[50] WTS, "Truth of This Time," *New and Selected Poems*, p. 4.

he was interested in writing poetry and in making a name for himself as a poet. "Yes, I know the kind of belief you want," Bill Gerry wrote him from California, "the belief of others. . . . Of you, I can repeat, using EA's words . . . I have never doubted." But Robinson was dead, and purely local fame could not assuage the young poet's thirst for approval and recognition. With *Traman*, Scott took the first, longest, and most difficult step toward commanding that much-prized belief of others. His range of reputation now extended far beyond Brown and Providence. Stephen Vincent Benét hailed him as one of the nation's most promising young poets.[51]

[51] W. H. Gerry to WTS, 16 December 1938, Scott Collection, John Hay Library. *Biography for Traman*, dust jacket (1937).

Thirty wakes me, and what have I done?[1]

6. Gathering Clouds

LESS THAN FIVE MONTHS after the publication of *Traman*, Horace Gregory wrote Scott a letter advising him to make haste slowly: "As to your own work which I respect at its best, I think you should not run too fast with it; it's again a technic of concentrating energy . . . from time to time a select process should be used, gathering together the best elements of several poems into one—and making that one do the work of a dozen poems that have gone before it. . . . One of the horrors of American literature is that so many younger writers use themselves up before they reach middle age: this art of reserving forces was well understood by Robinson."[2] Conserve your forces, don't use yourself up, take your time. Wisely, Gregory appealed to the beloved ghost of Robinson, and of course he was right. For, as Scott grew older, he was first troubled and then obsessed with fear that his talent was oozing away, that he had lost his artistic vigor. But when Gregory's letter arrived in

[1] WTS, "Sonnet II," *Collected Poems: 1937–1962* (1962), p. 103.
[2] Horace Gregory to WTS, 18 August 1937, Scott Collection, John Hay Library, Brown University.

August of 1937, it made little impression. Here Scott was, finally a published poet, and nothing seemed more important than to publish another book as soon as possible. He was after all but twenty-seven: no use to talk to him.

In fact, by the time *Traman* came out, Scott was already formulating what he jocularly referred to as "a booklength perm, blank verse no less, about 3 people—a professor, his friend the young poet, and the professor's wife." A conventional triangle theme, he admitted to Jeff Werner, "but it also pretends to be (amidst the deaths and illicit love) a study of the creative mind and the teacher-mind; the love, in fact, should be subordinate in idea—when the poet who writes (and the prof *don't*) grabs off prof's wife, he's getting hog's share and getting one more thing the prof wanted for himself. I hope it to be all a bit more subtle . . . than this précis sounds . . . the prof is no straw man and the poet no blemishless hero. In fact that prof's a *better* guy than the poet or the prof's wife." And no, he went on to assure Werner, he was not taking liberties with him (as an academic), or with his wife, Elizabeth. Nor was he writing out of experience: there had been no such affair in his own life.[3]

Scott worked on the 2,500-line poem, which he titled "Day of Unkind Farewell," over the summer, got an endorsement from Hillyer during a Pomfret visit, and sent it off to Covici in the fall of 1937. It was not, exactly. what Covici had been hoping for. In August he had written Scott inquiring about a novel, but the young writer declined the suggestion. With understanding and generosity, Covici immediateiy approved Scott's decision: "You are quite right. Don't write a novel unless you absolutely want to, and that should not be until you are past forty. In fact, nobody should write novels until the age of forty."[4] But Covici had reservations about the long narrative poem that reached his desk in November; it needed a good deal of work. Still, he wrote Scott in reassurance, "I want to see anything you want me to see. If I don't think it should be published I shall tell you so and try to convince you, but should you insist on having it published, I shall publish it. And I mean exactly what I say."[5] These were words to buoy the spirit of any struggling young

[3] WTS to H. O. Werner, 1 April 1937, Scott Collection, John Hay Library.
[4] Pascal Covici to WTS, 19 August 1937, Scott Collection, John Hay Library.
[5] Ibid., 29 November 1937, Scott Collection, John Hay Library.

writer, and Scott quoted the letter euphorically to Werner. Unfortunately, however, the firm of Covici-Friede, despite or perhaps because of its adventurous list (including John Steinbeck and Muriel Rukeyser, as well as Scott), went into bankruptcy, and Pat Covici, though he immediately found a place with Viking Press, was unable to live up to his guarantees. Not for another twenty-five years was Win Scott to find an editor who would so believe in him.

In any case, "Day of Unkind Farewell" turned out to be yet another false start; it was never published and the manuscript, like that of the Whittier biography, simply evaporated. Undaunted and full of projects, Win went on to try another long blank-verse narrative, this time on the Norse voyages to America. "I'm writing a verse story primarily—because it's a good story, and to see what one can do these days; but I hope it has some meaning above the action (thru the action?): the clash of Christianity and paganism, of the Iron and Stone Age in America briefly, and over all the change that came in the Viking voyages from adventurous exploration to attempted wealth-getting that ended in murder."[6] So he wrote Gregory in March of 1938, and in May, finished, the Norse poem went to Covici. "I pray to God about Covici and the Viking poem," he wrote Werner. "I reason it out—it's for my friends' sake, really, since how awful it would be for you all to know a failure-poet."[7] But by this time his editor's firm was on the brink of bankruptcy, and though he liked it better than the triangle narrative, Covici could not publish the poem. Twenty years later, after many revisions, it finally saw print as *The Dark Sister.*

Still another proposal went by the boards when the Guggenheim Foundation rejected Scott's application for a 1938 fellowship to write a play in verse about Woodrow Wilson. Letters of reference from Gregory, Hillyer, Stephen Benét, *Poetry* editor Morton D. Zabel, and Professor Ben Clough were of no avail, nor was Scott's proposal: "Wilson offers, it seems to me, perhaps the most excellent 20th century example of high tragedy—the tragedy of a man who, because of inner failure and outward forces, saw the wreck of a very great ideal of which he was capable."[8] Both the preoccupation

[6] WTS to Horace Gregory, 30 March 1938, Syracuse University Library; WTS to H. O. Werner, 10 May 1938, Scott Collection, John Hay Library.
[7] WTS to H. O. Werner, 17 May 1938, Scott Collection, John Hay Library.
[8] WTS, application for a John Simon Guggenheim Fellowship, acknowledged

with failure and the pursuit of "very great ideals" were characteristic of Scott. In several essays of this period he explored the theme
of failure in American letters; as time wore on, he began to see
himself, because of his own ambitious ideals, in the role of failed
poet.

In his early years, Win Scott could joke about the trials of the
poet:

> The goddam literary life is stupid; you're up one day with an idea
> and collapsed the next one with, mind you, the same idea. Or, the thing
> gets printed at last; whereupon it's (1) excellent and (2) stinking; both.
> Or, you try something different from anything you've done before;
> you're going to pieces. You print something else: you're not Getting
> Anywhere . . . And something else: it's influenced entirely by (1)
> Robinson, (2) MacLeish, (3) Eliot, (4) Hopkins, etc. You work at a
> daily job: that's bad, interferes with your art. You don't work at a job;
> that's bad, you're in an ivory tower.

"I perceive," he concluded to Werner, "in suddenly writing this all
out, that what I'm talking about is other people's reactions, prejudices, foregone conclusions and occasionally honest criticism; and
I suppose that's all so much chaff. One of them may be right, but
which one? So I imagine that a great deal of maturing as an Artiste
is in learning to say the hell with all that."[9] Unhappily, Win Scott
never learned his own lesson; pores open, antennae extended, he
picked up the reactions, prejudices, conclusions, criticisms of others
—and, though knowing better, tended to accept their often shallow
judgments. At times, in fact, he heard remarks unspoken and saw
the invisible smirk that did *not* hide behind the smile.

Book reviewing provided Scott with a foothold on the literary
ladder and brought him within hailing distance of the great and
near-great. Distinguished writers came by the office; at the Charles
Connicks' in Boston, Win and Savila attended literary teas where
Robert Frost read his poems, or simply talked, both brilliantly;
Scott himself was in demand to talk about books—or, sometimes,
to read his own poems—on the chicken-and-peas cultural circuit

by the Guggenheim Memorial Foundation, 4 September 1937. Winners of fellowships in poetry for 1938 were Asher Brynes, Rolfe Humphries, and C. F.
MacIntyre.
9 WTS to H. O. Werner, 21 October 1937, Scott Collection, John Hay Library.

of Rhode Island. Each week he had something to say, in the *Providence Sunday Journal*, about the latest books. Often, in *Poetry*, he
took on the reviewer's role, turning out two notable essays on
E. A. Robinson in 1937 and 1939. But there were disadvantages,
too. One of them was that editors tended to think of him more as a
writer about poetry than a writer of poetry. John Crowe Ransom
at the *Kenyon Review*, for example, frustrated Scott regularly by
asking for poems, returning them and asking for more ("We didn't
like the poems quite enough though we liked them, and would like
to see others"), and by the way inquiring if he'd be interested in
doing a review ("Not long ago I read and admired greatly your
Poetry review of the life of Robinson. That was fine writing, and
I wish you would some time propose a book review for us . . .").[10]
Kerker Quinn, first at *Direction* and later at *Accent*, also kept turning down poems and asking for reviews. And there were inevitably
those, less knowledgeable than Ransom and Quinn, who reacted
in wonderment when Win Scott published a book of poetry: "I
thought he was a book reviewer."

Approaching his thirtieth year, Scott still had not contracted for
a second book of poems, and self-doubt weighed heavily on his
mind:

> When I was twenty and a man of promise,
> Innocent of time, at ease with it,
> Nowhere by moonlight, I remember this
> Friend of mine who said—he was explicit—
> That I'd do my best work in the next ten
>   years.
> Even though he spoke—of course I knew—
> Less of my than his expected cheers,
> Designing epics when my rhymes were through.
> Thirty wakes me—and what have I done?
> Shelley and Keats are younger now than I,
> Chatterton's a child sure of the sun,
> Only Yeats and Hardy comfort me:
> These days, a river darkening and slow—
> The nights a dream of it fired in the
>   snow.

[10] John Crowe Ransom to WTS, 29 May 1939, Scott Collection, John Hay
Library.

Scott's ambition remained extraordinarily active. In a portion of "The Brittle Street," written in 1939, he analyzed himself with a harshness that predicted a coming hatred of self: "His own ego expressed itself very often in concern for others, in remarks of self-deprecation; oh, he was always the last to enter the office elevator, the first to step aside in a crowded street, the quickest to praise in others what he seemed to lack. In fact—he knew, when he thought about it—he did nothing but seize the simplest ways of differentiating himself from others, and what he found to praise in others was nearly never a quality that he felt rivalled his own most valuable ability." He would select teachers or newspapermen as superior to himself. But as for his writing, "there his admiration of his contemporaries (and even of long dead writers) stopped always somewhere short of admitting their ultimate superiority over himself. As he grew a little older he realized how altogether possible it was that he might not become as great as Shakespeare; but even at thirty he thought "possible" and not "probable." . . . He remembered that Shakespeare at thirty was nowhere and writing badly. In short, his vanity was colossal."[11] Happily, Scott's best work lay ahead of him, along with most of his cheers. But he could hardly know that, in 1940, when discouragement over his career as poet combined with domestic difficulties and the impending worldwide eruption to darken the future.

Win Scott and Savila Harvey married for love, and, at least to some of their friends, it seemed an ideal match. "Remember," Bill Gerry wrote Win when he and Savila were breaking up, "that I was utterly devoted to you two, as individuals and as a unit. You represented a kind of perfection so near that to me it just had to happen." In the early years, Win's satisfaction with the marriage was reflected in his unhesitatingly advising Jeff Werner to get married. "Possibly," he wrote Jeff in March 1936, a "thorough drag-off-by-the-hair" would be the best way (to make Elizabeth Ward his wife). Win missed Savila on those infrequent occasions when they were separated. "Savila went to New York for a few days—very long ones, while I kept bachelor hall: me and the cat," he wrote Jeff in November 1933. In June 1936, when Savila again went to New York, Win announced, "I miss you very much, but

11 WTS, "Sonnet II," *Collected Poems*, p. 103; WTS, "The Brittle Street," manuscript (11 May–28 June 1939), p. 19, Scott Collection, John Hay Library.

somehow find myself awkward in the expression thereof: *that* is the chief cause of marriage." Six months later, she was in Darien, and "we are," Win wrote, "about to find out what kind of person I'd be if I were left alone. So far the results ain't encouraging. . . . The burden of this is that it is very true I'm in love with you because I miss you very much even within this time in which it's been practically impossible to miss anybody."[12] For a Yankee, that was eloquent testimony indeed.

Even in its first years, however, the marriage encountered difficulties. Win was used to being spoiled—and dominated—by women, and he had married an exceedingly strong and potentially dominant woman. Blunt, insistent upon honesty, Savila eschewed euphemisms and made it abundantly clear to everyone what she thought of them. Her open dislike, often reciprocated, extended to such companions of Win's as Frank Merchant, Linnell Jones, and Victor Ullman. Where Win would go to almost any length to avoid social conflict, Savila's brilliant, sometimes acid tongue cultivated it. Meeting her in Haverhill, Daniel Smythe was baited by that tongue: "We were discussing Emily Dickinson, and I said I didn't care for her poetry. Savila said, 'Oh, I'm so glad you agree with me that she stinks.' I said, 'I didn't say her poetry was no good. I think it's great! However, I don't care for this style of great poetry.' Savila's answer was, 'Oh, you're pretty cagey, aren't you?' " Predictably, Smyth remembers no participation of Scott in this byplay, though it was *his* idol—Emily Dickinson—who was under attack. When he was at the MacDowell Colony in 1965, Win learned that "old, old Prof. Huntington [had died]—who taught 'argumentation' so much more successfully to my first wife than to me."[13]

Savila refused, in short, to conceal her feelings about others, and she used her considerable verbal gifts to demonstrate how she felt. It made her angry that Win was underpaid and his work taken for granted at the *Providence Journal*; she could not understand, then or later, his apparent lack of indignation about that and other real or imagined slights. "The whole point about him," she said later,

<hr />

[12] W. H. Gerry to WTS, 31 May 1944, WTS to H. O. Werner, 27 November 1933 and 21 March 1936, Scott Collection, John Hay Library; WTS to Savila Harvey Scott, 1 June 1936 and 19 January 1937.
[13] WTS to EMS, 28 October 1965; Daniel Smythe to SD, "Memories of W. T. Scott," 10 January 1970.

"was his incapacity for bitterness."[14] Or, rather, his unwillingness to show bitterness, to let his anger come to the surface.

To her, a case in point was the marriage of Win's sister, Jeannette, in 1936, to Robert D. Wolfe. Savila clearly disapproved of the marriage, and proclaimed that it would not last six months. Wolfe, a Brown man who served for a time as business manager of *Smoke*, wrote Win asking him to be his best man at the large wedding he and Jeannette had planned. Win wrote back caustically that he would be nobody's "rented gentleman," and his brother-in-law-to-be responded in understandable heat:

> During the two and a half years I have known Jinny (Jeannette), I have been well aware of Savila's dislike of me. The gibes and sneers made against me to mutual friends were repeated, probably as she intended they should be. The criticisms she made of Jinny, in her presence and behind her back, such as that Jinny was "chasing" me, took on a peculiar sort of humor, particularly as it was well known, even among your mere acquaintances, that Savila (by your own admission) had been "chasing" you for some time before she caught up with you.

Having dealt with Savila, Wolfe went on to attack Win for his indifference to and lack of interest in his sister, and concluded that "your insult to me, about hiring oneself into being a gentleman, was gratuitous in the extreme." Perhaps, as Jeannette Wolfe believes, it was only with Savila's encouragement that Win made the "rented gentleman" remark; certainly it was uncharacteristic of him to invite so open and bitter a quarrel.

One reason that the Scott family (though not Win) might have been supposed to disapprove of the wedding was that Bob Wolfe was Jewish, and as such more or less foreign to their social experience. But Bessie Scott had more than forgiven the young man his exotic religion because his family was rich. Your mother, Savila wrote from Haverhill during wedding preparations, "has been regaling me constantly with little scraps of pleased information about the Wolfe family; about their wealth, their kindness to Jeannette, their trading in Tiffany's, 'do you have to pay to attend Horace Mann school?'—their prospective reception for J. and Bob . . . I thank almighty god that you escaped this prevalent regard for the dollar bill. It is too bad that your family hasn't got more sense; it is

[14] Savila Harvey Kaufer to SD, 12 September 1969.

not surprising that Jeannette's head has been badly turned." To make her disapproval manifest, Savila spent most of the wedding day on a pilgrimage to the Whittier birthplace and turned up, at the last minute, to insist that her dress needed pressing.[15]

Honesty in all such matters was part of Savila's code; in later years, she impressed that lesson unforgettably on Lindsay, the son of Win's and her marriage. It is probably healthier in the long run to show anger, as Savila did, than to bottle it up beneath an untroubled façade, as Win had been taught to do. But two people so different temperamentally must necessarily have been powerfully incompatible. Even before Win met and fell in love with Eleanor Metcalf, Helen Moffitt DeJong recalls, almost "everyone felt that separation was inevitable."[16]

Prospects for a happy union may also have been compromised by a climate of competition, for Savila had literary aspirations too. While still at Pembroke, she had demonstrated real talent in writing poems and stories for *The Sepiad*, the campus literary magazine; among her best works is a short story about a young girl whose enthusiastic first love is stifled by an unfeeling, professorial father. She wrote poems as well, with a rapidity and ease which amazed Win: "Savila has been pouring out light verse the past ten days. I don't know how she does it so fast."[17] Her poem, "To Edwin Arlington Robinson," shared space in the March 1932 issue of *Smoke* with contributions by her husband, by J. V. Cunningham, and by Conrad Aiken. *Poetry* took a lyric of hers in 1937, and the *Literary Digest*, in one of its last issues, "picked [it] up and boxed it as 'Poem of the Week.' "[18] To the Wolfes and Frank Merchant it seemed as if Savila deprecated Win's work, but to such other observers as the Gregorys and Victor Hill it did not seem that way at all.

According to Win's later reports, there must have been sexual

[15] Robert D. Wolfe to WTS, 15 August 1936, Scott Collection, John Hay Library; Savila Harvey Scott to WTS, 20 August 1936; interview, Mrs. Jeannette Wolfe, Los Angeles, 2 February 1970.

[16] Interview, Helen Moffitt DeJong, Providence, 25 August 1969.

[17] Savila Harvey, "The Professor's Daughter," *The Sepiad*, November 1928, pp. 17–27. The same issue carried two of Miss Harvey's poems, "Helen on the Walls" (p. 30) and "Rebuke for a Poet" (p. 38); WTS, 1944 Journal, 15 March 1944.

[18] WTS to H. O. Werner, 12 January 1938, Scott Collection, John Hay Library.

maladjustment, too. Not entirely sure of himself and given besides to a certain Yankee reticence, he lost all confidence as he failed to inspire in his wife a full measure of response. He even spoke of Savila as a castrating female, but if ever a man invited such a relationship it was Win Scott. To friends he maintained that when he first slept with Eleanor Metcalf he was "a technical virgin," in the sense that he had never, up to that time, satisfied a woman.[19] Neither he nor Savila were much good at pleasing each other; sexual incompatibility accompanied their temperamental incompatibility.

In the late thirties, the Scotts took steps to keep their marriage from disintegrating. They took a trip to Europe; they bought a house; they had a baby.

When the *Statendam* left Hoboken on 24 June 1938, Win, Savila, and Dave DeJong were on board, traveling companions for a two-month tour of England, Scotland, and Holland. The Werners had agreed to stay in the Roome Lane apartment for the summer and to feed the cat. During the voyage, Win awoke in terror at his own insignificance and the vastness of the ocean. In a poem reminiscent of Stephen Crane in its attitude (the man as bug reference) and of John Donne in its diction ("battered my heart"), he later recorded his terror:

> And so awoke at midnight at midsea
> Deep in the shuddering ship, and knew the
>   chill
> Black waters pressing in upon my blood
> That tore me out of sleep and battered my
>   heart;
>
> . . . .
>
> And thought, whatever made us hope to voyage
> Safely: no more than bugs a moment clinging
> To a thin fin once arched out of this
>   wallow . . .[20]

Here, Scott expressed that fear of travel which was to become so troublesome in his middle age that he avoided airplanes and had to be chauffered the sixty miles from Santa Fe to Albuquerque.

[19] Interview, Donald Dean Eulert, Denver, 27 December 1969.
[20] WTS, "How Voyage Safely?" *Collected Poems*, pp. 98–99; WTS, 1944 Journal, 20 January 1944.

The Scottish part of the trip was pleasantest for Win, for, in the
graveyard at Annan, he found part of his ancestry recorded. By
amateur genealogy, he traced the paternal line back to Simon Scott,
a mariner who died at sea (a matter to give Win pause) in 1800,
and his Grandmother (Agnes Hogg) Townley's forebears back to
her great-grandfather, William Hogg, and from there to his only
literary ancestor, William's cousin James Hogg, a poet called the
"Ettrick Shepherd."[21] He liked the Scots for their dignity and their
closemouthed way; the English seemed boorish by comparison. A
trace of Anglophobia, perhaps inherited from or encouraged by
his parents, manifested itself then, as in this note from his 1944
journal: (N.B.: remember the airy Englishman at The Piccadilly:
question: why are so many Englishmen you meet in this country
lying foreflushers [sic] ? Curious thing, I've met so many of
them.)"[22] To be sure, England was the land of Shakespeare and
Hardy and Keats, and he felt strong emotional ties to these great
writers and to the language they shared. But his inevitable direction was westward toward home, and when, en route to Holland,
they came upon a boat flying the American flag, Win was deeply
moved. On board the *Statendam* for the return trip, he wrote that
"All walking against the sun is dream; I turn with time/ And
ascend the night toward morning in the west."[23]

The trip accomplished little by way of bettering the relationship
between Win and Savila. The following spring, in another attempt
to alter surface conditions, the Scotts moved from their apartment
on Roome Lane to a small house at 56 Olney Street. Though located
in anything but a fashionable neighborhood (a public housing
project now occupies the land), the house promised more spacious
living-quarters—three bedrooms and bath, big living-room and
kitchen, and a "beautiful square study on garden with fireplace."[24]
Ensconced in their new house, they set about to have a baby after
six years of childless marriage.

[21] WTS, "No Amusements of an Artificial Kind," unpublished essay
(1939[?]), 14 pages, Scott Collection, John Hay Library.
[22] WTS, 1944 Journal, 23 February 1944. For a rarity, Scott misspelled a
word. It's fourflushers. He did not play poker.
[23] WTS, "Letters of Our Travel," *Collected Poems*, p. 48; EMS to SD, 15
February 1970.
[24] WTS to H. O. Werner, 21 February 1939, Scott Collection, John Hay Library.

When at last the grandchild Bessie Scott so clearly wanted from Win was on its way, Savila suffered through a difficult pregnancy. For a time it looked as if she might have a miscarriage; throughout the summer of 1939 she lay "very steadily and carefully abed" while Win did the household chores. The birth of their son, when it finally came, on 13 February 1940, was nearly as difficult as Win's own, thirty years before. Tumors interfered with the birth, and "the marvelous modern pills had almost no effect on S at all—that was tough, and you may imagine," the new father wrote Jeff Werner, "she had none too good a time." Nor was Lindsay Bothwell Scott, as they called their new son ("by god, there's nothing like not being subtle about racial ancestry," Win commented), a healthy infant. "We're having a weird life with no baby, who is 5 weeks old this morning," Win wrote Jeff. "He had so much formula trouble we had to leave him at the hospital and week has followed week without our getting him. He tossed up one thing after another. . . . It's been a worrisome time; now he's all right it's merely annoying. I pay him a visit every other day, which is apparently no edification to him. Savila of course has had a much better rest than she otherwise would have had, and she's looking very well—albeit this baby business is getting her down."[25]

The financial burden occasioned by Lindsay's arrival was quickly—and pleasantly—eased but a week after his birth. "The Hand of God shewed itself," Win informed Jeff in a letter of February 22, "in yesterday afternoon's mail. I am one of the 2 recipients of the annual Shelley Memorial Award for Poetry, and got a check for three hundred and ten dollars. (I like to write it out.)"[26] However, taking care of the baby, when he finally joined his parents, did impose a burden; he remained unhealthy and cranky, and so did his mother. Early in June, Win wrote Jeff in exasperation:

Class Night has collapsed. As far as we are concerned, and our usual Class Night style. In spite of his good weight and progress, Lindsay is making a wreck of his feedings and in turn a wreck of his mother's nerves. Starting tomorrow (god knows on what capital) we are moving in here a very excellent nurse: an elderly woman, an M.D. who retired upon marriage and now upon widowhood takes baby cases because she

[25] Ibid., 28 July 1939, 22 February 1940, and 19 March 1940, Scott Collection, John Hay Library.
[26] Ibid., 22 February 1940, Scott Collection, John Hay Library.

likes babies. . . . If nurse-Dr. Elliott has things well in hand and life is quiet here, we may have cocktails for 6 or 8 people in the early evening; I don't know. I hate to be uncooperative, but I'm at the stage where I can't ask Savila to take on anything reasonably avoidable until she's rested and sane again. (Of course, there'll be fairer days this summer and I expect us all to foregather at sometime.)[27]

If anything, relations between Win and Savila worsened after the birth of their son. There were petty quarrels that Win recorded in letters to Jeff: "Lindsay and I put in the morning at Prospect Terrace. We watch the trains—of which there are many these days, —and learn how to climb along the iron fence. But when we got home at 11:30 I gave him a lollipop and three peanuts for behaving well and keeping dry, but then his mother arrived and was displeased with me for that." There was the inevitable loss of privacy and quiet: "I should get back into the habit of writing letters from the Scott home, but I don't seem to. It's got so much easier to take a few office moments and type letters than to fight Lindsay off the typewriter. I have a study, socalled, but it is not sacred to anybody I've encountered."[28] Savila remained on edge, often ill. Win found no peace. Lindsay's parents drifted farther and farther apart.

"I haven't written a line in four months, between Lindsay and Hitler."[29] So Win wrote Jeff Werner in June of 1940, as his concern over the gathering war clouds deepened into personal despair. On the dust jacket of *Biography for Traman*, Scott's publishers had announced that "in politics his sympathies are Red; in literature, most deeply Yankee, in the Emerson-Thoreau-Whittier-Robinson line."[30] The second half of the description was more accurate than the first, for Win Scott was never, by any stretch of the imagination, a Communist sympathizer (though he undoubtedly had friends who had joined the party during Depression days). His lack of political sophistication may be gauged by his comment after hearing a lecture by Communist leader Earl Browder, "a gentle, attractive fellow, a bit less radical probably than he should be. Far as I can figure out, the Communists are now for working gradually

<hr />

[27] Ibid., 11 June 1940, Scott Collection, John Hay Library.
[28] Ibid., 31 July 1942, Scott Collection, John Hay Library; WTS to Dilys Bennett Laing, 20 November 1942, Dartmouth College Library.
[29] WTS to H. O. Werner, 3 June 1940, Scott Collection, John Hay Library.
[30] *Biography for Traman*, dust jacket (1937).

(via Farmer-Labor party and the like) while the good old Socialists (the left stream ones anyway) would start by upsetting the apple-cart; so you may vote most radically by voting for N. Thomas, I'm not sure."[31] In fact, Win *had* cast his first presidential ballot for Norman Thomas, but the key words of the letter are the last three. He was not sure what was going on, politically; he liked Browder, but he was fuzzy about what Browder stood for.

Besides, Win was certain that literature and politics didn't mix. "There were contemporaries of mine," he reminisced thirty years later, "such as Muriel Rukeyser (but she is only one among a dozen, one of the better ones), who wrote a great deal of political verse. I only edged toward it, and I am glad that is all I did, because most of that stuff is awfully dead and dated." Such writers, he believed, failed to distinguish between a preachment and a poem. "And a lot of so-called verse went down the drain just because it was all tied up with current events and could not possibly be of interest after awhile, and was on the whole pretty badly written."[32] These sentiments he had expressed in an article called "Pianos in the Street," which had been sent off to (and had come right back from) Philip Rahv at the *Partisan Review*, in 1935. It was heresy, to the truly left-wing of the thirties, to maintain, as Scott did in that article, that "poetry is a stronger thing than politics; it is larger than economics and, at its best, more lasting than all social schemes."[33]

After college, Win had stayed close to the literary crowd he had known at Brown (Merchant, Vliet, Gerry, and Professors Damon and Clough), but had lost touch with the more politically inclined group. As Scott and his companions put out *Smoke*, W. M. Frohock writes,

Meanwhile, up on the Hill, we in graduate school were very caught up with the social thing—as was natural in the trough of the Depression—and our idea of literature was changed rapidly in the process: all Dos Passos, Steinbeck, Caldwell and such in America, Malraux, Bernanos, and Celine in France . . . The point of all this is that I don't think Scott and the guys downtown went with us. When he reviewed

[31] WTS to H. O. Werner, 22 October 1936, Scott Collection, John Hay Library.
[32] Donald Dean Eulert, "Winfield Townley Scott: Conversation on Poets and the Art of Poetry" (Ph.D. dissertation, University of New Mexico, January 1969), p. 159.
[33] WTS, "Pianos in the Street," unpublished essay (1935), 9 pages, Scott Collection, John Hay Library.

Agee's *Permit Me Voyage* he wrote that he didn't "care what Agee believes so long as he writes good poetry." Agee, working for *Fortune* in New York and in the process of dropping poetry—the writing of it— for good, just said bullshit. So far as I remember, neither of us saw Scott after that, not out of any intentional avoidance but because our paths didn't cross.[34]

Writing to Win after the publication of *Biography for Traman*, Victor Ullman complained that the poems had not come to grips with the issues of the time, and added, "When you do the Journal work inevitably you are being transformed into a Journal non-activist. . . . I do know that you aren't a member of the Newspaper Guild and therefore it is a sure bet that the Journal has negated some pretty strong ideas you used to have on trade unionism."[35] Predictably, Win dodged the controversy: "Let me waive all argument with you till I get stronger and generally rest up for that sort of thing. All I ask of you (aside from my personal deficiencies) is to remember that . . . it's first and foremost a question of poetry . . . my anarchic ragards (if those Red-religious will still accept them) to Meyer and Abe."[36]

Preferring his own individualistic bent, Scott ignored the party line to follow his own convictions. But he yielded to no one, no matter how radical, in his passionate support of pacifism.

As early as February 1938, Win confided his misgivings about the impending conflict to Jeff Werner. Vacationing in New York, he had been interested "to see my contemporary college pacifist liberals—Dunc Emrich is the best example—deciding that there will be a war, *this* time to defend democracy against fascism, and *this* time justified: so they're going. O my god! The same catch phrases, the same exceptional case argued." What was happening in Nazi Germany was terrible, he agreed, but Britain and France and America had also behaved dishonorably by standing on the sidelines during the Spanish civil war. "What a fine stew of dishonor, hypocrisy, treachery and crucifixion it all is: Hitler and all he does I hate; but I likewise hate the British and French greed that, long ago, did so much to make this. The whole century has been

---

[34] W. M. Frohock to SD, 21 December 1969.
[35] Victor Ullman to WTS, 20 September 1937, Scott Collection, John Hay Library.
[36] WTS to Victor Ullman, 23 September 1937.

bitched. One bunch of thugs trying to hold all they can, the other trying to grab all they can—and both of them, sooner or later, will send the people against each other." In a gesture unusual for him, Win signed (at Dwight MacDonald's request) the 1939 antiwar statement of the League for Cultural Freedom and Socialism, a statement which concluded by calling "upon all American artists, writers and professional workers to join . . . in implacable opposition to this dance of war in which Wall Street joins hands with the Roosevelt administration."[37]

In an eloquent column for the 11 October 1941 *Providence Journal*, Scott prophesied, more rightly than he could have known, that "it was too late now, that the aggressive forces of cynical tyranny were triumphing, that they could not be stopped, and millions more were yet to die or be crippled or to be enslaved, and that never, never in his life would [a man born in 1910] know happy mornings or pleasant afternoons or peaceful evenings—that those and all they meant were all gone, as far as he was concerned, forever."[38]

Even after Pearl Harbor, Scott refused to commit himself to the war. "I no longer believe that any definitely older man who publicly wishes he Could Go is anything but a Goddam hypocritical liar . . . I wrote a whole column the other day about thinking and speaking responsibly during war; the paper wouldn't use it."[39] What he could print in October was suppressed in December; the machinery of thought control characteristic of wartime had already stirred into operation. But the *Journal* did secure a deferment for Scott, as for other newspapering fathers on its staff, and he felt no sophomoric regret at having missed his chance in combat.

Of course, there was no escaping the war, even in Providence, and one of Win Scott's best and most often anthologized poems derived from the visit of a young sailor to the *Journal* offices in January 1944, bearing with him a ghastly souvenir: the skull of a Japanese soldier. "He'd acquired it simply enough. At Guadalcanal, he'd hacked off a dead Jap's head, then put it through various peeling and scrubbing processes. A boy of 20—an Italian, I think. Very

[37] WTS to H. O. Werner, 23 February 1938 and 20 September 1938, "War Is the Issue!" statement of League for Cultural Freedom and Socialism (1939), Scott Collection, John Hay Library.

[38] WTS, "In Perspective," *Providence Journal*, 11 October 1941.

[39] WTS to H. O. Werner, 19 December 1941, Scott Collection, John Hay Library.

breezy and gay about it. . . . At first I was disgusted and horrified:
by the next day it had also struck me as a thing to use."[40] Use it he
did, in what he would later describe in public readings as his "ugly
poem."

> Bald-bare, bone-bare, and ivory yellow: skull
> Carried by a thus two-headed U.S. sailor
> Who got it from a Japanese soldier killed
> At Guadalcanal in the ever-present war: our
>
> Bluejacket, I mean, aged 20, in August strolled
> Among the little bodies on the sand and hunted
> Souvenirs: teeth, tags, diaries, boots; but
>   bolder still
> Hacked off this head and under a Ginkgo tree
>   skinned it:
>
> Peeled with a lifting knife the jaw and cheeks,
>   bared
> The nose, ripped off the black-haired scalp and
>   gutted
> The dead eyes to these thoughtful hollows: a
>   scarred
> But bloodless job, unless it be said brains
>   bleed.
>
> Then, his ship underway, dragged this aft in a
>   net
> Many days and nights—the cold bone tumbling
> Beneath the foaming wake, weed-worn and salt-
>   cut
> Rolling safe among fish and washed with
>   Pacific;
>
> Till on a warm and level-keeled day hauled in
> Held to the sun and the sailor, back to a
>   gun-rest,
> Scrubbed the cured skull with lye, perfecting
>   this:
> Not foreign as he saw it first: death's
>   familiar cast.

[40] WTS, 1944 Journal, 29 January 1944.

Bodiless, fleshless, nameless, it and the sun
Offended each other in strange fascination
As though one of the two were mocked; but
  nothing is in
This head, or it fills with what another
  imagines

As: here were love and hate and the will to
  deal
Death or to kneel before it, death emperor,
Recorded orders without reasons, bomb-blast,
  still
A child's morning, remembered moonlight on
  Fujiyama:

All scoured out now by the keeper of this
  skull
Made elemental, historic, parentless by our
Sailor boy who thinks of home, voyages laden,
  will
Not say, "Alas! I did not know him at all."[41]

Certain words carry a heavy burden of meaning. It is "our" sailor
boy and bluejacket, the skull rides "safe" in Pacific waters after a
savage taxidermy in which it is "hacked," "skinned," "peeled,"
"bared," "ripped," and "gutted." But this inhuman ugliness serves
a wider purpose. "My experience in reading this poem," the novelist, poet, and critic George P. Elliott wrote, "is not just esthetic: not
the least of the reasons I like it is that it has shown me a truth about
something that matters." That is:

In the image of the U.S. sailor cleaning the skull of a beheaded
Japanese, and in the last line of the poem, are contained a horror at the
sailor's indifference and a pity for his alienation from his enemy whom
he has dehumanized, that have not only moved me but have taught me
to see something about the attitude of Americans towards their enemies
generally . . . when on certain occasions I have repeated to myself,
"Who will not say, 'Alas! I did not know him at all,' " I have done it

[41] WTS, "The U.S. Sailor with the Japanese Skull," *New and Selected Poems*
(1967), pp. 50–51.

less because it is beautiful inside the poem than because it is true outside as well.[42]

Win Scott was done with estheticism, too. "Not to make something
'beautiful' but something true—which in time will be beautiful":
that was the task he had set himself. The U.S. sailor was one of us
after all: "It was a revelation," Scott recalls, "to see men and
women flock . . . from all over the Journal building to 'see the
skull.' " It was their reaction as well as that of the methodically
craftsmanlike sailor that his poem told a truth about: a truth about
human nature, not about politics.[43]

No one influenced Win Scott's political education, such as it was,
more than Joe Coldwell. Old (he had been born in 1869, along with
E. A. Robinson and Esther Wilbar), poor, crippled of body but
exuberant of spirit, a devout Socialist who had shared time at the
Atlanta penitentiary with Eugene V. Debs for speaking out against
World War I, Joe Coldwell would hobble into the *Journal* office
with an invariable greeting, "Hello, you pampered pets of plutoc-
racy!" Then he would inveigh against the capitalist press: Why
hadn't they printed this? Why *had* they printed that? and leave an
inflammatory Letter to the Editor in his wake. Coldwell, a labor
leader when labor leaders' lives were frequently in jeopardy, a man
whose life style matched those of the poor workers in whose behalf
he worked, represented a world that Win Scott, in his scrupulously
middle-class upbringing, had never known. Though sometimes
bored by Joe's repetitive rhetoric and incessant organizing zeal,
eventually Win came to love him: an essay, "Portrait of a Free
Man," movingly testifies to that affection. Coldwell would chide
Win about his job as literary editor: "You can write pretty nothings
that offend nobody and please the same number of persons. Or you
can write articles that will cause persons to think. And that should
be the big job of writers, to *cause people to think*. . . . Keep your
ideals. . . . If you think you can exchange them for wealth, position,
or easy living, you will be getting the worst of the bargain." Similarly, he berated Win after his marriage to Eleanor Metcalf: "Sorry
to learn of your illness, especially when you are living on the East

---

[42] George P. Elliott, "The Sky and a Goat," *Accent* 13 (Summer 1958):
153–155.
[43] WTS, *"a dirty hand": The Literary Notebooks of Winfield Townley Scott*
(1969), p. 147.

Side among the plutes. . . . Of course I should say it serves you right, a proletarian living among the plutes." But there was no malice in what he said; Joe Coldwell was, simply, a born evangelist. Win admired Joe somewhat for the place he occupied in the history of American radicalism, but principally because of his idealistic individualism:

> The tradition he embodied was that of the free individual roaring his beliefs from a soapbox. Joe was intelligent, but not an intellectual: he represented that passionately emotional conviction that all men are created equal. He wanted a world in which there was no war, in which people were paid fairly for their labor, and in which they would hold unmolested whatever beliefs they chose. From Tom Paine on, Joe had some shining antecedents in American history. Now in a more apprehensive world [as of 1960] it is hard to find shining descendants and easy to find within our own democracy all manner of enmity to the benign individualism Joe Coldwell stood for. . . .

Every penny Joe Coldwell made went to the cause he espoused; there was not a selfish bone in his body. To Win Scott he represented, personally and therefore meaningfully, the best of democratic idealism.[44]

Still another kind of democrat attracted Win as well: the class traitor. In his young years Jack Wheelwright, the poet born to the Boston aristocracy, best exemplified the type. "He was a rebel. He was a devout Episcopalian and also he was an active member of the Socialist Workers party. He was a proletarian poet on Beacon Street. He was an aristocrat and a radical artist. . . . He was, simply, not like anybody else; but he did have a regional, identifying characteristic—he was an old-fashioned New England individualist overbred to eccentricity."[45] In Washington, it was FDR, that man in the White House, who, in his genuine concern for the downtrodden, outraged the gentry he belonged to by birth. Later, Adlai Stevenson and Jack Kennedy would play similar roles, as it seemed to Scott. In *The Sword on the Table*, a one-thousand-line dramatic-narrative poem published by New Directions as its poem of the month for April 1942, Win Scott found in Rhode Island history still another

---

[44] Joseph M. Coldwell to WTS, [?]1941 and 8 February 1949, Scott Collection, John Hay Library; WTS, "Portrait of a Free Man," *Exiles and Fabrications* (1961), p. 142.

[45] WTS, "John Wheelwright and His Poetry," *Exiles*, p. 126.

class rebel to apotheosize. Appropriately, Win dedicated the book to Joe Coldwell.

The Sword on the Table tells the story of the Dorr Rebellion, the clumsily executed 1842 attempt of Thomas Wilson Dorr and his followers to extend the franchise in Rhode Island (even at that late date only male property owners and their oldest sons could vote). The hero, and class traitor, was Dorr himself, who took to the sword, when persuasion failed, and was later tried for and convicted of treason. Written hurriedly against a deadline in Ben Clough's office at Brown, the poem hardly ranks with the best of Scott's verse. But it does tell a fascinating yarn, and it gave Scott an opportunity to lobby for the cause of democracy, one hundred years after the abortive 1842 uprising. Cast in rough blank verse largely derived from the transcript of the trial, *Sword* ends with Dorr's statement in behalf of those he wanted to enfranchise:

> The rights a people have are those they care
>   for—they
> Must be worthy of their innate rights or they
> Shall get only those that they are worth.

Let them exercise these rights, and the public (not the law) shall have the last, late, lawful word, for "where the people are, there is the sun."[46]

Critical reaction to the poem was mixed. The *Nation*, stoutly and opaquely leftist, opined that "its value as propaganda for the people's cause is somewhat dubious." John Holmes, reviewing for *Poetry*, suggested a reason for the *Nation*'s displeasure: Scott (thus showing his preoccupation with failure) did not reveal that Dorr was freed and the franchise extended, but let *Sword* end in a falling rhythm "of gallant men and noble hopes come to nothing." Still, the book sold much more successfully than most books of poetry (1,315 copies in the first two months). As Peter Monro Jack wrote in the *New York Times Book Review*, "Mr. Scott has been there in his imagination and has made an uncommonly good story."[47] Besides, *Sword* had a timeliness few poems could match, telling almost

---

[46] WTS, *The Sword on the Table* (1942), unnumbered pages.
[47] Reviews, *The Sword on the Table*, Scrapbook 8, pp. 47–56, Scott Collection, John Hay Library.

exactly one hundred years later the tale of one democratic rebellion which represented in microcosm a present worldwide conflict. In a 6 May 1943 speech on the floor of the United States Senate, written mostly by Scott himself, Theodore Francis Green drew the historical parallels. On 4 May 1776, in advance of the nation, Rhode Island declared its independence of England, but not, unhappily, of the restricted franchise inherited from the English. On 3 May 1842, Thomas Wilson Dorr was formally—but illegally, because he allowed the votes of all adult males to be counted—elected "people's governor" of the state. On 2 May 1843, Rhode Island adopted a new, more liberal constitution extending the franchise (rebellions then, as now, had their political effect). And on 3 May 1943, one hundred years later, Dorr's portrait was officially hung for the first time with those of other governors in the Rhode Island state house. Though wealthy and successful, class-traitor Dorr "was incapable," Green said, "of compromise of principle. In that lay both the tragedy of his defeat then, and the glory of his triumph now." That last rhetorical flourish was undoubtedly supplied by Win Scott. He turned to gallant figures from the past, and such feckless adventurers of the present as Coldwell and Wheelwright, for his political idols.

It was part of Scott's New England heritage to admire the independent man, the Thoreau or Emerson who went his own way heedless of the predominant drumbeat. A statue of the independent man stood atop the Rhode Island state house in downtown Providence. Senator Green himself, a Democrat among far-right neighbors, friends, and family, had gone his own way. Such men possessed a self-sufficient spirit, like Rhode Islander Ned Hazard, who wrote to Emerson in 1845: "I have ceased to have friends. I have put a lock and bolt on my office door. But do not think, Sir, that I am not in the best of spirits. I have good books, good newspapers, and a bottle of Rhode Island rum. . . . I am thinking of surrendering liquor that I may look upon the disasters of my enemies with a clearer eye."[48] If Win could have, he would have been a man of independence, a man of principle, himself. But he could not: he desperately required the approval, the reassurance, and the support

[48] Theodore Francis Green, in the *Congressional Record*, 89 (6 May 1943): A2376–A2377; Margaret Emerson Bailey to WTS, 22 February 1945, Scott Collection, John Hay Library.

of others. To please her, Win sent a copy of the *Congressional Record* containing the speech (and a mention of *Sword*) to his mother in Haverhill.

Actually, Scott had begun an artistic rebellion of his own the previous year, stirring up the stodgy local arts establishment with a diatribe in the *Providence Sunday Journal* of 23 March 1941. As he wrote Jeff, his piece "assailed, it pointed with scorn, it gibed; called on the young to get together and make Providence, Rhode Island, a Dublin. Much excitement. Much fun." His essay did not so much attack the past as lament that it had not been put to proper use: "Where age and tradition are, the soil can be richest." It was praiseworthy to enshrine the past, but artistic death to "impose it as a pattern on new creative work." If the young would unite, and blast that official attitude, which was "indistinguishable from the odor of the Providence River," the city might become an American Dublin, "a living, working cultural centre instead of a chill tomb." Who would be the Yeats of this unlikely renaissance? Well, if need be, Scott would accept the onus. Partly, of course, his article was an attempt to enliven not only the arts, but the literary page of the *Journal*, and in that it certainly succeeded. Probably, Win's newspaper colleague Brad Swan proposed, the diatribe provided the first real evidence that the old walls were crumbling. "It woke up Providence," Swan said. Letters, both angry and approving, came in from readers. Win was invited to speak at the old-guard Providence Art Club, and did so to mixed reactions. Later, the Art Club opened a show of modern Rhode Island artists, accompanied by boogie-woogie piano. Waldo Kaufer, one of the artists, hung a picture upside down. An experimental theater group performed original plays of Frank Merchant and others at 30 Benefit Street. Scott himself launched a weekly "New Verse" column in the *Providence Sunday Journal*. All this furor someone—probably Kaufer—characterized as "Scott's rebellion," and the tag stuck. "It was this," Win wrote in 1965, "that made me look up material on the very different 'Dorr's Rebellion' and . . . I went on and wrote my poem called *The Sword on the Table*."[49]

49 WTS to H. O. Werner, 25 March 1941, Scott Collection, John Hay Library; WTS, "On the Possibility of Providence Becoming a Dublin," *Providence Sunday Journal*, 23 March 1941, sec. 6, p. 3; interview, Bradford Swan, Providence, 16 July 1969. (Kaufer later married Savila.)

Mostly, Scott stayed on the sidelines after firing the rebellion's first shot, but the "New Verse" column was strictly his project. Begun in the 4 May 1941 issue of the *Journal*, the weekly column offered poets an opportunity to publish their work for nominal pay (one to five dollars a poem) in the pages of a major American daily newspaper—an unprecedented market for serious, unsentimental, hitherto unpublished verse. Once a week for seventy-five weeks, "New Verse" printed original and interesting poems, until wartime space restrictions brought the experiment to a halt on 27 September 1942. The very first column presented work by William Carlos Williams, John Ciardi, John Russell McCarthy, and (in translation) Rainer Maria Rilke. Distinguished poets happily sent their contributions; those less well known, for whose work the column was intended, happily sent even more. Among them were Theodore Spencer, Tom Boggs, Rolfe Humphries, Robert Hillyer, Byron Vazakas, Josephine Miles, Randall Jarrell, Robert Fitzgerald, Richard Eberhart, Herbert Read, Eve Merriam, Weldon Kees, John Malcolm Brinnin, Dilys Bennett Laing, Meyer Liben, Leonard Bacon, C. F. MacIntyre, Carol Ely Harper, Keith Thomas, Henry Treece, DeJong, Merchant, and Gerry.[50]

The selections reflected Win's catholic taste in poetry. On the one hand, "New Verse" offered a forum for the experimental. Dr. Williams's poem, in the first issue, provided a "Defense" for this direction:

> I'll tell you what to do
> You that blame me for
> Illicit pleasure in the new verse.
>
> . . . .
>
> Take your beauty out
> Of a Sunday afternoon
> To some quiet corner
> Of the Park, kiss her—
> Slip your hand tremblingly
> About hers, discuss with her
> The inner recesses of the soul—
> And leave me and the insolent children
> To mock you from the shrubbery.

[50] "New Verse," *Providence Sunday Journal*, 4 May 1941–27 September 1942, Scrapbook 10, Scott Collection, John Hay Library.

But Scott was not inhospitable, either, to poetry that smacked of the traditional. He always agreed with Frank Lloyd Wright that there was no such thing as "modern architecture"—there was only *architecture*, and Scott believed it was the same with music, or painting, or poetry: to be an architect, or a poet, one must know and understand what has gone before. In "Time for Our Lesson," written the year he died, Win summed up his feelings about the old versus the new in art:

> "There goes the sun in splendor down."
> How did that Victorian line
> Crop in my unwary head?
> It never could be mine.
>
> The order in which words are set
> Denotes a poet much given to rhymes.
> Shall I search books of quotes? Shall I
> Write to *The New York Times?*
>
> No. I know better. The words came
> As though they were a thought I had
> Phrased in another's ancient brain
> Either for good or bad.
>
> And that's no matter either. What
> Concerns me are the changes rung
> By disparate generations of poets
> Upon the common tongue.
>
> So I, no longer young, would say
> To the younger tribes: *Don't scorn what's yours—*
> *Know all the ways the sun goes down.*
> They will pay no heed, of course.[51]

Win made an anthology of the column's best poems and secured a preface from Louis Untermeyer: "[Scott] belongs to no 'school,' he does not pit one tendency against another . . . a glance at the contents will show how skillfully he has maintained his course between the dangerous Charybdis of experiment and the alluring Scylla of tradition."[52] Indeed, Win Scott never belonged to a

[51] William Carlos Williams, "Defense," in "New Verse," *Providence Sunday Journal,* 4 May 1941; WTS, "Time for Our Lesson," typescript (11 January 1968).

[52] Louis Untermeyer, Preface, " 'New Verse' Anthology" (1942), Scott Collection, John Hay Library.

"school" of poetry, and always resisted the lure of literary dogmas. James Decker's press in the midwest agreed to publish the anthology on a royalty basis, but Decker went off to war, his press collapsed, and with it still another of Scott's projects ended in limbo.

While still a civilian, however, Decker had brought out *Wind the Clock*, Scott's second book of verse, at the end of 1941. Despite troubles at home and overseas, 1941 was a successful year for the young poet-critic from Providence. In the spring his essay against old fogeydom in Providence arts had produced the beginnings of an artistic revival. Late in May, Bert Hart died, and Win Scott took his place as literary editor, at least, he wrote Gregory, "in a sort of bastard way . . . That is, they've made me Acting Literary Editor following a long talk from the boss [Sevellon Brown] on Is there any sense in having a Lit. Ed. In cold fact it seems to mean having a Lit. Ed. at bargain rates." Still, there was a raise involved, and it meant "a marvelous change after 5 years of news broadcasting." In recognition of his new, albeit acting, title, the Providence Public Library elected Win to its board of trustees in August, a recognition from the established order that pleased him more than he was willing to acknowledge. The "New Verse" column was off and running well. He was publishing poetry and reviews in *Poetry*, *Accent*, the *New Republic*, and other magazines. He was in demand for readings at Brown, Pembroke, the Rhode Island School of Design, and elsewhere. In October, he passed up a chance to attend the first annual Inter-American Poetry Pilgrimage in San Antonio, Texas, but the occasion provided him—and *Journal* readers—with a memorable column, its satire softened by empathy. The Pilgrimage, according to publicity releases, would feature a tournament (each poet would submit "a clearly typed copy of one poem on any subject, not to exceed eight lines") and a burial service (contemporary poetry "selected in a year-long international contest" would be buried in a timecapsule for five hundred years). "This unique gathering," the release stated, would not only attract many nationally known poets, but great numbers of lesser known ones, "of whom there are over two million in the United States." None of the nationally known were named, Scott wrote, but as to the others, "the figure— 2,000,000—is itself impressive, and gives one, at least, pause . . . Two million of anybody is almighty impressive: two million plumbers, engineers, bricklayers, professors, Sunday School superintenders—but two million poets lays over any other craft-census I can think of and I'll tell you why. Or, you can see it, anyway. Two million personalities, every one of them 'different' from the mass, every one of them defying nature and striving to record in his name some permanence in our mortal and impermanent world, and— perhaps—every last one of them doomed to failure."[53] In December, with the publication of *Wind the Clock*, Scott made his own, second, attempt to leave the world something permanent in his name.

Decker printed only 250 copies, so the book could hardly have had wide readership. But the reviews were excellent; not until the publication of *The Dark Sister*, sixteen years later, would a book of Win Scott's be so enthusiastically greeted. It was praised by Robert Hillyer in the *Boston Globe*, by Rolfe Humphries in the *Nation*, by Marshall Schacht in *Poetry* ("His progress since *Biography for Traman* is already great"), and, most flatteringly of all, by Coleman Rosenberger in the *Washington Post*. "It is an exciting book," Rosenberger reported, "full of poetic surprises yet poetically honest, a mature and provocative book . . . Scott spans the space between the poet and the public."[54] Perhaps still more rewarding to the author were personal letters, from John Ciardi: ". . . a wonderful set of poems. I kept wishing I'd written them—damn it. . . . I'm really excited about this book, though, to keep impressions straight, I'm not an enthusiast by nature"; and from Robert Fitzgerald: "I'd be very glad to have turned out the ones on la Argentina ['Spain Once Danced'] and on Buffalo Bill ['Indian Summer— Buffalo Summer'] . . . I think you have broken through and opened up some kinds of experience that others have left wrapped in cellophane, for instance that matter of recognition in the eyes of strangers."[55] The last poem Fitzgerald referred to is "Street Looks," which has something to say about Win Scott as well as about a universal human experience:

[53] WTS to Horace Gregory, 2 August 1941, Syracuse University Library; WTS, "In Perspective," *Providence Journal*, 25 September 1941. Note the Mark Twain idiom: "lays over."
[54] Reviews, *Wind the Clock*, Scrapbook 8, pp. 31–35, Scott Collection, John Hay Library.
[55] John Ciardi to WTS, 5 June 1942, Robert Fitzgerald to WTS, undated, Scott Collection, John Hay Library.

That street glance of human diffidence,
indifference, even of scorn
Will in all kinds of weather sometimes mutu-
ally fail: a face
Confronts me, really returns my real look that
I had not thought to give:
A knowledge, a questioning, a hope dilate the
air happily,
A mask dissolves, and someone strange and new
and known looks and goes by.
Why did I not say to her: Wait—you are
beautiful, and who are you?
And to that ragged young man whose home was not
anywhere here:
Wait—what are you—what were you going to say?
And make
A smaller hell, a warmer brighter hell here in
hell.[56]

In the subway, on a train or plane, simply walking to work, you see someone and there is a communion between you, though nothing is said. Yet if the silence were broken, if you had put the question, it would bring but little comfort.

Another poem in the book, "Grant Wood's American Landscape," concludes that the painter's figures "are not real./There is too much sun. There is too much peace." Scott does not talk to strangers, for to do so would only be to confine the space and intensify the heat of his hellish universe. For him, personally, as for the rest of the world generally, there was no peace, and it was no good to pretend that Grant Wood's landscape was representational. Once, such a time of peace had existed for him, and several poems in *Wind the Clock* look back nostalgically to boyhood in Newport. But, as even Gatsby found, you cannot repeat the past, and it was to art that Win Scott looked for an ordering and quieting and cooling of his private hell.

In the opening poem of the book, "Five for the Grace of Man," he attempts to establish an artistic code by which to order his life. The poem is divided into five sections, the first of which begins:

[56] WTS, "Street Looks," *Collected Poems*, p. 40.

See this air, how empty it is of angels
Over O'Ryan's barroom. The bum thrown out
Shoulders the sidewalk, pushes it away,
His hat rolling and his baldspot gleaming
Under the rain and under O'Ryan's lights.

The poet, watching from the opposite curb, notes not only the absence of angels in the air, but the inescapable presence of the bum, who rises,

... arms at surrender pressing
Against the mucky glass, the jeering faces
He touches but cannot touch: they're in,
   he's out;
—Like a child's game: only he's sort of old,
And drunk and broke, alone, the game turned
   real.

The second section is introspective, the poet waiting at midnight for "for something I do not know / And may as well wait here as any place." The bar has closed, and

As the world pitches east I'm on a line
Between O'Ryan's darkened bar and the light
Storm-hid but drumming of the star Orion.
Romantic—Classic, and me in the middle:
Not much, but all there seems to be tonight.

Then, in the third section, the poet confesses to his daylight habit of visiting graveyards, as if from the names and dates and new masonic emblems and old cherubs he might learn "The possible answer to all our separateness," the separateness he feels from both the drunk (romantic) and the angels (classic). The climax of the poem comes in the fourth section, when Scott first restates the problem:

How shall I ever come to any good
And get my works in schoolbooks if I use
The rude word here and there, but how shall I
Let you know me if I bequeath you only
The several photographs, the family letters?

and then by gesture reaffirms his common humanity:

I turn in the comfort of the midnight rain
And as much for pleasure as for necessity
Piss in the river beyond O'Ryan's bar.

The fifth and final section resolves the romantic-classic dichotomy. Cold and wet in the midnight rain, listening to freight cars and to trucks roaring toward the Boston Post Road, he observes that though he's occupied investigating angels, "there's a power of prose draining the air." What is required is a corporeal angel, the merging of classic with romantic, and in the last ten lines of "Five for the Grace of Man" Win Scott states his poetic resolution:

> Poetry, I hear, is to be read aloud—
> Like epitaphs by cemetery strollers
> On Sunday afternoons? There's always Monday,
> Which interests me more: I want an angel
> Easy in the house on weekday mornings.
>
> I want the separated hand and voice
> Brought commonly together: flesh and word
> Concerning whether stars or buttonholes
> Only together can come through night and
>   death
> And move with morning light as with massed
>   liberating wings.

Bum and angel, hand and voice, buttonhole and star: they must be merged in a poetry that is at once common and remarkable. He will abandon his Sunday-afternoon angel of dead aestheticism, and pursue instead a Monday-morning muse, even if she inspires him with the rude word now and then.[57]

Somewhat in the spirit of the preacher's kid who turns out to be the most flagrant hellraiser in town, Win Scott tended, especially in his early verse, to thumb his nose at his conventional upbringing by choosing the shocking word or mentioning the usually unmentionable. Morton Dauwen Zabel at *Poetry*, for example, once asked his to recast the phrase "anal grunt" in his poem, "Passing a Steeple." For the magazine, Win substituted "rumbling" for "anal"; in *Biography for Traman*, he restored the more vivid "anal." Another poem in *Traman*, "And in the Evening," goes on at some length about the appearance of a used condom, "Man's

57 WTS, "Five for the Grace of Man," *New and Selected Poems*, pp. 11–13.

coat-of-arms, sagging and rotten." And in "Five for the Grace of Man," the shock comes when the protagonist relieves himself in the river. "The 'piss' poem is the only one I *don't* like," William E. Wilson wrote Scott, "but not for the same reason that the Old Lady from Oshkosh would disapprove. It's just that I don't think you 'piss' naturally in your poetry . . . But I can forgive you that sickly trickle when I think of the flow of the rest of the poem."[58] A writer himself, Wilson nonetheless objected; imagine the outrage of Old Ladies generally, from Oshkosh, Haverhill, Providence, or wherever. Though he eternally played the Nice Boy, and courted the approval of Old Ladies from Grammie Wilbar in Newport to Frieda Lawrence in Taos, New Mexico, Win Scott must have borne them a hidden animosity suggested by his willingness, in his poetry, to play the Bad Boy for a change.

In the summer of 1942, having published *Wind the Clock* and *The Sword on the Table* within the space of six months, Win Scott went off for two weeks of the literary life at Bread Loaf, the writers' conference in Vermont. It was his first experience with such colonies, though he had been twice nominated by Stephen Vincent Benét to go to Yaddo at Saratoga Springs. As a Bread Loaf fellow, he had neither to teach and lecture, like the distinguished staff, nor to mingle with the paying hopefuls. "Bread Loaf was extremely pleasant," he wrote Jeff Werner that fall, "beautiful Vermont country, on the whole very few wacks in the learning-to-write crowd, and a lot of fun with the staff . . . Our cocktail and drinks in the evening life was all with the staff: Untermeyer, Wally Stegner, DeVoto, Marquand, Fletcher Pratt, Frost, etc. etc. And that was most enjoyable. Frost is both a kind old man and a prima donna now—he has many people with gloves on, all around him; as far as I was concerned, he was extremely kind. Untermeyer I liked far more than I'd expected to: he's a day-long, night-long talker, and very amusing. It's largely unreproducible, punning nonsense."

At Bread Loaf Win met the beautiful and talented poet Dilys Bennett Laing, like himself one of the four fellows. She became immediately one of the most important people in the world to him. After that first encounter, they corresponded regularly until Dilys's death in 1960. They shared respect and affection, and had she not

[58] Morton Dauwen Zabel to WTS, 29 May 1935, William E. Wilson to WTS, 20 February 1942, Scott Collection, John Hay Library.

been happily married, perhaps Win would have fallen more than halfway in love with her. Instead, she became his confidante. In his letters to her, he looked back on Bread Loaf with open nostalgia. In a way, it was another Newport; he had cast off care and indulged himself in a "sort of over-all removal for two weeks from responsibility: doing as one pleased, loafing, gabbing, walking, taking it easy—all amid somebody else's linen and food and fires."[59] But the fortnight of escape ended, and Win returned to Providence, his workaday job, his troubled marriage. In another six months he would begin the love affair which marked a turning point in his life.

[59] WTS to H. O. Werner, 30 November 1942, Scott Collection, John Hay Library.

I speak of spring
Which came this year as hesitant as ever
Yet like a virgin half-bespelled, once touched,
Opened with such passionate responses
We were ourselves half-frightened, all amazed,
And said it never was like this before.[1]

7. Ultimate Spring

ON 14 APRIL 1943, some two weeks after they first became lovers,
Win Scott sent Eleanor Metcalf a poem called "Flowering Quince,"
with a characteristically self-effacing notation, "A slight thing, I
fear; but your own":

If right in front of me,
Slow motion—fast motion really—
The cold branch of the quince
Should all at once
Start with a rash of buds
Then the thin green nudge
The brown back, then the color

[1] WTS, "Contradictions in an Ultimate Spring," *Collected Poems: 1937–1962*
(1962), p. 94.

Of the waxen flower, the flame,
Open everywhere the same
Golden-centered swirl
Of odor, sweet burning odor—
Performed in one day, one hour
Or even one minute
Which would then hold in it
Far more than sense of praise
Could say, all April's days—
That would set my heart awhirl.
This stratagem
Of instant gold from green
I have never seen
On tree or branch or stem:
Never never never—only once;
Once, and it was a girl.[2]

Eleanor represented for Win Scott an awakening, a rebirth magical beyond the gift of nature in his most troubled of times. As his marriage to Savila had worsened, he had covered up the pain in coldness and cynicism; now all that seemed changed. "I have been freezing deeper and deeper for years," Win wrote Eleanor in the first wonder of rejuvenation, "and though I am utterly warmed by you—as I am—I feel awkward still, as though I were fresh from a shell and stupid in the sun."[3]

Like the sun, she brought him to life with unwonted intensity, and his creative powers reawakened with his sexual ones. "Instant gold from green"—often, in Win Scott's poetry, he adopts this color symbolism: green connotes "the state of creativity, most often potential" (as in "Come Green Again"), gold, "the actualization of potential, the climax realization of creativity."[4] And so it was with Eleanor. Loving her revived the poetic drive which had been drying up in his twin depression over the war and his marriage. Poems began to come in a rush; slam-bang, on a visit to Haverhill, he "got" the marvelous "Gert Swasey,"[5] and for Eleanor herself he wrote

[2] WTS, "Flowering Quince," *Collected Poems*, p. 116.
[3] WTS to EM, 12[?] April 1943.
[4] Jeff Todd Titon, "Gold from Green: The Poems of Winfield Townley Scott" (starred paper for the M.A. degree, University of Minnesota, Spring 1966), p. 12. Titon brilliantly develops the color symbolism in writing of Scott as a poet of heterosexual love.
[5] WTS to EM, 20 May 1943.

dozens of sonnets in the summer of 1943. She brought him a kind
of reawakening, and another poet might have done more:

> That last romantic poet of all,
> George Sterling, Age of Technicolor,
> For too many weeks kept scholar
> Of silence deep with alcohol,
> Once upon his knees did fall
> As to worship and to beg
> When he first saw Mary Craig—
> Though the drawingroom was full;
> Cried, his hand upon his heart,
> "You have given me back my art!"
> Then made a hundred poems, vesture
> For her superior loveliness.
> This is a duller age, I guess,
> That can constrain me from the gesture.[6]

Thirty-three years old, nearing the middle of the journey through
his threescore years and ten, wondering if he would live out his life
half-frozen in fearful acceptance of what he had, Win was terribly
vulnerable to the love of this girl, still in college and eleven years
his junior. She became for him indistinguishable from the light and
warmth of the sun:

> And I tell the sun
> Lie on this girl and be as my love's sun
> In whose possession she will not be stayed
> But walks arrayed among such towered ranges
> That make of light a special victory,
> Light moving with her, so I cannot say
> Which wakes the morning.[7]

The girl who so inspired Win was studying, appropriately, at
Bennington. Appropriately, for Bennington's reputation as an un-
orthodox institution exactly fitted the personality and desires of
Eleanor Metcalf. Born to wealth and position, she had rebelled
against her heritage: she was, in fact, a class rebel—in politics, in
life style—of just the sort Win admired. The family money derived
from the buccaneering success enjoyed by Eleanor's great-grand-

---

[6] WTS, "Sonnet XXVIII," *To Marry Strangers* (1945), p. 54.
[7] WTS, "The Dawn," unpublished poem (12 May 1943).

father Jesse Metcalf in the heyday of the Gilded Age. Jesse established the Wanskuck Company, the family textile firm. He obtained
controlling interest in the *Providence Journal*, where his great-
granddaughter met and fell in love with Win Scott. From the close
of the Civil War until his death at the end of the nineteenth century,
he was a commanding figure in the business world of New England.
But still he could not command preeminent social position among
the families who lived in the handsome red brick and still hand-
somer gray-tan clapboard houses of Providence's East Side. There
were two kinds of Rhode Island aristocracy—the old old rich going
back to the eighteenth century (the Browns, Hazards, etc.) and the
merely old rich who made their money in the post–Civil War
industrialization (among them, the Metcalfs). The old old conde-
scended to the merely old, who continued, in the middle of the
twentieth century, to act upwardly mobile. "A colorful character
on the Journal copy desk," newspaperman Ben Bagdikian recalls,
"used to say in his only somewhat fake English accent, 'Jesse
Metcalf would have given a million dollars for a grandmother.' "[8]

Eleanor, however, felt no lack of family. Quite the opposite. Her
father, Houghton P. Metcalf, had found it impossible to adjust to
his role as junior partner under his father and older brother. He
left the mills and the paper, and turned instead to hunting, to
flowers and landscape gardening, to art collecting, to oceanography
and ichthyology. Though hardly a notable success as a businessman,
or socially (he was never elected to the *Journal* board, nor to the
best clubs at Harvard and in Providence), Eleanor's father ruled
as an absolute god in his own home.

The house rules were strict for children; as if to demonstrate that
not even the Browns nor the Hazards could exceed them in propriety, Ellie's parents allowed no uproar, no offensive publicity, and
a minimum of communication in their houses at Providence and
South County, Rhode Island, and Middleburg, Virginia. Born 22
September 1921 (once again the oddly persistent twenty-second
of the month), like her father before her the youngest of three
children, Ellie soon demonstrated an independent streak. She
couldn't eat—or she couldn't keep down what she did eat, and at
five hovered on the verge of death when a Boston doctor came to

[8] Ben Bagdikian to SD, 28 June 1969.

see her at the Rhode Island Hospital. "I remember him standing by
the bed—blue suit, pince-nez, and respectful . . . saying: 'Take her
home and leave her alone. She'll fight her way back if you let her.' "
Fight she did (once, after Ellie threw up in the middle of the room,
a governess made her clean it up with a spoon), and, having fought
her way to health, she regarded herself thereafter as being a tough
and independent person.[9]

Frequently, she shocked the family's sensibilities. One memorable
summer day she and her brother Houghty decided to raise some
money for the unemployed by showing films. "He found an old
movie projector up in the attic, and we rented some films from
Anthony's Drug Store. I made a big sign—fancy pictures water-
colored—announcing the event, and hung it on a big tree outside
of 108 Prospect Street. Sure and the house was soon swarming with
pickaninnies plus the better part of Federal Hill [the Italian section
of Providence]. When Father came home . . . he beheld this terrible
sight, and afterwards damned near killed Houghty and myself."[10]
Like her sister, Kay, before her, Ellie was sent off to Foxcroft to be
polished prior to college, but she refused to let the rough edges be
smoothed. The inscription beside her senior picture in the school
yearbook reads:

> El fizzes like Gin
> At the slightest provokin'
> She's quite individualistic
> And often pugilistic—
> She sure ain't no cherabin.[11]

Still more independently, Eleanor refused to "come out" with the
other Rhode Island debutantes, and went off to an unconventional
college. At one time, she wrote Win, she had "tried to play the role,
normally mine, according to their rules—became quite orthodox
for a moment—and then outplayed them at their own game, drank
more, raised hell far more successfully than it ever had been raised
on the East Side before. All of which might have been amusing,
but . . . it disgusted me. . . . Then I knew I must leave the East Side

[9] EM to WTS, 27 May 1943; interview, Ben and Betty Bagdikian, Washington, D.C., 15 March 1970.
[10] EM to WTS, 7 June 1943.
[11] *Tally-Ho*, Foxcroft yearbook (1939), p. 21.

. . . I couldn't stop being whoever I was."[12] Even allowing for the self-dramatization of her account, it is clear that Eleanor's rebellious youth stood in sharp contrast to that of her lover, who had conformed so meticulously to the expectations of his parents and grandparents.

At the *Journal*, where she worked summers and during the work breaks in the Bennington calendar, Ellie used *fuck* and *shit* so often that one of the more fatherly staffers threatened to spank her. Assigned to women's news, she often slipped the bonds of reportorial restraint. In covering the annual tennis tournament and social outing at Newport, for example, she talked mostly about the tennis, hazily about the costumes of the ladies, and ended with a thumb of the nose at the socially obsolete: "Then the rains came. The brilliant scene dissolved. Soon perhaps the cold waters of necessity will extinguish it forever."[13] At the very least, *Journal* readers must have been startled to find revolutionary rhetoric on the woman's page; one wonders how many cub reporters would have been forgiven such license. Soon she was shifted from society to social welfare and court reporting, sobsister features, and biographies of men killed or missing in action—stories that better suited her interests.

While working on the paper, Ellie fell in love with Win Scott. Sharing the near-worship of the artist typical of many Bennington products, she would watch him fill a pipe, light a match—admiring his hands "white upon the dark table, delicate and yet quite strong."[14] She took walking routes that traveled by the Scotts' house at 56 Olney Street and stood looking a long time at their windows. When, infrequently, they talked at the office, she turned "a most becoming, blushing pink," but for a long time Win attributed the blushes to her shyness.[15] Then he began to notice her more closely. Eleanor's older sister, Kay, was the acknowledged beauty of the Metcalf family, but Ellie had her charms as well: shoulder-length blonde-to-brown hair, high cheekbones, a coltish way of walking, and what women call a stunning figure. She looked, Win wrote her, like Veronica Lake; Ellie professed to be annoyed.[16]

[12] EM to WTS, 14 April 1943.
[13] EM, "Newport Tennis Attracts," *Providence Journal*, 16 August 1941.
[14] EM to WTS, 7 May 1943.
[15] Ibid., 18 May 1943, WTS to EM, 8 April 1943.
[16] WTS to EM, 6 May 1943, EM to WTS, 7 May 1943.

The first lovemaking was a revelation to Win. He had not known what completeness and joy he could bring to a woman. It was Sunday, 28 March 1943 (the incident, like the rest of their long affair, is recorded in the love letters they exchanged). Savila and Lindsay being out of town, they went to Win's house, where he read poems aloud and finally crossed the room to ask, "Are you easily shocked, Ellie?" She was not. He could not recall in detail, later, just how it had all come about; he had drunk too much Scotch earlier in the evening:

Darling, I still don't know *how* I got across the room that Sunday . . . I am all wonder and delight to have you tell me that you were really waiting all the time; that you wanted me to come. My clearest, though still Scotch-y, recollection is that you said something or some things to give all that reasonable talk of ours a we-must-be-good-friends finishing off. Am I crazy? (Probably.) But I did cross the room. But how? Did you say something? When you came downstairs—before I read— you stood so close to me I could feel my whole arm burn with your side, your breast: and I merely kissed you with a sort of now-go-and-sit-down-over-there kiss. (Yes, I was crazy.) But when I quit that interminable reading, did I just get up and walk over? Didn't I say anything? Didn't you? All I can remember—and I remember this explicitly— begins when I came down upon you with my hands and my mouth— and the wildest happiness.[17]

Was he crazy? If so, it was with fear of rejection, a fear so deep that no gesture, even from a lovesick girl, could entirely reassure him. Win's dread of failure (could he jump the fence in Newport? did she—whichever she—really want him?) led to a sex life curiously unventuresome for a poet, and especially for a poet many women found sexually attractive. In the journal he kept at the MacDowell Colony in 1966, Win queried himself: "Fear = evasion; therefore liquor? I was drunk when I seduced El; I was drunk when I phoned Savila and proposed marriage . . ."[18]

It was but one of many fears he confessed to Eleanor in the outpouring of letters from Providence to Bennington, Vermont, in the climactic spring of 1943. To her, as to a psychiatrist, he revealed his deepest doubts about himself; with her, he thought, he might be

17 WTS to EM, 11 May 1943.
18 WTS, Peterborough Journal 2, 23 September 1966.

able to eradicate those traits he found contemptible in himself. "I want to be as strong and wise as you, and perhaps more so on some occasions. I want to be male, for god's sake. My impulse is to be somewhere with you, to lie down and put my head in your lap—it's very real, that impulse; but I should also want to stand up again, beside you—taller than you are, physically stronger than you are, older than you are. . . . There is something about you which challenges me to be grownup at last. . . . *Does* this make sense? It isn't anything I sat down to write: it's been . . . rambling out of me."[19] Perhaps it was not too late to change, to be a man, to take a chance, to assert himself in a way forbidden to him as a child: "For a long time I used to think, in view of one or two completely disintegrated lives of mothers' boys, my contemporaries, how odd it was that with all the mother and grandmother adoration I was bathed in all my life I wasn't so wrecked, so badly spoiled. Later I got less sure. If ever there was anyone with a fierce impulse—at times—to return to the womb, it has been I. To be safe—safe—safe. But more and more I have not approved, have wanted very much to break that." In Newport, he had huddled in the corner between bed and wall; at school, there was the drainpipe corner of the yard at recess "—and all the long rest of it; I never could take part, I feared competitive games of all kinds because I dreaded being out-classed, couldn't bear the idea of any defeat or inferiority. In all honesty, I have never been able to lose these lousy little fears. And with them, you see, the need to be adored."[20]

He was no bargain, he insisted. "You seem to think I'm kind and gentle and thoughtful, and god knows what. I'm afraid I'm not. I am thoughtless and arrogant and self-centered. I feed on praise and daydream on ambitions; I'm cowardly; I'm vain. . . . It strikes me . . . that I perhaps have never done a reckless thing in my life—what an awful commentary that is! I want to be reckless," and in Ellie's youth Win Scott saw new hope. "I think your being so much younger than I is good for me: I mean it combats my tendency to let someone else do all the deciding."[21] Ellie wrote back that she had observed all his fears, and the roles—the bright-young-man role, the little-boy role—he played under the spell of these fears. "I

[19] WTS to EM, 11 May 1943.
[20] Ibid., 14 May 1943.
[21] Ibid., 26 April 1943.

was afraid that when the time came for you to stop being 'America's promising young poet,' when the time came for you to do the big piece a bona fide American poet must do, these roles, this fear would stand in your way."[22] The past tense is significant; Eleanor would teach Win to express his feelings, cast off "shame, self-disgust, and too great consciousness of an ever-watchful audience." Through her, he would learn that it "is not wise to hate oneself."[23] Yet even in these early letters, she showed what later became abundantly clear: that if Win wanted to "do all the deciding," if he wanted to play the dominant partner in marriage, Eleanor Metcalf was ill cast for the part of the complaisant young girl.

The difference in their ages—and its effect, sexual and otherwise —remained a persistent source of concern to Win, although Ellie insisted that the issue was beneath notice. "Darling I would dare you to speak of 'inevitable failures' while looking down into my eyes," Ellie wrote him. "That is a challenge." A challenge Win was often unable, as the years passed, to meet. But for the moment it was wonderful to be passionately wanted by an attractive, intelligent younger woman. Certainly Win was keenly sensitive to slighting remarks about his masculinity. "I remember," he wrote Ellie, "a drunken Biltmore entertainer showing up once at a cocktail party; several years ago. She gazed at Savila, then at me, then said in a loud tone to S: Well, I should think you could have done better than that for yourself! Which is no doubt true." He was issuing a cry for help, and Eleanor responded that after all the entertainer could not know what *she* knew and must be forgiven her error. He was developing a bald spot at the crown, he knew, but avoided "all mirror arrangements that would show [it]—as though, if I can't see it, it really isn't so bad." Before they were married, however, he and Ellie visited Lu and Nat Adler in Cambridge, and Win for the first time looked in a mirror from the wrong, revealing angle. "He flew into a rage," Eleanor recalled. "We were supposed to spend the night but he drove back to Providence that night through an ice storm. Once back at the Colonial Apartments he raged, drank, threw a glass out of the window, could not be mollified." He hated the idea of aging. Perhaps most revelatory of all was a dream he, in-

[22] EM to WTS, 13 May 1943, 23 November 1943.
[23] Ibid., 23 November 1943.

credibly, told Eleanor about, in November 1943: "I dreamed last night—as I have once before—that I lay abed with you, and that someone else was asleep in a bed a few inches away; only last night —I ought to be a-freud to tell this, but I'm nothing if not honest! —you were, for god's sake, a boy. I woke up, then went to sleep again, and I dreamed you (all you this time) and I were sitting in a field looking at pictures of somebody. It was nice: we were just quiet, and close to one another."[24]

Still another source of troubling reflection to Win was the Metcalf clan itself. With the unconscious snobbery derived at least partly from his boyhood among Newport tradespeople, he worried that the Metcalfs might not "accept" him. Three weeks after their first lovemaking Win rummaged through the *Journal* files for clippings and pictures of Eleanor and her family. Of Ellie he found only a negative, but there were "a lot of pictures of your family, and neither Mr. nor Mrs. Houghton Metcalf reminded me of you; but Houghton Jr. does. It all put me into something, I'm ashamed to say, of a cold sweat. All I could think of was my god how these people would have none of me. H. Jr., excepted, I hope. . . . Darling, Darling, Darling, where *are* we headed?" And what of Eleanor herself? Did she realize what it was like *not* to have plenty of money? "Darling, marriage is dusting and dish-washing and rent or taxes to pay, clothes to buy, and rugs and oil and god knows what; coal to get and ashes to be taken away—on and on: it's all that . . . we must be sure never to dive into anything that will threaten your dignity, be so foreign to you that you would surely be miserable."[25]

For Win, the prospect of marrying Eleanor seemed to promise a place of peace, a very specific place that existed in his dreams and may have represented, in the silent language of dreams, a symbolic return to the womb. The details of the place he described in his 1944 journal:

Yesterday I was thinking of—indeed I actually see it, as though it were a picture in a women's magazine—a beautiful hallway in a beautiful house. (I have decided to make a note of it here because I have thought of it now and then for years: it is a regular picture in my escapism.) I see it from just inside the front door—it is broad,

[24] Ibid., 7 December 1943; WTS to EM, 8 June 1943 and 15 November 1943; WTS, 1944 Journal, 7 May 1944; EMS to SD, 28 October 1969.

[25] WTS to EM, 20 April 1943 and 16 May 1943; EM to WTS, 17 May 1943.

with rooms off each side, and a stairway—broad, too, and light, going up on the right-hand side, about midway; but the great and changeless feature is that it leads directly toward a broad, open door that lets on a back garden. That is the look and the feeling of it: light, spacious; and it is a cool—and sunny—forenoon atmosphere, summer; doors (and no doubt windows) open—and sweet and countryish, quiet and peaceful—rich yet not gaudy—a little (I blush for my Frank Lloyd Wright enthusiasms!) Georgian. If (1) one foresees the future and (2) gets what one greatly desires in this world, I shall someday live in that house. But (1) and (2) are very unlikely. Especially, however, (1).

Even to the most amateur of psychologists, the passage sounds Oedipal, traveling back through the vaginal hallway to the open, sweet, quiet womb where one may be sure of peace and protection, indulge his emotional inertia, and become totally dependent. Win and Ellie Scott never lived in such a house; perhaps Wawaloam, her family's farm in South County, most closely approximated it. As he wrote Jeff Werner in August 1944, "yesterday for the first time I went to the South County farm. O my God, what a beautiful place! A long, low rambling house, white-shingled, in part a really old farmhouse, with big additions in similar style—low ceilinged, up-and-down-stairs and all around halls and rooms, wood panelling. And woods and a big pond. Peace, by heaven! We ate lunch E had made, walked along the pond, stripped and swam, made love in a pine grove, swam again—that sort of day."[26] Win had never been so happy.

In Robert Frost's "The Death of the Hired Man," Mary and Warren debate the definition of home: "Home is the place where, when you have to go there, / They have to take you in," Warren declares, and Mary replies, "I should have called it / Something you somehow haven't to deserve."[27] It is both odd and telling that Win Scott, who of course knew this poem well, did not for many years grasp the meaning of Mary's reply. Apparently, he could not conceive of not behaving in such a pleasant and accommodating way as to *earn* his home. He had to *deserve* whatever place of peace he might one day be restored to. But how to deserve the Metcalfs, and Eleanor herself? He thought briefly and despite his pacifism of

26 WTS to H. O. Werner, 21 August 1944, Scott Collection, John Hay Library, Brown University; WTS, 1944 Journal, 20 March 1944.
27 Robert Frost, "The Death of the Hired Man," *Complete Poems of Robert Frost* (New York: Holt, 1942), p. 53.

wangling a commission in the Navy, a step which, Jeff Werner had pointed out, would at once widen the breach between him and Savila and confer a kind of status on which the more easily to meet the Metcalfs. "I pass this on without comment," he wrote Eleanor, "having none at the moment. (Yes I have: the action involved doesn't *sound* like me. But that, alas, may be nothing against it.)" He finally confronted Sevellon Brown, editor and publisher of the *Providence Journal*, for a raise and a change in title from Acting to just plain Literary Editor. He investigated the possibility of becoming an editor at Little, Brown or Atlantic Monthly Press in Boston.[28]

But the best way of all to deserve Eleanor was by way of poetry, and in the summer of 1943 Scott wrote a sonnet sequence for Ellie, later published in *To Marry Strangers*. Here is the central sonnet:

Take my hand. Your hand was chill as mine.
Now both are warmed. So. We draw apart
From others. Our intent is isolation
If necessary. But everybody, every street
Is beautiful. At once. We touch the world.
This immense tenderness. Why, this
Would be the way, wouldn't it! Go out
By going in. Go everywhere, coming close.
The hands are only ours. Touch everywhere,
Birthmark and childhood scar. Also
Hidden somewhere, tissue of death growing.
Go little that tragedy—it sweetens us.
Now we are awake. We know. We are.
We warm the sun. We have invented spring.[29]

Once again, with staccato excitement Scott strikes the note of awakening, but now "it is through the state of being in love—heightened and real communication with another person—that the connection with the 'world' is made." No matter that the world is in chaos: in the development of love, at first selfish and isolated, he sees that the world and everyone in it, is after all beautiful. Even Whitman's "delicious" death "sweetens" by paradoxically reminding the lovers both of their puny mortality and of their immense, supernatural creative power.[30]

28 WTS to EM, 1 June 1943.
29 WTS, "Sonnet XXIV," *Collected Poems*, p. 114.
30 Titon, "Gold from Green," pp. 6–7.

The sonnets of "Go Little My Tragedy" (twenty-six of them survived Win's blue pencil and stand in his *Collected Poems*) celebrate a love affair that seemed in the summer of 1943 to be drawing
to a close. In mid-June Win decided to confront Savila about a divorce. "How many times have I told you that I know what I want
but not if I should try to get it?—Well, now I still know what I
want, and I know at last I shall ask for it. . . . I am not afraid of
anything anymore." So Win wrote Eleanor on June 15, adding that
he knew he was asking a great deal of her: "The possibility that I
can begin by bringing you only a perilously small stake in the
world's goods—less than enough for us both without some help
from you that I would prefer not to ask for; and the probability of
unhappiness between you and your family; but—but, I hope not
unhappiness with me."[31] That same night, he put the question to
Savila, and the answer was Yes, but . . . but she wouldn't be saddled
with Lindsay (an immediate, soon-repudiated reaction) . . . but she
wouldn't sue for divorce herself (if Win wanted it, he'd have to get
it himself—a position Savila did not retreat from for a long time).
There was no talk of another woman the night of Tuesday, 15 June,
but the next morning at breakfast Win told her he intended to re-
marry. "And Ellie, she hadn't—she really hadn't: I believed her—
the slightest idea whom I intended to marry."[32]

The next weekend, Eleanor came to Providence and she and Win
spent forty-eight hours together. "My mind and memory are so full
of you. It seems as though my veins themselves are full of you,"
Win wrote Ellie on Monday, 21 June. She responded from Bennington that "perhaps people are not meant to be that happy, but I
don't know why not. Let us never destroy [those hours] with doubt,
regret, or the attempt to smother memory and feeling." But on
Wednesday, 23 June, Win and Savila (she had been in Haverhill
with Lindsay over the weekend) met in Boston for lunch, and
agreed to try a reconciliation for Lindsay's sake. "When I phone
you tonight," Win wrote Ellie on Thursday, "I don't know how I
shall tell you I've done what I hate to do—nor what you will say to
me." The letter, despite its message, was the most moving he ever
sent her:

You are all around me. Most of all, I think, you are sitting on the
floor in nothing but your pajama trousers and I am kissing your feet.

[31] WTS to EM, 15 June 1943.   [32] Ibid., 16 June 1943.

You are so lovely, Ellie: your wide shoulders with their beautiful bones and hollows under your throat, and your savage breasts, and your hair, eyes, mouth. —I have to write slowly, thinking about you. It is so much harder to keep writing than to stop and stare, seeing you. I remember how amazed I was, looking up from your feet, to find your face all passionate and burning, all filled with—wonder, was it?—and a sort of fearful happiness. O my darling, I shall think of you so forever. . . . Do you suppose I am insane? —doing what I have done: giving you up, as the saying goes, but all the while in my heart I cannot give you up. Returning to a marriage—but I do not want it. . . . We must agree, darling, that it will work. It would be *insanity* not to say that much. I must not deliberately achieve only a prolongation of a wreck, making it worse. Perhaps the sight of Lindsay, the reason for all this, will really make it work. I must honestly try, unless I am a madman.

His resolve of a week earlier had melted away, and his fears returned: "When Savila's and Lindsay's future seemed so hard and insecure, I could not take it. I have let myself be frightened: no doubt. No doubt some arrangement would have been reached and it might not have been a bad one; but since I could not know, I was scared and couldn't go on." Of course it was guilt as well as fear that motivated Win. The guilt went largely unexpressed, consciously, but found an outlet in his dreams. Shortly after his affair with Eleanor began, for example, he dreamed he'd got Lindsay a baby pig for Easter—a pink pig, alive. "But the point was he (the pig) was supposed to be eaten on Easter: and I put him in a little dish, all pink and curled around, but I couldn't imagine how to kill him and I didn't want to kill him. That was all the dream." He had done something so heinous, taking to bed a young girl in the absence of his wife and child, that, he feared, most respectable people could hardly conceive of it. And still he could not really cut loose from Eleanor. "I must talk as though there were finalities between us, but all the time I seek to establish them I do not want them, I cannot yet imagine them. Do you understand? How wonderful that you came to me last weekend, that we had that. It is so much, Ellie: I tell you it is more than I have ever had." Would she write him one last time?[33]

The phone call and letter hit Eleanor hard. "All day I have been

---

[33] Ibid., 24 April 1943, 21 June 1943, 24 June 1943; EM to WTS, 22 June 1943.

trying to teach myself that this is final—so far as our marriage goes
...I am very tired, more weary than I know. I see that I walk
slowly as if afraid of jarring something loose, which would move
and tear and hurt. But all this is what I knew might be, and I accept
it. ...." She would not dismiss the possibility, however, of a second
miracle, or even of her becoming Win's mistress: "I shall never be
afraid to come to you. And you to me? Win remember I am yours."
So Eleanor reminded him in that "last" letter, but of course the
correspondence continued. As Ellie finished her exams and prepared to go to New York, Win advised her to "wait. Wait and wait.
I feel so much nearer to you than to anyone else. All my other relations seem passive, but this one is so active, as it has always been.
Some times there's agony—*you* know about that. Some times are
easier, quieter somehow: I hope you have that too. Some times I
think we shall never come together again. Some times I feel sure
we shan't be able—whenever it is, in a little while or a long while—
to stop ourselves from coming together. Sunlight opening on another hill." And Ellie asked a despairing question: "But to give up
one's title to life, against deepest things believed in, to wake at night
with only the dream shape against one's flesh—can this be right?
I don't know, Win. Someday you must tell me, and explain these
things to me, for (perhaps I am still very young) I do not know."[34]
After exams in July, Eleanor left for Greenwich Village and the
resumption of the affair that had been implicit even in their letters
of renunciation.

In New York Ellie found an apartment on Bedford Street and a
number of friends (including Marguerite Higgins, later a foreign
correspondent), and took on a succession of jobs—bookseller in Doubleday's in Grand Central Station (she was fired, with nice irony,
for reading on the job), editor for the liberal magazine *Common
Sense*, cataloguer of the books on William Rose Benét's shelves. She
looked up Win's sister Jeannette and her husband, and soon demonstrated to the Wolfes that she had lost none of her unconventional
ways. One steamy September afternoon they lay on a hill in Central
Park, Ellie in a lemon yellow dress, and gazed down on the park-
goers walking along the path below. Oddly enough, the walkers
stared back up at them. "Why?" Jeannette wondered. "Oh, probably

34 EM to WTS, 26 June 1943, 19 July 1943; WTS to EM, 12 July 1943.

because I have no pants on," the incorrigible Miss Metcalf explained.[35] In October, Win and Savila came to the city for a week,
and inevitably he and Eleanor resumed their affair. They barged
around the streets of Greenwich Village, dined together, loved together, and, as Ellie wrote him after that week, "Much more agony
would be a fair price for what we have had." But the tone of their
letters changed subtly. Win clucked over the plight of a young girl,
"so small and so much alone, walking on into the goddam friendless
canyons of New York. O my dear, I am all bad for you: I do you
no good—no good at all. What kind of love is it that has a man
standing about saying Take care of yourself Take care of yourself—
over and over, a helpless fool." In a poem written some years later,
he re-created that time:

> How young and unhappy and lovely you were
> How uselessly in
> Love we were; and there
> Walking alone in New York in the snow
> You had nobody anywhere to see to
> Talk to nowhere to go.[36]

For her part, Eleanor chided him for worrying about her catching
cold, about unraked leaves in the yard. "It's a funny thing but often
lately Win you've sounded like an old man whose life is almost
done. . . . You have many years to live, for darling, did you ever
think you will see me when I am 55 or 60 or yet more? . . . When
the verdict will be in, and we will just be living out the sentence,
good or bad. But if good, how very good."[37]

That was the accommodation, then. Some very indefinite day in
the future, they would be old together, and then "the sky will burn
so slowly in all the golden light, and everywhere a silence and a
peacefulness shall rest." In the meantime, Ellie had in effect become his mistress. It would be nice, they agreed, if they "had a
place of [their] own in that sinful city, Providence." Lacking that,
when El came to attend a wedding in November, they made love

[35] Interview, Mrs. Jeannette Wolfe, Los Angeles, 2 February 1970.
[36] WTS to EM, 26 October 1943 and 27 December 1943; WTS, "Chapter
Two," *Collected Poems*, p. 276.
[37] EM to WTS, 4 January 1944.

surreptitiously in a "dingy cellar room, and the door locked, and danger somewhere."[38]

Win couldn't accept the ambiguous relationship between them. He wanted Eleanor, but could not have her, and that tasked him, that heaped him:

I couldn't help thinking as I walked through Benefit street at 9 a.m. —in all that low, slanting sunlight that strikes across the smoke and mists of a fall morning—what dangers we all run: how possible, maybe probable, it is that we will arrive at our deathbeds and know that most of the days were spent in the wrong places doing the wrong things. Thoreau remarked, I discovered just the other night, that the "mass of men lead lives of quiet desperation." And you remember, Babbitt tells his son—suddenly, at the end of the whole book—that he'd never really done anything he wanted to do. I wonder why it has to be that way, and if it does. Some people seem to get away from it; artists of all sorts ought to—and I'm sure some do—if anyone can.[39]

Could *he* get away from his quietly desperate life to do what he really wanted to do? More to the critical point, *should* he? Eleanor supplied him with a rationale which, like the experience of Henry David Thoreau and George Follansbee Babbitt, carried the more weight with Win by deriving from literature—a quotation from the letters of Abelard and Heloise: " 'I know she is not one of those affected females who are continually oppressing you with fine speeches, criticising looks, and deciding upon the merits of authors. When such a one is in the rush of her discourse husband, friends, and servants all fly before her.' Fly for your life, my darling."[40] In his uncertainty, Win began to fear for his sanity. In January 1944 he once again broke off with Eleanor, this time (he thought) permanently. At the same time, and for the first time in his life, he began to keep a journal.

Scott's entries in the journal were made in his near-indecipherable handwriting, "as though this were an earnest of my wish for privacy in this writing." If he was keeping a journal for any audience—so he worried the issue—it would be for himself at a future date. And when he did read the journal, nineteen years later, it

---

[38] Ibid., 12 November 1943, 17 December 1943; WTS to EM, 22 November 1943.
[39] WTS to EM, 7 October 1943.
[40] EM to WTS, 29 December 1943.

brought back "an almost appallingly total recall" of his "most crucial winter—to spring. . . . I scarcely know whether to burn it—to
leave it in its semi-decipherable state—to type it out and seal it under lock and key." As it happened, he followed the simplest course,
leaving the journal in his own handwriting, and so it remains to
stand as a document more revelatory of Winfield Townley Scott
than any other he committed to paper.[41]

Perhaps most revelatory of all is the distinction between what he
wrote Eleanor and what he confided to the journal. We must break
off, he told Ellie, "if we are not to go mad" (and again, unwilling
to close doors finally, "I would like you to write me once again,
if you will and if you wish to"). But, he insisted, she had given him
a new self-respect:

> I know myself as a little unlike what I was before I knew you; there
> is some knowledge in me that was not there before—and a lurking sense
> of physical inferiority and an uncertainty mentally have gone: I do not
> mean that I now consider myself as a sexual god or a first-rate brain!—
> rather that somehow from knowing you, from being with you, from all
> that we have said to each other, from our lovemaking that was always
> wholly ours, and deep and good: from all of this I have (it is so difficult
> to express this) got some acceptance of myself. And it isn't a smug satis-
> faction at all: doesn't feel at all like that. It is different. Rather, that
> knowing you and all that you are and that to you I could bring many
> satisfactions, now I envy no one, feel apologetic to no one.[42]

So he wrote Ellie on 11 January 1944, but his journal notation for
that date demonstrates anything but self-acceptance: "Is my love
for E less than I supposed? Is my love for L (Lindsay) less than I
suppose? Is it still my love for myself that is operating here most
powerfully?—my fear of change, confusion, upheaval, insecurity
(in these times!)? I do not really know. I do love E, but I do not
know what capacity I have for love; sometimes I fear it is very little." Still another introspective passage on 15 January underlines
Win Scott's inability to come to terms with himself. "It seems to
me," he wrote, "that every life I have touched has been to its sorrow: that always I have seized upon someone at once more vulnerable and *finer* than I—that I have not deserved any of the people

[41] WTS, 1944 Journal, 12 January 1944 and 4 April 1963 (an addendum).
[42] WTS to EM, 11 January 1944.

who have loved me." Note once more the notion that he must *deserve* love, and the guilt in what follows: "Almost never have I wept—but there have been so many tears for me. Deep down, I am unhappy, confused. There is something very wrong with me: something evil and selfish—unreckoning of others. Only the other night Savila cried out—and not for the first time—'Do you have feelings as other people do?' But if I perceive that something is wrong, why can't I do something about it?"[43]

His sense of inferiority was only compounded by Eleanor's valedictory reply to his letter. If you have loved me, she wrote:

> I would have you confront your life in simple nakedness. I would have you take it up and permit it to touch your flesh until knowledge of your life permeates every point of your body, of your brain. I know this is an agony. I know this is something you have rarely done. Also I know this is the only way you can escape bitterness, self-contempt, and an eventual sterility that can only hurt Savila, Lindsay and myself most grievously. . . . You can do little for Lindsay if you think that by simply keeping a home and a marriage going in fact, but not in truth you have done enough. A home filled with either quarreling or coldness—and both are equally bad I can assure you from my own knowledge—grants a child only doubt, fear, insecurity and pain. . . . You cannot forget me. I know that nothing good that has happened to one, can or should be forgotten. But you can come to think of all that might have been, finally, as a dream and impossibility. In time you can come to look upon me as a symbol of a woman who loved you, and lived correctly with you for a little while, but who is now a person involved in her own life and work; yet still she looks upon you with the simple understanding and the love human beings should have from one another. Nothing more, and yet this is a lot god knows. . . . I am not ashamed of the tears such necessary brutality forces from me.

This letter led Win to wonder, to his journal, "how someone 22 can be so much wiser and clearer-headed than I, 33. And so much stronger, so much finer."[44] He was fully prepared—perhaps even compelled—to feel as guilty about abandoning Eleanor, the more so because he had only himself to answer to, as about the prospect of abandoning Savila and Lindsay, a course that would leave him stigmatized (he felt sure) in the eyes of others.

[43] WTS, 1944 Journal, 11 January 1944 and 15 January 1944.
[44] EM to WTS, 13 January 1944; WTS, 1944 Journal, 15 January 1944.

Soon, it became clear that Eleanor was returning to Providence, and a job at the *Journal*, and though Win insisted that propinquity would not alter his resolution, that he indeed did think of Ellie now as "a dream and impossibility," Savila was justifiably alarmed: "S is sure that E's reappearance in Providence means not only awkward occurrences but above all that 'everything will begin all over again' . . . S's reaction . . . is that she as a woman knows precisely what E is 'up to'; and as for any protestations she concluded that either I am a liar or a fool. —I think finally she decided on the fool thing. . . ."[45] Win was, of course, fooling himself; as the winter wore on toward spring, he turned more and more to thoughts and dreams of Eleanor.

Meanwhile, his emotions scarred, Win Scott behaved in extraordinary ways. He drank still more than usual, and lectured himself about it. "Night before last," he set down in his journal,

I finished up a bottle of rum—for no good reason. Had one drink as I sat, late, and read; then felt I had to keep gobbling them up. Last night . . . Ben (Clough) took me to his house, and Elsie (Clough), Ilka (Chase) and I from 10–2 completely finished a bottle of rye. This morning I got up at 10, my eyes bloodshot, and for the first time I noticed two veins—one each side of my forehead. . . . They subsided quickly; but I think they will be there when I am abed. I seem to crave liquor so whenever I have it: not that I can't be without it, but that once it's there I want to drink it all. I want to inhale—bathe in it—drown in it. Most of the next mornings—like this one—I feel physically pretty well, but my conscience bothers me: I am uneasy at having no control over my drinking. I should try having one, or two, drinks sometime, and no more. But of course I never *want* to drink myself: and the party is so jolly!

Alcoholism lay ahead of him.

He indulged in a homosexual encounter with a young poet visiting Providence, an incident he found most painful to record in the journal. How difficult it was to put down the truth, not merely to say it but to know it: "The point is not that I deliberately suppressed it [the encounter] in writing here, but that I *subconsciously* suppressed it: it did not 'occur to me' when I wrote the journal entry. That . . . aptly illustrates the perils of truth . . . Sure it makes

45 WTS, 1944 Journal, 17 January 1944.

us free. But we do not want to be free. We are afraid to be free."[46]
On the verge of madness in his uncertainty, he caught himself "on
several occasions . . . mentally playwriting E's death—her funeral
—my anonymous appearance there—my secret visit to her new
grave after her family has departed. On one or two occasions I have
so playwrote my own death—but never E's. Now in God's name,
why do I do that? I don't think I am mad. I don't believe I desire
E's death. I *do* believe I desire self-dramatization. But why E's
death? Is my ego finding some ghastly pleasure in the thought of a
real finality there? —No, I don't think I've wholly tracked it
down."[47] What he did not admit, in so many words, was that if
Eleanor were dead, the need to make a decision would evaporate.

On April 11, Win received a letter from Dilys Laing that helped
move him toward resolution of the dilemma. To her husband Alex's
remark that "the New Englander's inability to show emotion does
not mean that he doesn't experience it," she had replied, "if you fail
to express emotion you end by failing to experience it. If you don't
practice courtesy or the piano or love or tennis or touching your toes
in the morning, you become after a while incapable in all these directions." The letter, Win replied, was "a bullseye hit . . . I think I
am not so deeply in that state as once I was; but a little, still, I
guess." How could Yankees be otherwise, unless . . . unless they
could let go in a way he and Savila had never learned? The very
next day he went into the *Journal* cafeteria, and there was Eleanor.
"I swung round to the counter . . . and could not think: stared at
the menu and tried to perform naturally, but felt as though I'd been
struck dumb, or that in a moment I might go blind, or at least that
I might fall flat . . . It was a kind of joy, a kind of excitement and a
kind of terror to see her . . . but . . . I was—to borrow Dilys' phrase
—not *expressing* any emotion and therefore I cannot say what emotion I experienced. . . . On the 24th—12 days from today—she will
start work here at the Journal."[48]

Though he was not writing, the winter and spring of 1944
brought Win Scott substantial evidence of the respect he had earned

---

[46] Ibid., 8 February 1944 and 1 March 1944.
[47] Ibid., 15 February 1944.
[48] Dilys Bennett Laing to WTS, 10 April 1944, Scott Collection, John Hay
Library; WTS to Dilys Bennett Laing, 11 April 1944, Dartmouth College Library; WTS, 1944 Journal, 12 April 1944.

as a poet, and his final decision to quit his marriage for Eleanor was influenced by this recognition. No job in publishing had come his way, but the *Journal* provided a $600 raise to go with his status as literary editor. Then, on 22 January 1944, still another in the series of momentous events on the twenty-second of the month occurred: in the mail came an invitation to be Phi Beta Kappa poet at Harvard in June. "It's a god-awful *respectable* role," he wrote in his journal, "but I guess I'll chance it . . . I shall have to get all togged out. I have striped pants, but no fancy coat. . . . There can't often have been so young a poet for the occasion, and of course of all Phi Bete affairs none is so distinguished as Harvard's. For sure gaudy predecessors, too: Emerson, for one. Robinson refused, I believe, and that year Vachel Lindsay was the poet. I think they've had Sandburg, too. *And others*—in case that turns out to be my department!" He would get $50 for the reading, but the money hardly mattered: it was recognition he thirsted after.[49]

Still other gratifying invitations followed. In March he read at a Wellesley poetry festival, along with Muriel Rukeyser, William Rose Benét, and Ted Spencer. The event, which alternated a "speaking choir" with each poet's solo performance, turned out to be a great success: Scott's "Mr. Whittier" proved "the great adornment of the evening."[50] Phil Horton, a Providence native who had recently written a biography of Hart Crane, brought Win up to Cambridge to put some of his poetry on the Harvard Vocarium disks."[51] Locally, his researches into the life and Poe-like fantasies of Howard Phillips Lovecraft led to several much-applauded speaking engagements. And on April 22, incredibly, arrived a note from John Holmes inviting Win to serve as Phi Beta Kappa poet at Tufts.[52] In the spring he could not find a publisher for the "Go Little My Tragedy" sonnet sequence, but even that cloud lifted in midsummer, when there came a letter from T. Y. Crowell Company—"right out of the blue. They'd been, they said, deciding to publish an American poet and they'd gotten themselves pretty certain I should be

[49] WTS, 1944 Journal, 23 January 1944.
[50] Ibid., 5 February 1944 and 29 March 1944.
[51] WTS, "Four Sonnets," *Winfield Scott Reading His Poems*, Harvard Vocarium Records, P-1090, H.F.S., 1806; and WTS, "The Stake," "The Game," and "Natural Causes," Ibid., Harvard Vocarium Records, P-1091, H.F.S. 1864.
[52] WTS, 1944 Journal, 11 February 1944, 28 February 1944, and 23 April 1944.

their baby."[53] The next year, Crowell published *To Marry Strangers*, containing not only the love sonnets but a number of other poems as well.

Buoyed by these auspices, Win Scott regarded the future with something like equanimity: "I sometimes think of myself at 60 as a smalltown newspaperman whose early poetry has come to nothing—who is of no consequence in American writing—who has only his circle of friends and his parties and his own second-rate wits. And sometimes, too, I *suppose* that at 60 I may be widely considered the best American poet of my generation, that I may have a box full of honorary degrees. . . . Either . . . seems to me possible." Whichever his fate, he confided to his journal, he felt certain that he could live with "about as much happiness and as much unhappiness as I feel now. . . . I hope these pages survive for me at 60 so I can make some sort of proof of it, whatever happens. . . . Of course—vanity being what it is—I hope—I hope—for the fame and acclaim. Yet—in short—I feel certain that I am the kind of person who would see the ambitions fail and die and could bear that, too."[54] Sadly, he overestimated his ability to bear frustration, and did not live to read his self-prediction at sixty.

To Win, Eleanor seemed to offer the better chance to fulfill his ambitions. With Ellie, he felt, he could let go in the way Dilys Laing (and, independently, John Holmes at Tufts and John Crowe Ransom at Kenyon) had been advising him to do. In feverish anticipation, he wrote in his journal for April 21: "This is Friday; Monday E will be back at the Journal. I think constantly of it, and had dreams of her last night. —I do not know how it will be, the two of us there day after day. What does one cultivate?—indifference? calm acquaintance? gay friendship?—all of them false." He had just read an appropriate lyric by Dorothy Parker "about how bearable it would be if 'you' were loving, adventuring or whatever across the sea—'But, oh, to have you down the lane / Is bitter to my heart.' "[55] A week later, after a few days with Eleanor down *Journal* lane, a feeling recurred that he had

. . . had every time I left her, each day, last October in N. Y. Simply:

[53] WTS to H. O. Werner, 21 August 1944, Scott Collection, John Hay Library.
[54] WTS, 1944 Journal, 11 March 1944.
[55] Ibid., 21 April 1944. The poem is Dorothy Parker's "Distance," *The Collected Poetry of Dorothy Parker* (New York: Random House, 1959), p. 158.

that I was going away from her and there was something ugly about it. Invalidation took place: either what I was doing—going away—was *wrong*, or what we had been doing together—walking, talking, drinking, eating, shopping, making love: in short being all alone and utterly self-sufficient and happy—was *wrong*. (There are morals.) Something was ugly. And I think it was then that the end began: my feeling of madness began to take me as never before. And I kept going deeper until, the first of January, came the climax.[56]

With Eleanor back, Win was again torn by his own indecisiveness. Possibly, and despite his knowing what he wanted, his marriage to Savila might have weathered even this crisis—possibly, but for Savila herself.

Savila brought matters to a head within a week after Ellie resumed work at the *Journal*. On Sunday, 30 April, the Cloughs had a party to which in all innocence they invited both the Scotts and Miss Metcalf. Learning that Eleanor would be there, Savila not only refused to attend but forbade Win to go, threatening to take Lindsay and leave the house at once. In the ensuing argument, Win confessed to his wife for the first time that he had gone to bed with Eleanor. The next day, Savila suddenly phoned Eleanor, "This is Mrs. Winfield Scott . . ." and she then went to call on her. "After you," she warned Eleanor, "there will be others—younger ones and prettier ones." She demanded an apology, but that Ellie would not give, and Savila assured her that she would never again consent to a divorce.[57] War had been declared, but it was a war Savila was in no position to win. For sixteen days after that confrontation between the women in his life, Scott in his distraction maintained journal silence. Then he confessed that "desire for E has been steadily advancing in my consciousness: and there it is—yearning with all that militates against it. Maybe I have lost all perceptiveness (never my strong point)—but I feel that E will do anything I ask her; anything at all. This supposition increases the fires, of course . . . In short, I want her—the thought of possessing her again turns me over inside. And, in short, it would be madness begun again to have her."[58]

Madness, perhaps, but when Savila and Lindsay retreated from

[56] WTS, 1944 Journal, 27 April 1944.
[57] Ibid., 2 May 1944; EMS to SD, 30 May 1970.
[58] Ibid., 20 May 1944.

the field on 26 May, Win and Ellie inevitably came together once more. On 29 May,

E had come over here, bringing some Scotch, and we drank and talked till 12. Then we went to bed and made love and slept. About 1:30 we woke up and I said "I'd better get you the hell home;" and E said "O, not yet. I can stay later." And then, I think, we had our deepest, closest loving ever. At the last it was a sort of death. I think there was nothing it did not touch and consume. It began bestial and ended on a mindshaking ecstasy. It was rut and it was also the "love-death" music. It was worth a whole life—or two—if such a price were demanded.

Later still we came downstairs and talked, read poems, kissed now and then, laughed, drank coffee and beer, and E ate bread and jelly and I ate crackers and peanut butter, and we were very happy. At nearly 5:30 when all the streets were bright with rising sunlight, and cool and full of birdsong, I took her home—and came back and had two hours' sleep. It was a very wonderful night.

An artistic resurgence accompanied the sexual one. "Just before E arrived I wrote a poem about her beginning 'Since after all we were born to marry strangers.' "[59] It was the title poem for his next book. When Savila returned from ten days spent visiting relatives in Darien (her father was very ill), Win moved out.

Returning to obvious indications of infidelity (Ellie had used her hair brush), Savila understandably became bitter. In emotional turmoil, Win wrote with unwonted speed a long, partly confessional poem to read at Harvard, named "Contradictions in an Ultimate Spring" and dedicated to Lindsay. He brought a typed copy to the house at 56 Olney Street (from which he was now exiled) for his son to save against the day when he might be able to read it with comprehension. Badly hurt, Savila Scott lashed back at Win for his effrontery. If he wanted a divorce, he could whistle for it. Savila would grant no more than a legal separation, at least for ten years, she insisted. From the South Pacific, five thousand miles away, Jeff Werner assured Win that he could not "imagine that Savila will carry such a grudge as to attempt to extract her last split second out of ten long years," and Win's lawyers concurred.[60] But Win was less sure, exposed as he was to the fury of a woman

---

[59] Ibid., 31 May 1944.
[60] H. O. Werner to WTS, 13 August 1944, Scott Collection, John Hay Library.

scorned. For example, Win asked to stay at 56 Olney (to save room rent) while Savila was out of town, and promised not to bring Eleanor there. No, Savila replied, she would trust Win no further than the length of a shoelace. More in self-pity than in anger, Win replied:

> What is it that you want of me? You have at least 50% of my cash income. You have practically all of such property as we accumulated in 11 years of marriage. You have your good name and the satisfaction of feeling more sinned against than sinning. You have . . . pretty much exactly the separation you desired. Above all, you have my son; and under the conditions necessitated by this separation, there is no way of my having him at all. Why do you insist on keeping me at arm's length and—as it turns out—kicking distance? Why do you demand so much on the one hand and on the other continually worsen our relationship with every sort of jibe and insult? If I am, as you say, more of an asset outside your life than in it, why don't you let me go altogether?

The letter was grist for Savila's mill. She disputed him, point for point, adding that everytime he asked why she wouldn't release him completely, it gave her a great deal of pleasure. Very rapidly, the point of possible reconciliation was reached—and passed.

It cannot be enough emphasized that leaving Savila constituted the one decisive action in Win Scott's life—the one time when he behaved, if not recklessly, at least with uncharacteristic firmness. It was for him an agonizing decision. He was troubled by his conscience, by the prospect of losing his son, Lindsay, and by his deeply imprinted fear of change. Most of all, he was disturbed by What Others Would Think. From the South Pacific, Jeff sent an offer of financial help (refused) and his blessing: Win should do what he thought best. "What an antidote you are," his friend wrote from Providence, "to those who pleasure themselves moaning over my possible failures as a poet, my lust for money, position and power. . . . They *do*, you know—they do get some sort of satisfaction out of talking that way. They are sorry I am a 'weak' person—they tell this to S, not to me of course—and yet, and yet there's something *not* quite sorry about it."[61]

As ever sensitive to opinion and wanting to please, Win canvassed family and friends for their reactions. Win's father in Hav-

[61] WTS to H. O. Werner, 21 August 1944, Scott Collection, John Hay Library.

erhill and his sister in New York, hearing of the separation, tacitly approved by advising him to seek legal counsel, a course Win at first, naively, thought unnecessary. Grandmother Townley was incensed, and tended to regard Eleanor as a scarlet woman, but Bessie Scott came fiercely to the defense of her son in a 28 August 1944 letter to Savila. With less accuracy than conviction, she told Savila that if she hadn't acted "like an unreasonable child" her home would still be intact:

> Instead you would not listen to reason and go to a party with Winfield that your friends had seen fit to invite a person you did not like. Then you had to insult Miss Metcalf whom I have never met but do not think you had any just cause to insult at that particular time, and third you started proceedings against Winfield. He has always been a kind person to you and to your family and what thanks has he ever received from you. You know Savila that all your married life you have insulted Winfield I have heard you and Winfield is like my father, he will go just so far then he is done. . . . Do not forget Winfield is my son and he is Jeannette's brother and we are not going to fail him when he needs us.

Then, after a plea that Winfield be allowed to bring Lindsay to Haverhill for visits and a wish that Savila might find future happiness, Bessie Scott signed herself, pointedly, "Mother Scott."[62] There was a legend that the Scott men were weak and easily led, but the tendency did not extend to their wives; Mother Scott supported Win with a loyalty and firmness that helped stiffen his own backbone: "The trouble with S.," Bessie wrote her son, "is she now knows you are in earnest and the Scotts are not soft after all."[63]

Inevitably, the separation caused Win and Savila's friends to take sides. On one side were those who considered it unjust of Win to leave his wife and son for a rich young girl and her money; on the other, those, like Brad Swan at the *Journal* who thought it entirely justifiable for him to leave a woman who didn't love him (as Win believed) for one who did.[64] Dave DeJong took Savila's side. During the separation he escorted Savila to an unpleasant confrontation with Win and Eleanor; he wrote a short story painting

[62] Bessie Townley Scott to Savila Harvey Scott, 28 August 1944, Scott Collection, John Hay Library.

[63] Bessie Townley Scott to WTS, 29 August 1944, Scott Collection, John Hay Library.

[64] Interview, Bradford Swan, Providence, 16 July 1969.

Ellie in unpleasant colors; finally he testified for Savila in the divorce proceedings. All this hurt Win, for DeJong was a writer whose work he respected and a man he liked and had often confided in. Still more painfully, their strained relations stretched to the breaking point in a dispute over a review DeJong did for the *Journal* book page in 1947. DeJong had complained in a letter about the niggardly, and often late, pay given book reviewers, and when word reached Win, he cut him off from further reviewing. A nasty correspondence ensued, including threats by DeJong of a lawsuit. As late as 1952 he rehearsed his case against Scott (not by name, but the intention was clear: "Rhode Island can't boast of one respectable poet") in an article for the *American Mercury*, and it was not until 1956 that DeJong wrote Scott "that all these animosities and recriminations are silly and ought to be evanescent," bringing their quarrel to an end.[65]

The defection of DeJong and others (Victor Ullman was so charmed by Ellie that he was able to forgive her both money and capitalist background) distressed Scott. Nor would Dilys Laing give him, in writing, the reassurance he obviously sought. Her sympathies lay with Lindsay: "Poor Lindsay, poor Savila, poor you, but above all, poor Lindsay . . . Will you have him at least part of the time? I couldn't bear for you not to, after reading your poem ["Contradictions in an Ultimate Spring"], or even remembering how you talked of him at Bread Loaf." Couldn't Win have kept both wife and mistress?[66] Lindsay, of course, was very much on Win's mind. In a "letter" dated 10 July 1944, with the scribbles translated by Savila, his son implored Win to "come back tomorrow" and asked, "How do you think this letter looks? Does it look terrible? all misserable? I write on this side and odder side, and that's all it says: nothing more."[67] Guilt-stricken, Win began to playwrite Lindsay's death:

[65] WTS to David C. DeJong, 18 March 1947; David C. DeJong to WTS, 19 March 1947, 14 April 1947, 17 April 1947, and 7 September 1956, Scott Collection, John Hay Library; David C. DeJong, "A Day in Rhode Island," *American Mercury*, May 1952, pp. 25–32.

[66] Dilys Bennett Laing to WTS, 9 July 1944 and 6 October 1944, Scott Collection, John Hay Library.

[67] Lindsay Bothwell Scott to WTS, 10 July 1944, Scott Collection, John Hay Library.

To L. B. S.

Sometimes, tired, I imagine your death:
By childish illness, reasonless accident
Stopped still forever, gone; until I loathe
Fool dramatizations of the brain—I won't,
Though I could, write them into pictures here.

My child, outlive me! Stay beyond my times
Which—how I see now—could be worse than
    these,
As they are worse for many who had sons.
Death I can bear for myself once, not twice.
I am out of bed at midnight to beg this.[68]

He sent this poem to Dilys and supplied her with current reports on
the separation, the divorce, and his impending remarriage, but she
adamantly withheld approval: "So it is the Lady Eleanor. Well, I
am glad for you. But sad, very sad, for someone else. I'd wish you
happiness but I'm not sure it's what you want, or that it would be
very good for you. I don't wish you luck. Bad luck makes good
poetry. Let me see. What do I wish you?—Life. But *that* hurts."[69]
Obviously, theirs was no casual correspondence. Sparks flew. Still
more intensely than usual, Win *cared* what Dilys thought.

Win had better luck in securing the blessing of the older women
who always hovered around his life, offering praise, affection, and
encouragement. As a boy, he had turned to Essie and Grammie
Wilbar, as an adolescent to his grandmother Townley, and as a
grown man to Esther Willard Bates, for many years E. A. Robinson's secretary at the MacDowell Colony, for unstinting admiration. When his marriage was breaking up, for example, Elsie
Clough jocularly remarked, "Well, I really didn't know whether it
was Ellie or Essie Bates." Certainly, Win felt an extraordinary
closeness to Miss Bates, who became a kind of surrogate mother
after the death of Bessie Scott. As Eleanor said of Win, "he did have
a thing about old ladies," and in the course of his climactic spring,
he met, charmed—and in turn was charmed by—still another such
lady, Maud Howe Elliott of Newport.[70]

[68] WTS, "To L. B. S.," *New and Selected Poems* (1967), p. 37.
[69] Dilys Bennett Laing to WTS, 20 June 1945, Scott Collection, John Hay
Library.
[70] EMS to SD, 30 September 1969.

When he met Mrs. Elliott in her Newport home in March 1944, she was ninety years old and the author of a memoir of her early life in the resort colony, which Win, with his combined interest in the past and in a style of life foreign to *his* Newport forebears, found fascinating. The daughter of Julia Ward Howe and the sister of Laura E. Richards (at one time E. A. Robinson's mentor in Gardiner, Maine), Mrs. Elliott read from her book about the Newport of "Pussy" Jones (Edith Wharton), James Gordon Bennett, the Astors, and the Lorillards. She told of her father's correspondence with Lafayette and of his having fought alongside Byron in Greece. Then, Win recorded in his journal,

> I waited my turn afterwards to speak to her. Turning from handshaking such oldsters as Perry Belmont—(it is essential that I note that!)—she came a step toward me and asked, "Now who is this handsome boy?"
>
> . . . .
>
> "Do you come to Newport often?" I said that I went very rarely: my grandparents dead—etc.—and she said "Would you come down and have lunch with me sometime?" I said I'd love to. "Yes," she said, "you come some time and have lunch with me—and I'll be your adopted grandmother!"
>
> All this was within a few minutes [among] the gilt chairs. And then off I went to get my bus back to Providence. What a woman!

On the bus, all Win's old nostalgia for his boyhood home flowed back. "I love Newport . . . always, just . . . a few minutes away, that magnificent rock-rimmed sea."[71]

But there could be no escape from Providence yet. For more than a year (but not for ten) Savila refused to take steps for a divorce, and when she finally did so, the divorce was granted for extreme cruelty and on her terms. Win was to send her $25 a week and an additional $35 on the 15th of each month (despite Savila's eventual remarriage, Win was still making these payments at the time of his death). He was to purchase a life insurance policy in her name and to pay all legal fees, and she of course kept the house, its furnishings and furniture. (Win retained his books and records.) Most stringent of all, however, was the clause pertaining to visiting

[71] WTS, 1944 Journal, 9 March 1944.

rights. Win might see Lindsay at Savila's home or on day trips not interfering with school, and he might take him on visits to the grandparents in Haverhill "not more than one week every two months." But Lindsay was never to be exposed to Eleanor: "The husband shall at no time take or keep said son in the presence of a certain person, now known to both parties to be objectionable to the wife." The clause stood firm even after Win and Eleanor were married; plates of cookies would appear mysteriously from the kitchen when Lindsay was visiting, but not the baker, Ellie. Though he ate the cookies, Lindsay conceived of Ellie for a long time as an ogre. Not until 1950, when Savila was married to Waldo Kaufer, was the clause modified; eventually, Lindsay and Ellie came to know and be fond of one another.[72]

The divorce was granted on 12 September 1945, and only then did Eleanor reveal to her family the marital plans she and Win had made. Her father's response to the news, in a letter of 20 October 1945, betrayed some of the coolness Win had been afraid of from the beginning of his affair with Eleanor Metcalf: "Your letter of the 20th is received. You seem to have no doubt in your mind as to your plans and feelings, so, as you say, more need not be said, except to wish you well and congratulate you. . . . Win's dossier sounds interesting and I look forward to meeting him with no more trepidation than he may have for same." Rather more warmly, Eleanor's mother wrote Win that she sincerely believed "you two were made for each other . . . In a way I think a couple is lucky who has had the chance to fight for each other literally." In colorful language, Essie Bates agreed: "To see you both together is to see something that warms my very gizzard."[73] The divorce became final early in April 1946, and on 26 April Win and Eleanor were married, moved to the house at 312 Morris Avenue that H. P. Metcalf had bought them, and began a life together that lasted for twenty-two years.

For once in his life, Win had taken a gamble for future happiness, and he never repudiated his decision. In 1964, a younger writer, whose own marriage was tearing at the seams, asked Scott for ad-

[72] Family Court Divorce Record 45358, 1945 term, Family Court Clerk's office, Providence, Rhode Island.
[73] Houghton P. Metcalf to EM, 24 October 1945, Mrs. Metcalf to WTS, 15 October 1945, Esther W. Bates to EM, 19 April 1946, Scott Collection, John Hay Library.

vice. Go ahead, Win wrote, change your life, and your marriage if it's what you really want; and in that counsel he voted in favor of his own decision two decades before. But no one cuts all ties, and in 1965 Win Scott looked back on his ultimate spring and the bitter split between himself and Savila in a poem called "Questions out of the Cellar":

> Smell of mold from the cellar—rat dung—dust
> Stain letters of that quarrel years ago
> Here all typed out to keep and be forgotten,
> And now they spread as legible as pain.
>
> I read them carefully, as if I must
> Run fingers down an unremembered scar
> Which long since shut across the wound of
>   pride
> Cut crooked with malicious jealousy.
>
> Sad and sickening not to feel it now.
> Did we care so much we had to hate so much?
> Was there so much time that we had time for
>   that?
> Is regret indifference or resurrected love?[74]

Perhaps that poem, written on Eleanor's birthday at the Mac-Dowell Colony and as yet unpublished, will serve as the apology Savila Scott never had from Win.

[74] WTS, "Questions out of the Cellar," unpublished poem (22 September 1965).

A pet dogma of mine is that literary success . . . is not a matter only of literary talent; it is a matter of character. The world is full—at least, sometimes it seems so—of people of talent who don't amount to a hill of beans. No guts.[1]

8. Cutting Loose

MORE THAN IN ANY OTHER BOOK, Win Scott sang his song of love in *To Marry Strangers*. Its thirty-seven sonnets celebrated the reawakening to joy and wonder Eleanor had brought him. Win asked a good deal of that rapture; he asked that it remain timeless, fixed, unaltered:

> I want to show you a young girl in an orchard
> Face down to a book, hair fallen forward,
> The May apples' shift of white and green
> Lifted around her, sun let out and in;
> Such day as you may remember for unnameable
> Fragrance and the long slow sound of it all,

[1] WTS, "Bookman's Galley," *Providence Sunday Journal*, 10 December 1944, sec. 6, p. 6.

As though it were the unopened heart of summer
Somehow known. The girl is at its center.
She is out of herself and into the book,
And she and the book and the day together make
A page that holds the sun, and may be so
Forever but that of course I cannot show you
Or know myself. But I can look as long
As I grow older, and none of this will move or change.[2]

This ecstatic vision—the young girl reading in an orchard—would stay with him forever, but the girl perceived and the man perceiving inevitably aged and coarsened and wrinkled until reality warred with romance and Scott closed his eyes in order to hold steady in his mind's eye his unrecapturable vision.

The seeds of disillusionment had been planted (Win could no more repeat that first spring with Eleanor than he could summon back childhood summers by the ocean), later to sprout. Meanwhile, in poetry if not in life, the moment could be captured, all could come green again if the words were right and the voice unstrained. Scott committed no love yelp in *To Marry Strangers*; but the poems are not less unabashedly personal for being spoken sotto voce. Love ordered Win's world, and awoke him to others. "What happens is, that you are not alone. / Can you understand that?—you are not alone."[3] Or, as he writes in "Poem," "I walked through town with a dirty face and, on the whole, / More strangers spoke to me than usual."[4] *That* was worth celebrating, and in committing his own emotional experience to verse, Scott began to find his own voice. The critics were divided on the merits of that voice, but they recognized it as a distinct and different one; there was no longer much talk about influences and borrowings.

In a review for Scott's own *Providence Journal*, Horace Gregory explored the merits of that voice. It was, he found, an independent one, deriving not at all from any group or school of poets. It was authentic, honest: it commanded belief, and if, "as Jean Cocteau once said, 'a poet wishes to be believed rather than praised,' then Winfield Scott has accomplished more than any poet of his immediate generation in America, and today one cannot name an Amer-

---

[2] WTS, "Sonnet XVIII," *Collected Poems: 1937–1962* (1962), p. 111.
[3] WTS, "Sonnet XVII," *Collected Poems*, pp. 110–111.
[4] WTS, "Poem," *Collected Poems*, p. 100.

ican poet under 40 who with more courage and more fortunate results has written a better book than Winfield Scott's 'To Marry Strangers.' " It was unpretentious; his poetry disarmed the reader with its lack of artiness and its plainspoken manner which at once found its origin in New England speech and yet was peculiarly Scott's own.[5] Hollered up to the skies by Gregory, Scott was brought crashing down by Robert Lowell's judgment, in the *Sewanee Review*, that he had no ear, that his lyrics were slow, professional, and pedestrian, and that only in such poems as "The U.S. Sailor with the Japanese Skull" did he escape from his customary vagueness, whimsy, and sententious daydreams.

No ear, or a keen ear for New England rhythms? Well, Scott *was* becoming a plainspoken poet, whose diction was at the farthest possible remove from Lowell's (a man whose work Scott never much cottoned to). "As a modern poet," a newspaper reviewer in Springfield, Massachusetts, concluded, "Mr. Scott falls into the common error of 'talking' his verse down to the level of prose ..."[6] There was no more tinkling water in his best poetry than in Robinson's, and like Frost he was working toward talk-song. "My present conviction as a writer of verse," so Scott expressed his code, "is for an essentially simple, direct language, and one that carries its intellectual significance—such as it may be—on an emotional utterance. I am interested in the elevation of seemingly common speech to 'poetic' power." Still, adverse judgments hurt, even when he could joke about them. "Consider me annihilated by all this news," he wrote Dilys Laing of the Lowell review.[7] Mrs. Laing reassured him, and so, in acknowledgment of a copy he had sent her, did Florence Williams Potts, the woman Win had wanted to marry during and just after his college years at Brown. "When we walked up the snowy hill at Northfield and you said in the first 5 minutes after we had met that you were going to be a poet," Mrs. Potts recalled,

[5] Horace Gregory, " 'To Marry Strangers'—A Book of Poems," *Providence Sunday Journal*, 29 April 1945, sec. 6, p. 6.
[6] Robert Lowell, "Current Poetry," *Sewanee Review* 54 (Winter 1946): 147; Margaret Cobb, *Springfield Sunday Union and Republican*, 29 April 1945. These and other reviews are pasted in Scrapbook 8, pp. 65–88, Scott Collection, John Hay Library, Brown University.
[7] WTS to Dilys Bennett Laing, 18 January 1946, Dartmouth College Library.

"I must confess I smiled to myself at your assurance—but you were right."[8]

From Cid Corman, a poet himself, came a largely ill-tempered letter concluding "Scott, you are not completely a poet, you are more a lover," but suggesting that he should turn his narrative skills to advantage: "Why don't you tell stories in verse; you have the power to evoke emotional responses, so why talk about them; write *longer* works, don't be afraid of giving yourself elbow-room, if you want to say something fully and decisively."[9] Again, a matter of taste was involved: Corman's obvious preference of narrative to lyric verse. But he was partly right. Among Win Scott's best poems, "Mr. Whittier" and "Gert Swasey" brilliantly weave storytelling and capsule biography. Scott had withheld "Mr. Whittier" from *To Marry Strangers*: it did not jibe with the lyric mode of the book, and it was always well to have something in reserve toward the next book of poems. And, of course, unknown to Corman, Eleanor was urging Win in the same direction. If he were to become a major American poet, he would have to produce poems of greater substance and bulk. Win resisted the notion. Had he thrown up his job soon after he and Eleanor were married, tongues would surely have wagged: See, the uncharitable would say, he *did* marry her for her money. Win feared those voices, and still more he feared the echo they found in his judgment of himself. He and Eleanor were to be married five years before Win finally broke with the *Journal* in favor of full-time occupation as poet and man of letters. But he, too, sought the time to write at length and without the daily interruptions of his job. Once again, encouraged by I. J. Kapstein, Brown professor and novelist, Win applied for a Guggenheim fellowship in the fall of 1945.

Win proposed in his application, to write two long poems, one "a dramatic-narrative based on the Norse sagas of voyages to North America," and the other "an autobiographic-philosophical poem of an individual's mental and emotional growing-up in the past 20 years of American life." The first proposal, obviously, would have given Scott yet another whack at *The Dark Sister*. The second,

[8] Florence Williams Potts to WTS, 19 May 1945, Scott Collection, John Hay Library.
[9] Cid Corman to WTS, 13 May 1945, Scott Collection, John Hay Library.

under the working title "Walpurgis the Autobiographical Night," he never carried much beyond the planning stage. He confided to the foundation:

> . . . its theme of going-toward-maturity will be worked out on three intermingled lines: Superficially the events will be those of a man's journey from inland to the sea, from evening of April 30 to dawn of May 1. It will also mirror his growth of 20 years and, in a series of escapades and incidents, his varying reactions to society, religion, sex, love, poverty, wealth, etc.: his maturing from selfishness to selfhood. And also, by implication, it will reflect the 20 years in general in the U.S.A. —approximately 1925–45. It should contain what I have to say after getting to be 35 years old in my time and place.[10]

Kapstein, Gregory, and Henry Beston wrote in support of the application, but once again it was no go with the Guggenheims. If the fellowship had gone through, Win and Ellie had planned a year in the Southwest, probably Santa Fe; it was a place Eleanor had been briefly happy in as a girl, and one that fascinated Win. Nine years later they moved there permanently.

Though spurned by the Guggenheim Foundation, Win Scott was in demand for sundry cultural occasions in the New England of 1945. Late in January, he represented poetry—and eloquently upheld the cause of nationalism in literature—during the the third annual "Cultural Conference" at Middlebury College. Snow and bitter cold greeted him in Vermont. The snow "creaked when you walked it. It shone like great shields in the sun under the ice-blue sky. It lay marvelous upon the mountains, there dimmed as by a perpetual snowfall of white birch, here riddled with firs and pines . . . Vermont is a dramatic country in its Winter. I think if a painter dreamed up, as an idea, cubes of strong-red buildings set in valleys of white snow we should accuse him of some prettiness." At Middlebury he met and made a Saturday night of it with Granville Hicks, whom he admired for the "smalltown flavor—sense of locality" in his novels. Next morning, they "walked down across the Common. . . . Still, cold, bright, blue-and-white, the morning shone: the very heart of a country town's Winter. Beyond the little bandstand and

---

[10] WTS, application for a John Simon Guggenheim fellowship, received by the Guggenheim Memorial Foundation, 6 November 1945. Winners of fellowships in poetry for 1946 were Gwendolyn Brooks and Randall Jarrell.

the Grand Army monument, the bells of the white steepled church clattered twice over with the music of 'A mighty fortress is our God.' Maybe no one but a Yankee would have felt like breaking right down and crying—or kept from doing it."[11]

In May, on an occasion that moved him more to exasperation than to tears, Scott went to Boston for a New England Poetry Club reading. The club met at the Mt. Vernon Place palace of Mrs. Fiske Warren "filled . . . with loot from renaissance Europe." After some talk lamenting the lack of tradition in the United States, thirteen anonymous poems were read, each "by a clergyman with a resounding voice." Discussion followed, with John Holmes of Tufts leading, and then balloting, to rank the poems one, two, three, while Mrs. Warren improved on the time by reading various " 'thoughts' she's recently copied out from Blake, Plato, and similar characters."

It is now 7:10 and Scott, who has been told to come and read 45–50 minutes, is introduced by J Holmes, who says the buffet supper downstairs should begin at 7:30. Follows, thereupon, —from, I should be sure to tell you, a throne chair—a nervous, hectic reading during which S tries (1) to read tough, ugly American poems, such as they are, (2) to decide while going on what to drop out of the program, and (3) how to rearrange what's left. Follows a gorging by 60 people of cakes, sandwiches, ice cream and coffee in a sultry downstairs room.

So Win wrote Dilys Laing, with the superfluous warning, "Dilys, my dove, don't ever let them do it to you; don't ever!"[12] Scott obtained still other glimpses of cultural life in Boston at the Sunday teas of Rollo Walter Brown, where one might meet literary luminaries and, often, listen to Frost. "If Robert Frost's talk for the past thirty or forty years had been recorded, what shelves of speculative wit and wisdom we should have! . . . Of course much of the charm, the invigorating zip, of [his] talk is that it arises like a . . . fountain from moment to moment; it is immediate, but it moves from profundities. . . . It is a playing of the mind. It even plays with decisions—just to see how they look from all sides. It could be irresponsible, but I think it is not; and there is always the responsi-

---

[11] WTS, "Bookman's Galley," *Providence Sunday Journal*, 4 February 1945, sec. 6, p. 6.
[12] WTS to Dilys Bennett Laing, 17 May 1945, Dartmouth College Library.

bility to personality—and it's a natural one, not an act."[13] By 1949
Holmes had organized an informal club in Boston of the poets there-
abouts: Richard Eberhart, Richard Wilbur, May Sarton, John
Ciardi, and Holmes himself, and he asked Scott to join the group.[14]
Such gatherings of real poets held considerably more appeal for
Scott than the membership of the New England Poetry Club, but
Boston was an hour and longer away and he did not really like the
process of comparing notes and critical remarks. He stayed on the
periphery of that cultural ambience.

What he had to say about literature he confided to print, not only
in reviews, but also in a *Providence Sunday Journal* column called
"Bookman's Galley," a column he wrote almost every week for
seven years, from 25 June 1944 to 6 May 1951. Many "Bookman's
Galley" columns consist from start to finish of news from the publishing world: comments on and gossip about new books and their
authors. As such, the columns represent a kind of personalized literary history of the time: the postwar Modern Library and paperback boom, the Fitzgerald revival, the Faulkner rediscovery were
all chronicled. And occasionally a column was enlivened by Scott's
willingness to write of himself (the Middlebury visit, for example),
to tell of trips to New York and meetings with William Carlos Williams and E. E. Cummings, dinners at Cavanagh's and Louis
Scribe's, and evenings at the theater.

Occasionally, too, the "Galley" became a forum for the discussion of issues that especially troubled Scott, none more than the censorship which flourished in Boston. Censorship, like pacifism, was
one of those issues on which Scott never wavered, and he repeated
his missionary convictions again and again, sometime in debate
with readers, more often in response to particular violations of the
canons of free speech. "Massachusetts," he lamented on 15 July
1945, "has gone and put its book censorship nonsense into written
law. Instead of the Watch and Ward Society warning booksellers
about this or that allegedly dangerous volume, now the Attorney
General or a district attorney may ask the Superior Court to rule on

---

[13] WTS, "Bookman's Galley," *Providence Sunday Journal*, 17 December 1944,
sec. 6, p. 6. Oddly, it was Scott's Haverhill High School classmate who later
brought out a book of Frost's lectures and conversations. See Daniel Smythe,
Robert Frost Speaks (New York: Twayne, 1964).

[14] John Holmes to WTS, 3 April 1949, Scott Collection, John Hay Library.

a book. . . . This makes stupidity as official as purgatory, and I was never gladder that Roger Williams got out of the place when he did. Out of the Bay Colony, I mean." With the end of World War II came another outrage: "the Allied purge in Germany of books glorifying the Nazi theories and the Germanic military tradition . . . If the book-burning program stands we shall be as meanly guilty before the world as were the Nazis themselves 13 years ago at their famous book-burning . . . How many times must it be insisted that you cannot burn ideas." And in one of his last columns, on 28 January 1951, after hearing that the works of Mark Van Doren had been banned because of their author's presumably left-wing sentiments, he cried, "How long, O Lord, how long!" and continued with an eloquent and prophetic statement of the dangers of official hypocrisy:

> I don't think I can say simply enough how important this is. All the yammering ever done here about little flurries of censorship has really intended to be about this great question of how to live as we say we mean to live. You can go on just so long saying one thing and doing another—just so long, and then it catches up with you; then the rest of the world cynically judges us and why should they not? And it may be—most serious of all—that our own youth will ask: Defend what? . . . I don't say we are that far gone. But every little meddling committee member who bans you because you don't think as he does—or . . . bans you because he supposes (but doesn't even know) that you don't think as he does—takes us farther along this ruinous way. . . .[15]

Professing an ideal and then flouting it cheapened the ideal; as Scott predicted, in time the nation's youth came to question the values for which they were supposed to fight. The problem was only exacerbated by the gradual degeneration in communication. "You can't hear, week in and week out, that each new movie is the most stupendous, most colossal, most terrific, most beautiful and have these words mean anything. Like money, words without any agreed standard of value become counterfeit; and presently you get a complete amorality of language. . . ." When the *Ladies' Home Journal* had announced in large letters on the cover of its August, 1944 issue, "Pastoral—COMPLETE NOVEL—Nevil Shute," and

[15] WTS, "Bookman's Galley," *Providence Sunday Journal*, 15 July 1945, sec. 6, p. 6, 19 May 1946, sec. 6, p. 6, 28 January 1951, sec. 6, p. 8.

printed inside but one-third of the novel, Scott was troubled less by the shoddy commercial morality than by the instance as

> . . . a symptomatic illustration of one of the evilest and most dangerous characteristics of our time. That is the divorce of words from what they actually mean. I think it has been brought about principally by people who have something to sell. That is a great many people. But the evil doesn't stop there; it impinges upon all our lives. It endangers nothing less than man's communication with man. In turn, therefore, it threatens the very peace of the world, that peace which the vast majority of mankind desires. . . . A regard for the meaning of language is a moral obligation. The habit of saying what you do not mean, what is not so, or what you think somebody else wants to hear, is a destructive and terrible thing.[16]

In other columns, he inveighed against the fake, the imitation, the work of art altered for profit. The range of Scott's targets extended from classic comic books (*Macbeth* was the first to come to his attention), to *Reader's Digest* book condensations ("The Digest plans to issue one of these little monstrosities every three months . . . How would you like [the] eyes and nose cut from a Rembrandt painting? . . . Or—to come closer to home—the guts torn out of as fine a novel as 'Cry, the Beloved Country'?"), to the architecture of the ambitious mid-1940's building program at Brown. In the last, Win was aiming at a target very close to home, and his criticism produced a spate of angry letters, mutterings on the *Journal* board of directors, and a dressing down from Sevellon Brown. Win's 14 July 1946 column launched the controversy:

> It is at once evident [from a brochure about the $4 million building program] that more of 18th century Williamsburg is going to get piled up on the Brown campuses in mid-twentieth century . . . The new Pembroke dormitory looks like a dungeon for the Revolutionary-era French upperclass; the interiors put one on the alert for sudden entrance of a bevy of Brown men in silk knee-breeches and flowered waistcoats and powdered wigs, and for Pembrokers mincing about in hooped crinolines. It's all very pretty—and utterly fake . . . Is our time so timid, unimaginative, sterile that we can express ourselves only in assembled fragmentations of these far pasts? . . . Alma Mater, I hail thee with

[16] Ibid., 6 August 1944, sec. 3, p. 6, 3 February 1946, sec. 6, p. 6.

loyal devotion, —but I think thee deserves a good kick in the seat of thy 4-million-dollar pantalettes.[17]

As it seemed to Win, he had merely stated strongly held artistic principles. It did not occur to him that in attacking the architectural plans he was also attacking the accompanying fund drive for millions of alumni dollars; nor did he anticipate that his opinions would be construed as those of the *Journal* itself. Subtly, since his marriage to Eleanor Metcalf, his status on the paper had changed. Overnight, he was expected to be more circumspect. He had not realized that, either: a memorably aroused Sevellon Brown enlightened him.

The marriage had begun with trips to Wawaloam, the Metcalfs' summer place in South County, serving as a honeymoon. "El and I are down county now and I'm paring commuting down to a nice minimum," Scott wrote in May. "We've just been out at the pond side observing what seems to be the mating season of pickerel. They appear to be excited about it, chasing round and round, and floating over each other and/or over eggs." But frankly, he added, unable to resist breaking the mood, "I doubt that it will ever replace fucking." In its natural beauty, the place enchanted Win. Swallows danced over the pond, lady slippers grew abundantly wild in the woods, and sand violets bunched along the woodland roads. "I wonder yet again: Would it be so insane a life to spend it all just sitting around looking at the natural world? Comparatively not, I think."[18] In the fall of 1946, another pair of honeymooners came to stay with the Scotts at Wawaloam: John and Judith Ciardi.

Scott had met Ciardi for the first time in December 1945 at John Holmes's house in Medford, Massachusetts. Tall, dark, well built, aggressive, confident, determined to make money in his impecunious trade, Ciardi was as unlike Scott as another poet could possibly be. But each admired the other's work, and they immediately hit it off. Ciardi wrote the first "general essay" on Win's poetry, for the *University of Kansas City Review*. "If there are ever any more I hope to have as good luck," Win wrote him in gratitude on 2 October 1946. Later in the month Ciardi brought his new bride for a

---

[17] Ibid., 14 July 1946, sec. 6, p. 6, 23 April 1950, sec. 6, p. 10.
[18] WTS to John Ciardi, 15 May 1946, Scott Collection, John Hay Library; WTS, "Bookman's Galley," *Providence Sunday Journal*, 15 June 1947, sec. 6, p. 8.

South County visit, and a subsequent thank-you note, subtitled "The Good Old Days," called up the charm of the place: "Life becomes appallingly complicated, and automatically my mind retreats from the stern and overwhelming present to the memory of times when life was sweetness and light by the shores of Pond Wallaloam (or whatever it is). There in that pastoral setting, with Spot the Great Dane curled peacefully in the sun (after a stiff battle with a cricket), ducks dive in the middle distance, Eleanor the good charms the blonde air and too many dishes, and Win, master of autumn colors, master of martinis, doctor of weather arrangement puffs his thoughtful pipe."[19]

Win began to develop a host's manner which put visitors entirely at ease. Byron Vazakas, a poet who visited the Scotts early in their marriage, was struck by Win's comfortableness. "There was this extra thing about his personality. He was physically and psychologically restful, rounded but not heavy, usually puffing on a pipe, and dressed in the usual corduroy trousers and tweed jacket. He struck me as the gentleman-poet-scholar-teacher type,"[20] and he impressed others in much the same way. Win Scott played the genial host, unmistakably, by his kindness and attentions, approving the guests who came to call. Ben Bagdikian, who also had met Win during the first years of his life with Eleanor, called him "the best host I have ever known." And so he was, when things went smoothly. Let an argument start and he would carefully stroke it to quietness; let someone else commit a social gaffe and he was all courtesy and gentleness, but let *him* do or say the wrong thing and there was no consolation. All of his peacemaking talents were called into service, one evening in 1951, when Mary McCarthy, her husband, Bowden Broadwater, and Elliot Paul came to a dinner party at the Scotts' in Providence. The Bagdikians, also on hand, reconstructed the occasion: Paul, who had recently suffered a heart attack, brought along his secretary-wife-companion and announced that he must leave by 10:30. While Broadwater lay on the floor, stroking a cat, the brilliant and beautiful Miss McCarthy engaged Paul in a fierce argument about the Spanish civil war. Win, as mediator, took the

[19] WTS to John Ciardi, 2 October 1946, John Ciardi to WTS, 7 October 1946, Scott Collection, John Hay Library; WTS, "Bookman's Galley," *Providence Sunday Journal*, 16 December 1945, sec. 6, p. 6.
[20] Byron Vazakas to SD, 14 April 1970.

edge off the argument, drew the combatants to one side, papered things over. But Miss McCarthy's tongue had not been stilled. As Paul, on doctor's orders, prepared to leave after Cognac, she commented sweetly, "Oh, Mr. Paul, I hope you're not leaving just because you lost the argument." Paul turned white with anger, but even then, Bagdikian recalls, Win managed to say something supportive of Elliot without its being a rebuke to Mary. Such tolerance, though, extended only to others, not to himself. During the Ciardis' visit, for example, John spilled his coffee on the rug one day, and Eleanor moaned something about its being her mother's rug. "To hell with your mother's rug, El," Ciardi boomed. "Where's my cup of coffee?" The tension broken, everyone laughed. But Win, had he spilled the coffee, would have been furious with himself, perhaps to forestall the criticism of others.[21]

In March 1947, Holmes and Ciardi were inspired by a rumor of Win's death, followed shortly by a vigorous denial, to commit doggerel elegies to their fellow poet. Holmes's effort, entitled "Elegy That Had to Be Laid Down, or Weep Ye and Bow Down Your Heads for the Lately Late Mr. Scott," contained these couplets:

> He was a good guy, I always thought, but he got
> tooken dead,
> And a letter came from Kansas in which this news
> was said.
>
> Among modrun American poets he had only a very
> few dozen peers.
> And when they told me he was no more I could not
> believe my ears.
>
> Many was the fine conversation full of wit and
> poetry we had,
> Such as, "How about it, Win?" that being his name,
> the one he had,
>
> And he would say "Okay, with a little water," or
> something quick
> Like that, he being always full of bright wit and
> he was no hick.

· · · · · · · · · · · · · ·

[21] Interview, EMS, Santa Fe, 6 September 1969; interview, Ben Bagdikian, Washington, D.C., 15 March 1970.

I was feeling very fine only yesterday, not even
    thinking of Scott,
But today I feel terrible, with the bad news I
    suddenly got.

Henceforth this poem was caused to be written,
    and I am sorry
And every time I shall hear his name I will feel
    bad and worry.

He was a good guy, but he was called to a better
    land of rest.
What is sadder at his comparatively young age than to
    have to go west?

In similar spirit, Ciardi produced his "Elegy for an Abandoned
Elegy for Winfield Townley Scott, Erstwhile Esteemed Friend and
Colleague, Who Churlishly Sabotaged Ten Fertile Elegiac Stanzas
(Long Labored at by John Holmes and by Me) by Telephoning
the Most Bare-faced Denial of a Most Authentic Rumor":

Scott, whom we thought the best,
Is living yet—the beast:
There's nothing now to carve on any stone.
That's ten good stanzas lost
On an inconstant ghost:
Lay that elegy down, John; Scott is on the phone.

.   .   .   .

Oh, there's no one you can trust,
Even dead and in the dust.
I could say—though I won't—we might have known.
After all the tears we've shed
He deserves to be cut dead.
Tear the damn thing up, John; Scott is on the phone.[22]

Win was not yet ready to assume the status of a vital statistic, but
death—and birth—were very much on his mind in 1947. Early in
the year, Bill Gerry died in California. It was with Gerry and Wade
Vliet that Win had started the little poetry magazine, *Smoke*. After
Scott's senior year, when he lived in Gerry's apartment, Bill had
moved to the West Coast, where he continued to write verse and

[22] John Holmes to WTS, 12 March 1947, John Ciardi to WTS, n.d., Scott
Collection, John Hay Library.

short stories, one of which appeared first in the *Yale Review* and then in the Martha Foley and the O. Henry collections of the best short stories of 1946. Gerry "lived always with the excitement of one who expects something wonderful around the next corner," yet in his last letter to Win, in November 1946, he "remarked that if he should die the next day that was all right with him—he was indifferent . . . on the matter." Scott may have suspected self-dramatization on his friend's part. In any case, he did not believe there was any imminent possibility of Bill's death. It came as a shock. Win didn't like sickrooms and tried to shut out unpleasantness. It was easy, he decided, "to write only of the deaths of those who were not one's friends."[23]

On Thanksgiving Day, 27 November 1947, Eleanor gave birth to their first child, Joel Townley Scott, who weighed a healthy eight pounds, seven ounces. El's mother sent a chaise longue for the bedroom, and novelist Edward McSorley sent a telegram which read, "Wonderful news congratulations love. When is the wedding?" Western Union, to the parents' delight, delivered the wire in one of its Sender Requests an Answer envelopes. Temporarily a bachelor, Win took meals with the Swans, with the Cloughs, and with Charles and Deborah Philbrick. Win glowed with fatherhood in a letter to his mother in Haverhill, but another difficulty loomed. On Saturday, after Win had taken Lindsay to a children's play to break the news of his brother Joel's birth, Savila spoke of her financial problems and talked of moving to live with her family in Brooklyn.[24] Leaving the state, however, was one thing Savila had agreed not to do in connection with the divorce; if she decided to move, Win proposed, perhaps they could renegotiate the custody clause so that Lindsay might visit Win and Eleanor openly and for more extended periods. Early in 1948 a lawsuit settled the matter: there would be no change in custody, nor would Savila be allowed to take Lindsay away from Rhode Island. The court battle reopened wounds, and did nothing to improve relations between Win and his first wife.

Drugged and waiting to enter the delivery room in the crowded hospital, Eleanor was nevertheless intent on taking orders "for my

[23] WTS, "Bookman's Galley," *Providence Sunday Journal*, 26 January 1947, sec. 6, p. 6.
[24] WTS to Bessie Townley Scott, 2 December 1947, Scott Collection, John Hay Library.

husband's new book Mr. Whittier and Other Poems, $1.75." Any
who placed orders, however, would have had to wait ten months
before Macmillan (of six books, Win Scott's fifth commercial publisher) brought out the book on 28 September 1948. Once again,
Win stood in Horace Gregory's debt for his favorable report on the
manuscript to Macmillan, though how much of a favor Horace
had done remained in some doubt. In May 1948, Win went to talk
with his publishers in New York and reported to McSorley that
"the people at Macmillan were quite decent—though as Marya
Gregory says, having a book published by them is a lot like dropping
the MS. in a slot. You never, she says, meet anybody at Macmillan
. . . who's ever read your book.—Not literally true, but I see what
she means."[25] Still, Win was grateful enough, for he had learned in
New York "that for a volume of verse to clear expenses it now has
to sell around 3000 copies. When you realize that you can count
almost on one hand practicing, reputable poets any of whose books
will sell even that modest figure, you can see how slim poetry's
chances are with book publishers. . . . Dead or alive, it's a hard
road."[26]

Macmillan introduced Scott, on the dust jacket of *Mr. Whittier
and Other Poems*, as "one of the best of New England's young poets"
and "an heir of the Whittier, Robinson and Frost tradition." The
accompanying picture shows a man of thirty-eight, ubiquitous pipe
in hand, with his face fleshing out, but still slim enough for one
reviewer to note a resemblance to Frank Sinatra. Though the book
did not achieve a Frostian sale, inside its covers appear more of Win
Scott's best poems than in any other book he published.

Following the poetico-historical line of the title poem, Scott composed a bitter dramatic monologue in which the impoverished
Christopher Columbus, dying, damns a fickle public:

> I do not want your praises later on.
> When I am dead I shall rest easier
> In lack of borrowed breathing; and you will
> Be tempted—never doubt—to sweeten up

[25] WTS to Horace Gregory, 2 November 1947, Syracuse University Library;
Horace Gregory to WTS, 14 November 1947, Scott Collection, John Hay Library; WTS to Edward McSorley, 15 May 1948.

[26] WTS, "Bookman's Galley," *Providence Sunday Journal*, 23 May 1948,
sec. 6, p. 10.

Your own names with the fame of praising mine.
Even your scoffing mouths that so reviled me
Can learn again the shape of knew-him-when
And claim a talking share in India.

"Why," the poem's last line asks, "did you hate my finding India?"[27] The theme—recognition and reputation—was one Scott would return to, many times over, in his later poetry. In other poems, Win brought Gert Swasey to life, and lamented the tragic failure of Woodrow Wilson to command public support after World War I. Casting back to his artistic heritage, he wrote of Winslow Homer and of Emily Dickinson, in a poem borrowing its title from Miss Dickinson's own "After Great Pain a Formal Feeling Comes." Like many another late-comer, Win's feelings for Emily Dickinson bordered on adoration, an emotion deeper felt because of the emotions she had denied to herself and sublimated into art:

What is rejected becomes a greater thing.
All things referred draw drama from its size.
So Amherst can become the fabulous sun,
One yard a kingdom and one house a castle,
One room a throne, and dry within that room
One closet be the casket of a name.[28]

Another set of poems in *Mr. Whittier* dramatically condemns any and all wars. "The Ivory Bed" ironically contrasts the union of Venus and Mars with the casual copulation of soldiers and girls on the Green. "Pvt. John Hogg" relates the death of his great-grand-father (demoted from sergeant to private "to make him more common, and therefore more accommodating to poetry") in the Civil War: "It was all for nothing—running through the sweet dust to his death in a fevered bed off New Orleans harbor./Nobody has anything now of his except some blood."[29] Most telling of all is his "Three American Women and a German Bayonet." Here, Win Scott reminds the reader in erotic language of the sterile relationship between Venus and Mars:

---

[27] WTS, "May 1506," *Collected Poems*, pp. 130–131.
[28] WTS, " 'After Great Pain a Formal Feeling Comes,' " *Collected Poems*, pp. 127–128.
[29] WTS, "The Ivory Bed," *Collected Poems*, pp. 148–149; WTS, "Pvt. John Hogg," *Collected Poems*, pp. 149–150.

Outweighing all, heavy out of the souvenir bundle
The German bayonet: grooved steel socketed in its
    worn wood handle,
Its detached and threatening silence.
Its gun-body lost, the great knife wrested to a
    personal particular violence—
Now bared shamelessly for what it is, here exposed
    on the American kitchen table and circled with
    wreath
Of his three women, the hard tool of death.

And while Mary his mother says, "I do not like it.
    Put it down"
Mary the young sister, her eyes gleaming and round,
Giddily giggles as, the awkward toy in her left hand,
She makes impertinent pushes toward his wife who
    stands
Tolerant of child's play, waiting for her to be done.
His mother says "I wish he had not got it. It
    is wicked-looking. I tell you: Put it down!"
His wife says "All right, Mary: let me have it—
    it is mine."
Saucily pouting, primly frowning
The sister clangs bayonet on table; walks out
And her mother follows.

Like a live thing in not-to-be-trusted stillness,
Like a kind of engine so foreign and self-possessed
As to chill her momently between worship and terror
It lies there waiting alone in the room with her,
Oddly familiar without ever losing strangeness.
Slowly she moves along it a tentative finger.
As though to measure and remember its massive,
    potent length:
Death deep, tall as life,
For here prized from the enemy, wrenched away cap-
    tive, his dangerous escape and hers.
Mary his wife
Lifts it heavy and wonderful in her hands and with
    triumphant tenderness.[30]

[30] WTS, "Three American Women and a German Bayonet," *New and Selected Poems* (1967), pp. 58–59.

Fame, art, war: Win Scott's poems touch on these themes, as again on love and on nostalgic backward glances. One such memory, deceptively understated in the spirit of Robert Frost's "After Apple-Picking," Win recounted in "Day of the Russets":

The boy, the man, and the old man in the orchard
Gathered russet apples all day long.

Their feet printed frosty grass of the morning,
Boy's running, man's steady, grandfather's scuff.

The little grove, fragrant with ripened russets,
Took them in just as it took the sun.

Grandfather picked what he reached, father on
    ladder;
The boy filled burlap from the brown-green ground.

There were big fall-defying bees, I remember,
And grackles that kept sorting the field.

Too fast at first for talk, too tired later,
They worked, and also too much at ease.

Afternoon resumed sound of small punches
Apple by apple now not quite so cold.

But the day grayed with the sun southwest,
Northeast the dull clouds beginning to shut.

The boy quit, to start eating the harvest,
Sitting half asleep except chill hands.

Toward the last grandfather went picking
    flowers,
Coming back burdened with asters in the dusk.[31]

The reviews of *Mr. Whittier and Other Poems* baffled Scott. Selden Rodman in the *New York Times Book Review* found in him "a real craftsman working the main stream of American poetry—and working it steadily toward mature accomplishment." But the Kirkus Service ill-temperedly could not but wish that "this talent would at last mature and take some shape of definite outline."[32]

[31] WTS, "Day of the Russets," *Collected Poems*, pp. 152–153; John Ciardi, "Letter from Harvard," *Poetry* 74 May 1949: 112–113.
[32] Selden Rodman, "Verse in the Main Stream," *New York Times Book Review*, 7 November 1948; Virginia Kirkus Service, 1 July 1948. These and other reviews are pasted in Scrapbook 8, pp. 88–118, Scott Collection, John Hay Library.

There were so many contradictions of this sort, in fact, that Scott
devoted an entire "Bookman's Galley" to rehearsing them. In effect,
the reviewers described different books. "The poetry is clear; it is
obscure; it is prosy; it is lyric; it is local; it is universal; it is new;
it is old . . . And what have you if you add it all up? Zero." To the
author, such contradictions were of course frustrating, but Scott
fell short of advocating the abolition of criticism—and his job along
with it. As he confessed at the finish, there was much to be said
against book reviewing, but after all a good deal to be said for it,
too, and besides, on the Sunday the column appeared, he was sitting
"on a beach in Bermuda and not thinking about book reviewing."[33]

Bermuda became for Win Scott a magic place, after that fortnight
at St. George's over Easter of 1949. "Somewhat to the chagrin of
my Yankee conscience," he rhapsodized on return, "I'm finding
re-application to earning a living a very difficult exercise. The died-
and-gone-to-heaven feeling which you have in the islands of Bermuda leaves you stunned, I find, upon return to earth and real
life." It was hard to put his enthusiasm into words. "Writing about
Bermuda seems an almost useless task; a painting of the lily; an act
of supererogation." Still, he found an objective correlative for the
magnificent weather: it had been like "a perfect summer day in
Newport." And in his five-part "Bermuda Suite," he paid poetic
tribute to the islands, where kites traditionally flew, taut strings
humming in the wind, on Good Friday. If the custom did not renew
his faith in God, it did restore Scott's conviction that man did not
and should not, Robinson Jeffers to the contrary, "take second place
to other animal life on this planet":

> Swiftly by ancient custom all
>   over the Bermuda islands
> The sky fills—thousands of many-colored kites
>   staining like marvels of windows the great blue
>   air.
>
> .   .   .   .
>
> Between all lifted hands and the kites such
>   intense power strains,
> Which holds? Which is held?

[33] WTS, "Bookman's Galley," *Providence Sunday Journal*, 27 March 1949,
sec. 6, p. 8.

> The power flows up the strings into the sky out
> of the hands that have set this glory there.
> All faces lifted to love what they have made.
> Even all the islands for this little while
> Lifted between the waters and the sky.

In this passage, Scott later remarked, "I really let loose. And I remember so well—you know you don't often remember things like this, but I remember I wrote it I think it was on a Sunday morning, and I wrote it with tremendous rapidity (I mean the "Kite" section) and came out into the kitchen where Eleanor was getting lunch (this was in Providence) and just hot off the griddle and read it to her and broke down at the end over my own work." Then, apologetically, "I was in a very high state, you know; and I don't usually go around crying at my own work but I broke down, and I still remember that very well."[34]

In the summer of 1949, Win and Eleanor abandoned the idyllic Wawaloam, with its regular comings and goings of Metcalf relatives, for an equally idyllic but less trafficked retreat forty miles due west of Providence in the hills of Hampton, Connecticut. Win cut down his summer schedule to a three-day, Tuesday through Thursday, work week; and the Scotts liked Hampton so much that they stayed on well into the fall "amidst a welter of flaming woods and fired hills." Walking one October morning, and "I hardly expect you to believe this," Win confessed to *Journal* readers, they stumped through roadside brush to discover a field with hundreds of fringed gentians in bloom. "Now I am aware," Scott continued, "that the closest most of us come to the fringed gentian is the laborious memorizing in Grade 6 or thereabouts of a poem by William Cullen Bryant—a bearded old gentleman who lived long ago when, it seems reasonable to suppose, there grew a very beautiful flower named the fringed gentian on which one could hang a moral; flower, like moral, rarely seen since."[35]

In 1949 and 1950, on the heels of the publication of *Mr. Whittier and Other Poems*, Win read occasionally for such groups as the

[34] Ibid., 17 April 1949, sec. 6, p. 8; WTS, "Bermuda Suite," *New and Selected Poems*, pp. 88–93; Donald Dean Eulert, "Winfield Townley Scott: Conversations on Poets and the Art of Poetry" (Ph.D. dissertation, University of New Mexico, January 1969), pp. 155–156.
[35] WTS to Edward McSorley, 12 July 1949; WTS, "Bookman's Galley," *Providence Sunday Journal*, 16 October 1949, sec. 6, p. 8.

Rhode Island Historical Society and the state's colleges. On prestigious occasions he shared the platform with Robert Fitzgerald (a
poet Win very much admired) and John Berryman (a poet he
didn't) at the New School in New York; and with Richard
Wilbur and John Ciardi at Pembroke (Harvard 2, Brown 1, Scott
announced before reading recently composed poems). A solo performance took him to the Elizabethan Club at Yale in February
1950. It was Win's first trip to New Haven, and he renewed acquaintance there with Donald Gallup, curator of the university's
vast American literature collection, and with the witty and sympathetic Norman Holmes Pearson—teacher, critic, editor, anthologist—encourager and friend to Scott, as to so many twentieth-
century writers. There was a delightful lunch at Mory's, with new
Yale president Whitney Griswold at the adjoining table; and the
successful reading that night cemented the admiration of Scott for
Yale, and vice versa. "You now rank by popular acclaim with Eliot
as the two poets most successful at reading their own works," Gallup
wrote in high praise.[36] (Eliot had read his poetry to the massive
postwar class of 1950 in their freshman year, to thunderous applause.)

In March 1950 Scott went to New York with bookmen from
throughout the country for the first presentation of the National
Book Awards. He talked briefly with William Carlos Williams, who
won the first NBA poetry award. There was an opportunity to meet
E. E. Cummings and to chat with Elizabeth Bowen. He and Eleanor
reveled in that most remarkable of Broadway theater seasons: they
saw *Lost in the Stars*, O'Casey's *The Plough and the Stars*, Arthur
Miller's devastating *Death of a Salesman*, Win's favorite, *The
Member of the Wedding*, with the triumphant Ethel Waters, and
finally and least liked, Eliot's *The Cocktail Party*. Like many another theatergoer, Win went to see Eliot's aptly named play after
attending a cocktail party, this one given by Dutton's for out-of-
town critics and publicity people, and he "literally saw double
throughout the play. Coming home—we were walking and it was
snowing—Win lurched to a stop in the center of Times Square and
refused to budge. Cars swerved, honked, cabbies hurled invective,

[36] Donald Gallup to WTS, 24 February 1950, Norman Holmes Pearson to
WTS, 25 February 1950, Scott Collection, John Hay Library; WTS, "Bookman's
Galley," *Providence Sunday Journal*, 19 February 1950, sec. 6, p. 8.

while Win stood his ground stubbornly and insisted 'I want to go
home and roll a red ball across the lawn to my little boy.' " So
Eleanor recalls the evening, most uncharacteristic for a man who
greatly feared that he had never committed a reckless act. "It was
funny & sad & a little scarey."[37] Scott was unaccommodated to New
York: he liked the food and the drink and the theater and the music
and the galleries and the publishers' gossip, but he felt out of place
and insecure there. At times he would lament to Ellie that he'd
never had a Greenwich Village period, but the regret was more
literary than real. He was not tough enough for New York, and
opted in the honesty of liquor for the security of home and family
and rolling a ball across his lawn.

It was in 1950, too, that the work of Winfield Townley Scott,
who had now reached forty, was collected with that of his contemporaries in an anthology called *Mid-Century American Poets*. In the
way of successful anthologies, this one, edited by John Ciardi,
brought Scott's poetry to a much wider audience than his own books
had done. It also solidified his position as one of the generation's
candidates for canonical status. In the anthology he shared space
with Richard Wilbur, Peter Viereck, Muriel Rukeyser, Theodore
Roethke, Karl Shapiro, John Frederick Nims, E. L. Mayo, Robert
Lowell, Randall Jarrell, John Holmes, Richard Eberhart, Elizabeth
Bishop, Delmore Schwartz, and Ciardi himself: a comprehensive, if
not complete, list of distinguished American poets writing in 1950.
"I do believe they are the best of their generation," Ciardi asserted
in his foreword; from wide consultation he drew "the substantial
assurance that no name that incontestably belongs on such a list
has been omitted." In his review, Dr. Williams, a very great poet
of the previous generation, singled out Scott's talent for "fixing the
eye first on the object, an accurate placing of the object to make it
stand up in its private conditions. His work is indispensable to the
make-up of this book." Such praise, and from such a source, gave
heartening assurance to Win Scott, but he knew how fickle and un-
reliable contemporary judgments could be. In the "Bookman's
Galley" for 23 July 1950, he reported the results of an 1884 poll of
the American literary great which ranked Holmes, Lowell, and

[37] WTS, "Bookman's Galley," *Providence Sunday Journal*, 26 March 1950,
sec. 6, p. 8, 2 April 1950, sec. 6, p. 8; EMS to SD, 27 October 1969.

Whittier one, two, three, Henry James thirteen, Mark Twain fourteen, Walt Whitman twenty, and Emily Dickinson (of course) and Herman Melville not at all. "That whole ballot," Scott commented, "was just about perfectly upside-down."[38]

Each poet represented in the Ciardi anthology was asked to submit a statement of his writing principles; Scott's remarks, among the shortest, took the form of a letter to "Dear Jeff," his old friend H. O. Werner. In the letter he worried the problem of discovering his difference from other poets. Without wishing away influences, which were necessary to learning the craft, Scott saw that his first book had been "much disfigured" by persistent reading that took him "farther than ever from knowledge" of who he was. Who was he? What was his difference? Well, he was "against footnotes in poetry, obscure sources of reference, misquotation of older poems, resort to foreign languages, and the general clutter which ensues when intellectuality attempts the primary position." Ideas mattered, but not conclusively: "the emotional power of the poem *is* its power." His vocabulary was basically simple. "I know dazzling effects can be got with the strange and esoteric, but they are not my kind of thing. For me the possibility of richness in the unexpected juxtaposition of common phrases, or of such phrases put at a fresh slant, is always exciting. (I admire Wallace Stevens at his distance —for example—but I love Thomas Hardy, warts and all.)"[39]

So he did not like, for example, the verbal involutions of Henry James. "I tried reading "The Wings of the Dove,' . . . just reissued, and at long last I must confess, if I may make bold to do so, and, indeed, in what may be called some peril of arousing his, no doubt, happy admirers, that I despair of discovering any joy in the style, so, to use the vernacular, backing and filling, or rather, perhaps, pulling and hauling, of Henry—if I may so call him—James." Scott preferred instead the novels of Willa Cather, whose books had in them not only a plainspoken manner but "a solidity, a feeling for

[38] *Mid-Century American Poets*, ed. John Ciardi (New York: Twayne, 1950), pp. xxvi–xxvii; William Carlos Williams, "Voices in Verse," *New York Times Book Review*, 16 April 1950, pp. 6, 28; WTS, "Bookman's Galley," *Providence Sunday Journal*, 23 July 1950, sec. 6, p. 8.
[39] *Mid-Century*, pp. 107–109.

place and people, very like the best of Scandinavian novels."[40] Here, also, though he did not say so in his statement for Ciardi, was a goal Scott strived for himself, and a quality he compulsively sought out in other writers. It helped to account for his extravagant enthusiasm for the novels of Booth Tarkington, with their "flawless surfaces of neighborhood, streets, sectors of middle class society, houses and rooms, and of people," though only, he acknowledged, the surfaces.[41] As with Tarkington, so with Thornton Wilder's *Our Town*, and so with Eugene O'Neill's *Ah, Wilderness*, the film version of which contained a scene which Scott thought,

> . . . no doubt for sentimental reasons, the most beautiful I've ever seen in a movie. Dawn on the little main street. Scarcely any light, but gradually growing, and filled with a drifting mist that floats—hangs— lazily across the road and the white picket fences, the still sleeping houses. Utterly silent. And the silence is held while the light steadily and yet still faintly increases. . . . And then suddenly, somewhere out of sight, a firecracker goes off! Fourth of July! . . It is beautiful, and oh, how it takes you back!

Back he went in memory, then, to the old-style Fourth of July in nostalgic contrast to modern exhibitions of fireworks, to the time when children started pinwheels whirling on the telephone pole, set their own sparklers going to the pungent odor of punk, and pump-pumped their own Roman candles skyward:

> Now it is dark enough
> For fathers to come out
> To firefly-stippled lawns
> And set real sparklers there.
> Be careful, children, say
> Mothers on the porch steps.
> Then the fountains burn.
> Then the fences spin
> With fiery golden whirls.
> Then the night curves tall
> With rockets' arching climb
> And over all the town

[40] WTS, "Bookman's Galley," *Providence Sunday Journal*, 8 December 1946, sec. 6, p. 6, 4 May 1947, sec. 6, p. 8.
[41] Ibid., 26 May 1946, sec. 6, p. 2.

> Their many-colored stars
> Splinter on the sky
> And dwindle slowly back
> Toward damp grass and us
> Though never quite to reach.[42]

Win liked writers, in short, who could transport him on waves of nostalgia back to his own childhood. "The past is always beautiful," he quoted Mark Twain, but realized that "it is made so—wholly so—by deception." Fifteen years later, in an introspective conversation, Scott wondered if his tug toward nostalgia might not represent "a secret longing for irresponsibility—that's what childhood means to a lot of us, and the wears and tears of adult life make the past seem more beautiful than it really was." He could think that, and say it, but such self-perception could not alter his fondness for the nostalgic mood, both in what he read and in what he wrote. Gertrude Stein, he knew, had cautioned against the power of association in literature: "If she wrote 'brook,' she wanted it new, abstract, a Platonic 'brook'; and she did not wish you to call up at her word a particular brook familiar to you." But it was a caution Scott rebelled against: why give up one of the warmest responses to be got from reading? For him, even the names of places carried nostalgic magic; he could conceive of a poem which murmured over and over "Haverhill, Newport, Providence, Peterborough . . . letting it go at that." Perhaps, he admitted, "it is a little too easy for me to slide back into writing out of memories," but slide he did.[43]

In his *Journal* columns he praised the work of Margaret Emerson Bailey, whose *Goodbye, Proud World* was the kind of memoir—a piece of Americana—that especially appealed to Scott. When she died, he wrote a warm reminiscence of her—like Maud Howe Elliott another of the old ladies he so regularly fell in love with. A handsome woman, she had a streak of the actress in her. "I remember her saying happily to me," Win recalled, " 'Why, Jack Cady

---

[42] Ibid., 4 July 1948, sec. 6, p. 8; WTS, "Fourth of July, Old Style," *New and Selected Poems*, pp. 109–110.

[43] WTS, "Bookman's Galley," *Providence Sunday Journal*, 12 November 1944, sec. 6, p. 6; Eulert, "Scott," pp. 160–161; WTS, "*Our Town* and the Golden Veil," *Exiles and Fabrications* (1961), pp. 78–79; WTS, "There Was an English Poet," *Religious Humanism* 2 (Spring 1968): 52.

looks at me as if a circus had come to town!' And so there had."[44]
With such a bias, Win had little tolerance for condescension from
across the sea. When he heard, via Hilary Masters, a young friend
at Brown and the late-begotten son of Edgar Lee Masters, that Irish
poet Patrick Kavanagh thought America "floundering in a cultural
backwash," Scott responded in a "Bookman's Galley": "The likes
of Kavanagh go blandly on mouthing the same sort of insufferable
condescension Yeats himself once got off when he said "Oh, we
never read American poetry." My answer to that is that it's too
damned bad . . . The attitude attempts to preserve a conviction that
the Americans are all very well as sources of royalties and lecture
fees but of course pigs in the parlor when it comes to the creative
arts."

A decade later, Scott ran afoul of that lioness of British letters,
Dame Edith Sitwell. In editing an anthology of British and American poetry, she had entirely—and to Win's way of thinking, incredibly—omitted the work of E. A. Robinson. He wrote a review
of the anthology for the *Saturday Review*, calling attention to the
omission and comparing Sitwell's collection unfavorably to ones
by W. H. Auden and Norman Holmes Pearson, and Louis Untermeyer. "By the way," Dame Edith responded in a sarcastic re-
joinder, "who *is* Mr. Winfield Townley Scott?" Delighted, he included the quotation on the dust jacket of his 1964 book of poems,
Change of Weather.[45]

A handsome and talented older woman whose work Win also
praised was the American novelist Anne Parrish. Week after week
in his column he boosted her book, *Poor Child*, as one of the great
postwar novels. Finally, in 1948, he had an opportunity to meet her.
Alexander Woollcott, he noted, had spoken of her as "the lovely
Anne Parrish"; but he found the phrase inadequate. Win was enchanted by her and by her fiction, which unostentatiously "achieved
some of the sharpest satire and profoundest compassion in contemporary writing." She had that spareness of diction and keen

---

[44] WTS, "Bookman's Galley," *Providence Sunday Journal*, 6 November 1949,
sec. 6, p. 10.
[45] Ibid., 1 January 1950, sec. 6, p. 8; Letters to the Editor, *Saturday Review*,
28 February 1959, p. 23. Scott's review of the anthology appeared in *Saturday
Review*, 3 January 1959, pp. 12–14, 32.

sense of place that so disarmed him. And she wrote with rare understanding, he felt, of love—"love and one kind of failure or another
to sustain it. . . . She has moved from wit to feeling, from sauciness
to pity."[46] It was the direction he hoped to move in his poetry,
renouncing easy cleverness for mature compassion.

Keenly conscious of his role as a localist singing of love and art
and death in an entirely American context, Win received from
Eleanor as a gift for Christmas 1949 a book which reminded him of
his personal literary heritage. The book was *The Private Memoirs
and Confessions of a Justified Sinner*, published in 1824 by his
distant ancestor James Hogg, the Scottish poet known as the "Ettrick
Shepherd." Hogg, like Win's other Scottish forebears, had come
from humble stock. There was a story that he could not read and
write until he was thirty, but that then, thrilled by hearing some
Scottish ballads, he set out to become a writer. He'd written a book
about Sir Walter Scott, who had befriended him, and he had collected and edited books of native songs. And in the novel Eleanor
had found, Hogg produced a study of psychological evil in peculiarly modern terms.

Literary folk were scarce in Win's background, and he may have
overrated the Ettrick Shepherd in consequence. "From slow beginnings," he wrote, his ancestor had become "a very well known man
of letters in his time, productive and prominent."[47] Though writing
of Hogg, Win was exploring his own situation. Would he become
"very well known" in his time? And how could he do so while
spending his workaday energy in the employ of the *Providence
Journal*? Eleanor urged him to make the break, to work for himself,
to produce the long poems the Guggenheims had declined to finance.
There would be no difficulty about money, and Win owed it to himself to see how far he could go, how productive and prominent he
might become as a full-time poet. His job as literary editor seemed
a dead end, and the week-in, week-out chores of assembling the
book page had begun to bore him. Win worried about getting old,
about not accomplishing enough; gradually and painfully he came
round to Eleanor's point of view.

[46] WTS, "Bookman's Galley," *Providence Sunday Journal*, 2 January 1949,
sec. 6, p. 8; WTS, "Anne Parrish's Novels," *University of Kansas City Review*
17 (Autumn 1950): 52–59.
[47] WTS, "Bookman's Galley," *Providence Sunday Journal*, 15 January 1950,
sec. 6, p. 8.

But breaking with the *Journal* was difficult. After twenty years of reviewing books and putting together the book page, he had earned a reputation as one of the nation's best critic-editors. He had adopted the practice of sending writers tear sheets whenever they or their books were mentioned on the book page, and they were properly grateful for this unusual service. "I know of no other publication that is so faithful in this detail," John Winterich wrote, "—it is, of course, perfect public relations (a locution, I hasten to add, that turns my tummy)."[48] What was printed on the tear sheet, of course, was what really mattered. Time and again, authors happily acknowledged reviews, not so much because they were favorable as because they indicated that their work had been read and understood. On the publication of Nathaniel Hawthorne's *English Notebooks*, to take but one example, editor Randall Stewart thanked Win for a review which was "the best—I mean the most intelligent —which the book has had, or, I imagine, is likely to have."[49] As a reviewer, Win tended toward affirmative judgments; he loved books and knew how to savor them. He also had a knack for blending anecdote with criticism, making use of an otherwise not especially valuable memory for trivial information—"how many colors of typewriter Katherine Brush had, how young is Erskine Caldwell's new wife, what's the name of Booth Tarkington's latest French poodle"—to enliven his comments with the specific concrete detail which best suited the case.[50] Irita Van Doren at the *New York Herald Tribune* read and liked his work in the *Journal*; in February 1949 she inquired if Win would like to do occasional reviews for the *Tribune*. Win would, of course, and began a long if erratic association with the New York paper.[51] Scott began in these years to contribute to the *Saturday Review* as well. Whatever his status as poet, by mid-century Win Scott had established himself as one of the most perceptive and prolific reviewers in the country. He was, as anthologist William Cole pointed out, "that very rare thing . . . a

[48] John T. Winterich to WTS, 22 May 1951, Scott Collection, John Hay Library.
[49] Randall Stewart to WTS, 30 December 1941, Scott Collection, John Hay Library.
[50] WTS, "Bookman's Galley," *Providence Sunday Journal*, 29 October 1944, sec. 6, p. 6.
[51] Irita Van Doren to WTS, 3 February 1949, Scott Collection, John Hay Library.

truly literary man, an enormous reader and one who cared deeply about books."[52]

With Scott's leadership, Cole added, the *Providence Journal*'s book page was the nation's best outside of New York. It was a judgment echoed by many, not least the (London) *Times Literary Supplement* in October 1954: "Under the editorship of the poet Winfield Townley Scott and his successor, Mr. Maurice Dolbier, the *Journal*'s page has become the first in New England and is considered by many to be the best in the country. . . . It is in the pages of the *Providence Journal* that middle-brow reviewing makes its closest approach to criticism."[53] Among the regular contributors of *Journal* reviews were Ben Clough, Charles Philbrick, Esther Willard Bates, Frank Merchant, and Dolbier, Win's successor. During the 1950's the *Journal* won a series of Pulitzer Prizes for the distinguished journalism of such staffers as Ben Bagdikian, but by then Win Scott had left the fold. The excellence of the book page preceded that of the rest of the paper.

On 6 May 1951, Scott put together his last book page for the *Journal*, and, as Dolbier recalled, "there was a kind of hush in New York" where publishers had relied so long on the taste and judgment of Scott for intelligent reviews. If there was a phrase to characterize the page, it was its "conspicuous honesty." Literary merit was applauded, promotional efforts were set aside. Clough, in a letter dated that last Sunday, called attention to that honesty and congratulated Win for the long artificial period under B. K. Hart "when he did so much less, you so much more" without reward.[54] In the May 6 issue, Win wrote a long summary, "Mr. Scott Looks Back Across 20 Years of Books." He had worked but one month less than two decades to build the paper's book page.[55] On Tuesday, May 8, Scott came in to clear out his desk, and send a last letter to his mother in Haverhill: "Just now I came downstairs after having a photo taken, and this room was full of people. They gave me tobacco, a new Kaywoodie pipe, and an 1876 edition of Leaves of

[52] Interview, William Cole, New York City, 10 October 1969.

[53] "Book Reviewing for Middle-Brows," *Times Literary Supplement* (London), 17 September 1954, p. lviii.

[54] Ben Clough to WTS, 6 May 1951, Scott Collection, John Hay Library; interview, Maurice Dolbier, Providence, 13 June 1969.

[55] WTS, "Mr. Scott Looks Back Across 20 Years of Books," *Providence Sunday Journal*, 6 May 1951, sec. 6, pp. 1, 6, "Galley," 6 May 1951, sec. 6, p. 10.

Grass, signed by Walt Whitman and with a Whitman letter pasted in. I was completely flabbergasted & found it hard to say anything sensible."[56]

When Win left the *Journal*, he gave up a substantial investment. And he agonized over what others would say. Actually, there was not much criticism. Dorothy Pratt, an old-timer in the news room, said to Eleanor: "Thank God you're getting him out of here before he is carried out feet first the way the rest of us will go." Clough asserted his confidence that Win was doing the right thing. Henry Beston extended the "old Outermost Householder's warmest good wishes . . . for the success of the new venture. I'm so glad you are trying it, and feel that the course you are taking is the only proper one to chart to the silent rock of the Muses." In less rhetorical language, Norman Holmes Pearson sent an understanding letter that Win particularly valued. He would not have to starve, Win had written Pearson, for his wife had money, and he somewhat defensively submitted a list of reasons for quitting his job. "I don't care what the reasons were," Pearson replied,

I only hope that it will actually give you a chance to write. I don't know who will do the starving; but I do know that American poetry has been starving for a long time. It does need people like you, who have their own convictions but don't spend their time drumming up trade for conservative-liberalism or liberal-conservatism or old-new or new-old criticism. In fact almost anything but poetry has prevailed, as you well know. There are plenty of things to be written besides poetry —the book on Whittier you ought to do, etc. etc. But most of all there are the poems. Believe me.[57]

For a man who found it so difficult to believe in himself, the belief of others—and especially of so acute an observer as Pearson—was essential.

Almost no one said he was selling out, but Win imagined voices he did not hear. No one was accusing him but himself, but that inner voice he could not still. Win would be living off his wife's income, and if that did not trouble others, it never ceased to trouble him. The day before he quit, Win drove down to Newport with his

[56] WTS to Bessie Townley Scott, 8 May 1951, Scott Collection, John Hay Library.
[57] Henry Beston to WTS, 24 July 1951; Norman Holmes Pearson to WTS, 10 May 1951, Scott Collection, John Hay Library; EMS to SD, 15 February 1970.

aunt Anna, agonizing over his decision all the way. He was afraid, she remembers, that he had made a terrible mistake. The car wobbled all over the road.[58] The next week, the Scotts—Win, El, Joel, now three and a half, and seven-month-old Susan—moved to Hampton.

[58] Interview Anna (Mrs. George C.) Scott, Providence, 3 July 1969.

Mark Twain said something like this: Once you have remarked of a person that he is a member of the human race, there is nothing worse you can say of him. That—it occurs to me—has become one of my mottoes, and my other is from Stendhal: Try to live without hatred or being afraid.[1]

9. Perils of Freedom

HAMPTON IS ONE of the picture-postcard New England towns. Heading west from Providence on ancient Route 6, you drive past miles of shoddy industrial suburb, stoplighted for better gazing on used-car lots. Finally, there is open country, and forty miles down the road—but no longer *on* Route 6—lies the village of Hampton. Settled in pre-Revolutionary days, the village has a distinctly English flavor: small, neat farms, scattered colonial houses, a sense of order and peace. From 1 January to 22 February 1954, Win Scott recorded his impressions of Hampton in an unfinished narrative called "The Country of a Cloud" (after Dylan Thomas's observation

[1] WTS, "The Country of a Cloud," manuscript (1 January–22 February 1954), p. 48.

in *Quite Early One Morning*: "And one man's year is like the country of a cloud, mapped on the sky, that soon will vanish into the watery, ordered wastes, into the spinning rule, into the dark which is light"). Like many another small town in New England, Scott wrote, Hampton's "land is enormously disproportionate to its population of about 500. . . . But the village itself is concentrated along the crest of the steep hill, 700 feet above sea level and rolling suddenly up from magnificent eastern pasturelands." Substantial and simple houses, the "schoolhouse, a fire station, a garage, the Catholic Church, a Public Library, a little store and the post office," a post office with its own beautifully tended flower beds. "And serene above the town's frequently unserene affairs, the sweet white steeple of the Congregational Church in the center." That was Hampton. What people remember about the village is its hill, and the view of pasturelands below, cows miniaturized, though quite near, by a drop in altitude unusual in that part of the country. "Oh, yes, that town on top of the hill."[2] It is no stretch of rhetoric to call Hampton beautiful; Win Scott though it looked like a re-creation of Grover's Corners, New Hampshire, in Thornton Wilder's *Our Town*.

The Scotts lived several miles south of the center of town, on a road which dead-ends after passing their house. The lawn slopes to the rear, with gardens where Ellie used to garden topless on warm summer days, and a pond. No other house is in sight; only dense woods and a quality of quiet isolation delicious to the bombarded senses of city dwellers. Here, Scott came to pursue the life of poetry, full time, for its own sake and for the satisfactions it might bring him. A poem, "Exercise in Aesthetics," tells of driving down an ill-populated Connecticut road in December and passing a house, "three miles from the last/ And, as it turned out, three miles from the next" but yet festooned with Christmas candles and ribboned door-wreath:

> My question was
> Whom were all the Christmas signals for—
>
> . . . .
> At most a stranger or two passed once a day,
> Like us, in a moment passing. For us, then?

[2] WTS, "Cloud," pp. 6–7.

Yes, if we happened by. But of necessity
First for the mingled joy of decoration
And whoever made it. How else could it be?[3]

Since 1949, Win and Eleanor had spent their summers in this
house, but when they moved there intending to stay, in the spring
of 1951, certain alterations were required: the place had been built
two centuries before, in 1751. Vivid new painting and papering
covered the walls, the milkshed became the kitchen, the old kitchen
with its six-foot fireplace was transformed into the dining-room.
Most radical of all, the Scotts built a modern addition to accommodate their furniture from Providence and about three thousand
books. Ira Rakatansky, a young architect who had studied under
Walter Gropius, was given the commission—and instructions. Win
and Eleanor did not wish to imitate colonial architecture. Here was
a simple eighteenth-century country house: would he add to it a
simple mid-twentieth-century wing? Rakatansky cut into the land,
so that his proportionally large addition would not loom; he con-
structed a small passageway from old to new, and he put up huge
south windows opening on a brick terrace. "Ira," as Scott remarked,
"put the whole thing *into* the earth" (much as Win's idol Frank
Lloyd Wright would have counseled); ". . . altogether it is a beautiful room." Not everyone in Hampton agreed: the convention was
to extend real colonial with fake colonial, following the example of
the Brown University building program. "Have you seen what an
awful thing the Scotts have done to that lovely house?"[4]

Exactly one week after leaving his job at the *Journal*, and on the
sixty-fifth anniversary of the death of Emily Dickinson, Win made
a pilgrimage to Amherst, where he sought, and found, a kind of
inspiration. His account of that day, in "The Country of a Cloud,"
follows:

A couple of springs ago E. [Eleanor] and I drove up through the
Connecticut and Massachusetts countryside to Amherst. Apple blossoms
and lilac all the way and a singing ballet of robins and thrushes in the
flawless sun. It was May 15, the sixty-fifth anniversary of Emily Dickinson's death; such a day as Thomas Wentworth Higginson's journal
described in recording her funeral:

3 WTS, "Exercise in Aesthetics," *New and Selected Poems* (1967), p. 87.
4 WTS, "Cloud," pp. 1–4.

"The country exquisite, day perfect, and an atmosphere of its own, pure and strange, about the whole house and grounds—a more saintly and elevated 'House of Usher.' . . . E.D.'s face a wondrous restoration of youth—she is 54 [correction: 55] and looked 30, not a gray hair or wrinkle, and perfect peace on the beautiful brow. There was a little bunch of violets at the neck and one pink Cypripedium; the sister Vinnie put in two heliotropes by her hand 'to take to Judge Lord.' " . . . I think it is Millicent Todd Bingham who remembers how small Emily's coffin looked as workmen carried it from Squire Dickinson's house across the fields to the graveyard; and the coffin was blanketed with sand violets.

I had stopped at Amherst, and only briefly, once or twice before. I love the town, though, and regard it as a model New England college town. On that May day it was peaceful under its new-leafing elms, its old houses facing each other across the immense run of Green that leads up to the campus. We strolled the campus and rested awhile within the most understated, moving war memorial I have ever seen. It is simply a great circle of stone laid into a hillcrest which looks abruptly down on a baseball field—the boys were playing there—and straight out across the land to a sawtooth run of mountains. Center, there is a solid wheel of slate sunk into the ground and on it in concentric circles the names of the Amherst dead in the two world wars. At intervals around the terrace are low stone benches carved with the names of famous battles; you read Chateau Thierry and, also, Okinawa. By noon the day had shot up into a heat wave, and the campus turned gods-like with half-dressed undergraduates lolling in windows and doorways—looking so brown and handsome and everlastingly young.

Apple blossom and lilac everywhere. We walked over to the Dickinson house and I sat literally inside the enormous hedge that fronts the street while E.—who will walk in anywhere, especially if it's private—shifted here and there in the garden and took pictures. A maid came out the backdoor and told E. the lady of the house would ask us in but her husband (a clergyman, I think) had died within a few days. . . . Richard Merrifield, great-grandson of John Wilkes Booth, told me he once did visit the Dickinson house and he was "surprised at how small Emily's room was." I know what he means. We both know better. But one understands the surprise. *All that out of this?* Then one resumes the sense of scale, remembers the tiny shack at Walden Pond, and how drama can "make a little room an everywhere."

Emily everywhere. I spent the day obsessed with her. Years before I had written and published a poem about her and her town, dancing her all over it; but only now had I walked into my own poem and sat down in it. Better still, into Emily's own poetry and the tactile sense of her life as close as my hand. But what I had imagined was reality. Many years ago, when I was in my twenties, I conjured up a similar emotion in the garden of Keats' house in Hampstead outside of London. After viewing the pictures, locks of hair and other mementos in the house I went out and sat alone for a long while, looked at the sprawled and propped-up ancient mulberry tree in which, perhaps, that nightingale sang for him one day and for us ever since and forever, and did nothing except *be there*. None of this, I know, has anything to do with criticism, new or old or higher; it merely has to do with literature.

From the time I was a youngster and first read Emily and fell in love with her, I have always felt I knew her perfectly well. There is the mystery of her genius, yes; but genius is always mysterious. I have never felt anything mysterious about Emily herself or her way of life. How pensions and state aids and social security and women's jobs and rest homes have changed the Yankee way of life I have yet to learn; but any New Englander my age—I was born in 1910—is sure to have known one or more of those valiant spinsters who lived a housebound existence caring for an aged father or mother: an existence deeply if sterilely rhythmical, year in and year out, with serving three meals a day, baking and mending, washing and ironing, tending the furnace, nurturing a garden bed in summer, shoveling the snowed-in walks in winter, and wearing out their lonely lives at the dictate of the parent who sometimes survived them. What pathetic, brave, admirable old maids! Emily's life was far less hard than these, but her day-to-day business suggests a thousand resemblances; and if she seemed a little cracked, so too did her untalented kind of whom I knew in my childhood more than one, and one I well knew loved and cared for me in a way which, now I understand it, moves me with a lifelong sad gratefulness. An unpayable gratefulness, for she died before I was 16; it was I who found her dead on the floor of the cold kitchen, the oil lamp still burning palely on the table in the February sunlight, and the paralyzed, 90-year-old mother calling and calling from the next room at last in vain. Like Emily, she was 55. And I have always thought, having been close to such a woman, that I knew—as I say—perfectly well what it would be like to walk into that Amherst garden and (if she did not flee) talk to Emily as she knelt on her Civil War blanket and fussed with the weeds among the tulips; or follow her into the kitchen fragrant with the gingerbread which, she just remembered, should be ready to take out of the oven.

Was I that day the only one in Amherst obsessed with Emily? Did anyone there recall it was Emily's death-day? Her niece Mme. Bianchi was dead. Mme. Bianchi's house nextdoor—Austin Dickinson's Gothic-wooden house which, I had heard, was to be torn down—still stood at the end of the path wide enough for two. Violets and lilies of the valley crowded along. (Robert Frost told me he once addressed that lady as *Mrs.* Bianchi and she never afterward spoke to him.) The center of the town as we returned to it, midafternoon, was busy with traffic and perspiring shoppers. Where was Emily?

"Called Back," her gravestone says. Except for the whirr of a work-man's lawnmower in a distant corner, the cemetery stayed still and unvisited all the hour or more we sat in the cypress shade at the Dickinson lot. It is a Squire's lot: iron fenced and gated; and the stones face very close to the iron—E. found it all but impossible to get decent photographs. The Squire and Mrs. Dickinson, poor badgering and badgered Lavinia who did *not* burn Emily's papers—to whom we owe everything; Lavinia, who alone among these dead had had knowledge of the immortality which illumined all of them; and Emily, that near-ness happening. I found at one edge of the cemetery a clutch of butter-cups, that most childhood among flowers, and brought them to her small ground. They lay bright and alone in the sparse grass above the long hidden Cypripedium, the bunch of violets and the two heliotropes. "This quiet dust was gentlemen and ladies . . ." How near we were for that little while. How much better I seemed to know her than many a person with whom I had talked.

Well, we did not strain our piety. We went to the Inn and sat in the garden there and drank Tom Collinses until "about 6"—Emily's time of departure on that day sixtyfive years before. Then in the special brightness of early evening we drove through the supper-hushed town and headed southeast toward Connecticut; and soon under a "May mess" of stars through the tunnels of lilac-apple fragrance all the way down that beloved countryside. I felt we had really been somewhere, touched something, almost seen.[5]

So that Win might have a place to work, undisturbed by children, pets, and telephones, Eleanor arranged to have a ten-by-ten-foot cedar shack built in the woods, a quarter of a mile from the house. Carved behind the door is the inscription, "17 July 1951, WTS from EMS." On the wall, the peeled-egg picture of Shakespeare (Scott always and insistently spelled it Shakspere) and a chip of wood from Henry Beston's Outermost House on Cape Cod. On the

[5] Ibid., pp. 12–15. An amended version of this account, "A Pilgrimage to Am-herst," appeared in the *Emily Dickinson Bulletin* (December 1970): 88–91.

desk, a big dictionary and a pencil sharpener. There Scott wrote his poems as always in penciled, nearly opaque longhand, then typed them out with one finger only—despite his years in the newspaper business, he had never learned to type any other way. (Prose he wrote on the typewriter, directly.) A wood stove heated the shack, and he worked there except when the weather turned bitter cold, or when his pencil refused to budge: "There is a great deal of sitting on the tail, waiting for things to get moving. An awful lot of looking out the window. But . . . I think there has to be all this apparent loafing and sitting around for eventual concentration."[6] So he put it in an interview for *Yankee*, but in fact that "apparent loafing" troubled him more than he would confess. According to Frank Merchant, Win "never realized that you can't write poems on a schedule, never abandoned the concept that poetry has to be a job."[7]

For the first time, Win was free to write, to work for himself and for whatever niche in posterity he might carve out, to strive full-time for the fulfillment of that ambition which had visited him in Haverhill High School more than a quarter century before. The link between 1924 and 1951 he spelled out in "Coleridge," a tribute to the poet who had awakened him to his destiny.

> Old father, blessed ghost, mariner
> Of my launching, fixer of the bloody sun
> Round which my condemned and lifelong voyage
> Serves and follows—follows again, ignorant
> What tropic oceans, what icy straits
> Hide ahead, or winds across the magnet
> Shudder deeper than engines, or tides
> Trouble the ways before the invisible pole
> Set under that unsetting sun:
>
>   old talker
> Glittering through my childhood—voice and eyes
> Compellent to hold, to send me out to
> Find home by way of Vinland, India, by
> Horns of undiscovered coasts that sounded

---

[6] Quoted in Richard D. Estes, "Full-Time Poet," *Yankee* 16 (September 1952): 31.
[7] Interview, Frank Merchant, Atlanta, 7 November 1969.

Music undeniable till the sea
Flamed with mirage that grayed all gold:
                                        old
Detective of death in the boy's hand in the lane—
Resolve my life again. By this invocation
Invoke me—blessed ghost, old father.[8]

The mood is one of resumption, of following "again" the icy or
tropic course where Coleridge, the Ancient Mariner, might lead his
enraptured disciple, "condemned" to a life of poetry. "Not that I
had ceased writing," Win explained, "but after twenty years of
newspaper work I was at last free to resign and to use my life, so far
as I was able, as my own." The poem, he wrote, was "a particular
case in point" of "that temptation, not too frequently offered us . . .,
to talk about ourselves."[9] But with what control, what restraint, did
Scott succumb to the temptation! Facing backward to that November day in 1924 and looking ahead with poignant accuracy to the
storms which would buffet his remaining years, "Coleridge," like
many other poems, is valuable as a gloss on the life of Winfield
Townley Scott. But only a few readers could possibly have known
what the ghost of the poet-mariner meant to him. "Sometimes,"
Jeff Werner told Win, "I wish that you would speak out more, and
this wish, more likely than not, because in some . . . poems I listen to
you talking to me and in others I only see you, at night, bent over
a table such as the one in Slater [Hall, at Brown], with a goose-neck
lamp, and a house gone to bed, and the world is only a vacuum outside the light of that lamp. You sit cross-legged, hair mussed, not
happy."[10] Very rarely, until late in his life, did Win Scott speak as
openly about himself in poetry as he had in person to Jeff Werner:
something was held back, few incautious leaps taken.

His poetry, for example, did not explore the reservations he
harbored about his new-found leisure and isolation. "Much is said

      [8] WTS, "Coleridge," New and Selected Poems, p. 94. The line, "Detective of
death in the boy's hand in the lane—" refers to the meeting of Coleridge and
Keats near Highgate and the older man's observation, once Keats had left, that
"there is death in that hand."
      [9] WTS, "Three Self-Evaluations," Beloit Poetry Journal Chapbook 2 (1953),
pp. 25–27.
      [10] H. O. Werner to WTS, 25 June 1945, Scott Collection, John Hay Library,
Brown University.

about the value, the necessity of solitude for the writer," he set down in his literary notebooks. "I believe all of it, and at last I am able to have a great deal of time to myself. Yet this kind of life has also a danger which I think is seldom if ever commented upon, and that is that a poet's standards may relax if he is so much by himself as to have no give-and-take with other minds, creative or critical, as absorbed in the seriousness of literature as his own. To be much by one's self is to be much bemused of course with one's own thoughts; and what a short step it can be to bemusement with what is easily written"[11] Especially, there was such a danger for Win Scott, who avoided close critical conversations. In Hampton he had met the writer and critic R. W. Stallman, teaching at the University of Connecticut in nearby Storrs. Stallman, who admired Win's work, proposed that they examine and discuss each other's work; Scott backed away from the exchange. Daily put to the task of himself, he was visited by persistent self-doubt. In November 1951, after six months in "retirement," he confided to Horace Gregory, "Actually I feel pretty shapeless and, probably in reaction to the resignation, have frequent sessions of wondering if my life is one long self-deception. I would like to know if this is not rare among writers."[12]

Persistent rejections from publishers exacerbated his self-doubt. The Hampton period, 1951–1954, formed the middle years in a long publishing drought which stretched from *Mr. Whittier and Other Poems* in 1948 to *The Dark Sister* a decade later. "Here I am, at forty-one," he reflected, "at last divorced from a paid job, free to be a writer—and once again I have no publisher. Five books, five publishers. And I have to begin all over again. Poets can't be choosers." His experience, he realized, was "probably not untypical," but it was nonetheless discouraging.[13] He came to Hampton with several book ideas in mind. He buckled down to turn out yet another version of *The Dark Sister*, the long Norse-voyage poem he had first begun in 1938. He had written enough shorter poems to

[11] WTS, *"a dirty hand": The Literary Notebooks of Winfield Townley Scott* (1969), p. 42.
[12] WTS to Horace Gregory, 5 November 1951, Syracuse University Library.
[13] WTS, *"a dirty hand,"* p. 32; WTS, "Poet or Peasant? Why Do Book Publishers Duck into Earmuffs When the Muse Twangs the Lyre?" *The American Writer* 1 (December 1952): 6.

fill up a small book. He assembled "Poems: 1932–1952," on the philosophy, as he confided to Bill Cole, "Why not take *all* of me?— In short, if *that* don't dismay a publisher, I don't know what will: but I'm tired of being on the dismayed end."[14] Dismayed he remained, however: Macmillan rejected the collection of short poems, repeated versions of *The Dark Sister* found no reception, no one was interested in the collected poems. John Hall Wheelock at Scribner's nibbled at *Sister* in 1954, but he warned that the house could not bring out the book for at least two years. Win was willing enough, but apparently Scribner's had second thoughts, and his decade as unbooked though full-time poet stretched out its painful length.[15] "I'm usually in the doldrums these days—" he wrote in May 1953 to Lee Anderson, who had brightened a Hampton afternoon by recording Scott reading his poems for the Library of Congress "—for no more original reason than that I'm looking for a publisher . . . and a kind word is like an unexpected bone for an old dog."[16]

Even the periodicals seemed less receptive, including the old reliable *Poetry*. "My god, things are tough all over," he wrote Merchant in April 1953. "I've just had the most in-F-able (I just thought of that!) rejection note from K. Shapiro . . . KS replies: This interested us very much and we considered taking it, but on rereading I have decided to ask to see other material. . . . Isn't that peachy? Meanwhile, sour & aging, I read his magazine, full of Jesus, Mary, most of the saints, and much of the bad writing now extant, & think Oh, well."[17] The *Paris Review* turned down a group of poems because he was "too well established." "Oh grave," this to Gregory, "where is thy sting?"[18] Win was appalled by (and may have blamed his lack of acceptance on) the literary-poetic politics of New York:

The sucking-up to editors and anthologists, the behind-scenes plots to put over this one or that, the homosexual links, the reputable

[14] WTS to William Cole, 23 October 1951.
[15] WTS to H. O. Werner, 10 February 1954, Scott Collection, John Hay Library.
[16] WTS to Lee Anderson, 27 May 1953, American Literature Collection, Beinecke Library, Yale University.
[17] WTS to Frank Merchant, 7 April 1953.
[18] WTS to Horace Gregory, 15 July 1954, Syracuse University Library.

houses publishing books of poems paid for by such authors as can afford it; and so on. So much maneuvering! I said to H.G. [Gregory]: "But don't all these people see that all this activity is nothing? That the only thing that lasts, the only thing that counts, is the work itself, well done?" He smiled patiently at me as he does whenever, I suppose, he thinks I am both correct and naive. "That," says Horace, "isn't what they want. They want power." "But it doesn't make sense." "No."[19]

He took heart from the reassuring example of Dr. Williams, whom he had visited in New York in January 1952: "I can't tell you how seeing you and *on the other hand* seeing the feverish ruckus of literary NY recharges my arrogance—reaffirms my conviction that the one & only important thing is, mostly, to stay home on one's behind keeping at 'the poem' (as you would say) the best one can. If one is self-mistaken, that's sad, or a little sad; but in any case all the rest is such waste & distraction—*that*, anyhow, is not the way to fail."[20] He stuck to his last.

Though Win Scott enjoyed little success with book publishers during his Hampton years, he solidified his position as a man of letters through readings, reviews, and several stints as a contest judge. Over Thanksgiving, in 1951, on a visit to Haverhill, Win renewed acquaintance with Dudley Fitts. As a boy visiting Haverhill, Win had once shared a house with the somewhat older Fitts, and had predictably pulled Dudley's sister Jane's pigtails. "Come prepared to Lay Plans for a Haverhill Renescence," Fitts wrote Win, the two of them "now the only extant Haverhill poets."[21] The men got along splendidly; both in 1952 and 1953 Fitts invited Win up to Phillips Andover to read his poetry and talk with the prep school students. Early in the winter of 1953 Win performed on a New York YMHA poetry center bill honoring E. A. Robinson. Malcolm Cowley gave a précis of Robinson's career; Lawrance Thompson "shook a little New Criticism around the Tilbury Town poems"; actor Walter Abel "did" *Flammande* and *Ben Jonson Entertains*, and Win "chatted . . . of odds and ends of personal recollections" and read his elegy for Robinson.[22] In 1954, Scott served as Brown's Phi Beta Kappa poet.

[19] WTS, "*a dirty hand*," p. 69.
[20] WTS to William Carlos Williams, 2 February 1952, American Literature Collection, Beinecke Library, Yale University.
[21] Dudley Fitts to WTS, 2 November 1951, Scott Collection, John Hay Library.
[22] WTS to Frank Merchant, 7 April 1953.

One of the advantages of leaving the *Journal*, Win had thought, was that it would enable him to read more widely and think more deeply before committing to print his impressions of other writers and their books. And, as it turned out, he reviewed books less often but more carefully. For the *Virginia Quarterly Review* he turned out omnibus reviews of new books of poetry. For the same publication, he wrote a thoughtfully incisive study of *Our Town* ("Mr. Scott," Wilder acknowledged to Essie Bates, "is the first person to have put on paper a recognition of the fact that the play is in counterpoint between the particular and the universal and he has found striking ways of calling attention to it").[23] For the *University of Kansas City Review* he composed an exhaustive analysis of the novels of Anne Parrish.[24] He continued, also, to contribute reviews to the *New York Herald Tribune* and the *Saturday Review* from time to time. In May 1953, *Time* contacted him about the possibility of becoming a part-time reviewer. The post, he learned, "would call for somebody willing to attend a book conference" in New York every Friday afternoon. "It would mean reviewing one book a week, and the compensation works out to something like a permanent double Guggenheim." The prospect was an alluring one to Scott, who had been "lowering & lowering in a mood of despondency," but he did not pursue the job, since to do so would have made it too easy to skimp the poetry. "I mention the mood of despondency," he told Merchant, "—the oh-hell-who-gives-a-goddam-if-I-never-write-another-line: why-try-anymore?—because I was tempted and disturbed for a couple of days." Then he sat down and wrote "Thanks very much, but No."[25]

Win and Eleanor made it a regular practice to spend a week or more in New York each winter. The new plays and old favorite restaurants called them, but so did more strictly literary matters such as the National Book Awards. Win served as judge for the 1952 NBA poetry award on a panel which included Wallace Stevens

[23] Thornton Wilder to Esther W. Bates, 16 March 1953, Scott Collection, John Hay Library. See WTS, *"Our Town* and the Golden Veil," *Exiles and Fabrications* (1961), pp. 78–91.

[24] WTS, "Anne Parrish's Novels," *University of Kansas City Review* 17 (Autumn 1950): 52–59.

[25] Jack Tibby to WTS, 18 May 1953 and 25 May 1953, WTS to Jack Tibby, 23 May 1953, Scott Collection, John Hay Library; WTS to Frank Merchant, 27 May 1953.

and Conrad Aiken. He went into the meeting determined to boost
Horace Gregory for the award, but Stevens and Aiken were 100
percent for the eventual winner, Marianne Moore, and Stevens,
"quite a steamroller," dominated the meeting. "I made my pro-
Gregory (not for a moment anti-Moore) speech; tried to say why—
in a negative way—since Williams & Stevens had had the Award
—it might be wise to shift to another generation ('ungallant,' said
W. Stevens)—& why in a positive way [Gregory] deserved the
Award (though I said at all times that of course M. Moore's getting
it was a perfectly highclass business: I would not oppose her per se;
etc.) The voluble one—S—took the trouble to reply ('these younger
men will have their turn in time' etc)—& even after some interval
resumed a sort of judicial rebuttal; Aiken Amen-d; but of course my
speech actually got nowhere & I knew it wouldn't." After the meeting, poet and executive Stevens, very handsome in gray fedora and
dark blue Chesterfield, made a phone call, announced "I'm going
to see a girl," and was off.[26] A few weeks later, upon meeting Auden
in Providence, Win mentioned that he had seen Stevens recently
and Auden replied, "Are you in the insurance business, too?" Win
tried to rationalize the slight ("In any case, he struck me as the sort
of person not really interested in people"), but it hurt. In *a dirty
hand*," Scott took his not entirely just doggerel revenge:

> *To Mr. A.*
> Our poems keep separate domains
> However fame befalls.
> Sir, you write yours with your brains
> And I mine with my balls.[27]

In 1953 and in 1954 Win was asked to decide on the merits of
candidates for the Bollingen Prize in Poetry. A prospect for the
1952 award was Theodore Roethke, who had taught Eleanor at
Bennington and whose work and personality ran counter to Scott's
tastes. (Win may, too, have been influenced by his persistent and
admitted inability to admire the poetry of contemporaries, with
certain notable exceptions: Robert Fitzgerald, Richard Eberhart.)
Meeting Katherine Anne Porter, another on the committee, prior to

---

[26] WTS to Horace Gregory, 31 January 1952, Syracuse University Library.
WTS, "*a dirty hand*," p. 40.
[27] WTS, "*a dirty hand*," p. 36.

the judging, Win mentioned the collected poems of Roethke. "Oh, yes," said Miss Porter. "Well, I won't vote for him." Scott said, "Wallace Stevens won't vote for him. And I won't vote for him." "Good!" Miss Porter responded, waving her highball glass. "Good! Let him bring out his old book for all we care:"[28]

Stevens and Win were on the committee again the following year, along with Randall Jarrell and Marianne Moore. Miss Porter, who was ill, was unable to serve. In "The Country of a Cloud," Scott records his impressions of the January 1954 Bollingen session at Yale. He was put up overnight at Davenport College, that architectural stupidity, "Georgian on its exterior facing the campus, Gothic along the street," where he was gratified to learn that the pretty leaded casement windows admitted sharp draughts. Otherwise, his suite was luxury itself: two bedrooms, large bathroom, book-lined sitting-room, a great living-room with more bookshelves and comfortable furniture, framed prints, rich rugs, many lamps. "The effect of it all was to increase the extreme, sweating nervousness I cannot avoid whenever I have to venture out alone into a strange world. I walked and walked the floor. I took a hot shower. I changed into other clothes. I wrote a letter. I looked at books and resisted the temptation to steal an autographed, limited, and uncut copy of Thornton Wilder's plays: after all it had the Davenport College bookplate in it. A wonderful suite in which to throw a party, but there was no party. I stared out the draughty windows."

Finally, at six o'clock, Donald Gallup drove him off to the dinner party at librarian James Babb's house. Among the guests were Yale professor Maynard Mack "and his very pretty wife; the Cleanth Brookses—I had expected to meet an icily severe critic and was charmed by a mild bunny of a man; and Robert Penn Warren and his wife Eleanor Clark. After dinner Thornton Wilder and his sister Isabel dropped in." And, of course, Stevens and Jarrell: Miss Moore would come up for the committee meeting in the morning. Some of this company Win had met before, but he nonetheless tended to regard himself as having approached close to heaven when in the presence, as on that evening, of such literary lights as Wilder and Stevens. On the one hand, he felt their equal; on the other, he was nearly consumed by the fires of hero-worship and would not let go unreported the exchanges between the two men:

Whenever I encounter Wallace Stevens—I have met him two or three times, all within recent years—I am never sure I meet the poet; perhaps momentarily; but chiefly the successful vice president of a Hartford insurance company. He is a big man, the massive, close-cropped head, the ruddy face, set upon a tall and heavy body. Add to this his poetic reputation. Add again Stevens' flat-out way with his very decided opinions. And altogether he dominates any room and company.

Thornton Wilder, whom I also admire greatly and whom I was delighted to meet, was a complete contrast. While Stevens, making a miniature of the little brandy glass he held, sat hugely, impassively founded, Wilder was a percher on edges, a waver of hands, a bouncer-up—slight, quick, all animation. Wilder was correctly deferential to the older man. Nevertheless with Wilder's appearance in the living-room we had two Generals at the party; this has always been thought socially unwise. And I suspect Mr. Stevens knows about this.

In any case it was good luck for the rest of us, and Wilder's various enthusiasms careened only once into the Stevens wall. Via Jarrell, Wilder began glowing conversation about Gertrude Stein but quickly abandoned it when Stevens said he thought her a self-deceived Buddha who conceitedly expected all other people to make pilgrimages to her and kneel at her feet.

Wilder spoke of having gone over a great number of John Marin's paintings. "Beautiful! Beautiful!" Stevens said, "Yes—but he depended too much on reality." And there was the poet for the moment. The remark may or may not be valuable as to Marin's watercolors but it leads directly—or you may say the obverse of it does—to Stevens' poetry. And I remembered once hearing a fantastic story of Stevens calling on Robert Frost one winter in Florida when the two vacationed, as it happened, near each other. Stevens had said, "Frost, the trouble with you is, you don't know Latin"; but also: "Frost, the trouble with you is, you write about *things*." Frost replied, "The trouble with you is, you write bric-a-brac." Months later, back in New England, Frost—who by the way is an excellent Latinist—received a beautiful black-leather-bound Latin Dictionary from Stevens and, subsequently, a copy of Stevens' new book, inscribed "To Robert Frost from Wallace Stevens —more bric-a-brac." So at least I was told.

. . . .

When Stevens referred to a French paper he has long subscribed to, the much-traveled Thornton Wilder made an allusion to something in Paris. "I don't know," Stevens said, "I've never been to France." Wilder was electrified. He waved his arms. He looked rapidly back and forth from Stevens to me. "Why," he stammered, "why—that's impossible! In your poems—the references—the élan—the bouquet—!" Stevens grinned and said "It just goes to show what an old faker can do. . . ."

I spoke of my plan to go to the Southwest for a year. Wilder said "I'll give you a letter to Mabel if you like." Meaning Mabel Dodge Luhan. "Those fires are pretty well banked now." Stevens, looming over me, surveyed me for a moment. "Mr. Townley," he said—I did not mind this occasional slip, since also he now and then addressed Jarrell (whose poetry he admires) as "Mr. Randall"—"Mr. Townley," he said, "I don't think you'll like the Southwest. You're built rather like me, and I couldn't breathe there. I was all right in the daytime, but at night I couldn't breathe."

The Brookses popped back in, having gone off for the evening with the Warrens to see T. S. Eliot's *The Confidential Clerk*, trying out in New Haven before its opening in New York. Brooks liked the play but Wilder, who had seen it the night before, was vehemently against it. "*Ladies Home Journal* concepts tricked out in Eliot style," he said. Again he was surprised; it was discovered that, besides never having seen Paris, Stevens had never met Eliot. "I tend to avoid that sort of thing," Stevens said. Then he said a thing which amazed me, coming from a poet so established in style, "I don't read Eliot," he said. "Eliot's a very potent influence, and if the least glimmer of him got into my work it would be detected at once."

The following morning, the Bollingen Prize committee voted to give the honor and the $1,000 to W. H. Auden. But not before Stevens had "laid about him in all directions," summing up one contemporary as "a mixture of Dryden and Josh Whitcomb Riley," another as "just a poetry machine," a third as "a professional. A book like that is deliberately written to get the Bollingen Prize." Most painful to Win Scott was the dismissal of E. E. Cummings, who, he thought, should get the prize. Jarrell said, "Oh, well, Cummings, it is April and I am in love." And Stevens said, "Ah, it is April, period." And that was that. Even Marianne Moore, gently presiding at the head of the table (Stevens had appointed her), said a little wistfully, "I suppose Estlin *is* something of a cooky-cutter." The day was rescued for Scott, however, when Miss Moore, "looking like your nicest schoolteacher or your most understanding librarian," told him she'd liked some of his poems. "It wasn't somebody just being pensive," she told Win. And at the last Stevens relaxed, unexecutive. "You know," he said, "I think the country needs a poet who is just that and nothing else. We have poets in the insurance business, and poets teaching in college. It's time we had a poet—off in a village, a Hampton, Connecticut—who does nothing but think of his life: that is to say, of his poetry." Win thought of Robinson Jeffers, and wondered why his colleagues never seemed to think of him, working steadily and alone on his poetry in Carmel. But he thought of himself, too. Stevens, he decided, had said a beautiful thing: "nothing but think of his life: that is to say, of his poetry."[29]

Hampton had its own literary-academic subculture, made up of nearby residents who taught at Storrs: Stallman, John Malcolm Brinnin, J. C. Levenson, one year Richard Eberhart. But the Scotts' closest friends were not among these. Dearest of all to Win was Essie Bates, Robinson's former amanuensis at the MacDowell Colony. Essie was the kind of woman who took it upon herself to organize the village children's Christmas play . . . and to cast Joel Townley Scott as an angel. Win went to the dress rehearsal on Saturday afternoon ("an odd time sense") in the steepled Congregational church. "The young minister and his wife had within a few days adopted a little boy, not much over a year old; the blond mop, smiling type who looks fine in church or anywhere. When no one seemed to be watching, the minister grabbed a gilt-cardboard halo and put it on the boy's head and nudged his wife to look. The child smiled up at his father and mother." The costumes began the miracle, Scott wrote, and then the organist "commenced playing that Christmas music which so takes us back and is soothing and rending all at once. . . . Within that music we are 'alone with silence and the trick of tears.' "[30] Though almost seventy years old, Essie kept her vitality and her enthusiasm. Often, she was the oldest person

[29] Quoted in Donald Dean Eulert, "Winfield Townley Scott: Conversations on Poets and the Art of Poetry" (Ph.D. dissertation, University of New Mexico, January 1969), pp. 102–103; WTS. "Cloud," pp. 32–37.

[30] WTS, "Bookman's Galley," *Providence Sunday Journal*, 24 December 1950, sec. 6, p. 8.

in a Hampton gathering, but, as Charlie Philbrick told her at such a party, "You know, Essie, you're the youngest one here."[31]

Essie provided Win with unqualified affection and admiration. No reviewer could exceed her praise. When *Mr. Whittier* came out, for example, Essie wrote Win that "even if I had never laid eyes on you . . . I think I should feel the same permanent sense of gratefulness to anyone who wrote such poetry, poetry that springs up as freshly after a dozen readings as it did at the first." His poetry ranked with the best of Edwin Arlington Robinson. "But why rank you with Robinson? Great as he was, you have something he hasn't. You're not afraid and you're warmer."[32] After the death of Win's mother, on 30 September 1952, Essie Bates became a second mother to him, and he a dutiful son to her. Win worried about her health, and after the move to Santa Fe he appointed spies in Hampton to report on how she was getting along. She visited Santa Fe several times, and no trip east for the Scotts was complete without a call on Essie.

When Bessie Scott died, Win was hit hard: Eleanor was fearful of what he might do in his depression. But some of his grief he dispelled in an elegiac poem, "Memento," which, significantly, concerns itself more with Newport's natural setting than with his mother. "You might say," he wrote, "it is an elegy in terms of geography, those terms involving childhood-place, the strongest associations with the beloved dead, and the strange involvements of memory . . . It is an obliquely written elegy; in any case, I was unable to manage it any other way."[33] Of the five sections of "Memento" (it was the poem Shapiro rejected for *Poetry*), only the third concentrates its attention specifically on his mother, and there the emphasis is on one of Scott's fixations—the idea that in "each death of those nearest us we die to some extent, yet we are also enlarged as sole carriers of memories once shared":

> This lady's memory of these things is gone.
> Of us and sixty-seven years her knowledge

---

[31] Interview, Paul and Francis Chadwick, Hampton, Connecticut, 26 August 1969.

[32] Esther W. Bates to WTS, 17 September 1948, Scott Collection, John Hay Library.

[33] WTS, "After a Certain Age One Wants to be Wary," *Beloit Poetry Journal Chapbook* 2 (1953), p. 27.

Is gone. While you stare down at her long-loved
   face
The nonexistence which shakes you is your own.

Now you have come to stare at the statue of death
Its terror is in your recognition of it and,
Unlike a real statue, its failure to change,
Its inability to respond. And this conceived you.

From what you know, from what you can bear to see
This must be buried soon. And only for you
Now and always light is everywhere altered,
And the colors of the world are otherwise.

Whom do the mourners see? A girl—a ghost—
A bride—an old and tired lady—a stranger?
They pause and make her momentary replica.
Whom do the mourners see? Themselves. Themselves.[34]

At the burial service in Haverhill, there were piles of flowers, a
hundred or more people, and then an "opening up of pouring rain
with a great crash of thunder & lightning" and the minister fairly
shouting "I am the resurrection and the life."[35] To keep his memories green, Win wrote a long account in poetry not of *that* burial
service but of a much earlier one in Newport, after Grammie Wilbar had died. Like his mother, Grammie Wilbar had told Winfield
countless stories in his childhood. "The women of the tribe and of
the neighborhood are generally the prime historians. And as a
youngster I was a quiet and avid listener, a sitter upon hassocks,
a drinker-in of lore. I must have absorbed hundreds of hours of
monologue. . . . If I have lost the stories and names, then they are
forever lost."[36] Win's widowed father decided to remain in the
house on Cedar Street rather than return to Newport; his friends
were almost all in Haverhill. Barely a year later, on 8 October 1953,
Douglas Scott married Bernice Kelly, who at one time had helped
to nurse Win's mother.

With Jeannette's arrival in June 1953 and more frequent visits
from Lindsay (now that Savila had remarried), Win's own family
commanded more of his time than ever before. Weekday mornings

---

[34] WTS, "Memento," *New and Selected Poems*, pp. 69–73.
[35] WTS to Bob and Jeannette Wolfe, 7 October 1952.
[36] WTS, "Biography at the Open Grave," unpublished poem (1953), 34 pages.

he drove into Hampton a little before nine to drop Joel at school and pick up the mail at the post office. On Mondays, when the mail ran heavy, he would walk along the main street until it was sorted; occasionally he would investigate the cemetery in the northeast corner of town. Intellectuaully, he could not justify his fondness for haunting cemeteries. Emotionally, though, he found them satisfying. "Is it because a cemetery is so definite—so definitive—a place, in a world where one can seldom feel much certainty? Is it because one likes a sense of finality—at least to stand and look at? Of course there is the silence and the sense of peace, both also rare."[37] After he moved to Santa Fe, Win said good-bye to Hampton and its cemetery, and, in the next-to-last line, good-bye to his mother as well, in a poem called "Love and a Season":

> And now farewell
> To the June town of ladies in cotton lilac
> Bending their frail look upon picketed iris
> In hopelessly-joined grids of scented yards
> That give on the valley view that gives on graves
> Tucked in the north corner of the sky. Farewell
> That little way down hill to the terraced stillness
> Where moss-pink stitches the anonymous scars
> To a brave indifference of forgetfulness
> Under this music thinned and long familiar
> Which is not yet exactly mine, for the grave—
>   transfixed,
> Oh, my loved ghost!—most mine is not among these
> And the house I have to go home to is a new house.[38]

Forever unhandy around the house, Win exemplified the bumbling, ineffectual male. Machinery recoiled from his touch; one summer afternoon, he mounted the power mower, and, unable to stop it, careened through flower beds until Lindsay and Joel, at first helpless with laughter, came finally to his rescue.[39] On bitter winter days, he tried to work in the house, but much of his time was spent listening politely to the monologue of the housekeeper. Loath to give offense, Win did not demur even when the housekeeper inter-

---

[37] WTS, "Cloud," pp. 10–12.
[38] WTS, "Love and a Season," *Collected Poems: 1937–1962* (1962), pp. 310–311.
[39] Interview, EMS, Santa Fe, 7 September 1969.

rupted him by using his desk phone rather than the one in the bedroom. As he accused himself in "Alas!":

> I was about to
> Shut off the garden spray
> When I
> Saw two pigeons bathing beneath it.
>
> .   .   .   .
>
> So I
> Waited them out, thinking
> O God, do I want to be liked even by pigeons?[40]

As time passed, Win began to be of two minds about Eleanor's continuing eccentricities. There were times, to be sure, when her boldness delighted Win. Ben Bagdikian told of one expedition to town, "Once . . . they drove into Providence for the day and while there picked up some garden supplies to take back. Ellie was to meet Win at the *Journal*, and so she entered the building carrying a twenty-five-pound bag of dried manure. In the vestibule she met the young publisher John Watkins . . . and though Watkins, in public, usually bore himself with an air of earnest solicitation like St. Francis of Assisi, Ellie treated him the way she did everyone else, by not recognizing the façade. He asked Ellie what she had in that big bag and Ellie replied, 'Horseshit, John,' and then added, 'I know it's silly. Bringing horseshit to the Providence Journal is like carrying coals to Newcastle.' A little later . . . Ellie told this story with Win present and Win shook his head in irritation. But some time later, Win told the story with obvious glee and approval. His was a contradictory mix of kindness-propriety and mischief, and though he was tolerant of Ellie's 'carelessness and deliberate unorthodoxies,' Win would periodically explode, 'For God's sake, Ellie, will you please for Christ's sake put on a *clean dress*!' "[41] Such explosions took their toll. Once, when Lindsay was visiting Hampton, Win got angry at El and threw his coffee cup against the wall. In the spirit of the occasion or perhaps to mock his father, Lindsay followed suit, and Win's rage found a new target. He was about to throw a cup at Lindsay, but Ellie stopped him. What impressed

---

[40] WTS, "Cloud," pp. 49–50, 53; WTS, "Alas!" *Saturday Review*, 7 July 1956, p. 13.
[41] Ben Bagdikian to SD, 28 June 1969.

Lindsay most about the incident was that Ellie could physically restrain his father.[42]

Perhaps the Scotts' closest friends in Hampton were Paul and Frances Chadwick. Paul was fiftyish, tall, slender, with gray hair and clipped mustache; Win told him he should go to Hollywood and get into movies whose plot called for a "distinguished-looking" writer. He toiled on weekly newspapers and wrote pulp stories: "a hard and precarious gamble of a living." Win liked the fact that Paul was no yearner, but was actually writing his western and suspense yarns and selling them. He also admired Chadwick's many talents: "He is a very good flautist; his reading tastes are first rate; he can build a bird house or, it may be, a whole stone porch for his own house. . . . He belongs to a type . . . whose variety of talents take them in many directions; but Paul is the only one of that type I have ever known who has not become confused and wasted, or soured and selfish. If there is one human being in our town whom everybody likes, then it must be Paul Chadwick." Everyone, Win wrote, recognized Paul's exceptional decency and his youthful capacity for excitement "grown around by a genuine maturity."[43] Win and Paul talked and drank long hours together; they were at ease with each other.

Among other companions were the Scotts' neighbors, Ed and Anne Osborne. To their house, on 4 July 1950, Win and Ellie mistakenly brought bergamot and not mint to decorate the drinks. The incident is amusingly recorded in "An Owed, or Fourth of July, 1950; or The Longest Minor Poem I have Written So Far This Summer; or Writing Time: 5 Min., Reading Time: 1 Min.; or For the Osbornes—the Least I Can Do. By Winfield Townley Scott, the Aging Bard":

> O, the lugubrious
> Non-salubrious
> Outcome of the Scotts' one responsible Forth of July
>   stint!
>
> It all goes to show
> The best people know

[42] Interview, Lindsay Scott, Washington, D.C., 26 September 1969.
[43] Interview, Paul and Frances Chadwick, Hampton, Connecticut, 26 August 1969.

And can grow
And bestow
Mint.
But scratch a Scott,
What you got?
Bergamot.[44]

Anne Osborne has kept the poem, framed with a sprig of bergamot. Frequently, the Bagdikians and Swans and Philbricks traveled from Providence to join the convivial company at Hampton. Annually El arranged a birthday party for Win, and there were informal summer picnics, with a good deal of drinking and horse-play.[45] Charles Philbrick was one of the first of many younger men whom Win served in a mentor-pupil relationship. Trying to find himself in his postgraduate years, he drove to Hampton one night to talk to Win and Ellie about his future. They advised him, after many drinks, to give up writing and concentrate on teaching. Philbrick never forgot, of course, and he re-created the evening in his elegy for Scott:

> You stood, placing your pipe on a mantelpiece
>   idly,
> In each of the four remembered houses you asked
>   me to,
> And a couple of my own; you spoke to me, a dozen
>   years
> Your younger, married to beauty, boyishly tangled
>   in soft
> Words—
>   and I drove myself blind through a night to
>   deny
> That I wasn't a poet, denying that you mattered,
>   arriving
> Within two miles of my bed before I ran out of gas
> Downtown, near the halfway hill of my justification.
> My empty apartment that kept a collection of sunsets.

Later, when Philbrick had published several books of poems and stories and had won the 1958 Wallace Stevens Poetry Prize, the relationship between the two Brown men subtly altered: without

[44] Mrs. Edmund B. Osborne to SD, 3 April 1970.
[45] Interview, Ben and Betty Bagdikian, Washington, D.C., 15 March 1970.

its ever being acknowledged by either of them, they became rivals. "Years later," Philbrick's elegy continues, "you read my published poems, and praised the earliest ones."[46]

Another Brown man and Hamptonian, Clarence Webster, wrote an only slightly disguised description of the town in his 1936 book, *Puritans at Home*. No copy of the book was available in the Hampton library; the town had resented the book, for all the usual wrong reasons:

> Degenerate poor whites, known in Clarence's book as the Gulls, are no ornament to Hampton; but they are here, and Clarence quite rightly took account of them. This particularly was resented by the respectable folk—I don't believe the Gulls ever read this book or any other; they are much too happily occupied buggering cows and committing fornication within the family circle.

Now this kind of class or racial resentment is not at all rare. The literary mind is fascinated by the truth of things. The non-literary mind—which is an overwhelming majority in Hampton as elsewhere— always assumes that the not-nice things are best ignored; especially in print. Life-is-bad-enough-without-writing-about-it.

"The females of the village may strip one of their sisters with gossip. The males may enjoy many a filthy snigger when gathered at the local garage. But females and males alike, they know where dirt belongs: in the mouth, not in books."[47] Win himself loved gossip that did not descend to the mean-spirited; but that is what happened in Hampton during 1953 and 1954.

The trouble started with a scandal involving the Congregational minister. It was very much a reenactment of the small-minded uproar which had deprived Harry Elmore Hurd, minister during Win Scott's high school days, of his Haverhill post. The Protestant core of the town split almost exactly in two. "The very slight minority that wanted the minister to stay" set him up in a little, long-disused church. "The very slight majority against him" held the fort in the church on the hill. In such a row, Scott observed, "there are bound to be troubled, saddened Christians; but . . . for the most part the blood is up and hearts glow with self-righteousness. This

---

[46] Interview, Charles H. Philbrick, Providence, 6 June 1969; Charles H. Philbrick, " 'Now That Lost April' (W.T.S. 1910–1968)," unpublished poem (Autumn 1968), p. 3.

[47] WTS, "Cloud," pp. 16–17.

is change and excitement, and how much of that do we have?" The Catholics sat amusedly on the sidelines while Congregationalists no longer spoke to each other; resentments of older families for new ones came out in the open, and at least one "real ugliness" took place: the high school age youngsters of one faction sneaked into the Grange Hall and destroyed the decorations set up for a dance by youngsters of the other.

There was the stuff of a novel in the row, Scott saw: "strong personalities at war, with jealousies, social ambitions, political revenges and scandal dripping in its own juice." In fact, there were "many stories in this town which I could not attempt without the disguise of fiction. Every American town is a Winesburg, Ohio," with its grotesques. "Take off our roofs and you will see a good average of young couples happily conventional with a brood of children and elders happily self-sufficient; you will find too the print of Oedipus, the shadow of Medea, the bewildered Sappho, the incipient Corydon, a part-time Messalina, a John Evereldown, a frustrated and therefore hateful Joan of Arc, in his quiet desperation an Ethan Frome." Win was not going to write the novel; if he had, he should then have had to move away; and though the Scotts planned to spend a year elsewhere, they fully intended to return. At first he and Ellie had talked of Italy, but then Win got cold feet, "thinking of traipsing four children, one still a baby, another only three, across the Atlantic and into a strange civilization and an unknown language." They decided instead on the Southwest.[48]

In "The Country of a Cloud," Win maintained that he was moving away "for a change: no other reason,"[49] but that was by no means the whole truth. The bitterly vigorous language with which he described the ministerial row suggests how much it must have troubled him. Besides, in many other ways, the year prior to his departure for Santa Fe in September 1954 had been a miserable one.

The autumn of 1953 was excessively dry, and the Scotts' "famously good" well ran dry for six to eight weeks. The weather twinned Scott's situation: sexually and professionally, he had reached a plateau of sterility. Approaching his middle forties, Scott began to wonder if he had not irrevocably lost the powers of youth.

---

[48] Ibid., pp. 18–19.
[49] Ibid., p. 57.

When he was a child, every house had its own peculiar identifying odor. "Now I scarcely ever notice anything of the sort, but I fear it is I and not houses that have changed. I believe this February morning my wife and I have walked about in is not the same morning in which our children walked about; I think—their heads, ears, eyes, noses, mouths, all their small bodies, so much nearer the earth—they walked a vivider world."[50] He was growing old, he felt, and he was visited with obsessions about aging. Win's physical appearance reflected the years: he was no longer the slim aesthete, his fondness for rich foods and steady drinking was taking its physical toll. Win's body fleshed out, and he cut his hair very short in reaction to spreading baldness (his mother had made him promise, when he was very young, not to comb thinning strands across his bald spot when he grew up). With self-deprecation touched with compulsion, he repeated over and over an anecdote about his appearance: "When I was living in Hampton, Conn., one rainy Saturday morning I ran into a youngster named Chris Nosworthy, home for the weekend from Trinity College. Chris said, 'Hey, we had a class the other day in Modern Poetry, and your name was mentioned and I said I knew you, and one fellow asked if you looked like a poet.' Pause. I said, 'Well, Chris, what did you say?' Chris said, 'I told him, "Hell, no: he looks like a nightclub bouncer." ' "[51] But of course Win cared how he looked, and even in the countryside dressed neatly: if bluejeans, pressed bluejeans, and a tweed jacket and tie to accompany. In a poem, "Two Lives and Others," Scott explored the coming of winter, and, in the wholly imaginary picture of the old man in the last five lines, projected what he feared for his private winter:

> Beyond the field where crows cawed at a hawk
> The road bent down between oaks, pines, and maples,
> Maples skimming the air with terra cotta.
> The oaks spat acorns over scurries of squirrels.
> Moss crunched stiff underfoot, and overhead
> The sky was freezing gradually, white across blue.
> We hurried our walk through shadows, yet it was
> A noticeable sort of afternoon:

[50] Ibid., p. 60.
[51] WTS to Anne Hutchens, 29 April 1961.

We honored a faded robin and considered
The importance of the color gray on bluejays.
A woodchuck, all an urgent clumsiness,
Made his tumbling run, then he saw us,
Plunged, hid, and screamed his whistle of fear.
Round the next bend to twilight we went past
A solitary house, one room lamplighted,
An old man at supper alone facing the wall.
If he was aware of us he gave no sign.
We circled home, that last day before snow.[52]

Nothing reminded Win more painfully that he was aging than his flagging sexual powers. As he wrote in "The Country of a Cloud,"

I am just now extra-conscious of all this, having been through a year or more of nervousness and irritability and fatigue more damaging to me—and more baleful to my family, I suppose—than my age should explain. . . . Is this that rickety, dizzying bridge between being young and arriving at middle-age?—arriving, I daresay, a maturer and happier person than one has been? (Who in his right mind would choose to go back and repeat?) And a person by no means superannuated for sex. And, if he be a good artist, at last a better artist. . . . I want some time to write a poem about the shock of impotence. If I do and if it's ever published, I shall explain one does not have to drink the whole Atlantic Ocean to know the taste of salt water.[53]

Writing to Jeff Werner in February 1954, he treated the matter jocularly: "For a month or so . . . I had a pooped-out feeling; not up to anything in bed or out. Not good, you know. But it's worn off. I'm all right again, boy, I'm all right."[54] Less than a month earlier, however, he had put the case to himself more cogently, in a catalogue of frustrations: "In sex, one quick accident of fatigue with . . . resultant fiasco, and then the frighteningly swift establishment of a pattern, the fear feeding upon itself and growing. Not permanent, but frighteningly there."[55] The fear of failure did not wear off, a month later or ever.

[52] WTS, "Two Lives and Others," *New and Selected Poems*, p. 74.
[53] WTS, "Cloud," pp. 38–39.
[54] WTS to H. O. Werner, 10 February 1954, Scott Collection, John Hay Library.
[55] WTS, "Cloud," p. 40.

An accompanying frustration, of course, was Win's continuing
inability to interest a publisher in his work. Given the economic
facts of life, it was a problem which confronted not only Winfield
Townley Scott but many contemporary poets: "The frustration of
having years of writing—I mean a particular job [*The Dark Sister*]
—rejected; praised by publishers who hope some other publisher,
so they say, will publish it—that is, they expect, lose money on it."[56]
Rejection had its pernicious consequences: "For myself, and for
every serious artist ever confessional to me, self-delusion is the
huge fear: the non-creative stretches grow indigo with that terrifying question— Am I a fraud? This can be repeated, recovered from,
and repeated apparently as long as one lives."[57] If he was not a
fraud, why was he so unreasonably concerned with reputation, afflicted by "a preoccupation with career, which is not at all preoccupation with one's art; it is rather a deadly opposite"?[58]

In this mood, Scott wrote movingly of Phelps Putnam, a poet who
promised much as a young man but failed to live up to his early
promise. Putnam's descent was into drink, and once, for only an
hour, Win had visited the older man at his shabby cottage in Pomfret, Connecticut. There Putnam twirled his whiskey in a child's
tumbler "dappled with a painted pony rockered." The doctors had
told him, Putnam intimated, that his heart was not strong enough
to write again:

> Then he shrugged his old-young face
> And poured more whisky in my jelly-glass.

> "One can be legendary even at forty,"
> He said, "but that is to be alive only
> In other people's pasts." He lit the lamp
> With careful down-adjustment of the wick.

> The tall bookcases righted themselves but all
> The uncommunicative countryside
> Pressed against the blackened windows closer;
> As though a vacuum listened. "If I could

> Remember," he remarked. "When I was young
> Why, all of us were going to be great men."

[56] Ibid., p. 40.
[57] Ibid., p. 39.
[58] Ibid., p. 40.

> He let his drink stand by the lamp and thought.
> I looked away. "But to recall one's self,"
>
> I heard him say, "—such ruthless appetite."
> Projected from the glass the light had made
> The painted toy gigantic—shadow of horse
> Massive, silent, living, real, on the wall.[59]

Bottles were strewn outside the cottage door.

In an essay on the death of Dylan Thomas, Win examined a very different kind of career from Putnam's—or his own. He had seen Thomas only three times:

First was at a huge publishers' party at the Waldorf-Astoria, New York; short, stout, curly-massed hair, almost pig-faced but jolly-looking, Thomas leaned against a brocaded wall; his beautiful blond wife stood nearby, and an infamous anthologist seemed to crawl up one side of him and down the other. I turned and looked the other way and beheld Mickey Spillane. It was that kind of a party. And last year and the year before [1952, 1953] E. and I drove over to the University of Connecticut—at Storrs, half an hour from Hampton—and heard Thomas read his own and others' poetry; magnificently, as everyone knows. But I never met him.[60]

The first words of Win's 1954 essay on Thomas asked a disturbing question, "Why do people *like* to have a poet die?" and supplied some bitter answers. Since Thomas's death, he pointed out, people who heretofore had known nothing of him "have read obituaries, have read memorial articles, have heard of memorial meetings, have listened to broadcasts of Thomas' recordings of his prose and verse . . . and they are impressed with Thomas and pleased with themselves. Why?" First of all, and here Scott was undoubtedly thinking of his own experience in Providence and Hampton, "they are illustrating the old saw that a dead poet is a great man while the fellow who lives next door and writes poetry is obviously a damned fool; they are acquainted with this one—how therefore can he be important or immortal?" But a still deeper psychology was operating, Scott believed. Poets were committed to truth, and truth was a dangerous thing avoided by most people. "A poet is a rebuke, a higher and more responsible consciousness in our midst. He is,

[59] WTS, "Phelps Putnam," *Collected Poems*, pp. 293–294.
[60] WTS, "Cloud," p. 54.

while alive, more alive than most people." But when a poet proved
his common humanity by dying, then "people have him where they
can use him, where they can control him, where they want him."
Especially if their skepticisms are borne out, "when as in Thomas'
case the death seems wilful and his children require (of course!)
the benefits of a Fund. This way, they can have a poet and eat him
too."[61] Like Thomas and Putnam, Win Scott tended to drink too
much. "I do not get drunk, but daresay I have become 'tolerant' of
a great quantity of bourbon. After drink there is fatigue. And in
drink there is self-dramatization." And liquor brought relief from
the worst frustration of all: not writing—"beginning things that
do not work out, accomplishing others that look thin, accomplishing
nothing at all."[62]

In "The Country of a Cloud," Win also delved into those qualities
he hated in himself, qualities which, he had fondly hoped, might
evaporate after his marriage to Eleanor. He deplored, for example,
his habit of remaining silent when provoked, of only occasionally
throwing the coffee cup which symbolized his unspoken anger. "I
have deeply a tendency—deplorable in an artist—for turning away
from the emotional scene, for blotting out the unpleasant episode.
I do deplore this. I blame my ancestry. For it seems a bondage I
have no power to throw off."[63] As he expressed it in "Definition,"
"This habit of avoiding unpleasantness; it avoids / Poetry, it avoids
love."[64]

Another cross Win inherited from his mother was her "extreme
apprehension . . . her timidity, her fear of change." She was quick
to dread; the sound of the doorbell alarmed her, and through her
long illness these fears only increased in intensity. So it was with
her son, though he tried to fight the inheritance:

> In some moods it seems to vanish. At other times it is on me like a
> sudden tiger. I awake to that craziness in the middle of the night,
> sweating in a nervous paralysis over the public reading I have promised,
> over the journey I must make (How could I ever have supposed myself
> capable of uprooting and going off to New Mexico? the details and

---

[61] WTS, "The Death, and Some Dominions of It," *Yale Literary Magazine*
122 (November 1954): 13–14.
[62] WTS, "Cloud," pp. 40–41.
[63] Ibid., p. 39.
[64] WTS, "Definition," *Collected Poems*, p. 148.

troubles seem insurmountable—and so on); I visualize, even, the bad curve on the short drive I must make tomorrow, and my brain pitches with fright. (Next day, I drive that curve calmly.) This terror comes and goes but it has caused, I suppose, many a bad management in my life. Perhaps, contrariwise, my tendency to make decisions when in liquor has not been as bad as it sounds: then, at least, the inhibitions are down.

"Every bit of this," Scott concluded, "if published, will be news even to my intimate friends."[65] He was right about that; the usually perceptive Ben Bagdikian, recalling the Win Scott of Hampton days, spoke of his inner defense, his air of serene confidence.[66]

Psychiatry, Scott thought, might help rid him of such timidities and fears, but what else might it not do at the same time? "I know I am old-fashioned in this . . . as Horace Gregory once said to me about an eminent critic who had experienced severe breakdown at mid-career and emerged 'cured' to a largely softened point of view, 'The tooth is still there, but the nerve is gone.' "[67] It would be more than a decade, and only after abundant evidence that his inherited fears were, like his mother's, aggravated by age, before Win sought psychiatric assistance.

Curiously, he found that he could soothe his apprehensions by entering the womblike world of hotel rooms; not alone, as at Yale, but with Eleanor. Sexual vigor returned with the sense of peace and the delicious being-cared-for feeling:

You know how it is. The carpeted arrival after journey. The boy puts down your luggage, snaps on lights, hands you your keys, pockets your tip: and as he leaves, the door which he closes locks. And there you are in a small, warm, private world. Impregnable world. Invasion comes only if you telephone for it and then, most probably, to secure you further with food and drink. You are in a kind of Eden: manufactured, synthetic, not many days to be enjoyed, expensive—yet not an illusion. Its care and tending are all the concern of others. There you are, soft on the carpet, lazy in big chairs, or stretched deep in the hot water of the huge tub. The bed—to you anyway—is a new bed. The other world of intrusions, demands, responsibilities has vanished. You have escaped. You can do anything you want to.

---

[65] WTS, "Cloud," p. 41.
[66] Interview, Ben and Betty Bagdikian, Washington, D.C., 15 March 1970.
[67] WTS, "Cloud," p. 39.

For the cost of a winter week in a New York hotel, he could purchase temporary escape, secure despite the snowstorm swirling
outside.[68]

One final difficulty—perhaps the most significant in the Scotts'
decision to leave Hampton, the most influential in shaping the
course of his life and death—troubled Win Scott: "The guilt-feeling
[that] after nearly three years since quitting a bread-and-butter
job, I have little to show for my leisure . . ."[69] He was no longer
earning his bread and butter; and if he knew, in his mind, that that
should not bother him, he also knew, in his emotional life, that it
bothered him terribly. Joel paid more taxes than he did, he told
the Chadwicks, but it was not quite a joke.[70] No one else in Hampton shared Win's situation; he was the town's sole example of the
artist supported by his wife. In Santa Fe, though guilt continued to
eat away at him, at least there was plenty of company: artists supported by present wives or absent parents, a number of millionaires
who "did not punch the clock and were thus akin to his socalled
indolence. *That*," R. W. Stallman believes, is why the Scotts quit
Hampton.[71] In March 1954, Win wrote a poem for Anne Parrish,
drawing an analogy, "From A for Artist to Z for Zebra":

> The zebra is a useless animal.
> I read so in a book and so I know.
> He's an ungrateful mammal and also
> Will not be trained for anything at all.
>
> .   .   .   .
>
> There's some pathos—that is: human touch—
> In that when hurt or dying, a zebra's moans
> Sound for all the world like a man's groans.
> Of this, I suppose, we mustn't make too much.[72]

Scott left New England for a year, for a change, and in the ad-
ditional hope that the Southwest might teach him to know his native
region still better. "Little as I know of the Southwest from books and

---

[68] Ibid., pp. 41–42.

[69] Ibid., p. 40.

[70] Interview, Paul and Frances Chadwick, Hampton, Connecticut, 26 August
1969.

[71] R. W. Stallman to SD, 14 October 1969.

[72] WTS, "From A for Artist to Z for Zebra—for Anne Parrish," unpublished
poem (10 March 1954).

pictures, I imagine it to have a glamour precisely because it is American and yet is American in ways so foreign to all I have grown up in. And there is a codicil to my positive wish. As a writer, I believe one's deepest sources lie where one happens to belong, and I think I may understand those the better if I go away for awhile."[73] But he left in disillusionment and despair as well; in the closing lines of a nightmare poem, "The Long Party," he confessed the torment of frustrated hopes:

> The lawn sloped down to the blue hydrangeas.
> The blue hydrangeas held the sea. Apart,
> I found a clump of laurel I remembered:
> But shriveled. I had dreamed that laurel tall.[74]

Blue hydrangeas grow in clusters of perfect flowers, but they have a peculiarity. All or most of the flowers are sterile.

[73] WTS, "Cloud," pp. 19–20.
[74] WTS, "The Long Party," *New and Selected Poems*, p. 84.

See by this summer sun
Circling our mountains like the vast twilight of the old gods
How, too, there is a growing light in the west.
We carry with us
That which we journey towards.[1]

10. Lunar Land

ON 31 AUGUST 1954, winds of hurricane force struck southern New England. The loft, roof, and back wall of the Matunuck (R.I.) playhouse, only just vacated by the tempestuous Tallulah Bankhead, blew down. Brad Swan, Ben Bagdikian, and Paul Chadwick, among hundreds of others, lost cars to the storm's suddenly swelling waters. Elsie Clough's book shop in Providence was a complete loss: nine thousand books and not a penny of insurance. (No insurance for downtown Providence was sold after the great hurricane of 1938.) And at 10:45 that morning, at the ominous height of the hurricane, the Scotts left Hampton for Santa Fe. Driving to catch the train at Willimantic, they dodged tree limbs flung by the sixty-mile-an-hour winds and negotiated flooded streets only to find that someone

[1] WTS, *The Dark Sister* (1958), p. 30.

had misread the schedule and the train had already left. Another frantic, wet-palmed drive and they overtook the train in Hartford; the *Twentieth Century Limited* waited in New York, and there was plenty of time—or there would have been plenty of time but for a washout. They missed that train, too, and Win's worst fears about travel seemed confirmed: in Grand Central Station finally, baby Jeannette "cut her lip going bang on the floor & kept trying to escape to the lights & big buildings on 42nd Street." But a night train landed them in Chicago in calmer weather, and, miraculously, in their originally assigned car on the *Super Chief*. And, despite the chaos of missed connections, Win "loved the whole damn trip." He had never traveled to the Midwest—or the Far West—before. The countryside was a revelation he insisted on sharing; he woke everybody at 6 A.M., to watch the silos and elevators and sunflowers of Kansas, and climbed the dome car with Joel for a better view of the Raton pass. They arrived on schedule in Lamy, New Mexico, the train stop for Santa Fe, where they were met by Nat and Lucile Adler.[2]

Lu Adler had been a friend of Eleanor's at Bennington, and she had found a house for Ellie and Win to rent. There were, in Santa Fe, she had admitted in a June 1954 letter to the Scotts, "fewer stimulating minds [than in New York, say], little that's first-rate intellectually; but then there's the country, and the space and—and no apologies."[3] No apology offered, none asked for: Win and Eleanor were immediately enchanted with New Mexico. Their rented adobe house at 575 Camino del Monte Sol—a road which winds up into the foothills from Santa Fe and is known to some townspeople as "Nut Row" for its collection of artists and bohemians living in "mud huts"—had been built thirty years before, with his own hand, by owner Jozef Barkos. The house rested "inside an adobe wall—you step through a big wooden door in the wall: into a little garden full of paths, spruce, olive, elm trees & lilacs," then the medium-sized house itself, hugging the land, but for view, and reached by a crude wooden outside stairway, an upstairs studio with windows on all four sides, and, beyond, the Sangre de Cristo Moun-

[2] WTS to Ben and Betty Bagdikian, 17 September 1954; WTS to Paul and Frances Chadwick, 16 September 1954.
[3] Lu Adler to EMS, 18 June 1954, Scott Collection, John Hay Library, Brown University.

tains ("Blood of Christ," so called because of their reddish hues at twilight) to the west, the Jémez range to the east.[4] The Scotts had been in Santa Fe only three months before they let it be known, at first only to Essie Bates, that they would be gone from Hampton longer than the year they had planned, that they might stay in the Southwest indefinitely.[5]

In "A Calendar of Santa Fe," a long autobiographical account of the year from September 1954 to September 1955 (*New World Writing* paid him $250 for the piece, more money than he had ever before made on a single writing project), Win sketched what were for him the wonders of the place. Most startling was the immensity of the landscape. "The breadth and height of the land, its huge self and its huge sky, strike you like a blow," and though there were those who at once disliked it, in a kind of dismay at so much inhuman space, there were others—Win included—who at first could "do nothing but stand and stare." As a New Englander, he had to reorder his sense of space. His first night on the Camino, Win "stepped out onto the road and looked at a cluster of lights in the northwest. I assumed they were the lights of downtown Santa Fe. It was several days before I discovered they were the lights of Los Alamos, thirty-five miles away, and that the Jémez Mountains I looked at with a casual admiration . . . were fifty miles away. This would be, back East, like standing in Providence and looking at Boston." Hampton, on its hilltop, had been seven hundred feet above sea level; Santa Fe stood seven thousand feet above the sea. At that altitude, sudden strong winds stirred up a reminder of "the facts of astronomy. In cozier country it seems that the sun rises and sets, the moon rises and sets, above a still and level world. But here, as on a great ship, you are more aware of the voyaging planet—the mountains wheeling upward to the sun, and the winds like encountered currents breaking across the turning earth."[6]

Despite its elevation, the land was far from arid; natural phenomena bombarded the senses. On the night of 11 December 1954, Win wrote Ben Bagdikian, " my bride & I have just come in from a

---

[4] WTS to Ben and Betty Bagdikian, 17 September 1954.
[5] Esther W. Bates to WTS, 21 January 1955, Scott Collection, John Hay Library.
[6] WTS, "A Calendar of Santa Fe," *Exiles and Fabrications* (1961), pp. 193–195.

walk up the Camino in the moonlight on the snow. . . . It seeped in slowly last night & this morning & it has cleared slowly: so we have not seen the dazzling quickies the oldtimers talk about; but this afternoon was a pretty shining affair close to, the foothills all grayed green of trees, since pines, firs, cedars and piñons have the monopoly and are just the trees to hold the powder; as though the mountains were smoking in a great fire."[7] The piñon wood burning in the fireplace provided a delicious aroma which smelled best of all when you left the house. "I don't think anybody has yet pointed out that the choice way to enjoy your fireplace in the Southwest is to go outside."[8] There, the piñon smoke mingled with the painterly light and the magnificent air, ". . . the clear, shimmering, golden, ordinary, autumn, evening air." It seemed that everything blossomed golden, Scott's symbolic color for realization of potential. "Walking the Arroyo Hondo, I saw dandelions, a yellow cinquefoil I cannot name, the sculptured mullein, chamisa, cactus with its yellow bud-like growths, and even yellow butterflies and olive-yellow birds."[9]

Every now and then, Win Scott reported, chambers of commerce in the Southwest received requests for information as to passport regulations for entering New Mexico, but the "ignoramuses" were "not altogether in error. If you were flown here blindfolded—not to the cities of New Mexico, but to any of the little mountain villages with their low adobe houses, their farmers with creased Spanish faces, their herds of sheep and wandering horses—you would justifiably assume you were in a foreign land."[10] Such a town was Chimayo, where you dropped down a thousand feet or so, "and there, though very much in sight of the bare brown mesas, the still snow-capped Sangre de Cristo Mts., are green fields; many blossoming fruit trees; men afoot at hand ploughs behind horses; birds singing. Ancient and new."[11] In Chimayo the pace of life was the Spanish *poco a poco*, little by little, no hurry, and not much worry. "Even if the eastern United States were destroyed and all industry paralyzed." José Ramon Ortega, a weaver, told Scott, "we could always

[7] WTS to Ben and Betty Bagdikian, 11 December 1954.
[8] WTS to Paul and Frances Chadwick, 1 December 1954.
[9] WTS, "Calendar," p. 195; WTS, "As I Took the Evening Air," *Religious Humanism* 2 (Spring 1968): 52.
[10] WTS, "Calendar," p. 192.
[11] WTS to Paul and Frances Chadwick, 2 May 1955.

be safe and independent here." Many visitors came to see the weaving, but Chimayo had not become a tourist town. "For all the modern roads and cars, for all the commuting of job holders [to nearby Los Alamos] and the visitations of strangers, Chimayo still keeps its sense of isolation, in no way an inferior sense of being out of things, but rather the strong sense of locality and self-sufficiency," Win wrote in admiration.[12]

Above the town, however, lay a source of terror. When they were first in Santa Fe, the Scotts used to picnic Sundays on tortuous mountain roads which looked down on Chimayo. We "got onto roads," he wrote the Chadwicks in May 1955,

that damned near made me die: little, one-track roads, sandy, winding up into *space*—terrifying drops into nothingness; erosions to rock & roll the car around corners where you couldn't see; upward pitches— nothing but air above the car hood; no way of turning around for miles; ghastly fear of what the hell to do if another idiot came driving the other way; etc. etc. Jesus, I've spent my life avoiding roller coasters & then get into stuff like that! Well, I get through it, but I'm drained empty hours later.[13]

"How alien," Henry Beston had written him, "that hostile, lunar region is to white men and their souls," and on Sunday picnic drives Win was ready to agree with him.[14] But he worked out his resolution of the East-West conflict in a poem, "Between Ironwood and the Sea," that he wrote late in 1955. William Carlos Williams saw the typescript of the poem, made some suggestions, and, when it had been changed, called it "one of the most distinguished poems I have seen in years." The poem was an attempt at "realizing one's humanity against the West," an amalgam, Win wrote Frank Merchant, "of my images of the drama of resemblances and contrasts for the goddamyankee settling himself in the Southwest. My country—my so different country":

> Black mesa and the Merrimack
> Adjacent in the darkened dream
> Split in the daylight world

[12] WTS, "The Still Young Sunlight: Chimayo, New Mexico," in *A Vanishing America*, ed. Thomas C. Wheeler (1964), p. 124.
[13] WTS to Paul and Frances Chadwick, 2 May 1955.
[14] Henry Beston to WTS, 9 March 1954, Scott Collection, John Hay Library.

> Till each man move between
> Salt womb and ironwood
> Sea and desert, the breathless places.
> Only between them marriage happens.

And with the marriage, a determination to remain in this lunar land:

> Look! I had been told
> There could be snow on the blossoming lilac.
> I have seen it now and stayed
> Because it is so.[15]

The lilacs usually bloomed in March, sometimes in April, and in such incredible profusion that all Santa Fe seemed "one massive bush of white and purple."[16] For Win, the ubiquitous lilacs, achieving bloom even after snow storms, symbolized a sexual and artistic renewal of his own. (One of his last poems, written in despair the year he died, was called "The Year the Lilacs Didn't Bloom.") Santa Fe, he delighted in informing easterners, was not the desert place many imagined it to be. On 11 November 1954, he and Ellie lunched outside in Burro Alley under a warm sun. Yet the next day the weather turned: snow fell hard on the Sangre de Cristos, and there was a spit of snow by the Scotts' house.[17] Later that month he wrote Philbrick that he went on liking Santa Fe, partly for the interesting people, the sunny days and chilly nights, but also because he was writing a poem a week and because "the city is a blend of leisure and sex . . . a blend of peacefulness and pricky excitement."[18] The walled-in house secured him against the immensity of the land, and the disproportionate "number of beautiful women from fifteen to seventy-five,"[19] from Spanish American, Indian, and Anglo cultures, made walking through town a sexual experience. Win's extensive correspondence with Philbrick was shot through with sexual innuendo, with the older man betraying more than a

---

[15] William Carlos Williams to WTS, 7 December 1955, Scott Collection, John Hay Library; WTS to Frank Merchant, 21 January 1957; WTS, "Between Ironwood and the Sea," *Collected Poems: 1937–1962* (1962), pp. 313–315.
[16] WTS, "Calendar," p. 209.
[17] Ibid., p. 197.
[18] WTS to Charles H. Philbrick, [?] November 1954, Scott Collection, John Hay Library.
[19] WTS, "Calendar," p. 214.

hint of pride in his bedroom exploits. "Speaking of anniversaries," he wrote 29 March 1958, 'last night was E's and my 15th . . . of knowing each other. Though I didn't celebrate it until early this morning." Then, in an asterisked afterthought, Scott added, "After all, I approach my 48th birthday; my hair is tremendously parted behind; still, I'd admire to walk along a Cape Cod beach and at least hear the mermaids singing to you."[20] The reference to Eliot hardly masked his sense of accomplishment at having satisfied a wife eleven years younger—and considerably more vigorous, physically—than himself. In Santa Fe he had begun to suffer from a series of minor ailments which, standing as proof of his aging, troubled him out of all reasonable expectation. In the spring of 1955, for example, he underwent a cartilage operation on his long-ailing left knee, and afterward a period of "scuffing, jerking, hobbling about, learning to walk," and twice-daily lifting exercises to strengthen the leg. "I suppose great characters would have employed such weeks for redoubled production of arts & letters," he wrote the Bagdikians in June, "but not the like of me: I lay and/or sat thinking about the The Knee."[21] Even in darkening moods, however, sex lifted his spirits. Thus, in a letter to Philbrick, "I feel old & injured and tired. But I did roger my wife at 7 this morning & wrote a new poem at 10, so maybe I shouldn't despair."[22]

And in the Southwest, at least in the first years, the poems came more rapidly than in a long time. "Sad news: El is not writing any book," he responded to Bill Cole in April 1955. "Sad news: I may be writing three or four [and] of course there are always The Poems . . . I have, new & yellowed, far more than enough for a decent-size book, but I'm doing nothing about that at the moment."[23] Among the other books Win had in mind were the memoirs of his Newport childhood, which he wrote during his first two years in Santa Fe; a book about painter "John Sloan's 30 summers of life here" and "around it the post World War I life of the whole crowd";[24] a book made up of his essays on American writers and settings; and of course, *The Dark Sister*, after its career of rejections for the moment resting in a closet.

20 WTS to Philbrick, 29 March 1958, Scott Collection, John Hay Library.
21 WTS to Ben and Betty Bagdikian, 20 June 1955.
22 WTS to Philbrick, 17 July 1961.
23 WTS to William Cole, 19 April 1955.
24 WTS to Ben and Betty Bagdikian, 23 March 1955.

The book on Sloan and Santa Fe never got beyond the stage of research, but the others eventually were published. None, however, saw print during the Scotts' first years in the Southwest. The happiest publishing event of those years was the issuance, in 1956, of *15 Modern American Poets*, an anthology in paperback which devoted twenty pages each to Scott and fourteen other contributors. Once again, as in the case of the 1950 Ciardi anthology, a substantial chunk of Win's work was made available to a wide audience—in this case composed principally of college students. George P. Elliott, who put the anthology together, warmly admired Scott's poetry, then and later; from a distance, the two began a friendly correspondence which resulted in Elliott's editing Scott's *New and Selected Poems* in 1967. The anthology included samples from Robert Lowell, Theodore Roethke, Richard Eberhart, Elizabeth Bishop, Robert Penn Warren, Randall Jarrell, and Josephine Miles, among others. Miles wrote Elliott that she had liked Scott's "20 pages best when she read the book through." And Witter Bynner, until Scott's arrival the unquestioned king of the Santa Fe poet-hill, wrote that for "intimacies quick-spoken between him and me—or the best objective portraits since E. A. Robinson—Scott [was] the outstanding poet in the book."[25]

Win's relationship with Bynner stretched back to high school days, when he had won prizes in the *Scholastic* magazine poetry contests judged by the older poet, but the two had never met before the Scotts moved to Santa Fe. Despite Bynner's open homosexuality, he and Win got along pleasantly. "Hal Bynner's all right," Scott wrote Bill Cole. "He's an old man now: it's El he embraces as the evening begins & ends." Besides, Bynner graciously introduced Scott to the sizable artistic colony in Santa Fe and, on one memorable occasion, drove him up to Taos, less than an hour away, for a meeting with D. H. Lawrence's widow, Frieda.[26] Scott was fascinated by the artistic heritage of Santa Fe, which had been headquarters for Sloan, Georgia O'Keeffe, and other painters. As he told Dr. Williams, it was "more a painters' than a writers' town, has been since the end of World War I." There were crowds of the tiny-talented, and "probably phonies & charlatans" as well, but at

[25] George P. Elliott to WTS, 27 May 1956, Witter Bynner to WTS, 3 June 1956, Scott Collection, John Hay Library.
[26] WTS to William Cole, 2 January 1956.

least a few genuine people—and connections with literary history that Win obviously savored: "The girl who was Brett in *The Sun Also Rises* used to come here—our landlady's son remembers watching her empty a pint in the moonlight out in the Camino. She died of TB in the local hospital."[27]

Current leaders of the colony included not only Bynner but Oliver La Farge (like Scott a one-time Rhode Islander), Haniel Long, and, occasionally, Paul Horgan. If writers must have other writers, as Essie Bates wrote Win, certainly they would do. And Win was rapidly accepted into the inner circle of the Santa Fe establishment. He even helped to mend a long-standing feud between Bynner and Long. "Welcome to the madhouse!" La Farge wrote Scott in February 1956 after his election to Quien Sabe, a club of twenty-four members, at least half of whom according to the bylaws were to be professional artists—painters, sculptors, writers, journalists, photographers, musicians, actors, directors, and so forth.[28] Members of Quien Sabe met occasionally for dinner, and for a time Win enjoyed rubbing elbows with his fellow artists, even acting as secretary of the organization. In the early 1960's, however, he quit the club after two candidates he had proposed for membership were blackballed. The Scotts made friends as well with a number of European emigrés, including the sculptor Aristide Mian, who lived next door on the Camino, Dr. Richard Landmann, who lived across the street, Rudolph Kieve, and Karl Larsson. These men had been drawn to Santa Fe partly for its strong cultural base: the local symphony and summer playhouse (both now defunct), and the summer season of the first-rate Santa Fe opera company (still very much in existence).

Attracted by climate, culture, the beauty of the land, and the Indian ceremonies, visitors descended upon Santa Fe throughout the year, but especially in the summer. The most important visit during the Scotts' first year there was that of William Carlos Williams. Williams felt a special kinship with the Southwest. On learning that Win Scott was spending a year there, Dr. Williams predicted in November 1954 that "you will be very happy there if

[27] WTS to William Carlos Williams, 15 April 1955, American Literature Collection, Beinecke Library, Yale University.
[28] Esther W. Bates to WTS, 21 January 1955, Oliver La Farge to WTS, 28 February 1956, Scott Collection, John Hay Library.

for no other reason than you have come from New England and
are so much a part of New England that your present environment
cannot be other than a perpetual shock to you." For his own part,
though he had only spent one night in Santa Fe, Williams had an
"overwhelming" impression of the place. "It took me all the way
back to the beginnings of our country, to the times of Coronado
and the Pueblo Indians and I was deeply moved. I envy you this
experience, make the most of it, I don't know of a city in the country
that I would rather visit."[29] Seven months later, in June 1955,
Williams and his wife, Florence, made that visit at the conclusion
of a reading tour. In a letter to the Bagdikians, Win described the
occasion:

The William Carlos Williamses flew in on the 4th, flew off to N.J. on
the 7th, and were—are: always will be—wonderful. Bill is rickety from
strokes & heart trouble, he tires easily; yet his just-finished west coast
readings represented an important recovery. For some time, he told us,
he couldn't "get" anything when he looked at a printed page; but
somebody in St. Louis offered him $500 to give a lecture. "For Christ's
sake!" he said. "Nobody'd ever offered me anything like that before:
I figured I had to do it." Floss says there are half a dozen reasons why
he could sit home in a chair but he and she decided that that was no
way to live. I noticed the other night here when I asked him to sign
a book for us, he wrote his trembly signature then said to Floss "I want
to date this. How do you make a 'J'?" So F traced "J" on the tabletop,
and then Bill went ahead & wrote June etc. For all this, he is immensely
alive and responsive—looking sharply at everything, playing with our
kids, kissing El on occasion, walking too much around town, kidding
me about my leg: "I imagine the doctor will beat hell out of it next
time you see him—that's the only way to handle these cases." Etc. We
put them up downtown, & left them alone each day till lunchtime. The
day before they left, we had 6 or 8 neighbors in, but otherwise did no
visiting firemen treatment. On the Sunday [we] drove up to Chimayo,
where we picnicked . . . and then up the mountains to Truchas. Both
these are ancient, little, Spanish towns—Bill, of course, is partly Spanish. Coming down from Truchas you are driving high in air with the
Rio Grande, sandy badlands, terracotta buttes & mesas, vast blue mountains beyond—all spread out. "This is it," said Bill. "O.K., baby," said
Floss. They were both enraptured by the city and the landscape ("It

[29] William Carlos Williams to WTS, 15 November 1954, Scott Collection,
John Hay Library.

looks like a preview of eternity," said Bill) and want to come back—
really want to. We've had wonderful letters from them telling how
much of their hearts they left here. Floss is bright, sharp—right there
beside him all the time, but never obtrusively, fussily so: just *there*.
I wish you could have seen them picnicking: Bill was waving to Chimayo boys riding bareback past us to see (oh, rare sight) water coming over the dam above us, and after he'd eaten he sagged back on the
blanket on the ground, and Floss put her arms around him and held
him. Few minutes later as he got into the back seat . . . he remarked
"I wish to God I were still capable." He has a new book of poems
coming out. He said coming down from Truchas, "I don't know how
I could use all this, but I have a notion I shall." He's about to be 72. . . .
I read him a few poems. I had no intention of doing so: by which I
mean the thought hadn't occurred to me. But El behind my back had
told him about one & started things going. I was scared—but later very
glad, for the things he said both that last evening & on the way to the
airport next morning constituted a *recharge*. Not least because he's—
for all his sweetness and gentleness—an unwaveringly honest man.[30]

The tone of this account borders on the worshipful, but Scott did
not feel quite the same way about Dr. Williams as he had, when a
college boy, about Robinson. "You get older and you don't get so
hero-worshippy that you rush home and put down everything,
and sometimes you wish you did." Clearly, though, he cherished
his friendship with Williams, and valued the older man's judgment
of his work, though he knew of Williams's tendency to overpraise.
Though no longer a schoolboy apprentice at his trade, Scott still
took almost as gospel Williams's comments on his poetry, and made
alterations accordingly. But Win felt no inclination to imitate the
Williams manner; he thought arbitrary the doctor's pronounce-
ment that American poetry should follow the three-step-down
stanza he himself used. Where Robinson had influenced Scott's
poetic voice, Williams stood as an example of the need to persist at
the life of poetry. Unrecognized and unrewarded for decades, Williams had finally attracted the critical—if not quite the popular—
notice he deserved. And he had come through all those long years of
frustration an extraordinarily kind, generous man, "a nice country
doctor who happened to have this touch of genius." Being with Bill
and Floss, Scott confided, was "like being in the most comfortable

[30] WTS to Ben and Betty Bagdikian, 20 June 1955.

old shoes you had ever had." The heartening thing was that the
genius *was* finally recognized, though, as Floss told Win, "more
than once in his life he would discuss with her giving it all up because he thought nobody cared really about his writing."[31] On his
birthday in 1958, Scott wrote a poem for Williams—and for himself—in which he affirmed the primacy of art as aging took its inevitable toll:

Paging Dr. Paterson

On this day I was born
Forty-eight years ago.
And what's it to you? or me?

I sit in a little house.
I can see on the sun outside
Apricot blossoming white
And the pink-blossoming peach
In cold mountain air.
I have come this far, this high,
From the slow hill of birth.

I have read the morning away
With an old man's youngest poem
Made in his seventy-fifth year—
A time when all is one—
To say that virgin and whore
Are as one, and Art is all:
The poem become at last
A vast meadow of flowers,
A brave dance of Yes.

That old man, mad for words.

I recall the day I said
"I am twelve! I am twelve! I am twelve!"
That day I knew I was twelve.
Who knows now what I am?
Or how far I have come?
But closer to this hawk-high sun.

---

[31] Quoted in Donald Dean Eulert, "Winfield Townley Scott: Conversations
on Poets and the Art of Poetry" (Ph.D. dissertation, University of New Mexico,
January 1969), pp. 53–59.

I should like to send these trees,
White and pink over black,
To the old man, to say
"Here, these are all for you."
And: "Neither you nor I
Are in the habit of prayer;
So will you *wish* me then
For the year I am seventy-five
The meadow, the measured dance."

I watch the flowered branches.
They curve to my one desire.
They bend toward my last desire.[32]

Perhaps Scott, too, could achieve the artistically satisfying old age
of a Williams, or a Yeats, or a Hardy. But especially of a Williams,
for he carved particularly in the American grain. English critics,
Scott observed, could not properly hear or evaluate such poetry.[33]

Later that summer the Scotts took a trip to California that ended
in an interview with Robinson Jeffers. First stop on the trip was
Los Angeles, where Jeannette and Bob Wolfe lived. Wolfe had arranged for the Scotts to watch Cecil B. De Mille direct a scene for
The Ten Commandments—"thunder, lightning, the Voice of God,
and Charlton Heston (as Moses) up on rocks receiving." That was
fun, and Lindsay, stagestruck teen-ager with autograph book in
hand, loved it. But Win didn't like the city, "so endlessly big, so
filled with six lanes of cars speeding along, so saturated somehow
with the Get Ahead falsy atmosphere." Ellie was more openly un-
impressed with L.A. On the De Mille set she was forced to remove
her Indian moccasins, for the bells jangled as she walked. On another occasion, she dressed in an old sweater for a night on the town.
Win, angry, refused to take her out; he and Lindsay went to dinner
alone. Ellie and Win alike felt much more at home at the Santa
Ynez ranch of Ellie's sister, Kay Perkins, a mile north of Santa
Barbara. Despite the chaos produced by ten children (six Kay's,
four the Scotts'), horses, dogs, and twenty-seven cats, Win found
the place restful after Los Angeles.[34]

[32] WTS, "Paging Dr. Paterson," *New and Selected Poems* (1967), pp. 81–82.
[33] WTS, " *dirty hand": The Literary Notebooks of Winfield Townley Scott*
(1969), p. 150.
[34] Interview, Mrs. Jeannette Wolfe, Los Angeles, 3 February 1970; interview,

It was Kay who suggested the drive up to Carmel. The trip offered a view of some of the most beautiful shoreline in the world, but Win was unappreciative; freeway driving terrified him almost as much as narrow mountain roads. Kay's teen-age daughter by a previous marriage, Wendy Wilder, came along, however, and shared his highway panic. More importantly, her young beauty took him back to college days and the memory of a golden girl, Marion Doescher:

> *Brief Encounter*
> What I had never imagined: your return
> In the guise of an actual girl: and there
> She stood so slender in the summer light
> And leaned—in such a way—the light came through
> Her thin white shirt and silhouetted her
> So I was shaken with remembering
> And silent with impossible desire.
> O I so heavy with years and all I knew,
> All that she could not know—she was not you—
> Yet shared (I thought) that vibrancy of silence,
> Then walked to me and touched me, as if she knew
> Something neither of us would ever say.[35]

At Carmel, Win sent a timorous note to Robinson Jeffers, hardly expecting a response, but Jeffers phoned and Win and Ellie went to see him. For years, Win had regarded him "as the greatest poet now living," admiring in his verse the evolution of a "style expansive enough to manipulate all occasions, from personal to universal. . . . He does not make a poetry which depends upon symbol, innuendo, or any kind of double-talk. Of its kind there has been nothing successfully like it since Whitman. It is direct. It is a man speaking."[36] At sixty-eight, Jeffers seemed "a quiet, withdrawn man; yet kind, gentle, friendly." He looked old, "but slender, tall: the hollow-cheeked face; and extraordinary eyes—light blue & (almost) hooded. A haunting face." The meeting was hardly momentous: not much was said to tell grandchildren. Still, it was "like walking into the poems: the stone house, the tower outside, the foggy sea

---

Lindsay Scott, Washington, D.C., 26 September 1969; WTS to Ben and Betty Bagdikian, 23 September 1955.

[35] Interview, Mrs. Kay Perkins, Beverly Hills, 3 February 1970; WTS, "Brief Encounter," *New and Selected Poems*, p. 102.

[36] WTS, "*a dirty hand,*" p. 20.

beyond another window." As the Scotts left, Jeffers asked them to call again if they came back to California. He had the look, Win decided, "of a man who . . . may feel pushed-aside, neglected, & lonely."[37]

The summer of 1955 was especially satisfying to Win Scott because his son Lindsay had come to spend the school holidays with him. Small and dark like his mother, Lindsay had established a reputation in school as a troublemaker. During 1954, for example, he wrote Win diary letters from Rhode Island (a few notes each day) that described his beating up a schoolmate, his report on "Five ways to Rid Yourself of Teachers," and his discovery of girls ("I am getting awful tired of sex. Every where you go is sex sex sex"). He berated his father for sending him a winter coat several sizes too large: "I love it. It's beautiful. It's peachy keen. It's gone. It's real cool and crazy. I *gota send it back*." But for all his antics and sarcasm, Lindsay clearly missed his father. "Did you know," the fourteen-year-old wrote, on January 12, 1955, "that in 146 days I will be in your arms at the air port in Albuquerque, New Mexico."[38] Once in Santa Fe he was able to pursue his theatrical bent; he did odd jobs for the summer theater, and even got a walk-on part as a bellboy ten days after arriving. Lindsay "seems happy & content," Win wrote, "and he has taken very well our plan to stay on another year.—I had to talk to him before making it definite."[39] Later, when Lindsay chose to enroll at the University of New Mexico, and to make Santa Fe his home away from college, his father was overjoyed.

Life in Santa Fe attracted Win, too, because of its spirit of tolerance. Attempting to fix upon the particular stimulus that has brought modern colonists to the town of thirty-thousand, Paul Horgan concluded that even beyond the bracing effect of the altitude, the air, the light, the color, the primary reason lay in "an insinuation of freedom in behavior . . . in an opportunity for an

[37] WTS to S. Foster Damon, 1 September 1955, WTS to Hilary Masters, 5 October 1955, Scott Collection, John Hay Library.

[38] Lindsay Scott to WTS, 22 September 1954, 17 October 1954, 20 October 1954, 19 November 1954, and 12 January 1955, Scott Collection, John Hay Library.

[39] Interview, Lindsay Scott, Washington, D.C., 26 September 1969; WTS to Ben and Betty Bagdikian, 20 June 1955.

individual man or woman to live a life of free expression."[40] Certainly none of the customary stigmas was observed. "The boy-and-boy, woman-and-woman arrangements are notable," Win wrote Williams. "They live together and run shops together; nothing much is made of it; some—both sorts—we are friends with are pleasant, seemingly unpredatory,—settled."[41] Nor was the artist living on someone else's income a rarity: Win had plenty of company in that role to soften his feelings of guilt. Still, he wrote disparagingly to Bagdikian of his "endowed escape" and to the Chadwicks of one of Ellie's many automobile accidents (a week after they arrived in Santa Fe she had smashed the fender of the new station wagon when she turned around in the car to "look for her pocketbook, which she discovered when the car struck an embankment & the handbag fell off the top of the fender") when, in April 1955, El drove smack into a truck. Though no one was hurt, he told the Chadwicks, the garage bills—characteristically, there was no insurance to cover them—ran to four hundred dollars. "El moaned the bills to her mother—who happened to telephone. El's Ma said: Why don't you get a job?—Which I thought in extreme delicacy: not, that is, suggesting *I* get a job!"[42]

Shaking his sense of guilt would not be easy, even in a town where the Puritan ethic operated almost not at all. Aware of the writer's need for self-discipline, Win lamented that he smoked too much, drank too much, loafed too much. "And then I worry in a frustration of morning wishes crossed up by evening entertainments. Never the other way around. And I feel like a bum and get frightened—though, so far, not frightened enough." Then, to reassure himself, "I bet Katherine Lee Bates had a hell of a lot more self-discipline than Baudelaire."[43] Even more ominous was the ease with which he could assume a pose: "He lights a pipe and in his hairy tweed suit sighs back against the upholstered wing chair by the fireplace where the mulled ale is kept warm on the hearth and

[40] WTS, "Calendar," p. 213.
[41] WTS to William Carlos Williams, 15 April 1955, American Literature Collection, Beinecke Library, Yale University.
[42] WTS to Ben and Betty Bagdikian, 17 September 1954 and 20 June 1955; WTS to Paul and Frances Chadwick, 2 May 1955.
[43] WTS, "a dirty hand," p. 24.

he quotes to a few academic companions, "Of the making of books there is no end." And they nod and twinkle in silent assent. This is (or was: am I old-style?) the Literary Atmosphere. —God save me. God save us all."[44]

Walker (Bill) Gibson, then teaching at Amherst, spent the 1955–1956 academic year in Santa Fe on a Ford Foundation teaching grant. He had heard from Richard Wilbur that the Scotts lived there, and one Sunday morning he stopped by their house, mentioned that he was a writer as well as a teacher, and was immediately asked to dinner. The Scotts and Gibsons saw a good deal of each other that year. "They were exceedingly kind to us," Bill recalls. "Indeed the Scotts' hospitality must have become during ensuing years one of the great tales of the West."[45] But Gibson was shocked at Win's impressionistic approach to literature; Scott, for his part, scorned the analytical methods Gibson had acquired in graduate school. At one small dinner party Bill provoked Win into a rare burst of anger by denigrating American literature. At first, Win wrote Dr. Williams, "like the nice, sweet, uneventful gent I am, I kept silent—but got, so to speak, silenter & silenter until I heard him say Sherwood Anderson was a 'vulgar and coarse writer.' Whereupon—much, I immediately gathered, to everyone else's paralyzed amazement—I began lifting the diningroom table rapidly up & down & laced the man out to the rhythm of it all. (It is a heavy diningroom table). Before I got through I had not only spoken of Anderson but damn near *all* American Lit; and *when* I got through the man remarked that after all he had never read Winesburg, Ohio." Gibson remembers the incident differently; the argument resulted from his disparagement of nineteenth-century American literature in contrast to British. Whatever the authors in dispute, however, there was no question that Win's literary nationalism led to the outburst.[46]

The Gibsons thought the atmosphere of Santa Fe both liberating and dangerous. Taking their first year off from teaching was a most pleasant experience, to be sure, but, as Nancy Gibson remarked,

[44] Ibid., p. 150.

[45] Walker Gibson to SD, 1 September 1969.

[46] WTS to William Carlos Williams, 3 June 1956, Collection of American Literature, Beinecke Library, Yale University; Walker Gibson to SD, 1 September 1969; interview, Walker and Nancy Gibson, Amherst, 4 December 1969.

"we were saved by the knowledge that we were coming back to Amherst." Saved, that is, from too much drinking, too many parties. With the Scotts and the Adlers, they went on Sunday picnics, where Win would ingenuously confess that he liked Sundays "because you could start drinking earlier." And there were plenty of companions to join him over drinks: "the number of people living on unearned income in that town was amazing." Altogether, the Gibsons thought Santa Fe a very unhealthy place to live. "It's easy to see," Bill commented, "how you could rot there."[47] Win himself was not unaware of this danger: "You could live a cocktail-party existence here; some do. For my kind of person it can be an overstimulating place—your head next morning is filled with too much conversation, too much personality of others vibrant with that freedom of be-havior. . . . And there are those—Robinson Jeffers, as a visitor, among them—who have told me that they find the atmosphere here conducive to pleasant coma but not to work." But during the first Santa Fe years Win worked steadily and well; "many of us," he wrote, "have reacted differently" from Jeffers.[48]

Late in 1955 the Scotts took the step that made their exile from New England permanent: they bought the handsome house at 550 East Alameda where Ellie and the school-age Scott children still reside. In a letter to Frank Merchant, Win described the place: "It's a biggish 3-bedroom house built of now-unprocurable 20-inch adobe, and it has 2 guest houses out back—a simple bedroom & bath one (for Lindsay) and another with livingroom, kitchenette, bath, & 2-bed bedroom (for Merchants, etc.) . . . The house is very near town, yet faces a dead-end, countryish, dirt road with nothing across it from us except cottonwood trees and the Santa Fe River. It has some lawn front & back, huge blue spruce trees & ditto black locusts. Its decor so to speak—its landscaping—could be New England. Make of that what you will!"[49]

They paid $45,000, cash, for the house. A check for that amount came from El's trust account in Providence on 28 November 1955, along with the "usual monthly draft of $1,400." Win's financial contribution was smaller. In February 1956, they moved in, and

[47] Walker Gibson to SD, 1 September 1969; interview, Walker and Nancy Gibson, Amherst, 4 December 1969.
[48] WTS, "Calendar," p. 214.
[49] WTS to Frank Merchant, 6 December 1955.

in the mail he received a permissions check for $5.50.[50] "Biggish"
at first, the Scotts increased their new home's size by adding a huge,
two-level bedroom, with a desk and floor-to-ceiling bookcase on the
upper level to house Win's collection of books of and about poetry
and poets, and with an outsize bed below, bathed in the light admitted by enormous windows. The desk was partly for Win's use,
since the larger of the two guest houses, though converted to a study
(the "etc." of his description to Merchant), was too often occupied
by visitors to serve effectively as a workroom.

As Win wrote Edward McSorley in April 1956, "Santa Fe is a
great place of guests." Already that year there had been visits from
El's sister and mother, the Selden Rodmans, Dick Eberhart, and
the Malcolm Cowleys.[51] In the spring Justin and Anne Bernays
Kaplan came to town, and though they did not stay with the Scotts,
they and Win developed a strong and persisting bond of friendship
and admiration. Justin, who later won a Pulitzer Prize for his biography of Mark Twain, was then an editor at Simon and Schuster;
Anne, a novelist, worked in the New York office of Houghton
Mifflin. Both of them tried, unsuccessfully, in the year that followed,
to place two of Scott's book projects (the poems published in 1959
as *Scrimshaw* and the book of essays that appeared in 1961 as
Exiles and Fabrications) with their respective firms. Later in 1956
the distinguished poet-critic M. L. Rosenthal, visiting professor at
the University of New Mexico, invited Win to come for a reading,
heard—and liked—the parts of *The Dark Sister* he read, and took
the manuscript back to New York University Press, which eventually rewarded that long poem, two decades in the making, with
publication, in 1958. With literary people like Mack Rosenthal and
Joe and Annie Kaplan, Win felt among his own kind; with them
he could, and did, make a commitment to friendship. In a magazine
article, after Win's death, Annie Kaplan tried to suggest how she
felt about Win Scott. "Imagine the closest thing to being in love,
with neither the sexual overtones or ambivalent undertones to
abrade the relationship. It hasn't happened to me very often; I
suspect it happened to him a lot, he was that kind of person. He

50 Donald S. Babcock to EMS, 28 November 1955, Walker Gibson to WTS, 5
August 1956, Scott Collection, John Hay Library.
51 WTS to Edward McSorley, 17 April 1956.

was generous."[52] And if such friendships helped to end his long period without a book on the market, there was no harm in that. But the succession of guests, of cocktail parties and dinner parties, hardly contributed to the writing of poetry. After they moved into the house on East Alameda, Bill Gibson observed, "It was clear that no author of any kind was going to pass through the Southwest without attending a party there." Win himself complained, in letters to Philbrick and others, of the hectic social activity, but he did nothing about it. The poet William Stafford, who stopped by the Scotts' home in the mid-1960's, sensed that Win "liked to know people, that he enjoyed the place he had—geographically, and in the swirl of literary visiting. In his place, I might have wondered sometimes if my home were not *too* easily a stopping place; but I could not tell from his manner that he was thinking such a thought when we were there!"[53]

Ellie, who had been active in Hampton civic and cultural affairs, redoubled her efforts in Santa Fe. The "girl," Scott wrote McSorley in April 1956, "is knee-deep in Santa Fe: PTA—cub scout mothering—League of Women Voters. God knows what all. She *still* has time for me, but I'm fearful it's running out."[54] Not entirely in jest, he committed a piece of doggerel in his notebooks entitled "The Aging Husband"; it expressed a complaint that would be aggravated by the passage of time:

> The ardent girl he used to lay
> Is now content to skip or skim it.
> In committee work she goes the limit.
> She is fulfilled by PTA.[55]

Win and Eleanor found common cause, however, in support of Adlai Stevenson's bid to unseat President Eisenhower. Stevenson had a style, and a command of the language, that made him a hero to Scott. During the 1956 campaign he participated in a political stunt with novelist Thomas Duncan. In October, the local Volun-

[52] Anne Bernays, "The Outer Shores of Love," *Boston* (November 1968), pp. 71–73.
[53] Walker Gibson to SD, 1 September 1969; William Stafford to SD, 30 January 1970.
[54] WTS to Edward McSorley, 17 April 1956.
[55] WTS, *"a dirty hand,"* p. 137.

teers for Stevenson held a White Donkey party—a combination
rummage sale and dinner, with local authors contributing autographed books for sale. Duncan acted as auctioneer, and Win,
secreted in the back of the room, as the Voice of Eisenhower. As
Duncan recalls the stunt, "from the platform I called out something
like, 'Mr. President, we are worried about the high cost of living.
What do you plan to do about this?' Silence. I carried on the gag,
asking the President all sorts of pointed questions, and there was
always silence. Finally I said, 'Mr. President, some of us are getting
up a game of golf. Would you like to join us?' Whereupon Win
shouted, 'I'll be right with you.' "[56]

"Is New Mexico so delightful," Win's father asked plaintively in
December 1955, "that you would forsake New England? Think you
would miss the green of N.E., and the water,"[57] And of course,
Win Scott did miss his home of forty-four years. To the Bagdikians,
living in the Scott's former home in Providence, he sent off a plea
to be kept informed about "marriages, separations, & divorces,"
and other news. "Yesterday was El's birthday," he wrote on 23
September 1955, and "were we amongst our lolling old friends at
Wayland Manor? at the Ben Grosvenor? We were —in case you
noticed—not. We were quietly at home with cake, ice cream, &
three kids."[58] The night before the birthday they had celebrated at
the Pink Garter in Lamy with Lu & Nat Adler, where El observed
the occasion by listening to the Rocky Marciano fight with the
kitchen help.[59] A picture of the Stonington waterfront, framed and
in the Scotts' living-room, bored "a hole 2,000 miles deep in the
wall."[60] As he got older, Win found himself further removed, but
never separated, from New England landscape and people. Even in
Santa Fe he sought out La Farge and other refugees from New
England for drinks and conversation. "Sometimes," he wistfully
concluded his "Calendar of Santa Fe," "we speak of the sea."[61]

Much as the Southwest excited Win and served to revive his
sexual and artistic powers, he was unable, of course, to escape those

[56] Thomas Duncan to SD, 22 August 1969.
[57] Douglas W. Scott to WTS, 4 December 1955, Scott Collection, John Hay Library.
[58] WTS to Ben and Betty Bagdikian, 19 December 1957.
[59] Ibid., 23 September 1955.
[60] WTS to Paul and Frances Chadwick, 7 March 1955.
[61] WTS, "Calendar," p. 215.

demons that had begun to pursue him in earnest at Hampton. In the
obituary columns, which he compulsively scanned, he found ample
evidence of his own mortality, and that of his friends:

> This is the time of What happened to So-and-So?
> And to all those other faces in the Class Book?
> And to me? Of knowing too frequently
> What happened to So-and-So: Death snatching among us
> With unexpected insult. Of the fatigue of friendship:
> How pleasant to meet, but everyone hangs around
> Longer than one wants. Of dwindling sex[62]

Neither had Win been able to shake off doubts about his masculinity. These tendencies were on display in December 1955, when
he and Bill Gibson motored to the western part of the state to attend
the annual Shalako ceremony at Zuni. It was, Scott wrote, a tremendous experience. Traditionally, six Zuni gods blessed six new
houses in the village:

There are other dancers . . . but all is dominated by the ten-foot-tall
Shalako figures. The huge mask rests on the shoulders of the Zuni. He
works its clattering beak by strings. In the dances he runs and swoops
with an amazing grace.

These factual matters are not the point. The point is you feel you
are in the presence of towering, barbaric gods. Never more so than
when they first appear. That is at dusk, across the river from the village.
You stand amidst other Anglos at the end of the village and peer across,
barely able to see the gigantic figures as they slowly approach from
the hills. Eerie cries sound here and there in the sudden dark, and the
bitter cold, which worsens all night, sets in. For an hour or more the
Zunis come and go propitiating the Shalako with gifts. The gods stand
very near, but the darkness is so thick you cannot see them, only hear,
now and again, the clack of wooden beaks. Then with a rush, surrounded by the seemingly pygmy men of the town, they enter it and
each goes to a new house. And then you have a cold evening to wait
while the Zunis' feasting takes place; the dances, which last till dawn,
do not begin until midnight or after. . . .

Two or three times in the night I weakened enough to wonder if the
adventure was worth it: we were so cold despite long underwear, re-
course to the heater in the car, cups of coffee, and forbidden nips of our

[62] WTS, "Notes to a Gentleman I Once Met," *The Colorado Review* 1 (Winter
1956–1957): 41.

secreted whiskey. Yes, it was worth it; and we stayed on, wandering from house to house, until the first streak of paleness came over the mesa to the east. We were back in Santa Fe by noon.[63]

Only between the lines does Scott begin to suggest the ceremony's challenge to his manhood, which he later put into poetry as "The Outcast":

> I belonged to that tribe but I never danced.
> I kept the eagle feather close to my chest.
> Off in the night I shook to the pounce of feet,
> Dancing dancing dancing dancing together.
> I shivered to the rattle of turtle shells,
> To the knock of the deerhorn, to the outcry
> Of ankle bells that could be instantly hushed.
> I carried with me hidden the pouch of seed.
> If I could not dance could I belong to that tribe?
> In the darkness I watched tremendous gods
> So tall they were silhoueted against the moon
> That chilled the tallest, farthest mesa; I knew
> Each ten-foot god masked its fill of a man.
> Bird whistles and clacking of beaks. Zero.
> Their tilting rush into the village dwarfed it.
> They ran to bless but towered like avengers.
> They moved so much like gods that they became gods.
> I shook to the dancing dancing I could not follow.
> Inside the masks I knew were naked men.
> Where the wind in that hollowed canyon moans
> "Zuni—Zuni"; where I crept: bury me with the women.[64]

Gibson remembers two incidents during the trip which Scott nowhere reported. They had taken two pints of whiskey along to ward off the night cold, but police stopped cars at the entrance to the reservation to check for liquor. When asked, Win admitted (Bill would have lied) they had brought some along, and he was most obviously afraid (but finally consented) to give up one bottle and secrete the other, a stratagem urged on him by Gibson. When they left the ceremony at dawn, they passed an automobile accident, and another person who had stopped asked for their help in freeing a woman trapped inside her car. Win evaded the request and drove

---

[63] WTS, "Calendar," pp. 200–201.
[64] WTS, "The Outcast," *Change of Weather* (1964), p. 4.

off instead to call the police. He and Bill proceeded down the road, tried to make a phone call, and finally kept going when they saw a police car speeding toward the accident. To Gibson, Win had seemed unduly timorous in the first incident, and almost immoral in the second, in his reluctance to be involved in a real tragedy.[65]

Trying to assess Win's reaction to Santa Fe, Ellie concluded that at first "it was very good for him, and then the magic wore off. He had certain recurrent problems (alcoholism, inability to write, impotency). They occurred in Providence, Hampton, Santa Fe. I'm not sure locale had much to do with it all, but perhaps I am wrong."[66] More likely not. To Webster Schott, Win would talk about the light, the air, the beauty of the land, in Santa Fe, while lamenting as well its distance from the center of the publishing world. But he came to realize, with Schott and Conrad Knickerbocker, the supremacy of psychic over real geography: that you carry the geography with you.[67]

[65] Interview, Walker and Nancy Gibson, Amherst, 4 December 1969.
[66] EMS to SD, 26 July 1969.
[67] Interview, Webster Schott, Kansas City, Missouri, 29 December 1969.

So October 27 is the day on which, as I think
Conrad Aiken once remarked about publishing a
book of verse, we drop the feather in the Grand
Canyon.[1]

11. Feathers in the Canyon

AFTER A DECADE without a new book, Winfield Townley Scott published four in the five years which spanned his fiftieth birthday.
The Dark Sister appeared in 1958; *Scrimshaw* in 1959; *Exiles and
Fabrications* in 1961; and *Collected Poems: 1937–1962* in 1962.
The history of these books, as of his previous work, bore testimony
to the tired observation that in publishing (especially of poetry),
it is not so much what you do as who you know that counts. As a
young man, Win had known Horace Gregory, and Gregory gave
two of his books of verse the needed shove toward publication. In
1956 and 1960, Win met two other men who helped see his work
into print. Gregory, as well as these others—Mack Rosenthal and

[1] WTS to Lucia Staniels at Doubleday, 26 July 1967[?]. What Scott was trying to remember, almost surely, was Don Marquis in the "Sun Dial": "Publishing a volume of verse is like dropping a rose-petal down the Grand Canyon and
waiting for the echo."

Bill Kelley—clearly thought Scott ought to be published, and they were right. Still, without their intervention, Win's long and frustrating unpublished years might have stretched on even longer.

Eighteen years before Mack Rosenthal read *The Dark Sister*, Win had started work on the long narrative poem about the eleventh-century voyage to Vinland-America of Leif Ericson's mad, ambitious, illegitimate half-sister, Freydis. "The first version," Win recalled, "was [in] very short lines and I was very young [28] and I didn't have the sense to clothe it, to body it forth in characterization of these people. But I kept fumbling with it over the years and finally got . . . the long line."[2] In the mid-1940's, he rewrote the poem completely to adapt to the long line, and in Hampton he rewrote again and expanded the poem to its final length of 115 book pages. Then *Sister* knocked around various publishing offices until, in the fall of 1956, Rosenthal took it back to New York University Press, which he wanted "to begin publishing good poetry."[3] The Press assigned Wilson Follett, an eminent arbiter of American usage, as a reader, and Follett turned in "the kind of once-in-a-lifetime report which should obviate all a writer's wretched days."[4]

"In one of the curious coincidences that can happen even in editorial corners," Follett's report began, "this magnificent narrative poem fell into my lap on what, in calendars of the Western world, passes for the Day of Discovery—Columbus Day." He was bowled over by *The Dark Sister*:

> It is a tale greatly told, and with a noble range of poetic effects, from the classic obscenities of the seamen . . . to the splendor of [its] description of the aurora borealis. . . . The experience of this poem—a great, sustained experience that begins in the first sentence and holds into the last—is like coming above a tree line. It is an experience outspread rich and thick over sustained passages, yet concentrated in stupendous lines and fractions of lines. . . . This is a piece of literature, and it may be around to make itself felt long after the Spenderists and the Audenarians have ceased from the business of tying knots in their own

---

[2] Quoted in Donald Dean Eulert, "Winfield Townley Scott: Conversations on Poets and the Art of Poetry" (Ph.D. dissertation, University of New Mexico, January 1969), p. 126.

[3] M. L. Rosenthal to WTS, 3 August 1956, Scott Collection, John Hay Library, Brown University.

[4] WTS, *"a dirty hand": The Literary Notebooks of Winfield Townley Scott* (1969), p. 112.

brains and ours in the name of poetry. It is for the instant recognition of such things when they come that we sit patiently in editorial corners, biding our time—and let us hope that the members of the University's editorial committee will know, too, what they are there for. Allah is being very good to us this week.[5]

But before he would commit himself, Allan Angoff at the Press asked Win Scott to summon up supporting evidence from a number of fellow poets who had read the poem in manuscript. Back came letters from William Carlos Williams, Malcolm Cowley, Richard Eberhart, Horace Gregory, and Lee Anderson, urging publication of the poem. The response of Anderson, who had arranged for Win's Library of Congress recording of the poem, was the most laudatory. "It may well be the best long narrative poem in our literature," he wrote. It was to the other, better known writers, however, that the Press turned for its dust-jacket encomiums. "Dramatic, passionate, written in modern verse that carries a suggestion of the Eddas," Cowley wrote, "*The Dark Sister* is not only an epic but truly a poem." Eberhart said simply that in *The Dark Sister* "Winfield Scott has written the best long poem to appear in a long time." And Williams, who did not much like the long line, nonetheless concluded that "the present story brushes all piddling questions of style aside in its headlong and dramatic career. I was fascinated by the story and eager to finish it."[6]

Fortified by the favorable opinions of this distinguished company, New York University Press decided to undertake publication in November 1956. To Rosenthal, Win acknowledged "The resurrection & the life that you have brought about . . . for the moment, I'm born again—it's 8 years since my last book—and I owe it, unpayably, all to you."[7] NYU Press took its time bringing the book out, and it was not until 19 February 1958, twenty years after Scott had first begun work on it, that *The Dark Sister* was published. The reviews, conceivably influenced by the authoritative praise on its

[5] Wilson Follett, New York University Press reader's report on *The Dark Sister*, 15 October 1956, pp. 1–5.

[6] Lee Anderson, prefatory note to a reading of Winfield Townley Scott's *The Dark Sister*, poetry archive of the Library of Congress; Malcolm Cowley to Barbara Hall (New York University Press), 17 October 1957; Richard Eberhart to Barbara Hall, 24 October 1957; William Carlos Williams to Barbara Hall, 1 November 1957.

[7] WTS to M. L. Rosenthal, 10 November 1956.

jacket, ranged from good to reverent. "Though Winfield Townley Scott has written admirable verse for over twenty years," Robert Hillyer remarked in the *New York Times Book Review*, " 'The Dark Sister' is his masterpiece and one of the remarkable poems of recent times. It has excitement and depth. With a control of his medium that never falters, he handles characterization, narrative and landscape with equal power in the flexible cadences of his verse." Judson Jerome, in the *Antioch Review*, proposed that Scott, like great artists of the past, had achieved anonymity. "In this poem you do not see the author nor his words: you see the saga itself, conceived greatly, delivered with unashamed excitement, and I, for one, throbbed with it to the end." Had this poem come down to us from the time it treats, James Dickey observed in *Sewanee Review*, "it would have been reckoned a masterpiece." For *Sister*, William Jay Smith wrote Win, "you should have the Pulitzer Prize."[8]

There were no prizes for *The Dark Sister*, however, nor did all the early enthusiasm for the book stand the test of time. Dickey, for example, on rereading the poem in 1969, decided it seemed "a fairly predictable kind of wedding—if that is the word—between Robinson Jeffers and Archibald MacLeish." Jay Martin's view of the book "is rather dim."[9] And those who most admire Win Scott's poetry, men like Ben Clough, George P. Elliott, and Webster Schott, find *Sister* less moving, less satisfying, than his shorter narrative or lyric verse.

What *The Dark Sister* does best is exactly what Dr. Williams singled out: it tells its story with clarity and boldness and sustained suspense. When Win had first come across an account of the voyage, in Edgar Lee Masters's long poem "The New World," he had been immediately excited. Later, tracking it down through Greenland sagas, he uncovered only the bare bones of a story. "No psychology, no motivation, but simply the page . . . just *outlining* the basic happenings . . ." That, he decided, was "a great advantage. You

---

[8] Robert Hillyer, "On This Voyage Death Went Along," *New York Times Book Review*, 9 March 1958, p. 10; Judson Jerome, "Through Thick and Thin," *Antioch Review* 18 (March 1958): 106–109; James Dickey, "The Human Power," *Sewanee Review* 67 (Summer 1959): 506–509; William Jay Smith to WTS, 14 December 1958, Scott Collection, John Hay Library. These and other reviews are pasted in Scrapbook 12, Scott Collection, John Hay Library.

[9] James Dickey to Webster Schott, 17 September 1969; Jay Martin to SD, 7 July 1969.

don't want too much."[10] From the sagas, he learned that Leif
Ericson had taken to Christianity very seriously, but that his sister
Freydis had not. Thus one of the themes of the book was the conflict
between the pagan and the Christian; if anything, Scott was more
sympathetic to the pagan point of view, as less productive of
hypocrisy. With no more than a hint from the narrative, however,
Win supplied the missing psychology for two other themes that run
through the book.

The first of these has to do with the nature of the land, Vinland/
America. Gudrid, who had lost her husband on a Vinland expedition, insists that

> there is evil in that place.
> That land was not meant for us—there is something
> against us,
> Something beneath the soft grass and the bright leaves,
> More than threat of savages native there. Some trick
> of the sun
> Gentles its uttermost kingdom and lures us into it as
> if it were
> A shining paradise beyond the black cold sea. Those
> who go in
> Are netted with a silken skein of light, move as
> dreamers in dream,
> Fancy themselves gods of a sort come miraculously
> to an earth-garden of Valhalla
> —And are welcomed with poisonous arrows, and
> yet dream still: those spared,
> Lulled to birdsong and the great shards of the sun
> on the coast rock,
> The way of the wind in the tall trees, the forested
> hills
> Sighing of peace and wealth and a kind earth
> flowering under their feet
> —They are sucked weak. I tell you trouble and
> danger weave in the air.[11]

But Leif refuses to believe this, and at the end, after the slaughter
of the disastrous voyage, he puzzles over the meaning of America:

[10] Quoted in Eulert, "Scott," pp. 125–126.
[11] WTS, *The Dark Sister* (1958), pp. 17–18.

'Did we find more than we were meant to find? Come
    by long westward sailing
Where we were never meant to go, since we could
    not stay? Once having walked that land
We knew all others harsher. And though it could not
    be ours we set names on its shores
And marked it with some of our dearest bones; but
    we knew all the same that it was not evil.
Only that it was not ours, only that it waited.'[12]

It was not America, waiting for another discovery, that was evil,
but the voyagers themselves—and worst and strongest among them
Freydis, the dark, malevolent monster feared by all. Win made of
Freydis a tremendously dominant woman, unscrupulous even with
her dignified, kingly half brother, Leif (whose legitimacy she envies
and resents), scornful of her weak, ineffectual husband, Thorvard,
as of all other men, monomaniacal in her lust for wealth, fame, and
power. She leads the Greenlanders on a joint exploitation of Vinland with a ship full of Norwegians. Through vicious cunning and
greed, Freydis pits Greenlander against Norwegian until, when it
is time to return, all the Norwegians (and many of the Greenlanders) have been slaughtered. She will share her booty, a cargo
of fresh-cut lumber, with no one. Scott felt in her "a vibration of
something as wild and mad and ambitious as Lady Macbeth," but
the vibration came from within. The dark sister of his American
saga may have represented an intensified projection of all those
well-intentioned women—Aggie Townley, Bessie Scott, Savila,
Eleanor—who had held Win, child and man, in apparently willing
subjection. Consider Scott's inherent self-contempt revealed in the
venomous thoughts of Freydis after she has been unfaithful to her
husband (obviously, there was no such language in the sagas):

—'Or do I despise all men?' said Freydis aloud,
    walking homeward alone
Along the wind-scuffed beach, ghosts of the dawn
    wavering over the coldly quiet sea.
'Their little jabbing trick in their moments of
    proud flesh. A woman permits it—

[12] Ibid., p. 114.

Permits the paddling of hands like a dog's paws
   on her and the jigging dance.
The bone digs for the god and he pants above it
   like a drunken emperor
Rubbing himself in victory.
                              'Short, shallow, soon done.
   How they wilt away.
As though they were the satiated conquerors—
   not the possessed and the spat out—
Snore back into dank-breathed sleep. What woman
   could like it and like herself?
Only a wench so hollow she feels empty without it
   to needle her vanity.
Let me be closed and cool and dry.

   'I know his kind, and they are all alike
Having had it, he'll come sniffing and skulking
   around to snatch an easy piece.
  .   .   .   .
   . . . once is always enough for me—
Once now and then with a new one as a reminder
   how weak they are.
But I was a fool to let wine make me forget that I
   need no more reminders.
Let me be left alone. I want to be rinsed head to
   foot, new-clothed and combed and left alone.'[13]

In January 1958, the month before his book was published, Win
stayed in Santa Fe with the children while El went to visit her
parents in Florida. In an angry letter to Eleanor, probably written
after considerable drinking, he talked about giving up book reviewing. Irita Van Doren had sent him "yet another unknown novel"
to review, and though Win resolved to do the job,

this one-a-week hack-writing business is not my program at all; I
am not ready to admit that I'm nothing but a lousy little tenth-rate
scribbler. Maybe—maybe I am. But I don't think so & I don't want you
to think so: which is what I think you think when you talk about
"keeping in touch with reality." Shit. Maybe I can't write anymore, but
I'd rather write nothing than be only a penny-a-liner whore turning

out skillful crap for Monday morning's garbage wrappings. Goddam it . . . I'm the author of The Dark Sister.

OK OK OK—don't be mad. I wish I were in bed with my hands on your breasts.[14]

Win was, of course, screaming for reassurance, but nothing Ellie could say would provide enough. Besides, she wanted him to continue his reviewing both as a way of keeping his name before the New York publishing world and as a preferred alternative to writing nothing at all. It was easy to kill time in Santa Fe, and the more time Win killed, the more guiltily he wanted to cut down on any activity which might interfere with poetry. As he wrote Dr. Williams on 7 October 1960, "I've had on the whole a wasteful year —that family trip back east last June and an ensuing summer of opera-going and too many parties here and I've got so little done, even including keeping up with my correspondence. No doubt it's mostly my fault—but it's been aggravated by a swarm of people 'dropping by' and an unusual spate this fall of NY editors asking me to review books—till, now, I'm wiring back No."[15] But his resolve was hardly firm; in 1961, he began (and continued for a few years) a weekly book column for the Santa Fe New Mexican.

El also urged Win to give readings, or to teach, when the opportunity presented itself. One came along when, in 1958 and at the suggestion of Rosenthal, he was offered a post teaching a summer course in modern poetry at New York University. The prospect of confronting a room full of students, or an audience come to hear him read, was sufficient to send Win into torments of apprehension. ("Winfield," Thornton Wilder, visiting the Scotts in 1958, told him, "you're a nail biter. Why don't you stop being a nail biter?"[16]) As if preparing for the gallows, Win would dress carefully, eat sparingly, and show unaccustomed affection to his children before a reading. Teaching was almost as bad. "I have, for Christ's sake, probably incautiously, certainly without regard to my capabilities, just wired NYU that Yes I will accept their offer to teach a poetry course for 6 weeks—from mid-June to late July," he wrote Bill Cole

[14] WTS to EMS, 26 January 1958.
[15] WTS to William Carlos Williams, 7 October 1960, American Literature Collection, Beinecke Library, Yale University.
[16] Interview, EMS, Santa Fe, 6 September 1969.

in New York. "Dammit, I *always* say No to jobs."[17] As the time for going to New York drew closer, Win became steadily more fearful. What would he say? How could he interest his students? To ensure at least two successful meetings out of twenty nine, he secured from Malcolm Cowley typescripts of poems he had revised since their publication in *Blue Juniata*, and from Dr. Williams a set of advance proofs of *Paterson*, V. "The one thing that doesn't get me sweating, if I wake at 4 A.M.," he told Williams, "is the thought of bombing the class with Book V—& without warning—after we've been doing WCW. There'll be nothing like it since Tom Sawyer and Joe Harper walked into church at their own funeral."[18] After a visit to the Williamses in Rutherford, New Jersey, early in July, Win had still one more effective bit of business with which to wow his class. "Yesterday," he could say, "when I was talking with Ezra Pound. . ."

In teaching, as in his readings, once Win got started he did beautifully. "Really, it is extraordinary how well I feel," he wrote El during the first week of classes at NYU. "I've got a nice bunch of kids, all around 20 I should think. We are all talking like crazy. The boys are getting real forthright. The girls are beginning to quiver as I read."[19] Annie Kaplan, who visited the class one day, was struck by how warmly the students responded to Win. And Essie Bates, reliable as always, supplied hyperbolic but not unwelcome praise: "*Of course* your course is a brilliant success! Of course! Of Course!"[20] Teaching, Win recorded in his notebooks, is "to be *there* when the 'wild surmise' happens."[21] David Swadey, like many of Win's students an aspiring poet, wrote to thank him for such revelations: "The workshop with you was one of those few experiences that sink almost unknown into the center of the being and steer one's thoughts with a quiet hand—would it had lasted all summer."[22]

[17] WTS to William Cole, 20 November 1957.
[18] WTS to Malcolm Cowley, 22 April 1958, the Newberry Library; WTS to William Carlos Williams, 7 May 1958, American Literature Collection, Beinecke Library, Yale University.
[19] WTS to EMS, 18 June 1958.
[20] Esther Willard Bates to WTS, 5 July 1958, Scott Collection, John Hay Library.
[21] WTS, "*a dirty hand*," p. 129.
[22] David Swadey to WTS, 24 October 1958, Scott Collection, John Hay Library.

Had Win been less financially secure or less fearful, he might well have functioned, like many first-rate poets today (Eberhart at Dartmouth, Wilbur at Wesleyan, Dickey at South Carolina, to name a few), as a university's poet-in-residence, offering occasional writing seminars. He would have liked such a life, after a while, Ellie believes, though he would have insisted that it was an intrusion on his time. For Win was an excellent teacher (Bob Kurth, at Santa Fe prep, wondered at Win's ability—during his one day as guest teacher at the school—to command the attention and interest of the students), and he was delighted when kids stayed and asked questions through the coffee-break, as at NYU. And, of course, such a pied-à-terre would have helped Win build his reputation and have given him a better base for his poetry.[23]

Unlike some teachers, he genuinely *liked* literature. To Dr. Williams he complained that he always got in trouble "with academic types," for they "all seem to be *against* so damn much. They narrow down . . . to so little."[24] He adopted a standoffish manner with Ph.D's, insisting that he had no brains at all, but thought in pictures, like a child (a phrase he stole from Whittier).[25] And in a bitter poem, ironically called "Master of Arts," Win satirized the kind of teacher he was determined not to become:

> Still liking poetry—although not of course this new stuff:
> "Browning
> Is heady enough, my boy, if you learn to accept some idiosyn-
> crasies—
> Ah, to be sure there's Frost (who isn't bad)"—
> He sits in the coziest office of what is known as the Depart-
> ment of English—
> Desk, soundless rug, a shelf of Oxford Dictionary, reading
> lamps, easy chair—
> And confers singly with his students in what is known as
> Advanced Writing.
> A bachelor with an income, thick in body and tweeds and im-
> ported tobacco,
> He arranges on his desk ten Dunhill pipes direct from London,
> and listens

[23] Interview, EMS, Santa Fe, 6 February 1970.
[24] WTS to William Carlos Williams, 21 October 1955, American Literature Collection, Beinecke Library, Yale University.
[25] Interview, EMS, Santa Fe, 6 February 1970.

Patiently to the boy reading a theme aloud. And his interruptions
Are kind and accurate, for, unmentioned, he wrote—just for
himself—when he was young
And over the years he has become a czar of the individual
word,
Of punctuation, paragraphing, and—as it were—of the sub-
junctive.
"Sheer?" he quotes, and gnaws at his mustache. "Sheer is a—
a good word not to use."
The boy will remember that and the taste of winter darkening
at the windows
But the room secure with the tidy fire that never seemed to
need replenishing;
Though most of all the pince-nez'd tolerant twinkle which al-
ludes
Through a most cultivated noncommittal air
To amusement at ambition in the yet undefeated undergraduate.[26]

Despite the summer heat, Win Scott walked down to Bedford
Street where he felt not altogether avuncular toward "the girls/
From last year's commencements" going off to their young jobs.
There, twenty four years before, he and Eleanor had made love.
But Greenwich Village is no country for the middle-aged. If he
could have, Win would have willed the old days back, but Eleanor
lectured him about his yearnings: "People are not static. Relationships are mutable. No marriage could remain in the Bedford Street
honeymoon-affair stage indefinitely unless it were to be an incredibly selfish affair, a morally destroying business removed from
all reality."[27]

By 1958, the honeymoon had been over for a long time. Win
relied heavily on El's love and protection. In New York he stayed
in the Park Avenue apartment of Helen Danforth, Eleanor's aunt.
When he phoned Santa Fe, El chided him for the expense. But
"don't wait," she warned him in one letter's P.S., "until you run
out of money to send for money."[28] The customary marital roles
had been reversed.

[26] WTS, "Master of Arts," *Change of Weather* (1964), pp. 11–12.
[27] WTS to EMS, 24 July 1958; WTS, "A Postcard from Bedford Street,"
Change, p. 31; EMS to WTS, 4 July 1958.
[28] EMS to WTS, 20 July 1958.

If the honeymoon could not be restored, at least he would try to recover his sexual vigor. He was really resolved, he wrote El on 3 July 1958, to cut down on his regular (non–party going, non–special occasion) drinking: "I hope I have the guts to do it. After only two days of moderation, what happens?—I wake up four times during the night with John Thomas like iron, & not the spurious but the real thing. The first raring up of impulse in all these weeks. I've tried too long to keep both those lovely things, liquor & sex. But at my age, certainly, it can't be *well* done—can't be more than sporadically done—and of the two there can be no doubt which is the better.[29]

In New York, of course, there were parties and special occasions enough to blunt the effect of Win's resolution. Wade Vliet, his friend from college days, escorted him to restaurants and bars. He paid sentimental weekend visits to the Bagdikians, living in the Scotts' former Providence house, and to George and Marge Hemphill, who occupied the Scotts' former Hampton house. The Kaplans gave a party for Win. There were lunches or dinners with Bill and Nancy Gibson, George and Jo Clifford (in Connecticut), Leonard and Helene Gans, and James Purdy. And there was the visit with Pound at Dr. Williams's home in Rutherford. In his dissertation on Scott, Donald Eulert has reproduced Win's taped remarks about that occasion:

I met Ezra Pound only once . . . when I was in New York for six weeks teaching at NYU. It was at that time that Pound was sprung from St. Elizabeth's hospital where he had been held for years in Washington. I was in touch with William Carlos Williams . . . and Bill Williams told me that Pound would be, so to speak, hiding out at his house for a night or two before he took ship back to Italy. So I went over, you know. It was a hot July afternoon and I just dropped in and spent an hour or more there. It was quite a thing to be in the same room with these two men. They had known each other since they were college age—they and Marianne Moore, H.D., had all known each other when they were really young. It was a hot, hot day, and Pound was lolling back on the sofa in Dr. Williams' living room. He had on a pair of blue shorts and a sort of brown silk shirt; but he just held that in his hand and sort of rubbed it around himself from time to time.

He struck me as a very arrogant man; he got into conversations with Bill Williams about little magazines. They seemed to know all about

[29] WTS to EMS, 3 July 1958.

little magazines, current from Australia to Canada and back again, as though they were two excited young men. They were both then in their seventies. . . . Pound seemed to me to make a great deal of sense, to be perfectly lucid, until he got into any form of the political field. He took off on the name of Winfield Scott, and the famous General Winfield Scott, American nineteenth century, and from that he went on into the Civil War, and presently he began to talk about the Jewish-Catholic plot to assassinate President Lincoln. Then I sort of took leave of the whole thing.

He had a small retinue with him that included a tall and, in a goon-like way, handsome younger man who was obviously one of the Fascist types who had hung around Pound while he was in the hospital in Washington. A young girl, with dark hair. . . . She was pretty, and he had a very rude way at times of turning and whispering to her (and they would laugh together) so that the rest of us couldn't hear what was being said—this was quite rude. However, he was cordial. I had two of his books with me, the first volume of *Cantos* and his *Personae*, which he autographed very cordially. . . .

He was perfectly splendid as long as we were talking literary matters, but very scornful, very arrogant. For example, he discovered that although I was teaching at NYU I was not a teacher, and that pleased him very much. He is very much against teaching—no, not against teaching, that is quite wrong, but against the formula of what he conceived to be most of contemporary teaching of literature. As I say, there was this goon-like Nazi who sold me a pamphlet by Pound for a dollar, right in front of Pound—one of his money theory pamphlets, something of the sort, and from him I had a very unpleasant feeling. . . .

It was literally the very next day that he boarded ship to return to Italy after all those years of arrest and the judgment of insanity and so on, and only a few days later that he landed, and all the New York papers were filled with photographs of him with the Mussolini Fascist salute as he greeted the newspaper men in Italy.[30]

To the Williamses, Pound seemed far gone, mentally. You couldn't talk to him at all, Floss complained. It was impossible. "The only one he ever talked to nicely was Win Scott."[31]

The following summer, at the urging of an old Providence friend, Bill Wilson, Win Scott took on his last, brief teaching job, at the

[30] Quoted in Eulert, "Scott," pp. 44–47.
[31] *Writers at Work: The* Paris Review *Interviews*, 3rd ser. (New York: Viking, 1967), pp. 21–22.

Indiana University Writers' Conference. Win took the job, he wrote McSorley, for two reasons: "I thought it might be interesting to try . . . once, and I wanted to be in the Middle West." Dropping back into the "campus atmosphere of pretty-breasted girls and long-legged boys and alcoholic faculty *and* the lovely knowledge that *you didn't have to stay there*" was pleasant enough, but Win emerged from his role as "Poetry for a Week" wondering about the morality of writers' conferences generally. "The middle-aging and aging who attend the conference drain one so, because what can one do for them?" Was it enough that the paying customers seemed to have a wonderful time, spending a week among people "whose names are actually on titlepages & book covers"? Stanley Young, a playwright also teaching there, remarked that he was "supposed to hand crutches to people who aren't even ready for crutches," and Win agreed. He had one poet in his class (Patricia Low) "but there was little if anything I needed to do for her work." For the others, there was nothing he *could* do; he knew no magic incantation that would make them poets, or even get them published. To salvage the trip, Win made it into a sentimental journey, visiting Indianapolis because he had brought himself up on Booth Tarkington; Springfield, Illinois, for Abraham Lincoln and for Vachel Lindsay's decaying house; and, best of all, Hannibal, Missouri, where he climbed Cardiff Hill and sat watching over Sam Clemens's town and the river. "I had waited a lifetime to be there."[32]

Win Scott could do nothing for the little-talented aging. But there was almost nothing he would not do, in his generosity, for the talented young. The meeting with James Purdy in New York, for example, resulted from Win's favorable *Herald Tribune* review of Purdy's *Color of Darkness* and his subsequent (unsolicited by Purdy) offer to nominate him for a Ford Foundation award. Then, in 1962, Scott recommended the young novelist for a Guggenheim ("Hate to bother you," Purdy wrote, "but, as you know, my books don't sell." "The recommendation," Win replied, "rates you just short of Jesus"). Purdy, like a number of other young writers Win wrote letters for, got a Guggenheim. He could get Guggenheims for others, but not for himself, Scott would complain.

[32] WTS to Edward McSorley, 25 July 1959; out of the visit to Hannibal came WTS, "Hannibal and the Bones of Art," *Exiles and Fabrications* (1961), pp. 183–191.

Purdy, of course, appreciated Scott's help. It came when he most needed it, at the beginning of his career, and it lasted until Scott's death. "You are one of the few," he gratefully observed, "who have stuck with me from the beginning."[33] But it was Hilary Masters, another young novelist, who most benefited from Win's encouragement and friendship. Hilary, the late-begotten son of Edgar Lee Masters, had come to the *Providence Journal* office in 1950, when he was still a student at Brown, to thank Scott for some kind words he had written about the campus literary magazine. Masters arrived in an old, filthy, paint-stained camel's-hair coat, "a god-damned angel in rags," as Win put it. After college, Hilary went to New York, where he tried, between jobs in theatrical press-agentry, to write a novel and to straighten out his private life. Through a long period of frustration and disillusionment, Win encouraged Masters by letter and by occasional visits. He read and commented on Hilary's manuscripts, always finding something good to say about them; he suggested potential publishers, and, above all, advised Hilary—what he most needed to hear—to keep writing. In the agony of a divorce, Masters came to Santa Fe from Reno for consolation and recharging. Then, happily married this time, Hilary and his wife Polly visited Santa Fe several times for the fellowship abundantly available at the Scott household. To Masters, Win was a kind of father figure, an artistic conscience who would occasionally chide him about his spelling but more often and more importantly praise him for his fiction, which in time was—and is still being—published.[34]

Masters was but the closest friend among the stream of young men who came and went, talked and drank, at their house on East Alameda. Eleanor called them, jokingly, "Mr. Tolstoy's pilgrims. Some I liked. Some I didn't. Some I felt sincerely sought Win's advice. Some, I felt used him."[35] But Win embraced them all and was unfailingly generous with his time and attention. "I know everybody writes you for help," the poet Philip Legler remarked

[33] James Purdy to WTS, 9 April 1958, 22 December 1962, and 24 October 1964, Scott Collection, John Hay Library; WTS to James Purdy, 5 April 1958 and 23 February 1963, American Literature Collection, Beinecke Library, Yale University.

[34] Interview, Hilary and Polly Masters, Provincetown, Massachusetts, 30 July 1969.

[35] EMS to SD, 30 September 1969.

to Win, and he was right.[36] Only occasionally Scott would lament the cost in energy of ministering to his pilgrims, but then El would bring him up short: "How would you feel if they didn't come?" For he needed these young men—who, by hanging on his words, conferred an elevated status—fully as much as they needed his words of encouragement and letters of recommendation. George Starbuck, on a speaking tour of the Southwest, called the Scotts and went by their house for a visit; he was impressed by Win's confidence, his control, his chairman-of-the-board manner, his knowing what he could do and doing it, his likableness and impressiveness. Another younger poet, Keith Wilson, who came to know Scott only in the last years of Win's life, when he was privately depressed, nonetheless admired Scott as "a man who had come *through*, intact, with a beautiful wholeness." And to Don Eulert, putting together a dissertation based partly on tapes of Win's conversation, Scott was "an unpretentious, civilized, warm friend, and the most gracious man I have ever met."[37] Partly, Win's generosity stemmed from his ingrained inability to be rude, even to the bores or boors among those who came to call; partly, too, his ego needed the tacit support such callers brought with them.

To these young men he did seem whole, even though he was privately disintegrating. Tom Mayer, a then aspiring writer who grew up in Santa Fe and spent many adolescent hours at the Scotts' home, felt that in 1959 it was a "chaotically healthy place," that Win had better control of his surroundings and himself than any other man he had met. "If you were any good," Scott Fitzgerald once observed, "you dominated life." To Mayer, Win appeared the one human being who had lived up to Fitzgerald's standards. There was chaos all right, produced by the collection of children (El and Win's fourth and last child, Douglas, was born 27 December 1958) and animals and visitors usually in, more or less, residence. "When I was a kid first starting to publish," Mayer recalls,

I practically lived at their house—it was a second home to me at the very least—and how clearly I remember their family, the conversation, El producing food as if by magic, the girls, both of whom have

[36] Philip Legler to WTS, 12 November 1961, Scott Collection, John Hay Library.
[37] Interview, George Starbuck, Williamsburg, Virginia, 14 April 1970; Keith Wilson to SD, 21 September 1969; Eulert, "Scott," p. 7.

known exactly how to handle men since infancy, crawling over me, Doug with his blond hair and intentness looking like some mod conception of a child movie star, the dogs and mice and monkeys and for awhile a very distinguished goat named Rita (I gave it to them one Xmas) and her offspring. It was a place that was almost idyllic, perfect in a mad and very healthy way, and Win was always at the center of it, the source of its strength, the eye of the pinwheel, calm and witty and level, a tolerant and very wise gentleman who knew and understood more about things practical (by that I do *not* mean that he was an amateur plumber of any ability), about how to make people and the world around him go in pleasant and worthwhile and rational channels, than any psychiatrist or politician or professional parent (El is the original professional parent) who ever lived. I always felt he had things sorted out, squared away, both in his head and his surroundings.[38]

Certainly Win was blessed with wit. In the mornings, especially, he would tease Eleanor (who looked at life from a child's point of view—with honesty and recklessness), and the children loved the teasing. In January 1958, while El was in Florida, he took Joel to cub scout meeting one night, and reported on the event in terms that suggest the Mark Twain flavor of his humor:

To think you missed pack meeting. At 7:30—following steak, corn & peas, potato chips, milk—my children and I attended. There was a goodly throng, mostly children. Up front, talking, was a bald-headed old geezer complete with uniform & pot belly & various sewed-on decorations from a lifetime of guiding little boys in the Right Way. That was not enough. Lights were dimmed. A row of candles on an arrow was lighted. Mr Henderson—that's his name, & he neither smokes nor drinks & he is a member of Christ Church—reappeared wrapped in a huge horse blanket and wearing a band around his head with a very tall feather in erection at the rear of it. He then gave a speech about Cub Scouting, & I don't recall rightly what he said; but I recall that the speech went down, down, down—mostly, I think, on the theme of parents who do not appreciate cub scouting—and as the speech went down Mr Henderson, rather gingerly, pinched out candles, one at a time. But he left one lighted. And then Mr H. began to come up, up, up and as he did so he relighted the candles, one at a time. It was, I thought, r e a l sexy, and perhap's that's why I can't exactly say what

[38] Interview, Tom Mayer, Santa Fe, 28 March 1970; Tom Mayer to SD, 19 December 1969. [Mayer and Susan Scott were married in December, 1970.]

he talked about. But it was in favor of cub scouting, generally speaking.

Then Tom Galt read out the names of new award winning Cub Scouts, including Joel Scott, and by request as each Cub went forward to the candle lighted table & Mr Henderson, the parents were requested to come too & stand behind the victors. I went up. So, as a matter of fact, did Jeannette. (Susan remained seated, possibly through modesty but probably because, after all, *she* wasn't getting any prizes & the hell with it.) There were damned few parents, & Mr Henderson gave a little speech on how fortunate were the few little cruds whose parents *had* come. (I don't know how the little boys felt whose parents were absent.) Pins were then presented *to the parents.* . . . There was even one parent *without* the cub scout, but Mr. Henderson didn't seem to give her any particular credit. . . . As for Joel, he got a Two Year Pin and also a Silver Arrow. He still has the Two Year Pin. He lost the Silver Arrow before arriving at home.

But that arrival was delayed. Lights went up. Mr Henderson stripped down to his basic uniform—privately of course—and called upon an Air Force Officer to show us a movie of planes & missiles. (Are movies now taken of anything else?) It was full of atom bombs & other noises. When it got over, Tom Galt—at Mr Henderson's prodding—asked for a demonstration *if* the boys would like to see still another film. He got it. The second film was about the same, I thought, but in color. Jeannette was going to sleep in my arms. It was now 8:30. Suddenly I recalled that, while clearing up the kitchen at home, I had put on a kettle of water to boil for coffee, & I couldn't remember doing anything further about it. I pushed Jeannette into Jeanie Reed's bosom & said Here, I gotta run home but I'll be right back. . . . So, out into the night. I got into the kitchen just as the kettle began to smoke.

Then I went back. (Which, when you think it over, is perhaps the most remarkable event in this entire saga.) Film #2 was blasting to its finish as I got to my seat & regained Jeannette—not quite asleep. . . . Lights up. And *there* was Mr Henderson, looking as happy as though he'd just arrived. Now the numerous cub scouts, especially characters like Billy Eide (parent present) and Marshall Girard (no parent present), were manifesting real restlessness, as though it were time for the liquor and the naked girls to be brought on. But I don't think this had occurred to Mr Henderson. He squatted down and led the throng in a song about Acquila—The Leader—and how we all follow him. The squatting, you understand, is an important part of the song: *the* important part, I guess, because it ends with Acquila—in this case, need I say, Mr Henderson—leaping up with both arms in air in a sort of

Nazi salute, doubled. . . . Jesus, I thought, we have had it. But no. Mr Henderson then summoned the scouts in a circle around him & I'll be damned if he didn't summon the rest of us too. Each of us had to cross arms and take the hand of the person on each side of us. (Fortunately I had Jeannette—just barely awake, but on her feet—to one side; but some man I certainly don't know & have never even been introduced to, on the other side.) Well, we all held hands. Mr Henderson announced he would speak the Cub Scout benediction, and then we would all repeat it. It was brief. To the best of my recollection it went something like this: "May the Great Cub Scout Master of us all watch over us until we meet again."

I have a feeling I've forgotten some of the details, but this is the gist of it. It'll at least give you the idea, and you'll know how sincerely I wish you had been here to attend and take part.[39]

A good-natured geniality underlay Win's husbandly grumbling. The cub scout account was but another way of saying what he always said explicitly as well, that he was lost without Ellie, that he loved her and the children. But, occasionally, the genial, chairman-of-the-board manner would drop away, to be replaced by sorrow, or more rarely, an almost petulant anger. Dining with Purdy in New York, Win saw a photograph of Sinclair Lewis and pointed out how "alone" the man looked. "He kept coming back to this point," Purdy recalls. "I felt there was a deep sadness in him."[40] As Win wrote of himself, "I lead a bourgeois life—wife, children, a rather big house—all that—plenty of money. Poetry out of this environment? One's mind and heart can supply sufficient suffering anywhere."[41]

The rare fit of anger overcame Win most often in moods of nostalgia which others could not, or would not, share. Hilary and Polly Masters, for example, had spent a delightful two weeks visiting the Scotts, in September 1959. But on the night before they were to leave, after a marvelous meal, lots of drinks, lots of talk, the evening suddenly fractured. As Masters reconstructs it:

We got talking about family . . . and more particularly, Ellie's family. It was all light hearted tipsy and fun. I remember that she got out some pictures of herself as a child with some of her family. *Then,* Win

[39] WTS to EMS, 22 January 1958.
[40] James Purdy to SD, 27 August 1969.
[41] WTS, *"a dirty hand,"* p. 148.

left and returned with some pictures of his own, and I believe they were either of his mother or father—I'm almost certain they were of his mother. These were passed around and received the same attention as the others—just the sort of casual perusal of family photographs, with accompanying general comments, that you might expect. However, this did not seem to be enough for him, in fact, he seemed deeply hurt, insulted, and his eyes flashed, the pipe puffed and he paced around with his chin high with affront. It happened so suddenly, and we were so completely unprepared for it and really unknowing of what had actually happened to make him so. The evening was blasted to smithereens in a matter of minutes. The next morning, when we left, it wasn't any better. He was still petulant, sulky, and we felt terrible without knowing why.[42]

Later that day, overcome with remorse, Win sent his apologies for "being as icily hurtful as possible to everyone within reach. It was childish of me."[43]

What had hurt Win was the sense that no one cared about his past, that no one was willing to share his childhood memories: a form of persecution he visited upon himself increasingly in the years before his death. As early as 1943, he had written Eleanor of dreaming that "my great-grandmother's glass sugarbowl broke all to pieces, and nobody cared but me." Reality copied illusion seventeen years later when Douglas, still in his infancy, inadvertently broke a shell from the beach at Newport that Win's grandmother had given him nearly half a century before. Scott was devastated. Recollected in relative tranquillity, the incident became a poem, "Broken Shell":

> My smallest and last child smashed the shell
> That had been given me when I was a child:
> So long, so carefully kept: a pearl shell
> That filled my adult hand, its immaculate
> Inner dome flushed with miniature rainbows:
> A tiny cave carved in far-off seas
> Whose dazzle of sun-struck gold-green
> Here incredibly fixed; and the sound of seas
> Which was, I grew to learn, my pulse's sound.

[42] Hilary Masters to SD, 20 October 1969.
[43] WTS to Hilary and Polly Masters, 21 September 1959.

Now dropped and broken by that child of mine
Too young to know what he has destroyed;
Too young to tell me what I should have known.[44]

His tendency was to look backward, to consult, even to worship the past. Reporting in the *Herald Tribune's* annual roundup of "Books I Have Liked" for 1961, Win listed Frank O'Connor's *An Only Child*, Howard Fast's *April Morning*, and Harper Lee's *To Kill a Mockingbird*—two of them novels focusing on childhood experience and O'Connor's a memoir of his youth.[45] The same year, he wrote the Bagdikians, who were moving out of his and Eleanor's first house in Providence, wondering if he would ever send a letter to that address again. "Did I ever tell you—yeah, I probably have, for I'm sentimental & loquacious about such things—that when we acquired #312 we were given the original blueprints & they were dated the week I was born? . . . Ah well—*my* walls are cracking now, & there are draughts in the corners."[46]

With his children Win tended toward the kind of protectiveness that had characterized his own childhood. He had, as one poem puts it, a "fearful love of children." He wanted more babies even after Douglas was born in 1958, and took pride in his role as paterfamilias. Occasionally he would talk about building a family compound, so that all the children, grown up and married, might live with their families in houses nearby. Susan never doubted her father's love, though it found expression more in Win's protectiveness than in demonstrations of affection. "It was a damn hard thing for him to take his daughter's hand," she recalls, yet Win would work himself "into a real state whenever I went out."[47] Another poem, "The Children," begins:

Here come the children like tricky leaves let loose;
There they go down the hill on a meadow wind.
We the begetters watch but cannot say whose.[48]

Win wanted to catch and arrest the slippery leaves, but the task

[44] WTS to EM, 24 June 1943; WTS, "Broken Shell," *Change*, p. 46.
[45] WTS, "Books I Have Liked," *New York Herald Tribune*, 3 December 1961.
[46] WTS to Ben and Betty Bagdikian, 17 June 1961.
[47] Interview, Susan Scott, New York, 10 October 1969; WTS, " 'We Are So Fond of One Another, Because Our Ailments Are the Same,' " *New and Selected Poems* (1967), p. 60.
[48] WTS, "The Children," *Collected Poems: 1937–1962* (1962), p. 91.

was an impossible one. Eleanor, in reaction against her own tightly controlled childhood, was a most permissive mother—and, as Susan said, "Mother ran things—usually she did the deciding, and Dad sat back a bit."[49] Given a minimum of direction, sometimes ignored in a house often full of visitors, the children grew up very rapidly. Joel, very quiet, kept mostly to himself, cracked up motorcycles, and practiced the French horn—on one occasion, as his aunt Jeannette Wolfe will never forget, at six-thirty in the morning. Brilliant and intense, Susan started dating very young, usually much older boys, and men. At sixteen, she left home to study at NYU's School of Theatre Arts, and to live alone in the East Village. Beautiful and radiating a sense of peace, Jeannette took up smoking and drinking in her early teens. The towheaded Dougie, allied to Susan by temperament, early acquired a wide range of experience and knowledge. At six he hummed a few bars of "La Donna e Mobile" while Susan was rejecting a suitor in the front hall. At eleven he had perfected a clever imitation of an adult homosexual.

Often Eleanor's permissiveness clashed with Win's protectiveness, but they were both guilty, El has come to realize, of exerting other real and demanding pressures on their children. The kids were expected to be remarkable. In such households, as Eleanor put it in an essay written after Win's death, one is "told of each small talent, each sign that a creative being has been born. . . . Nothing is said of how the children feel—only accomplishments are totted up like a Bill of Obligation. 'We are exceptional beings, and our children must be exceptional.' They never say it flat out, but it is inferred, and the family friends and school teachers go along with the idiocy. Well, they do produce exceptional children, exceptional in their loneliness, and unhappiness, and in their anger."[50] So Joel Scott was encouraged, almost expected, to become a virtuoso hornist, and his teacher housed in the guest quarters that might otherwise have served Win as a writing retreat. So Susan, showing talent in ballet, was pushed through years of two-hour daily lessons after school, sent to study dance in San Francisco and Europe, and compared by her father, when she was nine, to Pavlova. Similar pressures were applied to Jeannette and to Douglas, who appeared on

[49] Interview, Susan Scott, New York, 10 October 1969.
[50] EMS, "Where Are the Children Tonight?" unpublished essay (fall 1968), p. 11.

stage with the Santa Fe Opera as a preschooler. "If I don't dance,"
Susan came to feel, "I won't have a place in the family."[51]

Reflecting on what a "sad limping lot" the unhappy children of
poets made, Eleanor located the malaise at home:

> For we the parents of the children of poets, have removed ourselves
> from Main Street. If our children church go [and in the Scott home
> they did not; Win would not allow it], play Little League, join the
> Scouts—it is as outsiders. We do not participate in such activities, and
> our children soon quit them, knowing that they really do not belong.
> Their sense of loyalty may be involved, certainly their desire to belong
> to us, not the others. Thus at an early age they learn the role of the
> outsider, the different one, the shy introspective. Rarely do they inherit
> a supporting talent. Bad nerves yes—but poetry is rarely sustained by
> the genes.[52]

Bitterly, Susan wrote of her hatred for the children of other poets
who came to call. "Their parents talked with Dad and drank and
talked and drank hour after hour, and nobody remembered to feed
them, or they were handed an orange which they dribbled around
the house, getting everything sticky. . . . The children of poets are
grubby and their noses run and their dirty hair hangs in their eyes
and their blue jeans are torn and they go to the bathroom in their
pants. . . . My Christmas toys were all broken by poets' children."[53]
Only half knowing it, she was writing of herself.

For what was intended as a permissiveness calculated to develop
self-reliance in the children struck some as simple neglect. Like
Win, Eleanor was rarely given to displays of affection; with the
children, she acted more like a playmate than a mother. She hiked
and picnicked and swam with them; on board the *Gripsholm*, in
1964, fellow passengers took her at first for the children's governess. But, she now realizes, Eleanor "did not really know how they
felt," and by the time she sensed their unhappiness, the marriage
had so worsened that she "withdrew into silence or busywork."[54]

The kids kept late hours; Web Schott remembers Dougie, as a
baby, toddling around in diapers at midnight. Despite the efforts
of a housekeeper, the Scott home was always in a state of disarray;

[51] Interview, Susan Scott, New York, 10 October 1969.
[52] EMS, "Where," p. 6.
[53] Ibid., p. 9.
[54] EMS to SD, 7 September 1970.

to Win, brought up in an unusually tidy house, El's lack of concern for neatness represented a sore point. Win drank excessively, and his diet tended toward rich foods— omelettes, soufflés, seafood and jonnycakes, fancy stews and casseroles cooked with wine and herbs, sweetbreads, eggs Benedict, roast beef and Yorkshire pudding.[55] Once a walker, he now never exercised, and his weight ballooned until the slim aesthetic youth took on the appearance of a voluptuary, his body outsized for his head. El, too, drank and ate too much; occasionally, much to Win's consternation, she would borrow his underpants. Conrad Knickerbocker, visiting from Kansas City, described Ellie, uncharitably but with some accuracy, as "a one-woman slum."[56]

But the disorder of the household hardly mattered when Win's writing was going well, or when his work was being published. Again through the recommendation of Rosenthal, who served as the publisher's poetry adviser, Macmillan decided to bring out *Scrimshaw*, a collection of the short poems Win had written in the past decade, early in 1959. How do I thank a man, Win wrote Mack in April, who "brings breathing to a whole ten years of my work (and so, it may be, to me as well)?"[57] In September the book came out to excellent reviews. The Kirkus service, usually unfriendly to Scott's work, praised Win for depicting the contemporary scene "with a self-conscious but subtle awareness of his American heritage in language that is both fresh and vivid."[58] Web Schott, who had met Scott earlier in 1959, praised *Scrimshaw* both for the *Kansas City Star* and the *Christian Science Monitor*. "Scott," he wrote, "is the major undiscovered poet in the United States today."[59] Robert Hillyer struck the same note in the *New York Times*: "In spite of his long masterwork, 'The Dark Sister,' published in 1958, Mr. Scott is not so well known as he should be."[60] Horace Gregory, in a letter, assured Win that *Scrimshaw* "is your best book. . . . This book has your language at last, and says what

[55] Ibid., 27 October 1969.
[56] Interview, Webster Schott, Kansas City, 29 December 1969.
[57] WTS to M. L. Rosenthal, 5 April 1959.
[58] Virginia Kirkus Bulletin, 15 August 1959.
[59] Webster Schott, *Kansas City Star*, 13 February 1960.
[60] Robert Hillyer, *New York Times Book Review*, 10 April 1960, p. 40. The Kirkus, Schott, and Hillyer reviews, among others, are pasted in Scrapbook 12, Scott Collection, John Hay Library.

you have to say. The book has charm in the true, not petty meaning of charm, and casts a spell. Therefore the title."[61]

For once, Win had hit on an absolutely appropriate title. Scrimshaw, the ingenious carvings in whalebone made by sailors on their long voyages, was a peculiarly American art. As Melville wrote in *Moby-Dick* (Scott quoted the passage opposite the title page of his book), "the white sailor-savage [with only a jackknife] will carve you a bit of bone sculpture, not quite as workmanlike, but as close packed in its maziness of design, as the Greek savage, Achilles's shield." However inspiriting that heritage, though, it could not supply answers to the hard questions posed by the present. Approaching his fiftieth birthday, Scott reflected on the difficulty of communicating, whether of answers or questions:

The Man at Mid-Century

We cannot guess how long he'll wait.
He paces in his room alone
Imagining someone must come
Whose voice will force the lag of fate.
He paces puzzled, helpless, dumb,
Or sits beside the telephone
Hoping it may ring his ring
And someone solve him everything.
Television, radio:
Sessions to watch and listen to
Lest someone there let slip the clue
Of what he needs to need to know.
All possibilities allowed,
He leaves the latchkeys in his locks
And walks among the city crowd
Seeking the face that will reveal
Someone whose questioning answers frame
His inarticulate questioning.
He hurries home to letter-box,
To rooms as empty, to the same
Expectancy of dreams and drink.
Pacing he waits for me or you
Or anyone to speak his name:

[61] Horace Gregory to WTS, 22 December 1959, Scott Collection, John Hay Library.

> Someone to tell him what to do
> Someone to tell him what to think
> Someone to tell him what to feel.[62]

The publication of *Scrimshaw* led at least indirectly to Win Scott's first honorary degree, conferred not by Brown (perhaps disturbed by Scott's attack on its architectural plans, Brown never awarded him such a degree) but by the neighboring Rhode Island College of Education. On 11 June 1960, Win was made an honorary Doctor of Education, with the citation observing that "you have, in your most recent book of poems, suggested that you are a maker of scrimshaw, an idle carver of bits of whalebone . . . [but] craftsmanship you have achieved in poems of a color and translucence not given to whalebone, however finely carved."[63] Two years later, the University of New Mexico honored Scott and Witter Bynner with Litt.D.'s.

In July 1960, on a trip to Kansas City, Win revealed that he was still, however unwillingly, in the grip of the American success story. Invited by Web Schott to speak to the editors and writers who worked for Hallmark Cards, Win met and was charmed by Joyce Hall, the founder of that massive firm. With delight, he wrote his father in Haverhill of the visit, and of "old J. C. Hall who *did it all.* An extraordinary man. He's 70. He started with $5,000—the boys tell me—and a suitcase full of card samples." With still more delight, he told his father what multimillionaire Hall had said of him to Schott: "Web, this fellow doesn't look like a poet .He looks as though he could earn a living in a legitimate way." Hall meant it, Win added parenthetically, to be funny.[64]

The Horatio Alger story of Mr. Hall was repeated, in miniature, over the Labor Day weekend in Santa Fe when William Kelley, novelist and Doubleday's West Coast editor, came to town to work on revisions of Thomas Duncan's novel. Discovering that Scott lived in Santa Fe, Kelley wanted to meet him. A dinner was quickly arranged by Duncan, whose account of the incident follows:

After dinner we adjourned to the Scotts', and Bill asked Win whether he had anything that Doubleday might be interested in publishing.

---

[62] WTS, "The Man at Mid-Century," *New and Selected Poems*, p. 83.
[63] Honorary Doctor of Education citation, *Providence Journal*, 11 June 1960.
[64] WTS to Douglas W. Scott, [?] July 1960, Scott Collection, John Hay Library; interview, Webster Schott, Kansas City, 29 December 1969.

Win said that he had compiled a book of his essays, but that only a day or so before it had been rejected by . . . Macmillan. Bill wanted to see it. Win fetched it, still in its envelope from Macmillan.

"I'll read it tonight," Bill said.

I might say here that publishers are coldhearted bastards—with always some notable exceptions. An author is likely to be kicked around, unless he has the high literary quality (and quite incidentally the money-making capacity, old boy) of somebody like Erle Stanley Gardner, and poets are kicked around a little harder than most writers. As for essayists—you might as well expect a warm welcome from a publisher if you walked into his lair with syphilis, mumps, smallpox and leprosy as with a manuscript of essays.

The manuscript was "Exiles and Explorations" [sic]. Bill read it that night in his motel room. He's a wild Irishman who moves fast, a writer by temperament rather than an editor; and next morning he told me he was accepting the book for publication with a thousand dollars advance. He had cleared this by long distance with the New York office, and the executive with whom he talked there was enthusiastic; the executive also admired Win's work; in fact, he told Bill that he had a copy of Win's *Scrimshaw* on his desk.

Bill and I went to a pay phone. When I got Win on the line, I told him Bill had some news for him. Then Bill took over and said Doubleday wanted the book with a thousand advance and would also like to bring out a volume of Win's collected poetry.

Bill kept assuring Win it wasn't a practical joke; it was all true; and then I took the phone again. Win was sputtering with joy. "But Tom," he kept saying, "things like this simply don't happen to a poet."[65]

For ten years, no one would publish his work. In 1960, however, Win was in the delicious position of being courted both by Doubleday and Macmillan. For Macmillan, getting word that Doubleday wanted to bring out his collected poems, reacted predictably. "Before Macmillan resigns your Collected Poems," senior editor Emile Capouya wrote Scott, "you will be exposed to homilies from me on old acquaintance, continuity, honor among thieves, etc. As a first step, will you entertain an offer from Macmillan for the book?"[66]

[65] Thomas Duncan to SD, 22 August 1969.

[66] Emile Capouya to WTS, 17 November 1960, Scott Collection, John Hay Library; Thomas Duncan to SD, 22 August 1969. Duncan and Kelley persuaded Win to take part in a literary hoax. On demand, and without much effort, Win composed a poem containing the words "virgo descending," the title of Duncan's forthcoming novel. The poem was printed at the front of the book, where it

In the end, Doubleday brought out *Exiles and Fabrications*, as well as two other books of Scott's. But Macmillan, which threatened to be uncooperative "about the material we control," published the *Collected Poems* in 1962. At Doubleday, as with no other publisher since Covici-Friede in the late 1930's, Win Scott worked with editors, Sam Vaughan and Anne Hutchens (McCormick), who cared for his poetry, his prose, and increasingly for him as a human being.

The omens continued bright throughout late 1960. In October Win traveled to San Francisco for two readings in one day, sandwiched around an afternoon hour with creative-writing students at San Francisco State. "I dread all such occasions," he wrote Frank Merchant, "but I must say that an hour or two bull-sessioning with college kids—the actual occasion, once I'm into it—*wakes* me. . . . I still am bemused by the boy who prefaced his question: 'Mr. Frost, do you–' "[67] Later that month the Scotts drove to Albuquerque for a Kennedy rally, where "the boy-o himself" displayed an "indefinable magnetism—good looks plus something else." When Kennedy won the election, Win found in him a hope for the future: "I like this Teddy Roosevelt youthfulness—I think it's just what we need. I think we are alive again. The Inauguration address was a great address, & I think we can't mistrust the man who made it." Somehow, President Kennedy managed to quiet Win's growing despair about the cold war. Over the Christmas holidays he was happily busy making tapes to be used on the Winfield Townley Scott record, in the Yale Series of Recorded Poets, for which Jay Martin wrote some perceptive liner notes.[68]

Despite these euphoric signs, however, Win printed in April 1961 his most damning review of the work of an American poet, Conrad Aiken's *Selected Poems*. It is difficult to account for the harshness of this *New York Times* review, which, as Aiken confessed, set him back with a wallop. Perhaps the attack on Aiken amounted to a re-

_____
would appear that Duncan had got the title from one of Win's poems. "This would instantly raise the novel in the estimation of the more snobbish critics who seldom read carefully the books they review." The scheme worked: ". . . at least one reviewer, who had never been friendly to my work . . . handled the novel a bit gingerly but with respect."

[67] WTS to Frank Merchant, 9 November 1960.

[68] *Winfield Townley Scott Reads His Works*, Yale Series of Recorded Poets, Carillon YP321 (1961).

pudiation of an early influence: critics had properly noted a similarity between Aiken's *Senlin* poems and Scott's *Traman* ones. Yet as late as the mid-1950's, Scott thought highly of Aiken's work, considered him unjustly neglected, and proposed writing an article on his work. Perhaps Win had simply changed his mind about Aiken. But such a change of heart hardly accounts for the nastiness of the comment, in "*a dirty hand*," that the trouble with Aiken's poetry was that it was "all lips and no teeth." Besides, it was always Win's tendency to write positive reviews, knowing from his own experience how easy (for the reviewer) and painful (for the poet) the unrelievedly negative notice could be. "I don't know if that review will disturb Aiken," he wrote John Malcolm Brinnin, "but it sure god disturbed me. I hate to write-down an elder of such serious intentions & deserved respect. Brief as it is, the work on that review damned near blocked me for a week—I got into a state of tension over it, such that I almost thought I couldn't write it. I didn't *want* to write it. You know? But I felt I had to be honest—as gently as I could." Aiken himself proposes an alternative explanation: professional jealousy. In 1958 R. P. Blackmur, Allen Tate, and Aiken had served as judges for the Wallace Stevens prize, which they awarded to Charles Philbrick. As a result Aiken and Philbrick met and became good friends; "perhaps," Aiken suggests, "Scott was simply jealous."[69] Or it may even be that Scott had learned of Aiken's recommending that Oxford University Press reject *The Dark Sister*, and bore a grudge on that account.

To all appearances Win had little reason to be jealous in the spring of 1961. Within the next fifteen months two books would be brought out, one of them collecting twenty-five years of his poetry, the other his first—and until then only—book of prose, his "little old middlebrow book of essays," *Exiles and Fabrications*. This book, which came out in August 1961, included essays on Newport and Santa Fe, on John Greenleaf Whittier and E. A. Robinson and Amy Lowell, on Jack Wheelwright and Joe Coldwell and H. P. Lovecraft, on Booth Tarkington and Mark Twain, on *Our Town* and *The Outermost House*, and it contained as well Scott's groundbreaking argument, from her letters and poetry, that Emily Dickin-

[69] WTS to Lee Anderson, 27 May 1953, Yale University Library; WTS, "*a dirty hand*," p. 131; WTS to John Malcolm Brinnin, 20 April 1961; Conrad Aiken to SD, 18 July 1969.

son had been in love with Samuel Bowles, the editor of the *Spring-field Daily Republican*, and not with Rev. Charles Wadsworth. "Your speculation," Millicent Todd Bingham, daughter of Miss Dickinson's friend and first editor, Mabel Loomis Todd, wrote Scott, "is so much more plausible than all the theories of all the biographers!"[70] In an earlier age, Win observed to Frank Merchant, the book would have been called "Some People & Places & Books That Have Interested Me."[71]

With very few exceptions, reviewers loved the book, though they were unable to persuade the public to buy it. "The personal essay," John T. Winterich commented, "has not gone the way of the dodo and the heath hen. He [Scott] writes with grace and charm, penetration and wit, and he is unfailingly interesting, which is the hardest trick of all." Henry Beetle Hough also singled out the essays' personal quality, which placed them at the opposite pole from the rigorous analytical approach of the new critics: "Mr. Scott is so articulate and companionable a sharer of his interest and experience . . . that it quickly becomes common ground with the reader, and straying is unthinkable. The essays are a venture of earnest volition, warmth, and personal involvement as well as of wisdom; moreover, the writing is a delight. There is not a stale or commonplace sentence in the book."[72] Letters from Thornton Wilder and Van Wyck Brooks, to whom Win sent advance copies, were lavish in their praise. "This is to thank you," Wilder wrote, "for every single page in *Exiles and Fabrications*, except the title page." (Wilder rightly felt that "fabrications" suggested nothing so much as fibbing; Win intended it in another dictionary sense, that of constructing or building up into a whole . . ." parts often made elsewhere.")[73] Certainly the title was a forbidding one, commercially.

In his preface, Win talks about the stain of personality he tried to achieve in his poetry; the stain permeated these prose pieces. James Gray, in the book's one bad review, charged Scott with introducing "chiefly the distractions of literary gossip," of being "concerned

[70] Millicent Todd Bingham to WTS, 20 February 1960, Scott Collection, John Hay Library.

[71] WTS to Frank Merchant, 16 January 1961.

[72] John T. Winterich, *Book-of-the-Month Club News* (August 1961), p. 12; Henry Beetle Hough, *New York Herald Tribune*, 27 August 1961.

[73] Thornton Wilder to WTS, 30 August 1961, Scott Collection, John Hay Library.

with personalities rather than with points of view," and with writing about trivialities that seem "quite beside the point."[74] ("Who
is this guy?" a friend inquired of Scott. "Did you repulse him once
in a Men's Room?")[75] In a way, Gray had a point. Scott was interested in the offbeat, in the little-known, in the minor writer like
Lovecraft. Early in 1962, he projected (but never completed work
on) yet another book of essays on such writers as Leonard Bacon,
Christopher Morley, Phelps Putnam, Louis Grudin, Ernest Walsh,
Anne Parrish, and Weldon Kees, among others. The lead chapter
would deal with what Win called the real lost generation of American writers—the poets Trumbull Stickney, George Cabot Lodge,
and William Vaughn Moody, and the novelists David Graham
Phillips, Frank Norris, and Stephen Crane—"a group of turn-of-the-
century American writers of great promise, all of whom died
young."[76] Sam Vaughan showed some interest in this project, but
was hesitant to propose the title which occurred to him: The Importance of Being Minor. For who could be sure that these writers—
and the man who wrote about them—*were* minor? If Win Scott
tended, as *The New Yorker* remarked, to discover masterpieces
everywhere, it was out of his conviction that literary reputation was
a fickle, chancy, and unpredictable thing.[77] It was the final judgment, not the immediate one, that counted. Macmillan had published *Scrimshaw* in paperback, as one of the first in a series to make
poetry more widely and inexpensively available; Scott was moved
to doggerel:

> Here is the poet, out in paperback,
> Just like Spillane and Kerouac.
> Let opinions on its merits vary—
> *His* worry: it looks so temporary.[78]

John K. Hutchens, in a publication-date (August 17, 1961) review of *Exiles and Fabrications*, best understood the book and its
author: "We have here, in the midst of our largely commercial
literary life, that old-fashioned phenomenon, a man of letters. The

[74] James Gray, *Saturday Review*, 23 September 1961, p. 48.
[75] WTS to Ben Clough, 1 October 1961.
[76] WTS, worksheet, 22 January 1962; WTS, "Lost Generation (Hamatreya),"
Change, pp. 7–8.
[77] *The New Yorker*, 14 October 1961, p. 224.
[78] WTS, "*a dirty hand*," p. 128.

written word is light and life to him, writers the most absorbing of people, poetry the noblest world to which a qualified talent could attach itself. If this suggests that "Exiles" is indirectly a book about its author—well, that is all right, too. The subject is good."[79] Win Scott was that rare bird, the intensely bookish man. When she was a little girl, his daughter Susan used to be very proud of her father as a writer. Then the questions occurred to her, as to her classmates. What does he look like when he's writing a poem? What does he *do*? And the only tangible image she could conjure up was of her father, in his study, reading.[80] Win liked to talk in quotations, and it was "amazing," Ellie remembers, "how often they applied to family situations." If he was not listened to at the dinner table, he would invoke *Death of a Salesman*: "Attention must be paid." On Thanksgiving, "Over the river and through the woods to Grandmother's house we go," and the rest of it. To encourage the children, he would recite "Somebody said it couldn't be done." From "Mr. Flood's Party," he would emphasize the need to set down jugs—and other objects—slowly and carefully, "knowing that most things break." Often, Win's habit of speaking in quotations would bewilder listeners. Was he talking or was he quoting? Often it was the book experience, and not the immediate personal one, that came to him.[81]

Win worried about this predilection. As another favorite quotation, from Housman, ran,

> My pleasures are plenty, my troubles are two,
> But oh, my two troubles they reave me of rest,
> The brains in my head and the heart in my breast.

" 'Teach us to sit still,' " as Louis Simpson has observed of Eliot's prayer, "is dangerous stuff; to use it properly you had better have, as did Eliot, spiritual resources."[82] Win, lacking spiritual belief, took his guidance from literature. In an interview with Don Eulert, he struggled with the problem:

I suppose one can take some comfort in that it is the end result that matters—and any literate person who reads and reads and so on, there's

79 John K. Hutchens, *New York Herald Tribune*, 17 August 1961.
80 Interview, Susan Scott, New York, 10 October 1969.
81 Interview, EMS, Santa Fe, 6 February 1970.
82 Louis Simpson, "Poetry in the Sixties: Long Live Blake! Down with Donne!" *New York Times Book Review*, 28 December 1969, p. 18.

no reason why he shouldn't derive experience, you know, from that kind of thing. It is a part of his life just as much as walking downtown or going to a whorehouse, I guess, or whatever; this is real. His mind is taking in things, and if it is useful, it is useful, and perhaps just as valid as falling down and cutting your knee. It is real experience. But I think one has to keep one's eye out—to watch out, wanting to *use* literary information, which is no good.[83]

Where else was the experience to come from? Typically, Win would try to write in the morning, have lunch and drinks, a nap, then read till cocktail hour, followed by dinner and drinks and reading until, with the help of medication, he was able to sleep. Children, animals, visitors cluttered the house, but he had no job, followed no cause, had no affairs, and no U.S. sailors carrying skulls walked through his door. In Hampton, Win used to take daily walks in the woods, but in Santa Fe, particularly in the last five years of his life, he rarely walked anywhere—not even to the Compound restaurant, two blocks away, where he usually lunched. He became an almost totally sedentary man. In a notebook entry, far less sure of himself than with Eulert, Win confessed to the feeling "of being off the main track—non-essential—of saying nothing to do with what is *basic* to our times; flirting with buttercups while the whole world burns. Have I shut myself away—not been aware enough— not lived enough?"[84] Had literature become an escape from life? In "Scarlet Runner Beans," Scott berated his metaphorical bent:

> He resembles the man in the novel
> Who never said what a thing was
> But always what it was like; because
> That is the way he behaved.[85]

But he was neither able nor altogether willing to change. "Do you realize the wonderful thing you have accomplished?" Win wrote a faithful reader in Providence. "You have somehow—right up to 75—preserved the excitement of a literary youth about books and writing and writers. It is one of the most delightful of all excitements. But very—very—few people even among the best of readers

---

[83] Quoted in Eulert, "Scott," p. 145.
[84] WTS, "*a dirty hand*," pp. 155–156.
[85] WTS, "Scarlet Runner Beans," *Change*, p. 42.

contrive to keep it through life. I congratulate you—and I hope I shall never have to envy you."[86]

Through the fall and winter of 1961–1962 Win labored over his collected poems—correcting, revising, and above all deciding what to excise altogether. As a strategy he determined to save whatever seemed at all worth saving; after all, his early poems had long been out of print, and here was an opportunity to bring them back to life. Still, he cut substantial portions of each of his first three books (excluding *The Sword on the Table*, which was preserved entire). In all, from 80 to 100 pages succumbed to blue-penciling, but a hefty 324 pages remained in the volume Macmillan brought out in July 1962. Planning ahead, Win held back new poems for the next book. And to ensure that this volume would not seem a final accounting, he insisted on the title, *Collected Poems: 1937–1962*. Still, as he inquired of Cowley, "Milestone—or tombstone?" Going back over the past, he added, had been "a ghastly bath of self-doubt."[87]

Scott realized the special importance of this book. Few poets' works are collected; fewer poets still could hope for more than one collection. What he wanted, and even expected, was what James Schevill predicted must follow from the book's publication: "a new consideration of his achievement" that took into account his gift for portraying character and episode, his insight into character and situation.[88] It was not forthcoming. In some places where his previous books had been reviewed *Collected Poems* was not noticed at all: the *New York Times* among them, though Jay Martin—and others—proposed a review to the editors. Schevill, Webster Schott, Ben Clough, and Robert Pack produced thoughtful, appreciative reviews, but, aside from their efforts, it seemed indeed that Win had launched a feather in the Grand Canyon. "Comparatively little has *happened* about the book," he complained to Schott in September.[89]

Win reposed his remaining hopes with the prize-givers: perhaps a Pulitzer, perhaps—even better—a National Book Award, and his *Collected Poems* was indeed nominated for the NBA. Though he

[86] WTS to Arthur (?) Roundy, 4 January 1962.
[87] WTS to Malcolm Cowley, 16 February 1962, the Newberry Library.
[88] James Schevill, "The Poets Speak from a Deep Personal Point of View," *San Francisco Sunday Chronicle*, 23 December 1962, p. 22.
[89] WTS to Webster Schott, 17 September 1962.

believed that in the scramble for prizes and awards ruthlessness and cruelty meant more than merit, Horace Gregory nonetheless wrote that he hoped the book would receive an award—"which it so clearly deserves—and which is the only way these days that books of poems get any recognition at all."[90] But the NBA went to William Stafford, though Reed Whittemore, the only surviving member of the three-judge panel (the others were Henry Rago and Rolfe Humphries) recalls that "both Scott and [William Carlos] Williams (who had just died) were leading contenders."[91]

Returning to Santa Fe for a visit in May 1964 after a two-year hiatus, Tom Duncan and his wife had lunch with Win and Ellie at the Palace restaurant. It was immediately apparent that

Win had changed. In the old days he had always seemed quite relaxed, but now he seemed under some kind of strain. He ordered a double Martini, drank it fast, then ordered another. Then he was more like himself. He told how shortly before our visit Thornton Wilder had been in town, depressed because he had not received the Nobel Prize. . . . And from something Win said—or left unsaid—I had the feeling that he too was wrestling with disappointment. . . . Telling how he had tried to cheer Wilder up, he said, "Of course, we all know that literary prizes are crap." I had the feeling that with his collected poems Win had laid his career on the line, so to speak; he had gone for broke. And he had been passed by.[92]

[90] Marya Gregory to WTS, 17 January 1961, Horace Gregory to WTS, 4 March 1963, Scott Collection, John Hay Library.

[91] Reed Whittemore to SD, 3 October 1969. The judges were considering books by nine poets, the others being Robert Creeley, Donald F. Drummond, Robert Frost, Kenneth Koch, Howard Nemerov, and Anne Sexton.

[92] Thomas Duncan to SD, 22 August 1969.

During a reading at Wellesley College, it was reported, Miss [Amy] Lowell revealed her displeasure at the girls' failure to respond after each poem. "If you like it applaud. If you don't like it, hiss. But for Christ's sake, do something!"[1]

12. A Dearth of Skyrockets

IN HIS NOTEBOOKS, Win Scott tells of talking to a "socio-psychologist" who had been interviewing "a couple of dozen poets." One of the researcher's conclusions was that no other professional group thought so frequently in terms of posthumous reputation. How else could it be? There was no objective standard to measure a poem's worth; it was all a matter of opinion, and opinion kept varying.[2] "The name of the game," as John Ciardi put it, "is impossibility. There is only one thing good about a poem: it is memorable. But there is no way of knowing, in one's own time, if a poem will cleave

[1] WTS, "Amy Lowell of Brookline, Mass.," *Exiles and Fabrications* (1961), p. 116.
[2] WTS, "*a dirty hand*": *The Literary Notebooks of Winfield Townley Scott* (1969), p. 5.

to human memory or not." So the poet lives with hope: an un-
confirmable hope. And so, in his necessary insecurity, he thirsts
after adulation. "If I told a hack contributor," Ciardi went on, "that
he was the greatest poet since Dante, he'd believe it," and wonder
why he had not been compared favorably with Shakespeare. The
final judgment lay in the future, but in the meantime the Nobel,
the Pulitzer, and National Book Award might temporarily satisfy
the unquenchable thirst. Still, as M.L. Rosenthal has said, "the most
successful poets I know are the least secure ones. They conceive
a range for their reputation that they only subconsciously realize."[3]

Consciously, intellectually, Win Scott understood that recognition in this world did not matter. "It's true, isn't it," he inquired
of Robert Hillyer, "that nothing outside one's self—prizes, lack of
prizes, whatever—proves anything?" Then he answered himself,
in his notebooks, with the observation that there was but one sane
wish a writer could make: "to write something better than he has
ever written before."[4] Posterity pays off for craft, not for earthly
reputation. One need only consult literary history to uncover multi-
ple examples of the neglected, underestimated, misunderstood, even
the unknown, resurrected to immortality. So Win avoided the topi-
cal, wary of "all poems that have news value" but lacked univer-
sality. So, carefully, from childhood on, he saved everything—
clippings, letters, journals containing his poems and essays—with
an eye cocked toward posterity. "As writers get older," he remarked
wryly, "most of us develop considerable interest in unappreciated
writers."[5]

Subconsciously, emotionally, it was a different story. "Beware,"
Win warned himself, "of becoming the kind of person who likes to
have his friends (or contemporaries) fail."[6] The warning did not
take. Wretchedly, Win watched as the careers of contemporary
artists were rewarded by prizes and critical acclaim. "Do you suppose any besides you and me have this feeling that the whole Berryman boom is a managed, phony thing?" he asked Horace Gregory

    [3] Interview, John Ciardi, Metuchen, N.J., 16 March 1970; interview, M. L.
Rosenthal, New York City, 10 October 1969.
    [4] WTS to Robert Hillyer, 14 May 1959, Scott Collection, John Hay Library,
Brown University; WTS, "a dirty hand," p. 97.
    [5] WTS, "a dirty hand," pp. 70, 110.
    [6] Ibid., p. 120.

in May 1964.[7] He had seen "an awful lot of skyrockets go up," he told Web Schott, and then, after a significant pause, added, "and come down."[8] Among them were pyrotechnical bursts for Peter Viereck, Paul Engle, Richard Wilbur, Theodore Roethke, and Randall Jarrell (a clever critic, Scott decided, but not a good poet), as well as John Berryman. When Win was sober, or among Santa Fe friends, he made light of rejections, unrewarded honors, the petty world of literary problems. But he cared—how he cared— and when much taken in liquor and talking to a sympathetic visitor, like George Elliott, he would reveal the depths of his bitterness about his reputation, as compared with that of others. "He suffered terribly from poet's envy, and the more so because he hid it, in his social manner and even in his writing."[9] Scott was especially criti- cal of what he regarded as the overpraise of Robert Lowell; but only posthumously, in "a dirty hand," did he try to dismiss Lowell—and his ancestors—with an epigram: "One famous American family seems fated to contribute, every generation, a prominent poet— and each time overrated."[10]

Scott's own work was by no means neglected, but it has not in- spired the kind of celebratory enthusiasm enjoyed by Lowell or Roethke. That is a pity, not only because his poetry deserved it, but for the humane reason that Win Scott more even than his fel- low poets longed for recognition. He set his goals extraordinarily high. "The last thing he wanted to be," Nat Adler recognized, "was a major minor poet. He wanted to be a major poet, period."[11] Per- haps most of those who know Scott's work would agree with J.C. Levenson that he was "a very good minor artist," though the books remain open on the question. What is a major poet? And major when? The point is that during his life Win Scott was regarded as a minor poet, and that he could not tolerate the judgment. "The good, serious minor artist," Levenson writes, "is a sort we have had too little of in America. The country does not know how to esteem him justly and as a consequence he may not even know how to esteem himself. . . . Instead of pride in his calling, he feels a con-

[7] WTS to Horace Gregory, 25 May 1964, Syracuse University Library.
[8] Interview, Webster Schott, Kansas City, 29 December 1969.
[9] Interview, George P. Elliott, New York City, 3 September 1969.
[10] WTS, "a dirty hand," p. 140.
[11] Interview, Nathan and Lucile Adler, Santa Fe, 7 September 1969.

stant, fundamental doubt."[12] Scott measured his every achievement
against the standard of immortality, of greatness, so that whatever
praise he did receive always seemed inadequate. "I wonder,"
Eleanor wrote after Win's death, "whether there ever could have
been enough, even as I believe there never could have been enough
love. The hunger was too great and too private in its sources." Perhaps, she suggests, the same thing "is true of all the artists historians
have marked off as destroyed by lack of recognition."[13]

Frank Merchant's wife, Christine, once told Win that she liked
to do things that showed—paper the walls, or fix things around the
house—and that she needed praise from her husband for the efforts.
"You have the temperament of an artist," Win said.[14] As a child, he
had earned the approval—and hence, he felt, the love—of his parents (especially his mother and grandmother) by his skill at reciting
verse and, later, his talent at composing it.

That childhood experience bred in Win a lasting and terrible
insecurity. "Eleanor tells me—quite rightly—that I'll forget a
dozen complimentary reviews and itch for years over some slighting
dismissal."[15] Sam Vaughan at Doubleday found it almost pitiful
that Win was so grateful to *have* a publisher, at fifty, for the first
time in his life. And Web Schott was struck by the lack of confidence in a man of such talents; from Peterborough, Win sent him
a postcard which ran something like this: "Here I am at the famous
MacDowell Colony where great artists have lived and worked.
Maybe I'll be able to write here in this distinguished company."[16]
As Win himself said, "I don't go around thinking of myself as *the
poet*. . . . In fact, rather ridiculously . . . I have always been terribly
excited and delighted having writers whom I respect sitting in my
living room, drinking and talking with me: I sort of forget that I *am*
a writer."[17] Win empathized with Whittier, "so successful and
seemingly simple a person," who had cried out in his old age, "O,

[12] J. C. Levenson to SD, 2 July 1970.
[13] EMS to SD, 18 March 1969.
[14] Interview, Frank and Christine Merchant, Atlanta, 7 November 1969.
[15] WTS to Samuel Vaughan, 19 January 1968.
[16] Interview, Samuel Vaughan, New York City, 3 September 1969; interview,
Webster Schott, Kansas City, 29 December 1969.
[17] Quoted in Donald Dean Eulert, "Winfield Townley Scott: Conversations on
Poets and the Art of Poetry" (Ph.D. dissertation, University of New Mexico,
January 1969), p. 114.

I'm a fraud! I'm a fraud! And someday they'll find it out!"[18] But he marveled at Emily Dickinson, who had been able to go on with no one to tell her that "she had written greater poems than any other woman in all literature."[19]

Win shared Whittier's doubts and lacked the ego-strength that made Dickinson's vast and abiding accomplishment possible. There is nothing very pretty or lovable about ego-strength, but it is a valuable—almost an essential—quality in an artist. Robert Frost had it, and behaved like a monster to those about him. Win Scott did not, and behaved—differently. As he realized, it was but a short step from self-doubt to self-pity:

> Poetry attracts the self-pitying type both as reader and practitioner. Why? In all the going terms of contemporary life poetry is a failure. Only the few (the "special") people want it. In these terms poetry is, therefore, "other than" all the accepted, successful, necessary things. To be devoted to it sets one apart. To spend a lifetime trying to write it removes one—all the cant within poetry circles to the contrary—from competition. "Competition" between contemporary poets is a fiction. Just because it is believed in and acted upon does not make it real. Confusion over these matters is confusion of fame. No man's "success" as a poet diminishes my own or mitigates my failure. Poetry has to be done in retreat from the world to deal with the world. Therefore the privacy—specialness—ego—self-absorption—(it may be) self-pity. ... The necessary arrogance of the artist is the other side, the healthy side, of self-pity. Self-pity is the shortsighted view of it all, the perversion of it, the sickness of it.[20]

But he could not muster the necessary arrogance of a Frost or, as this quotation implies, a Whitman: "Am I arrogant? Very well, then: I am small, I contain multitudes."[21]

Nothing better illustrates Win Scott's association of literary recognition with love than the telegram he sent Web Schott to thank him for a laudatory essay about his work: "I suppose I have always hopefully waited for someone to speak out for me loud and bold. I am more than grateful; I am reassured and deeply loved."[22] Love

[18] WTS, "a dirty hand," p. 53.
[19] WTS, "Afterword," to *Judge Tenderly of Me: The Poems of Emily Dickinson* (Kansas City: Hallmark, 1968), pp. 57–58.
[20] WTS, "a dirty hand," p. 126.
[21] Ibid., p. 31.
[22] WTS, telegram to Webster Schott, [?] January 1963.

as a child had been conditional—earned and apportioned out for
good behavior; as an adult Win could never get enough of it. On
rainy days in Santa Fe, Win would announce, "It's a gray day in
the book of the world" and then, Eleanor recalls, "he would be all
happy. He wouldn't have to go out—everybody was to stay home—
we could eat off the shelves—everybody hole in *and be safe*. He
loved rainy weather and snowy weather."[23] He could gather wife
and children around him. When his daughters first began to date,
Win was worried—and intensely jealous. When Eleanor, whose
normal gait is perpetual motion, ventured out into her many civic
and cultural activities, he was resentful—and intensely jealous.
"Never go off the Camino" remained a favorite saying, even after
the Scotts had moved from the Camino del Monte Sol to the Alameda.

Outside the family, Win courted the approval of others to the
detriment of his work and exasperation of his wife and children.
No matter how boring or foolish or rude they might be, he listened
to visitors with his whole attention. Dad "was so goddamned nice
to people, even shitty people," Susan remembers. One awful woman
in particular, with something of a crush on Win, used to invade the
Scott home with a regularity and tediousness that annoyed everyone. Though he'd rant and rave a little after she had left, Win was
never nasty to her, to her face.[24]

Those who knew Scott invariably comment on his extraordinary
kindness and gentleness. "One's abiding impression of him," writes
Charles Tomlinson, the English poet, "is his sweetness, his unfail-
ing kindness." To Schott he was "one of the kindest, sweetest,
gentlest men I've ever known." Keith Wilson observes that Win
was "a very kind man generally but, judging by my own experience, when he was drawn to someone his kindness knew no limits."
But all these men, and others, sensed as well that Win was possessed
by regret, a vein of deep subterranean sadness.[25] Nat and Lucile
Adler, among the Scotts' closest friends in Santa Fe, point out that
"in this town Win is loved and missed." Nobody could have been
more charming, easy, and gracious and warm, than he was. He was

[23] EMS to SD, 27 October 1969.
[24] Interview, Susan Scott, New York, 10 October 1969.
[25] Charles Tomlinson to SD, 9 May 1970; Webster Schott to James Dickey,
26 September 1969; Keith Wilson to SD, 21 September 1969.

socially lionized. But they suggest, as well, that Scott was playing a role: "He convinced a hell of a lot of people that he was a simple, kindly man, lovable and sad." He listened, and chatted of literary gossip, yet they could never get Win to really talk, and out of his vast circle of acquaintances and correspondents, there were few close friends. George Elliott, to whom he revealed a good deal more of himself than to most, never had the feeling that Win was totally opening up, revealing himself, even when drunk. The kindness, the geniality, the hinted-at sadness—all, the Adlers think, were part of a public role played by a man who desperately sought approval and love, but was unable in his fear and vulnerability to give of himself. It must have been terribly lonely, they think, to have lived that kind of role.[26]

Most poets make little money, and Win was no exception: he could not possibly have supported a family on the returns from his verse. Recognition replaces cash as the currency in which poets are paid, and it takes on an importance beyond its worth. This is especially true in the case of an artist who is supported by his own private income, or, as in Win's case, by his wife. Defensive about this reversal of roles, Win avoided queries about his status by the expedient of casually, and usually deprecatingly, telling others, before they had a chance to ask. He hoped that would close the subject. But occasionally he would discuss the matter at greater length. In the winter of 1963, for example, after a very successful reading at the Jewish Community Center in Kansas City, Win was riding with Web Schott alone when he began talking about the difficulties of being married to a wealthy woman. "Under the circumstances," he said, "it's possible to have the feeling of being kept."[27]

The feeling was difficult to escape. Dougie, the Scotts' youngest child, reported in 1966 that someone at school had asked him whether his mother was a millionaire. "Don't be stupid," the seven-year-old answered. "Just because my father's a poet doesn't mean my mother's a millionaire."[28] No, but in fact, Eleanor was a millionaire. During September 1965 Ellie withdrew $18,004.86, largely for charitable contributions. The previous month, Win had re-

[26] Interview, Nathan and Lucile Adler, Santa Fe, 7 September 1969; interview, George P. Elliott, New York, 3 September 1969.
[27] Interview, Webster Schott, Kansas City, 29 December 1969.
[28] EMS to WTS, 6 October 1966.

ceived from Sam Vaughan "a royalty check in the amount of $1.98, which represents the continuing harvest of a lifetime invested in American literature. Better you should sell used cars."[29]

Usually, royalty checks were somewhat larger than that, and Win endorsed them and sent them along to his aging father; at least he could help support him. At home, he could hardly compete financially. Lindsay, as a private in the Army, made more money than he did.[30] The situation had an emasculating effect. "I can't compete," he would say at his weekly lunch with Bob Kurth and Bob Saam, two intelligent and admiring prep school teachers. "I can't work against the trust funds."[31] Nor was his ego buoyed by the long-standing custom that he make out the monthly checks for El to sign. Early in their marriage, Win had got into this habit; he never complained directly to her about it.[32] Only in the last two years, on the advice of a psychiatrist, was the arrangement changed so that Win was allowed to sign checks.[33]

Whatever psychological ills Win Scott suffered from being a kept man were compounded by the widespread and peculiarly American notion that you get what you deserve, that hard work will be rewarded with hard cash. W. H. Auden, in 1962, noted the persistence of this concept, which is broadcast under the name of the Protestant ethic, in an essay on the Almighty Dollar. "The most striking difference between an American and a European," he found, was "the difference in their attitudes towards money." Europeans understood that wealth came only from the sweat of other men's brows, and, even in periods of economic upheaval, very few Europeans could rise from poverty to wealth. "In consequence, no European associates wealth with personal merit or poverty with personal failure." In America, however, because of its fund of natural resources, everyone, "until quite recently, could reasonably look forward to making more money than his father." If he did not,

[29] Blanche Cormier to EMS, 8 December 1965; Samuel Vaughan to WTS, 12 August 1965.

[30] On 28 April 1966, for example, Win sent his father a check for $136.81, as one-twelfth royalties from his part in the book *A Vanishing America*, with the note, "Happy Birthday *from* me!" Scott Collection, John Hay Library; interview, Lindsay Scott, Washington, D.C., 26 September 1969.

[31] Interview, Robert Saam and Robert Kurth, Santa Fe, 7 September 1969.

[32] EMS to SD, 7 September 1970.

[33] Interview, Mrs. Jeannette Wolfe, Los Angeles, 2 February 1970.

he was lazy or inefficient. "What an American values, therefore, is not the possession of money as such, but his power to make it as a proof of his manhood. . . . A poor American feels guilty at being poor, but less guilty than an American rentier who has inherited wealth but is doing nothing to increase it; what can the latter do but take to drink and psychoanalysis?"[34] Auden did not explore a still more culturally demeaning state: that of the man who neither makes money nor increases it, but is supported by his wife's estate.

In Europe, for centuries, artists had found patrons and if close to home so much the better. But it was different in America. Here, if you're an artist, Norman Pearson comments, "sometimes you feel you ought not to work, but to work your genius. But how do you keep your respect in a world given to people who stigmatize those who do not work? If you're a playboy, you can repay your wife by play, by doing things for and to her. But if you're an artist, you have to be a success, a very big success, to justify your role."[35] After a visit to the Scotts in 1963 or 1964, Merle Armitage wrote Win: "Something you said today about your well-to-do-wife having married a poverty-stricken poet leads me to believe that this has at times bothered you. Do not be caught in that old American idea that only money means success. You and I know that this is non-sense."[36] But it is the sort of nonsense that pervades the culture, so that even those who should have known better—Win's fellow artists—unconsciously accepted it as part of the American gospel. Stanley Noyes, a writer living in Santa Fe, once sat next to Georgia O'Keeffe at a dinner party also attended by the Scotts. During dinner she turned to Noyes and asked, "Just what does Mr. Scott *do?*" Noyes replied that Win was a very good poet, and Miss O'Keeffe just nodded. It was only later that he realized that she was really asking "How does Mr. Scott earn his living?"[37]

Worst of all, the Protestant ethic took hold upon Win himself. When he left the *Providence Journal*, in 1951, John Holmes warned him that

the coming years will have to be learned slowly and wisely—I mean

[34] W. H. Auden, "Postscript: The Almighty Dollar," *The Dyer's Hand and Other Essays* (New York: Random House, 1962), pp. 335–336.

[35] Interview, Norman Holmes Pearson, New Haven, 13 August 1969.

[36] Merle Armitage to WTS, n.d., Scott Collection, John Hay Library.

[37] Stanley Noyes to SD, 7 May 1970.

the use of them—the change of pace, and the difference in conscience and attitude, and satisfaction. . . . If I were you, meaning if I were now retiring, I know damn well I would waste some time and emotion with a feeling of guilt about seeming not to be doing anything. I'll think poorly of you if you do that.[38]

But of course that was precisely what Scott did, the burden of guilt only increasing as time went on. The young poet Keith Wilson, who met Scott in 1967, noted that

for such a liberal, open man, Win had much of his puritan heritage with him, carried it like a little brown paper bag which would fly open at the darndest times, always to his own embarrassment: he worried about his leisure, the fact that he didn't have to "work"; he worried about his drinking and party-going, though he dearly loved parties of his own special kind; he thought he talked too much, was always apologizing, all the while loving to talk and being very, very good at it. As death came near, these guilts, concerns intensified and drove him—or stopped him.[39]

Finally, the guilt deepened into the self-contempt apparent in "Man in a Rut," a poem Win wrote in October 1965 for "someone who wanted a 'happy poem' ":

> Just thinking how her ends
> Continually justify his means
> Makes him as proud-to-present as
> Any master of ceremonies
> Equipped with ball-pointed pen.
> It makes him feel—wonderful!
> There isn't a plumber in town
> With a slicker toolbox and
> He never forgets, he never
> Has to go back. He just comes.
> For all his skill, hers loves
> His amateur standing.
> It makes her feel—wonderful!
> O! he's seldom down in the
> Mouth. Except odd occasions.[40]

[38] John Holmes to WTS, 30 May 1951. Scott Collection, John Hay Library.
[39] Keith Wilson to SD, 21 September 1969.
[40] WTS, "Man in a Rut," unpublished poem (15 October 1965).

When Hilary Masters, who also married a rich wife, finished his first novel, Win congratulated him: "It must feel good to have that novel all on paper. . . . Us lucky bastards without a bread & butter worry who can sit on . . . our twinkly asses . . . have a special feeling, amidst all the lazy distractions, when for Christ's sake something, after all, gets done."[41] But other kinds of feeling when not much was getting written, or when the novel or book of poems was turned down, or when, duly published, it was greeted by dead sticks and not skyrockets. After Win's death, Masters reflected on the power of the work ethic to make rather unlucky bastards of artists supported by independent incomes:

Work is noble; therefore, so-and-so-deserves praise over another because he has worked hard. Not worked hard at his art, but worked hard at something else simultaneously. Remember all those book flaps listing novelists' past occupations, dishwasher, longshoreman, door to door salesman—that was earlier, during the WPA epoch, now the list contains things like teacher, librarian, newspaperman, etc. There's a reverse view: so-and-so has had an easy time of it; therefore, he could not possibly speak with any authenticity of . . . his times, or reflect any sympathy with most other people of his time. . . . And if you're a Win Scott, it is pointless to answer that many of those who pass such prejudices off as critical evaluation, or whose critical evaluation is affected by such prejudices, are also "living off" of a foundation grant, or playing the academic scene or practicing the Frostian form of prostitution on the reading circuit. And more practically, not to be engaged in the "work" of poets today, teaching, lecturing, etc., also removes one from the mainstream of poetry politics.

We shall never know but I wonder how many dark nights Win may have endured, thinking that he had been passed over for the National Book Award or some other recognition of his work because certain judges felt he had it "too easy." It's a horrible thought, and I would not wish it upon him or El, but we are all seized by paranoia like that occasionally, and once it bites it's hard to shake off.

Masters was moved to these reflections by an encounter with a well-known literary commentator who told him, authoritatively, that Win Scott had "married a rich woman and quit."[42]

---

[41] WTS to Hilary Masters, 22 October 1970, Scott Collection, John Hay Library.
[42] Hilary Masters to SD, 21 September 1969.

As he grew older, it seemed to Win that his opportunities for the most prestigious awards, for honorary degrees from the best universities, and for election to the literary academies had come and gone. He was tremendously sensitive to aging, a sensitivity sharpened by his marriage to a wife eleven years younger and considerably more energetic than himself. There was one story Win told on himself so often as to indicate a kind of obsession with his physical deterioration and a defensive desire to treat the subject with levity. Louise Wheelwright Damon, Foster Damon's wife, had painted portraits of Win, Wade Vliet, and Bill Gerry while they were still at Brown. Thirty years later, through arrangements made by Vliet, Mrs. Damon sent Win's portrait to Santa Fe. It showed a young man who seemed the very image of a poet—slim, full head of blond hair, features as fine as a doomed hero in an early Fitzgerald novel. One day Dougie, his youngest child, was looking at it and asked, "Daddy, who's that?" "Me," Win replied. Doug studied it a while longer and said, "What happened?"[43] What had happened was more dramatic in Win's case than in that of most men of fifty. He had lost much of his hair and added many more pounds than his body was made to bear. Liquor had taken its toll, too, around the mouth, the eyes, and the jowls.

Still more painful to Win than his physical decline were periods of artistic fallowness. Even in college he had suffered spells of dryness that inordinately troubled him; "I've written myself out," he told Frank Merchant more than once in his undergraduate days.[44] When blocked, Win underwent severe depression. In 1957, during one such period, he wrote letters to a number of other writers, among them George Elliott, Lee Anderson, and Paul Horgan, seeking reassurance that they too were occasionally blocked. Of course they all had been; but they knew with greater equanimity than Scott could muster that the dry spells always ended. In the meantime, as Elliott suggested, "there should be spiritual exercises for writers during periods of aridity, such as the trainee saints have."[45]

[43] William E. Wilson to SD, 28 August 1969; Tom W. Mayer to SD, 19 December 1969.

[44] Interview, Frank Merchant, Atlanta, 7 November 1969.

[45] George P. Elliott to WTS, 5 November 1957, Scott Collection, John Hay Library.

What especially troubled Win was that his periods of aridity grew longer as he grew older. "I'm slightly nuts," he told Jeff Werner in November 1964. "I write notes—notes—notes: but no symphony, no song. . . . I have 'ideas'—phrases—images—lines—but they stay *fixed* & I can do nothing. What a hell of a way to spend one's life. I sometimes wonder if it wouldn't have been nice if I'd inherited my Grandfather Scott's hardware store in Newport. I'll bet I could have run a very efficient hardware store. . . . I know this a somewhat phony remark. I wouldn't really swap. It's only I get so tired & dubious & discouraged at time."[46]

A multitude of distractions—the youngsters, the parties, the overseas artists the State Department sent to the Scotts to be entertained in Santa Fe (once a week or once a month in the early 1960's Tom Mayer would get a call to drive Win and a foreign visitor up to Frenchie's in Taos; hearing Win's voice on the line, Tom would inquire: "Hungarian or Rumanian?")—interfered with attempts to break through artistic blocks. "There was a circus quality to their social life," Nat Adler said. "It was always sort of startling that books did continue to get published."[47] The best remedy Win had found was to chore away at something other than poetry. So, in 1963, after three months in "that miserable, deadly state of being unable to write," he started doing research for an essay on the town of Chimayo (eventually published in *A Vanishing America*) and not only did he begin to touch "some of the form and some of the phrasing of the piece" but extraneously began to note ideas, phrases, for possible poems. "One's mind, beginning to work on *this*, seems to reach out toward *that*—and *that*. I begin to live again."[48]

Scott's book of poems, *Change of Weather*, which Doubleday published in 1964, was shot through with the theme of aging. He had begun what was to become an obsession with his own mortality, as the first poem in the book, "To the Old Men, Not to Praise Us," illustrated:

[46] WTS to H. O. Werner, 17 November 1964, Scott Collection, John Hay Library.
[47] Interview, Tom W. Mayer, Santa Fe, 28 March 1970; interview, Nathan and Lucile Adler, Santa Fe, 7 September 1969.
[48] WTS, *"a dirty hand,"* p. 146.

My generation: some swift and breathless off a
  bridge,
Some slowly down through many drinks. I don't
  know why.
Something's to be said I suppose for going still
  ball-quick.
Who awaits fake proofs, velvet on shoulders,
  medals?
And some twist in and out of madness and some
Like me don't quite do any of these deaths.

The poem ends, "I shall be old soon," and carries an epigraph from
Chaucer, "The lyf so short, the craft so long to lerne."[49] Had he
learned his craft, or was he carving statues in ice, of momentary
interest only? How long would he be able to continue carving?

Confidential

In the poet's vigorous fifties,
With prolific good work done,
He writes more virile poems
Secretly. He hides them
To be published in his seventies.[50]

Change of Weather is a book of middle age, exploring the effects
of the passage of time on art and sex. As always in Scott's verse, the
line between the act of making love and the act of making poems
is a thin one. In "Ritual Dance," published in Scott's 1967 book of
New and Selected Poems, the line is all but obliterated:

"Suppose," she whispered, "this were the last time,"
As I knelt in the darkness and leaned in
And lay there hardly long in the deep way
Of waiting for her and me until slowly
Each wondering if it might be the last time
We moved together and apart, apart and
Together, up up in the din of night
Driven by more than us, by the one that two
Become in the ritual dance; become!

[49] WTS, "To the Old Men, Not to Praise Us," *Change of Weather* (1964),
and *New and Selected Poems* (1967), p. 95.
[50] WTS, "Confidential," *Change of Weather* (1964), p. 10.

After many refusals—hers more? or mine?
And even after a thousand acceptances
I always suppose: Is this the last time?
Now shall I watch for or go look for her?
After the terrifying need to touch,
What else is worth touching now? And is this death
The one I dreaded? or just a little while?[51]

Polly Masters told Win that "Ritual Dance" excited her; he replied that the poem concerned the Poet and his Muse—his worry that he'd never be able to write another poem.[52] But the confusion was obviously intended; Scott's Muse is a carnal one, erotic love his metaphor for artistic creation.

A set of poems in *Change of Weather* ("Brief Encounter," "Postscript," "Another Return," "Dreamed Rain") looks back with nostalgia on a brief affair at Brown. "You have a middle-aged man who is not as sexy as he once was," Win said to Don Eulert in 1966, "and he is drawn by memory of early passions, by regrets of unfulfilled passions." As Yeats had put it, "One looks back to one's youth as to a cup that a mad man dying of thirst left half tasted." These poems are "filled with this regret for not fully realizing that full cup of water, and a sense of shame and failure and wistfulness, and the girl who keeps reappearing in the middle-aged man's dreams."[53]

The theme was not a new one for Scott; even in his earliest books, he had written poems focusing on a young, golden girl. In "Dream Penny in the Slot 6 A.M." (*Biography for Traman*) and "Natural Causes" (*Wind the Clock*), Eleanor points out, she is "seen as fiction, as image. . . . In *To Marry Strangers* she is of course all over the place and now she is (or is believed to be) 'real' "—in the person of Ellie.[54] Then, in later poems, the girl took the form of the girl from Brown, or her reincarnation in dreams. Almost always she is surrounded by mist, like a Newport morning. The golden girl, Eleanor believes, "contains the Eden Garden, a time of sufficient and abundant love, and physical as well as poetic potency,"[55]

[51] WTS, "Ritual Dance," *New and Selected Poems*, p. 118.
[52] WTS to Samuel Vaughan, 29 October 1967.
[53] Quoted in Eulert, "Scott," pp. 162–163.
[54] EMS to SD, 6 May 1969.
[55] EMS to SD, 18 March 1969.

and she occupied Win's thoughts and dreams and poems increasingly as his sexual and artistic power waned.

Scott's poems about sex are among his best. Walker Gibson wrote him in 1958 that he was "the best poet I know on the subject of sex," and William Cole included seven of Scott's poems in his 1963 anthology, *Erotic Poetry*.[56] These earlier poems celebrated sex, but in *Change of Weather*, now in his early fifties, Win contemplated youthful vigor with unwise envy:

> That pair lying deep there in exhaustion
> From hours of love-making: sprawled
> Young nakedness, half falling away
> Half clinging, on the couch in the
> Silenced room in late afternoon's
> Fading light: so I imagine them.
>
> O in my wiser moments I have written
> Not to look back in envy; it is waste.
> Yet how not shake with jealous memory
> So long as I'm still licked—briefer
> Infrequent—by intercrural fire?
> Perhaps some extreme quiet of old age
> Will let me look at such and dryly smile:
> That pair wet with sweetest wisdom.[57]

Win's father hardly approved. "Why so many sexy verses?" he inquired, and sent his son a poem called "Peonies" clipped from the *Haverhill Gazette*—"a nice clean poem about nice clean flowers."[58]

Change of Weather represented a departure in Win Scott's poetic voice. The book contained almost no narrative verse, instead concentrating on a lyric voice designed to reveal the innermost self. In some of the poems, Win wrote Edward McSorley in April 1965, "I was sure that . . . I'd dug deeper under my own skin than I'd ever been able to before," yet characteristically, leafing through the

---

56 Walker Gibson to WTS, 14 April 1958, Scott Collection, John Hay Library; WTS poems included in Cole's anthology were "Watch Hill," Sonnets XII, XIII, and XV from *To Marry Strangers*, "The Ivory Bed," "Wax," and the fragment from *Biography for Traman* that begins "Let us record/The evenings when were innocents of twenty."

57 WTS, "That Pair—" *Change of Weather*, and *New and Selected Poems*, p. 105.

58 WTS to Samuel Vaughan, 29 October 1967.

book, his conviction collapsed into "utter dissatisfaction."[59] Horace
Gregory singled out two poems for praise, one of them dealing sym-
bolically with the quest for that most hidden, inner self:

> When you come to the door in the wall
> It will do no good to knock.
> First you must find the door.
> It will be night, of course,
> And though many times before
> You have found and entered that door,
> It is never easy to find.
> It is never easy to enter. Wait:
> Full moon and a change of weather.
>
> .   .   .   .
>
> There are many doors in the wall.
> For you, all but yours are false.
> You must rediscover the door
> And then you must not knock.
> Do not beat on the door.
> Stand humbly, hopefully there
> In what seems immutable night.
> Perhaps the door will open. Wait:
> Full moon and a change of weather.[60]

What lay beyond the door? Once Thomas Duncan and Win were
"talking about science-fiction and horror stories. 'I have never cared
for horror stories,' Win said. 'Life is horrible enough without horror stories.' A door had opened a few inches and I had glimpsed a
long corridor where there were bats and cobwebs. Then the door
closed, Win lighted his pipe and we spoke of other matters."[61] Win
scarcely had more than a momentary glimpse himself. "I think,"
he wrote Gregory, "that I have a door which I have not pushed wide
enough open: a sewer-cover, not a door, is the way I usually think
of it. I am a Yankee, you know, since 1620. But that lovely Mr
Cummings found ways—and I live in hopes. At least, nothing,
however trivial, will be dishonest."[62]

[59] WTS to Edward McSorley, 26 April 1965.
[60] Horace Gregory to WTS, 17 August 1964, Scott Collection, John Hay
Library; WTS, "The One Door," *Change of Weather*, p. 3.
[61] Thomas Duncan to SD, 22 August 1969.
[62] WTS to Horace Gregory, 24 August 1964, Syracuse University Library.

He wanted, of course, not merely to open the door and explore the sewer, but to write about what he discovered, honestly and convincingly. It was not an easy task. "Nothing is more difficult," as Albert J. Guerard has observed, "than to write simply and unironically, fully and with a single controlled voice, about the things that have mattered to us most. . . . There are indeed no limits to the ways in which a man can avoid looking very closely at himself."[63] One technique of evasion was to substitute heat for light, the cry of pain for the pain itself—and this temptation Win carefully avoided. The poems in *Change of Weather* were shorter, written in simpler language, than ever before. "On Re-reading the Complete Works of an Elder Poet," written on 18 October 1962, set forth Scott's objective: "Ways to learn to be/ More casual in the poem/ Were what I searched for." He had begun to fear, Win confessed, that he had "Slipped on a New England streak/ Of grease and gesturing wildly/ Pointed morals," and had been charged with "Writing too much out of regret./ How reply to that?" But he was in search of "Any way to learn to live/ More casual in the poem." And "Despite 'the bomb'—and all that/ One wants—like Beethoven—to/ Conclude with the human voice/ In joy."[64]

Discussing this poem in his *Herald Tribune* review of *Change of Weather*, Elliott concluded that Scott had demonstrated "how vigorously casual he [could] be in his poetry, which yet his personality stains." The poet's voice, Elliott wrote, was "that of a reasonable man talking with an old friend. He has no desire to impress you . . . get you to change your mind, charm you, cozy up to you, or burden you with his secret troubles. You must pay attention to understand him, but if you do pay attention you will understand him."[65] Win was delighted: "To be *read* like that!"[66] Other adulatory reviews compared Win's work, directly or indirectly, with that of other, better known contemporaries. "His voice will be heard far longer than poets who now have the eye and ear of the critical fraternity." "Surely . . . Winfield Townley Scott is one of the wholly relevant

[63] Albert J. Guerard, "The Journey Within," *The Personal Voice*, ed. Albert J. Guerard, et al. (Philadelphia: J. B. Lippincott, 1968), pp. 2–3.

[64] WTS, "On Re-reading the Complete Works of an Elder Poet," *New and Selected Poems*, p. 98. The poet referred to is William Carlos Williams.

[65] George P. Elliott, *New York Herald Tribune*, 13 September 1964.

[66] WTS to Anne Hutchens, 17 September 1964.

poets in the United States. . . . He writes about the world in which we live, the world of people and their responses, rather than an abstract aesthetic." "Scott is revealed by this volume to be not just *a* worthy contemporary poet but one of the three or four most distinguished poets of our time and place."[67] Even *Time* Magazine, in a review which Win described as "a little stupid . . . but well-intentioned," called Scott the best of "a small group of American poets [who continue] to write mild, mellow verse in the Concord manner of Emerson and Thoreau."[68] A little stupid, perhaps, because if *Time* detected the role of memory in these poems, the magazine hardly took account of the empathic strain of yearning and regret that informs many of them—including the other one Horace Gregory admired:

> Whose dictionary? I bought it secondhand
> As the impersonal luggage of my language
> Used heretofore, but complete, as good as new,
> Unencumbered, as they say, by mortgage.
>
> Now here, like an unsuspected meadow
> Agape with frivolities of sun in a forest,
> Here at page fourteen-sixty-eight and -nine,
> Here between *luna cornea* and *lustless,*
> This palmful of pressed flowers like a cry:
> Hushed fringed gentians' faded purple hair,
> Three Indian pipe, grayed-frosted miniatures,
> And one embalmed-red plume of cardinal flower
> Of a most blood-like, death-like delicacy.
>
> Whose bookmarked book? Whose late summer
> Pressed and dried here from the scent of light
> And water-run and the shade-caring wind,
> From what other year and spin of the earth?
> And was it for the flowers or for the words,
> The passion to hold an afternoon forever?
> To fold it here—where else, lord speech, where else?—
> A personal garland blessed to anonymous grace.[69]

---

[67] Reviews by August Derleth, *Madison* (Wisconsin) *Capitol Times,* 6 August 1964; John R. Willingham, *Library Journal* 89 (1 October 1964): 3759; and Webster Schott, *Christian Science Monitor,* 10 December 1964.
[68] "Can All Come Green Again?" *Time,* 21 August 1964, p. 88; WTS to H. O. Werner, 18 September 1964, Scott Collection, John Hay Library.
[69] WTS, "Who's Been Here Before Me?" *Change of Weather,* p. 13.

Sometime in 1963 or 1964 the chaotic healthiness of the Scott household began to collapse. "And then somehow," Tom Mayer, who had earlier admired the control Win Scott exerted over his surroundings,

you could feel it all going bad, maybe stale, a little sour. Where he had been pink cheeked, almost cherubic if he hadn't been so solid, the flesh took on the consistency of damp flour and the jowls, which had been worn as a dignifying accoutrement, became the excess flesh of a tired man running to fat. The conversation was still witty, but there were pauses that grew longer and longer, and, as the children grew up and began to have adolescent problems and then young adult problems, he somehow emanated the feeling that he was losing control of other things as their need of his solidity, his presence, diminished and was perhaps less welcome. We had good times still and I used to put what I thought was happening as far from mind as possible, or, when I did consider it, mark it down to aging, to some inevitable process that eventually robs all of us, or at least changes us.[70]

It was aging, and more: a deep and abiding depression, the devastation of drink, and sexual impotence that crippled his marriage. Writing to Jeff Werner, the one man in the world to whom he could have said such things, Scott analyzed his own deterioration in February 1964:

I am tired—unambitious—I get (barring little hack book reviews) no writing done—in short I am pooped out. I have a great deal of indigestion "distress." My nerves are rotten—I'm pretty much all right if I stay here in my own house or just move about this little town—but if, say, I *have* to go to Albuquerque I get into a not really sane state of tension: I am frightened. I can describe this—know this—as a kind of nonsense but despite some pills I cannot control it.

These psychological woes were compounded by Scott's conviction that he was being neglected—at home as by the prize-givers.

My last year's checkup with my doctor was o.k.—a rising cholesterol business and a "difficulty" in digesting. No sign of ulcer. Of course I drink heavily—much too much. I keep resolving to cut it down but I don't. And I have no desire to go to a psychiatrist. I want— I know this is "weakness"—a mother-smothered case—someone who'd care about all this & so take care of me—but there's no such person in my life. I

[70] Tom W. Mayer to SD, 19 December 1969.

A DEARTH OF SKYROCKETS

have nowhere to turn. I've never written about this to anybody, so you please keep shut about it. According to some women—so I've heard— I'm the "most charming man in Santa Fe." I'm also a bewildered, rather bitter old bastard.

Enough of that. Forgive me. This may all be a phase from which sooner or later I'll emerge as the boringest male Pollyanna you ever endured.[71]

But it was more than a phase. The following August he wrote Essie Bates similar in terms: "What would I do without you? More generously than anyone else you distribute my books. You write me words that bolster my morale. You're the only person left on earth to spoil me—and I love it."[72]

The world outside offered further incentives to distress. As always taking such matters personally, Win was devastated by the assassination of President John F. Kennedy, the man who, he had hoped, would bring the nation to life again. Like many others, he "lived for days in front of TV and smoked and drank & sometimes wept." Kennedy's death seemed too ghastly a waste to be true; how "conclude in joy" when the nation's climate had turned to the heat of violence?[73]

In the summer of 1964, the Scott family took a cruise to Scandinavia, Russia, and northern Europe. In Bruges, in Belgium, Win "walked through a gateway—quite ignorant as to where I was going—into a nunnery called the Béguinage" and discovered, in the "great plaza of grass and trees surrounded by whitewashed little houses," such a place of peace as he had often dreamed of. Suddenly he "thought: this is where I want to come back and die."[74] Of the Nordic countries, Win particularly liked Iceland, where guides pointed out the houses of poets. "It seemed as though each hamlet . . . had its poet, and the poet was recognized, and he thought this beautiful."[75] But there was little sense of peace or recognition on board the cruise ship, the *Gripsholm.* "I was only depressed," Win wrote

[71] WTS to H. O. Werner, 21 February 1964, Scott Collection, John Hay Library.
[72] WTS to Esther W. Bates, 31 August 1964, Scott Collection, John Hay Library.
[73] WTS to Hilary Masters, 12 December 1963, Scott Collection, John Hay Library.
[74] WTS to Henry and Elizabeth Beston, 18 September 1964.
[75] EMS to SD, 7 September 1970.

Henry Beston, "by—say—90 per cent of our fellow Americans aboard: the ostentation of money and the stupidity which accompanies most of it." In their worship of the material, the passengers reminded Win that they neither cared nor knew anything about poetry and its practitioners. His only writing was "some outrageous doggerel about New Mexico for an 'entertainment' aboard ship." Afterward, an old lady came up to him and said, "Mr. Scott—promise me you'll go on writing. You *must* go on writing!" He said he'd try. More disturbing was "the 18 year old girl—pretty and rich and by no means stupid—who wants to write poetry—and who sat me down for a consultation and said: 'Mr. Scott, this is what I want to know: how do I start at the top?' "[76]

On the trip, as at home, Win continued to drink heavily. There was plenty of leisure time (in his notebooks, Win recorded Virgil Thomson's crack that "the trouble with being a poet [was] what to do with the other twenty-three and a half hours a day")[77] and the cost of liquor posed no barrier to Ellie's formidable wealth. Win's early fondness for liquor had developed into an unshakeable habit. When he visited Hampton in 1954, Hilary Masters thought Scott's drinking was under control. "I do drink a lot," he'd admit, "but they're very tall drinks—and weak ones." Ten years later, in Santa Fe, the drinking started with Bloody Marys at noon and continued through the party or reception or dinner that took place nearly every night. And Win's drinks had become dark, not weak, ones.[78] For brief periods he would cut down on liquor consumption, and in the spring of 1964 (shortly after he wrote his disconsolate letter to Jeff Werner) Win stopped drinking altogether, on doctor's orders, to nurse a diaphragmatic hernia. "I feel better," he wrote Web Schott, "but I can't sleep much. 6 a.m. is my most likely time to drop off."[79] It wasn't exactly the booze he longed for, he explained to Frank Merchant, but "the *habit* of certain daily & nightly hours" was hard to slough off.[80] Soon he was drinking as hard as ever.

Win never drank until lunch, as "proof" to himself that he was

[76] WTS to Henry and Elizabeth Beston; WTS to Anne Hutchens, 31 August 1964.
[77] WTS, "*a dirty hand*," p. 138.
[78] Interview, Hilary and Polly Masters, Provincetown, 30 July 1969.
[79] WTS to Webster Schott, 15 March 1964.
[80] WTS to Frank Merchant, 31 March 1964.

not an alcoholic, but he slept later and later in the mornings to shorten the hours without liquor; after a long lunch and a nap, the cocktail hour began and extended through dinner into a night of talking or reading and finally a drugged sleep. But he never went on binges and he never passed out at parties. Was he an alcoholic? In a medical sense, yes, his friend and physician, Dr. Richard Landmann, thinks; but not in the sense of being unable to function.[81]

It took his daughter Susan a long time to realize there was anything unusual about a man's going from afternoon to bedtime with a drink in one hand, his pipe in the other. One day, in biology class, she saw a film about alcoholism; alcoholics, according to the film, drank all day long. Susan objected: "My daddy drinks all day long, and he isn't an alcoholic." In time, she changed her mind about that, and came to dread the sound of the cap being unscrewed from a bottle of Bellows' Partner's Choice (her father's inavariable highball whiskey) and of ice cubes rattling in the glass. Toward the end, Win would slump into unconsciousness at the kitchen table and have to be put to bed, or, worse, would explode in anger at himself and Ellie.[82] But Win never admitted to himself that he was an alcoholic; it was only that he drank too much, just as he ate too much and smoked too much.

The drinking contributed to the frustrating impotence Win had so long feared. Unable to satisfy his wife, he could not respect himself as a man. The process of emasculation was spurred by El's aggressiveness: she was boss around the house. Win never scolded or yelled at the children; the most he would say, to the worst breach of behavior, was "You really mustn't do that." Win would tell Susan she couldn't go out, for example. Susan would say, "I want to and I'm going to." El, as arbiter, would decide; her word was final.[83]

In "a dirty hand," Win philosophizes on the relationship between women and artists in this country. For one thing, women make up most of the artist's audience.

And women—a great many women—are attracted to the artist as man; they love him, they want to marry him; sometimes several in a row

---

[81] Interview, Dr. Richard Landmann, Santa Fe, 28 March 1970.
[82] Interview, Susan Scott, New York, 10 October 1969.
[83] Interview, Lindsay Scott, Washington, D.C., 26 September 1969.

take turns (with some overlapping) marrying even one artist. He arouses the maternal in them and a temporary, uncharacteristic lust for an irregular, extracurricular, insecure, and remarked-upon life. But of course such lust doesn't last and furthermore the maternal instinct includes the dictatorial.

And even the artist who, like Win, wants desperately to be mothered, does not want dictating to. Unlike businessmen, artists are almost totally preoccupied with their work—and it is of necessity lonely, private work. "Wives of writers are wanted in so many ways by writers—and in some ways are not needed at all. There's the trouble."[84]

Eleanor ruled the household both by default (Win did not assert himself) and by temperament. Where Win was phlegmatic, she was volatile; where he was sedentary, she was energetic. As he told an interviewer for the local paper, "as far as Santa Fe is concerned, I have a hunch I'm known, to whatever extent I am known, as Ellie Scott's husband. Which is quite all right, too."[85]

El is always more or less involved in Opera work. She has just successfully run her 7th annual secondhand book sale that benefits the grade school Douglas goes to, and this week she's been gathering petitions to try to prevent the Public Service Co. from erecting a . . . steel tank on top of an open reservoir at a very pretty bend of Canyon Road. Also she attends a once-a-week adult night course with Dean Kramer at St. John's—and runs the house—and the rest of us. She's a busy girl.[86]

More and more, Win resented the time she spent on the Santa Fe Opera, PTA, and other organizations. "You care more about the Opera than about me." Eleanor thought him unreasonably possessive.

By 1965, when the Bagdikians were visiting Santa Fe, tension between Win and Ellie was evident. She "was completely absorbed in the Opera and the directors and singers in the Opera, to Win's obvious annoyance." She made a great deal of one particular singer, and though Win was plainly jealous, an "utterly bewildered" Ellie

---

[84] WTS, "a dirty hand," pp. 81–82, 141.

[85] "Winfield Townley Scott Stands for P-P-P," Santa Fe Scene, 6 February 1960, p. 7.

[86] WTS to H. O. Werner, 9 December 1967, Scott Collection, John Hay Library.

did nothing to relieve the jealousy. "I had never seen him," Ben Bagdikian recalls, "so distraught and tense, bordering on bitterness. . . . The Opera people seemed to bore and irritate him and Ellie's preoccupation with them even more so." Win withdrew, his face darkened, to walk alone in the garden outside the kitchen. He had lost his characteristic "quick responsiveness and rapport with others." It was, Betty Bagdikian remembers, "a horrible time."[87]

To Paul Horgan, Eleanor seemed "the eternal Bennington girl, following a cult of dressing like hell and being pretty smudgy as well as outrageously outspoken." This was not entirely pleasing to Win; he'd wince, or his countenance would cloud, but no more. "I always had the sense," Horgan said, "that he consciously restrained himself when irritated with her."[88]

Entirely aware of these shortcomings, Ellie now accounts for them, at least partly, as a consequence of their sexual difficulties. With advancing age, liquor, and fear, Win became regularly impotent. And when men don't react, how does a woman feel about herself? As men fear failure, El suggests, women lose a sense of themselves as women in such instances: hence her sloppy dress, unkempt hair, swearing, and more or less eccentric behavior.[89] She was married, she began to suspect, to a latent homosexual. There had been overtones of homosexuality, Win had told her, in his early relationships with older men, but they remained only overtones. His unusual kindness to the young men who came to call in Santa Fe suggested further overtones of this kind, and certainly his dreams reflected a terrifying insecurity about his own masculinity. But consciously, he thought homosexuality inimical to art (he bitterly complained about the extent to which homosexuals influenced literary politics), and the gay world repelled him. Eleanor knows of no single case where Win was unfaithful to her, with man or woman.[90] Imaginatively, he could conceive of such relationships, as in "Hong Kong Boy" and in "Poem," the latter published posthumously in *Poetry's* March 1969 issue:

---

[87] Ben Bagdikian to SD, 12 July 1969; interview, Ben and Betty Bagdikian, Washington, D.C., 15 March 1970; EMS to SD, 7 September 1970.
[88] Interview, Paul Horgan, Middletown, Connecticut, 5 December 1969.
[89] Interview, EMS, Santa Fe, 8 September 1969.
[90] Ibid.

The girl young enough to be my daughter
Walks with me in sweet dusk of spring woods.

Ignoring the common scrotal lady's-slippers,
The crone makes paintings of vulval orchids—
Huge immaculate blues not to be touched.

I ask: "Your painting is a celebration?
Its exaggeration is contempt for man?
Would you scare me back into my handkerchief?
Or to search a body which is twin to mine?"

Fixes me with cold orchid-color eyes
As one aware she has stirred a furtive terror
But is merely careless of her pleasure for it.

I—as they say—not so young anymore
Turn and protectively embrace the girl
And begin to tremble in astonished joy:
I had not remembered how slender, how weightless.[91]

The painter with whom the poet carries on an imaginary dialogue is Georgia O'Keeffe; the girl but another embodiment of youth, innocence, and full sexual and creative energy.

Finally, under the influence of liquor, a lifetime of keeping his emotions under control—particularly the taboo childhood emotion of anger—exploded in vicious attacks on his wife—and indirectly, on himself. Always the public Win Scott remained lovable. Going to a party, he might be metaphorically beating El to death in the car, yet for the next three and a half hours he would behave like a perfect gentleman, only to resume the tirade later. The trouble was confined to the home, where, in the last years of his life, almost anything could provoke a tempest. One night it was finding El out of bed and in the kitchen, reading. (Where had she been?) Furious, Win took glasses off the shelves and threw them at her; no one cleaned up until the next morning, when the great pile of broken glass forced him to acknowledge his drunken frenzy. If Eleanor served the children first at dinner, he'd blow up, in his rage launching question after unanswerable question. Why do you always have to insult me? Why do you always debase me? Why do you always have to be right? Why do you hate me so? Why don't you ever tell the truth? What is it like to be a marble

[91] WTS, "Poem," *Poetry* 113 (March 1969): 373.

goddess, incapable of feeling or love? What is it like to have the world run for your convenience?

Then, as if a litany, there would be remorse the following day. "I'm impossible to live with," Win would say. "You'd all be better off without me." He was told that it was not so, that it would not be so, if he would stop or slow down his drinking.[92] But that was hardly reassurance enough. In time he came to believe what had begun as the rhetoric of evasion. Perhaps he *was* impossible; perhaps he would be better dead. Win Scott began to hate himself.

[92] Interview, EMS, Santa Fe, 8 September 1969.

> In honesty—in speech—in love
> In what have I not failed
> So far?[1]

13. Triumph Disaster

IN A SPIRIT OF DESPERATION, Win Scott set out in the mid-1960's to rescue his writing, his marriage, and his self-respect. Doubleday, now firmly committed as his publisher (in all, the firm brought out three of his last four books), suggested a novel; even if the novel was not great, Sam Vaughan assured him, it would be sure to be beautiful. Win was not interested. Houghton Mifflin, on the strength of the essays in *Exiles and Fabrications*, proposed that Win might want to undertake a full-scale biography; again, he rejected the proposal. He would write no long prose. It was his poetry that mattered, and he accepted only those chores that might quicken his dormant creative drive. In 1964 he edited and wrote an Afterword to a collection of Emily Dickinson's poems; in 1965 he put together a book of Oliver La Farge's newspaper columns; he hired a young man to sort and file his literary correspondence and send it to the

[1] WTS, "Black Bean Soup with Hotdogs and Hard-Boiled Eggs," *New and Selected Poems* (1967), pp. 135–136.

John Hay Library at Brown; in 1966 he selected and introduced a volume of Robert Herrick's poems and wrote an introduction to a collection of Jack Schaefer's short stories of the West.[2] Interspersed with the 1964 cruise to Europe, a spring 1965 visit to the Metcalfs' house in Hobe Sound, Florida (covered with midge bites, Win vowed never to return), and a June 1966 journey to South County, Rhode Island, for the marriage of favorite niece Wendy Wilder to Jon Larsen, son of Time, Inc.'s Roy Larsen, these were minor projects. But Win also took a major step to revive his poetry.

In the fall of 1965 (and again in 1966), he traveled back to the MacDowell Colony at Peterborough, New Hampshire, "(1) to have a non-domestic life & try to write for a while and (2) to have . . . a New England autumn."[3] As he wrote Jeff Werner in August 1965, his poetry had "diminished to such a tiny trickle these past two years" that he was scared; so, with El's enthusiastic endorsement, he spent the months of September and October in Peterborough.[4] It was entirely appropriate that Win should have chosen the MacDowell Colony (with the support of letters of reference from Horace Gregory, Malcolm Cowley, and George P. Elliott) as the site of his first extended stay in an artists' colony. It was a place he cared about.

Established as a memorial to the composer Edward MacDowell by his widow, the Colony had been the summer home and workshop for many years of that idol of Scott's youth, Edwin Arlington Robinson. Peterborough, Win thought, was one of the prettiest towns in New England. "Dominated by the great Monadnock, its hilly streets climb and wind with neat white houses clinging all the way. Two rivers flood into the town in fall after fall, the pleasant rush of their brown waters a bright sound in the morning and a murmurous constant throughout the night."[5] At the colony itself, two dozen studios were scattered over some five hundred acres of

---

[2] *Judge Tenderly of Me: The Poems of Emily Dickinson* (Kansas City, 1968); Oliver LaFarge, *The Man with the Calabash Pipe* (Boston, 1966); *Poems of Robert Herrick* (New York, 1967); and *Collected Stories of Jack Schaefer* (Boston, 1966).

[3] WTS to Douglas W. Scott, 26 April 1965, Scott Collection, John Hay Library, Brown University.

[4] WTS to H. O. Werner, 9 August 1965, Scott Collection, John Hay Library.

[5] WTS, "Bookman's Galley," *Providence Sunday Journal*, 5 August 1945, sec. 6, p. 6.

woodland. At breakfast and again at dinner, the colonists assembled to dine and converse. The rest of the day was spent on their
own, in the studio, with lunch and mail brought to the door and
no unwished-for interruptions allowed. There, in a setting where,
for fifty-five years, much in American painting, writing, and music
had been accomplished, Win returned for renewal to his native
landscape. ("I know these trees, these plants, and the way the
weather acts and when fall comes on and the first frost appears
. . . and it all goes so deeply back into my life—how can I help it?")[6]

Byron Vazakas, a poet Win had not seen for two decades, rode up
on the same bus from Boston. Though he did not immediately
recognize Win in the bus terminal, Vazakas was struck by his appearance: "a slightly portly gentleman in quiet business suit sitting
on a bench, puffing on a pipe, and reading . . . Giovanni's Room,
by James Baldwin." The man reminded Vazakas of Mr. Chips. "I
was sure he wasn't a business man, very likely a professor. He
didn't fit in the bus terminal." On the bus, the reading and pipe-
smoking continued, until the bus was filled with clouds of smoke.
At Peterborough, in the evening drizzle, the two renewed their
acquaintance; on the way to the Colony, Win remarked lugubrious-
ly, "What am I doing here?"[7]

Any departure from home of more than a few days disturbed
Win. But he knew why he was there, all the same, and the two
months began auspiciously. Just after lunch of his first day in the
Sprague Smith studio (previous occupants who had signed their
names on slabs of wood included Esther Bates, Elinor Wylie, Sara
Teasdale, Thornton Wilder, Virgil Thomson, Lukas Foss, and
Aaron Copland), he "was surprised by writing a little." "I begin
to think this place will work."[8] By the end of October, according
to the journal which he kept at Peterborough, he had written
twenty-two new poems. (He might have completed more, but quit
at twenty-two, his magic number).

Life at the Colony settled into a routine. Win had breakfast at
seven-thirty, and was in his studio by nine or earlier. He ate lunch
outside in the sun just after noon. There would be a late-afternoon

6 Quoted in Donald Dean Eulert, "Winfield Townley Scott: Conversations on
Poets and the Art of Poetry" (Ph.D. dissertation, University of New Mexico,
January 1969), p. 130.
7 Byron Vazakas to SD, 14 April 1970.
8 WTS, Peterborough Journal 1, 2 September 1965 and 5 September 1965.

walk, followed by a few drinks, dinner, the New York papers in
the lounge, a highball while reading in bed. At Peterborough, as at
home, he assumed the role of kindly paterfamilias. Ignoring the un-
written rule that the artists should circulate, Win always sat in
the same place in the dining-room, his back to a window. "I don't
recall anyone else presuming to sit there," Vazakas, a regular at
the table, along with Janet Gemmell and Lael Tucker Wertenbaker,
reports. Scott's manner bore a certain courtliness; "his existence at
the Colony was like his personality, courteous, quiet, sedentary, and
gently sardonic."[9]
    At Peterborough Win exerted his customary charm; he was al-
most universally liked and admired by his fellow colonists. As always he listened with his entire attention and a predisposition in
favor of the speaker. "It was a pleasure to be around him, because
he had that ability to make *you* feel brighter and more aware rather
than impressing you with his intelligence and awareness," Lael
Wertenbaker remembers. Aspasia Voulis, closely drawn to him,
thought Win "a very kind, gentle, sensitive person . . . not hardened
or embittered . . . in any way." Harvena Richter, who met him
during the 1966 visit to Peterborough, placed him among the "very
limited number of people . . . in my life who are members of a certain radiant and angelic order." Hortense Calisher sensed all this
about Win, and more:

He charmed one with his understanding, delicacy and modesty. Unusual among literary artists, his ego was not most in evidence. I wrote
once "Authors should not be met." By which I mean that the man or
woman you meet on the surface may have little to do with the literature. At a place like MacDowell . . . Win was a companion on a different plane, enjoyable, interested, and interesting. His courtesy went
deep. And was always soothing—one meets that kind so seldom. But it
occurred to me there, and later in Santa Fe, that he was a margin too
deferential, too humble about himself. . . . I put it down to what I think
of as "the California syndrome"—in artists who are out of the New York
current. . . . I have also met it in artists of independent income, a
certain guilt for not having to hustle, or to suffer the privations others
may. . . . I've also met it in people who drink a lot—their humiliations
come nearer to the surface. Though I've no idea whether he did or not.[10]

[9] Byron Vazakas to SD, 14 April 1970.
[10] Lael Wertenbaker to SD, 9 July 1969; Aspasia Voulis to SD, 13 July 1969;

He was thought of as the "nicest man" at the Colony: Vazakas
laughed at Win's confession that he was "*mean*," he did not know
what Win was talking about.[11]
   In the journal Win kept, Vazakas might have found out. The two
months at Peterborough were marred by the word, received Sept.
6, 1965, that Macmillan would remainder his *Collected Poems* at
the end of the year—less than three years after publication! In
anguish, Win considered buying the plates. "It's my whole work,"
he told Tom Mayer. "Everything. If it was just a book, but it's not.
They'll melt the damn things down and there won't even be a
trace."[12] Bitterness over Macmillan's premature decision pervaded
his journal, where he damned some of the other colonists in language he would never have permitted himself in public. "I guess
the MacDowell Colony is to artists what a Bird Sanctuary is to
birds," he wrote, and among the exotic birds were those of unattrac-
tive coloration. "Note the nakedness of ego in many young col-
leagues. The eagerness to let you know how unique they are. Their
inability to say anything about anything without reference to themselves." Nor did the erratic behavior of his contemporaries escape
notice: "——— hid in the woods, late PM, and moaned and howled
as I walked by on the road. I didn't know who—or what—it was
and paid no attention. So he emerged. I told him I'd heard there was
a town idiot who roams these woods." Or: "———. I'm fed up with
his snooping. My new bottle of sleeping pills which I have not
touched is less than half full. . . . I suppose he's sick and I'm sure
he's broke and is therefore desperate, and no doubt I should be sorry
for him; yet there's no reason for his secret intrusions and his thiev-
ing. . . . This morning I marked the liquor bottle; it's that sort of
degradation I resent." Of the homosexuals in residence: "All the
amused asides. They can be so depressing when they gang up and
regard everything as laughable and all outsiders as inferiors."[13]
   Despite these annoyances, Win's work went well. In accordance
with his usual practice, he "fooled with notes all day and actually

Harvena Richter to SD, 11 February 1970, and Hortense Calisher to SD, 21
January 1970.
   [11] Byron Vazakas to SD, 14 April 1970.
   [12] Tom W. Mayer to SD, 19 December 1969.
   [13] WTS, Peterborough Journal 1, 5 September 1965, 14 September 1965, 18
September 1965, 2 October 1965, and 5 October 1965.

wrote nothing [on 3 September, the second day at Peterborough], yet it was a good day in that I *liked* the concentration—in the utter and uninterrupted stillness—and, aside from an afternoon nap, spent all my time contentedly irresponsible to everything else except the work."[14] An inveterate note-maker, Scott recorded his notes on one side of blue-lined ledger books, with poems (when they came) on the other. Then, as rapidly as possible, the poem was transformed into typescript, since no one could read Win's handwriting. Even he could see the poem better typewritten, as it might stand on the page, and would make revisions—anywhere from one to ten per poem—on the typescript. Then, almost always, the poem was frozen, done, "and neither next week or five years from now can I do any more, it's stuck."[15]

Win's notes came from books, from the dictionary ("sometimes an entire poem emerges from discovery of what one word really means"), but ideally from experience: "I am very fond of a remark that Goethe made, 'Let poems arise out of the events in your life.' I don't suppose that boxes the whole compass, but it is pretty much the way I operate. People I have known, places I have been, things I have read, emotions I have felt, despair, ecstasy, passing through me into what I hope is an objective statement that would have meaning to somebody else." As often as not it was a setting that called up the phrase or line which established the tone for a poem. "I want to start with a room—a house—a street corner—a town— a city—and see if I can be taken from there."[16]

Without such a phrase, ideas for poems would not move, but remained dormant on the ledger page. "Sometimes the phrase comes first—that is easiest, then. When the 'idea' comes first—and this is the more frequent experience as I get older—one often waits a long time for the language; and sometimes in vain." At first, "almost always a poem came like an orgasm, slam," but after his late youth, such orgasms almost never happened. Instead, poems came from the mating of two or more notes. "I have an intimation of an idea,

---

[14] Ibid., 3 September 1965.
[15] Sam Larcombe, "An Interview with Winfield Townley Scott," *Seven* 1 (March 1967): p. 6. This interview, published in the St. John's (Santa Fe) College literary journal, is an excellent one.
[16] WTS, *"a dirty hand": The Literary Notebooks of Winfield Townley Scott* (1969), pp. 145, 150; quoted in Eulert, "Scott," p. 113.

or I have a phrase, and I write it down, but nothing happens; and then a week later, or six months later, or six years later, two of these things copulate, and a poem happens."[17] At Peterborough he not only took notes but pored over and over the notebooks he had brought with him, waiting for two or more notes to mate. The imagery of mating, like that of copulating and the spontaneous orgasms, is Scott's; sex and art were inextricably linked in his mind.

One of the poems Win wrote at the MacDowell Colony, "Variations on a Line by Carlo Bettochi," nicely illustrates his process of composition. Here is the poem:

> "Shy as the grave of a child." —And I remembered—
> Beneath leather leaves the acorn-strewn ground
> Root-scrawled and starved among the granite names—
> Nameless in a corner the new-turned little patch.
>
> And I remembered how as early snow
> Began to hiss through the oaks the young mother
> Wove a little blanket of evergreens
> And hurried to the place and covered it.
>
> And I remembered too the living child
> Who in a first half-comprehension stared
> Wildly within the thickening snow and asked
> "Who would hold me there if I should cry?"[18]

At Peterborough Win had been reading a book of translations of the Italian poet Carlo Bettochi. The phrase, "shy as the grave of a child," sent his memory back to the death of Scott Merchant, infant son of Frank and Christine Merchant, ten years before (Christine is the young mother of the second quatrain), and still farther to the third stanza and a remark that Lindsay, four years old, had made two decades before.[19] The three experiences, separated by twenty years, joined together to make "Variations." How long he waited for their union!

By mid-October Win was ready to leave the Colony. "I had a shaky, palm-sweating time of it," he recorded in his journal for 14 October. "During last night I kept thinking of death." His digestion

---

[17] Larcombe, "Interview," p. 8; WTS, "*a dirty hand*," p. 11.
[18] WTS, "Variations on a Line by Carlo Bettochi," *New and Selected Poems*, p. 125.
[19] See Eulert, "Scott," p. 118.

went sour (on 21 October, "That stabbing in my belly is not really painful but the psychological depression because of it is very bad. What is wrong? I wish I were home"), and nervous legs kept him from sleeping, even with the aid of pills. He was afflicted as well with what he called LSD (leave-soon-distraction), which hindered concentration, and by the sense that New England pulled at him too strongly ("at the end of eight weeks I felt that I had to get out of there").[20] Yet it had been a productive time, and Win turned down the invitation of John Ciardi to spend two weeks on the Bread Loaf staff the following summer: "My feeling is that whatever weeks I take off from home next summer I should best spend by returning to the MacDowell Colony."[21]

En route home to Santa Fe, Win stopped in New York for a 31 October reading at the YMHA poetry center, under the direction of Galen Williams (Mrs. William Cole). For the occasion, he read "A Picture-Book for Zorina" in honor of the magnificent dancer Vera Zorina, whom Win had met—and fallen half in love with—in Santa Fe; sadly, she was ill and unable to come. But the Coles were there, and Paul Horgan, and James Purdy, and George Elliott, and Anne Hutchens, and the reading was a tremendous success. Looking old and tired, Win nonetheless commanded his audience; he poured out emotions which had been bottled up during two months at the MacDowell. Particularly effective was "Another Return," the "golden girl" poem Win himself best liked:

Why, when we were dressed for darker weather,
Did you walk in that slim green gown
That bared your shoulders and almost your breasts
And the young hair that way down to your shoulders?
As though you were quoting light.

Lie down. Lie down again beside me.
Was your reluctance for the others there?
Or, because you had not changed as I
You had forgotten me and all those times?
Lie down again beside me.[22]

[20] WTS, Peterborough Journal 1, 14 October 1965, 21 October 1965, and 28 October 1965. Eulert, "Scott," p. 130.
[21] John Ciardi to WTS, 21 September 1965, Scott Collection, John Hay Library; WTS to John Ciardi, 27 November 1965.
[22] WTS, "Another Return," *New and Selected Poems*, p. 103.

He spoke the words, "lie down again beside me," with an emotional vigor belied by his appearance. That evening, Cole recalls, Win delivered one of the two best readings he had ever heard; he had heard hundreds.[23]

The reading represented a kind of catharsis, but it could not purge the inner torments that haunted Win. On 22 November (the date was carefully noted as the penultimate entry in the journal begun at Peterborough), he began once-a-week psychiatric sessions in Albuquerque with Dr. George Lyon Ross.[24] El had to drive him; he was otherwise overcome by fear of the long roller-coaster hill which lay midway between Santa Fe and Albuquerque. He went to Dr. Ross, he wrote Merchant, "on the theory (much too belatedly arrived at) that there may be something better than pills to quiet my anxiety-ridden tensions." He went also to relieve what Rudolph Kieve called "one of the most disfiguring states of inferiority I have ever known in a well-established poet." But most of all, as he admitted to Lindsay, he went because of his impotence.[25]

The theme of impotence ran persistently through the series of dreams that he recorded, first in letters and journals and then in jottings for Ross. "A Ledger of Sleep" re-created one of his most characteristic dreams:

> Midnight. Rain blowing through the empty street.
> He is asleep. He dreams this over and over.
> He is there, waiting in the drenched lamplighted street.
>
> He runs with melting knees toward a train
> He can never catch. Never in time. Over.
> He trembles at the clock lighted high. Too late.[26]

This dream, like many others, suggested fear of impotence (melting knees) followed by despair and depression (he is never able to catch the train, characteristically an image of masculinity). Such an interpretation would be arbitrary, of course, without the support-

---

[23] Interview, William Cole, New York, 10 October 1969. The other superb reader was the Englishman George Macbeth. A taped transcription of the Winfield Townley Scott reading is available as *The Poetry of Winfield Townley Scott*, McGraw-Hill Sound Seminar No. 75996.

[24] WTS, Peterborough Journal 1, 26 November 1965.

[25] WTS to Frank Merchant, 11 May 1966; Rudolph Kieve to SD, 1 March 1970; interview, Lindsay Scott, Washington, D.C., 26 September 1969.

[26] WTS, "A Ledger of Sleep," *Change of Weather* (1964), p. 27.

ing evidence of other dreams in which, implicitly or explicitly, Win explored the same subject—and without the evidence of his life. Another recurring motif, for example, involved the threatening force of a stream of water. "I dreamed repeatedly during the night of water suddenly overflowing a second-story floor of a house—a grandfather-of-mine's house, I think. And me rushing to turn off the faucet. The last time I dreamed it the water was deepest & the faucet merely came off the wall into my hand: there was no pipe connection. What did all that mean?" It meant, probably, that he was afraid of his powerful, unconscious emotions, and sought to repress them by turning off the faucet. But the faucet-image was significantly phallic; there was no pipe connection, no true masculinity behind the merely ornamental faucet/penis.[27] The last poem Win Scott wrote in his life, on 5 April 1968, revealed his insecurity about the size of his penis:

> The man who thought his head was too small—
> He really thought his head was too small.
> Analysts tried hats on him—ordinary size—
> Which fitted perfectly. He was unconvinced.
>
> Young and handsome he wished not to be seen,
> Not to be touched if seen. He felt his hair
> Did not sufficiently disguise his shame,
> His head hung miniature among fortunate men.
>
> Unequipped midget he must remain secret—
> He thought he could handle only imagined love.
> Till a wise and beautiful woman—far from clinics—
> Embraced his head and showed him her delight.[28]

His 1966 journal demonstrated the persistence of yet another phallic symbol: the elevator/erection: "Read over the record of dreams I've kept for Ross: my god, the frequency of elevators!"[29]

Far more openly, another group of Win's dreams dealt with his sense of having failed Eleanor sexually. "I had waked up from a

---

[27] WTS to EMS, 3 July 1958. For assistance in interpretation of these dreams, I am indebted to Glenn Shean, professor of psychology and former director of the psychological counseling bureau at the College of William and Mary.

[28] WTS, "Not to Rely Altogether on the Medical Profession or Yourself," *Poetry Northwest*, 10 (Spring 1969): 54–55. The poem in manuscript is dated 5 April 1968.

[29] WTS, Peterborough Journal 2, 5 October 1966.

dream of starting between El's breasts, then sliding down and going into her, but after a few jouncing thrusts she said I was shriveling and promptly I shriveled. Very vivid." "Dreamed of love-making with El and that just before I was going to enter her, my erection dropped, and I was sad and bitter and wondered if I shouldn't find a man for her." "Fell asleep and dreamed I walked in on a power-ful-looking young man—full throat, neck—violently embracing and kissing El and she responding." Win conjured up imaginary lovers for his wife, possibly to expiate his guilt at not satisfying her, possibly as projections of homosexual desire. At the same time he was tortured with jealousy at the prospect, especially when the lovers, who remained imaginary in fact, became paranoiacally real to Win, in daylight thoughts as well as dreams.[30]

Was he no longer capable of heterosexual love? Dr. Ross assured him it was not too late, but Win—and Ellie—had doubts. On 7 September 1966, back at Peterborough, Win confided to his journal: "Couple of weeks ago El said 'Maybe you ought to turn homosexual' —not in a joking voice. I said 'I don't think I'd really like it.' I recalled this because last night I dreamed we were naked in bed together and she had a male erection and we mutually masturbated. I have had such dreams before. A return to my adolescent sex life? Yes, but with the weird ambiguity of marital fidelity: putting a cock on El. The dream disturbs me."[31] Perhaps Win's obsessive cleanliness had its origin in a persistent desire to eradicate the traces of guilt over youthful masturbation. "He washed his hands frequently throughout the day," Eleanor writes, "bathed daily, often twice a day, and was a real nut on the subject of deodorants. He was given to nervous sweating and often changed his shirt two or three times a day." He dressed casually but with great care. There is a picture showing Win on an Easter Sunday in Santa Fe, in western bluejeans topped by a tweed coat and tie. Often he would ask, "How do I look? How do I look?"[32]

Win's reaction to psychoanalysis was at first enthusiastic. He saw finally and conclusively that his "whole goddam life [had] been damaged by fear" and that he "must try everywhere, every

[30] WTS, Peterborough Journal 1, 19 October 1965; Peterborough Journal 2, 27 September 1966 and 1 October 1966.
[31] WTS, Peterborough Journal 2, 7 September 1966.
[32] EMS to SD, 30 September 1969.

way, to rid" himself of it. For a while, he seemed to be succeeding, casting off fears as successfully as he had been divested of his appendix (the source of digestive troubles) early in 1966. He began to drive the car himself to the sessions in Albuquerque. "What will ensue," he inquired of Jeff Werner, "if Dr Ross makes me *more* perfect than I am?" He dedicated his *New and Selected Poems* (which George Elliott was compiling for Doubleday) to Dr. H. Richard Landmann, who had referred him to Ross, and to Dr. George Lyon Ross, "two men who have done a great deal for me."[33]

But as the related problems of impotence and alcoholism refused to evaporate, Scott began to have second thoughts. He wondered whether psychiatry might not "remove the irritant which in the creative person begets the pearl in the oyster, but surrounds it with a protective coloring." If a man were perfectly happy, he reflected, he might "lack all impulse to paint a picture or compose a piece of music." So he held back, kept under control. Those closest to Win doubted that he ever really got into analysis. He treated Dr. Ross as he would have treated a visiting artist of considerable reputation: he wanted to please him, not open up to him. The irritants did not disappear, but neither did the long periods when no poems came. Analysis did not open the magic door to self-understanding, Win's "sewer cover"; perhaps he did not honestly want to climb down into the sewer. Win blamed Ross: "What the hell does he know?" He skipped appointments, including two of the three in April 1968, the month he died.[34]

The summer of 1966 was a rocky one for the Scotts. Susan, working nights backstage at the Santa Fe Opera, came home at all hours. Win sat up waiting, drinking, and agonizing: who was sleeping with his daughter? El drew most of the fire of the often-repeated indictment: it was her god-damned opera, her god-damned escape, anything about the opera was all right even though his daughter might be getting raped. A few days before going back to Peterborough (in 1966, Win spent six weeks, 1 September to 14 October,

[33] WTS, Peterborough Journal 2, 7 September 1966; WTS to H. O. Werner, 25 February 1966, Scott Collection, John Hay Library; WTS to George P. Elliott, 10 October 1966, the George P. Elliott Collection, Washington University Libraries, St. Louis.

[34] Interview, EMS, Santa Fe, 8 September 1969; interview, Robert Saam and Robert Kurth, Santa Fe, 7 September 1969; Eulert, "Scott," pp. 179–180; WTS, Peterborough Journal 2, 26 September 1966.

there), the long quarrel reached a climax with Win, drunk, suggested a divorce. You have perfectly good grounds, he told her: he'd consulted the legal statutes. He didn't know how she could stand to live with him. He'd go off to the MacDowell and she'd be resentful about having to pay his way. Win needed to be told that he was loved, no matter what. But El, deeply hurt, withdrew into a dark mood and reacted with "icy indifference." Encountering them on the way to the train, Stan Noyes was struck by the way Win "huddled in his seat like a frightened child. He was leaving the pleasant routine of his regular life, the security of his family life" and momentarily he resembled nothing so much as "a small boy at a stranger's birthday party . . . standing alone and not feeling part of the gang." Everyone, it seemed to Win, was "relieved to have me go away."[35]

The principal trouble was sex. It was "ridiculous and perhaps contemptible that a man my age should be so sex-obsessed," Win wrote in the journal he began keeping once more at Peterborough, but he could not help himself. For at the Colony, he dreamed regularly of sexual success—and failure, and began to have erections. "Confused and stupid though I am, I know of course what is going on: at home, faced with the availability of sex, my built-up fears inhibit me—off here alone I can indulge in fantasy." It was both perverse and humiliating, and he was ready to wish desire away entirely:

> Dawn rising. A last star trembles
> Slowly up the sky. The sky whitens.
> I limp with age by the window and watch
> The terrifying tenderness of the star.
>
> Flowers at the bedside begin to color
> Close to her face. She lies unwakened
> In this hour we used to know together often.
> If only desire would die out of the mind.[36]

Jealousy possessed him. On a joint visit to Dr. Ross shortly before Win traveled east, El had said, "in the situation, only lust is pos-

[35] Interview, EMS, Santa Fe, 8 September 1969; Stanley Noyes to SD, 7 May 1970; WTS, Peterborough Journal 2, 31 August 1966 and 3 September 1966.
[36] WTS, Peterborough Journal 2, 8 September 1966 and 15 September 1966; WTS, "Tender Star," *New and Selected Poems*, p. 137.

sible." If that were literally true, he thought, how could it matter
who the man was? In his journal, he

wondered what a woman feels like—how she feels, I mean—when after
many years of faithful marriage she goes to bed with another man? It
must be a tremendous decision (no matter what the circumstances of
the marriage?). Once it's made, if happiness follows, she probably feels
a wonderful renewal, but the period of succumbing to the decision must
be rending. Or am I forgetting the powerful propulsion of desire?

He began work on a long triangle poem—old husband, younger
wife, still younger man—called "The Woman Who Wanted Two
of Everything," in which he puzzled over the secrets of women:

> I don't imagine I understand women.
> The woman you know best in all your life
> Still can give you cause at times to wonder
> What it may be that she has never told you.[37]

Eleanor gave him some cause enough to wonder in her letters.
She reported the appearance at 2 A.M. of a young poet-motorcyclist
who "knew Win was away and thought she might be lonesome"
and the appearance at dinner parties of "the inevitable Sam Marsh
—honest I can't help it if he shows up only when you don't." She
reported each such incident, El has written, because Win would
become suspicious if he heard of them from another source.
Throughout, she reacted to his jealousy like a "dumb Desdemona.
Having no interest in other men, no desire for an affair . . . repeatedly I lacked awareness of when I was saying or doing something that would excite Win's jealousy and so was utterly unprepared for his attacks when they came." Whatever the intention,
such messages had their effect on Win: "Do you *try* to torture me
or are you just lucky? I think you have no idea—and who could
blame you, considering the mess I've been and the messes I've made
in recent years?—how much I love you." It wasn't so much that he
didn't trust her, Win wrote. "It isn't that simple. [The jealous fury]
comes rather from my own guilty sense of failure to one who is
after all a fiery woman—a sickening 'Who could blame her?' mood
that tears me to pieces."[38]

[37] WTS, Peterborough Journal 2, 23 September 1966; WTS to EMS, 23 September 1966.
[38] EMS to WTS, 2 September 1966 and 7 September 1966; EMS to SD, 7
September 1970; WTS to EMS, 9 September 1966 and 10 September 1966.

After two weeks of such letters, Ellie suggested they call a halt: "Let's simply chalk up one temporary aberration to you and give me a raincheck on a temper tantrum someday. It is funny how husbands select ancient gentlemen and homosexuals for lovers for their wives. Downright disrespectful." Her good-natured letter brought Peterborough back, Win wrote, "to 700 feet above sea level instead of 700 feet below. . . . I'll be all right now. Really—even if you report dinner with Charlie Chaplin."[39] At least he was all right enough, for the moment, to turn out poems. His numerological obsession gaining strength, he tried for no more after hitting twenty-two new poems on 7 October. And on 22 September, El's birthday, he wrote "North Easter," a poem which asserted the primacy of art in old age. A year before on the same date he had got "Variations on a Line by Carlo Bettochi." "This *particular* 22d seems a good day for me," he wrote. "Starting in 1921."[40]

Ellie joined him for a week in New York, and together they returned to Santa Fe. Win Scott came east but one more time, on the death of his father's second wife, Bernice. He wanted to ask his father to come live with them in Santa Fe, instead of going to a rest home; El argued that he would be uncomfortable and out of place away from Haverhill and his friends. Probably she was right. Certainly she won the argument.

For an artist less despondent about himself and his art, the year that followed Scott's second visit to Peterborough might have seemed unusually rewarding. To begin with, he discovered, in the mail for 22 October 1966 (and of course he made special note of the date), that *Poetry* had given him the Harriet Monroe Memorial Award for that year. Early in 1967 the family vacationed in Acapulco, and in May Win gave readings at the University of New Mexico in Albuquerque and at New Mexico State University in Las Cruces, where he met and immediately took to the young poet-in-residence Keith Wilson. At St. John's College, the Santa Fe branch of the Annapolis "Great Books" institution, he enjoyed two triumphs. One was the second theatrical performance of his life (the first had come when he read the part of the narrator in the Santa Fe Opera production of Stravinsky's *Oedipus Rex*, with Stravinsky

---

[39] EMS to WTS, 17 September 1966; WTS to EMS, 19 September 1966.
[40] WTS, Peterborough Journal 2, 22 September 1966 and 7 October 1966.

himself in the audience) as "Doc" in William Carlos Williams's
Many Loves. "The kids at St. John's—plying me with my own
liquor—seduced me into" taking the role, he maintained, but actually he liked being seduced: he was able to "play" Bill Williams, a
man he had known and loved, and the college students radiated an
infectious excitement. They also offered to share their marijuana
(Win refused).[41] He was a smash in the play, performed in June,
but drew a still greater ovation from St. John's students—and a good
many townspeople as well—when he read his poetry to a standing-
room crowd at St. John's in December. The applause, it seemed,
would never have stopped without his insistence; it was "like an
orgasm," he told Stan Noyes, and for a day or two he fairly glowed
with well-being. Then he sank once more into doubt and depression:
how could his poems have any real depth, if an audience could respond so warmly to but a single reading?[42] Early in December, too,
he got word from David Wagoner that he had been chosen to share
the Helen Bullis Memorial Prize of *Poetry Northwest* for 1967.[43]

The year also saw the publication of Scott's *New and Selected
Poems*, edited and introduced by George Elliott. This book, much
shorter than the *Collected Poems*, nonetheless brought back into
print what Elliott regarded as Win's best work, and it contained as
well thirty-five of the poems he had written at the MacDowell
Colony. Sam Vaughan, under the disguise of Doubleday's "L. L.
Day, Editor-at-Large," composed an ad for the book that would
have pleased any writer. The advertisement pointed out that Scott
was "overdue for the Pulitzer Prize in poetry and/or the National
Book Award" and that if justice prevailed eventually, Winfield
Townley Scott would, too. "I came into the office late one morning,"
Vaughan wrote, "determined to work through the lunch hour in
penance, and I had in my left hand a bagful of hot pastrami sandwiches and in my right a sheaf of Scott's new poems and life seemed
too good to be believed."[44] Hayden Carruth, reviewing the book for

[41] WTS to Elizabeth Werner, 13 May 1967; WTS to Charles H. Philbrick,
19 June 1967, Scott Collection, John Hay Library; interview, Robert Saam and
Robert Kurth, Santa Fe, 7 September 1969.
[42] WTS to Elizabeth Werner, 9 December 1967, Scott Collection, John Hay
Library; Stanley Noyes to SD, 7 May 1970; Eulert, "Scott," pp. 34–35.
[43] David Wagoner to WTS, 2 December 1967.
[44] "L. L. Day, Editor-at-Large," advertisement, *Saturday Review*, 2 December
1967, p. 2.

Poetry, remarked upon Win's "splendid talent for story poems and biographical poems, to my mind a talent the equal of Frost's and probably greater," but lamented that he had used the talent so sparingly, as in *The Dark Sister* and such poems as "Mr. Whittier" and "Four Old Boys." Why were there so few poems of this sort? "And why so many smilingly bitter lyrics about growing old, etc., that might just as reasonably have been written by somebody else?" Scott might have been "intimidated by the presence of Frost, always there on his doorstep, so to speak," Carruth suggested.[45]

But the smilingly bitter tone had more private sources. As early as "Traman Walks to Work," in *Wind the Clock*, Win had foreshadowed his later preoccupation with the theme of thwarted success:

> He confronts
> His possible failure, hates his hopes,
> Cartwheels into town: over and over,
> Triumph disaster triumph disaster.[46]

As he grew older, seeking the ultimate recognition that did not come and doubting his own powers, the theme of failure became obsessive. So, despite whatever good omens crossed the skies, for Win 1967 was a year of drought. Fallow, he wrote only half-a-dozen poems all year. The weather and the world reinforced his moods of despondency. Spring came late, cities burned at home, and villages burned overseas.

> The year the lilacs didn't bloom
> Frigid winds slung dirt in the air.
> Our nerves itched against the clay-colored sky.
> The weather went on being wrong.
>
> Those who'd lived half a century or more
> Worried, baffled by loss of lilacs. "There were always
> Lilacs," we said: for cemeteries, for dooryards.
> The weather went on being wrong.

---

[45] Hayden Carruth, "Critic of the Month: I," *Poetry*, 112 (September 1968): 425.

[46] WTS, "Traman Walks to Work," *Wind the Clock* (1941) and *New and Selected Poems*, p. 10.

We were too old to believe this was judgment;
Judgment, such as it is, belonged to us,
But to those of us really alive such blight was portent.
The weather went on being wrong.

There followed the idiot killings in our streets;
Arsonists crouched in the night; words helplessly looted;
We exported human violence into jungles.
The weather went on being wrong.[47]

Cemeteries, dooryards, killings, a coming apocalypse: Win could think of little but death. Suicide fascinated and repelled him: Weldon Kees off the Golden Gate bridge in 1955, Charles Fenton out a hotel window in 1960, Ellie's sister Kay's husband by gunshot in 1965, and in 1966 Teddy Landmann (the wife of Dick Landmann) and Conrad Knickerbocker with guns. "No steel," Web Schott wrote Win about Knickerbocker. "All spirit and feeling."[48] Had Win steel enough? He did not want to die like Wade Vliet, of "that goddam degenerative disease of nerves and muscles called amyotrophic lateral sclerosis. For which the medical profession can do absolutely nothing." At the urging of Vic Ullman, Win flew to Oklahoma City in February 1965 to be with Vliet, a bitter total invalid, while he eagerly awaited death.[49] Then, in March 1967, Jeff Werner died after a long illness, in the last months "very seldom responsive and wasted down to about 90 pounds. So of course the thing to say is Thank god, it's over. And it's true too. Still—you know—when one of these friendships that date from your teens is over there is an unfilled gap." He and Jeff had lived far apart throughout their adult lives, but still, as Win wrote Elizabeth Werner, their friendship had survived "all these years and all these other people and places" and Win had been warmed simply by knowing that Jeff was *there* and that he cared.[50] Now that warmth was gone; something irreplaceable died with Jeff.

47 WTS, "The Year the Lilacs Didn't Bloom," *El Palacio* (Spring 1969): 25–28. The poem in manuscript is dated 24 September 1967.
48 Webster Schott to WTS, 7 April 1966, Scott Collection, John Hay Library.
49 R. Wade Vliet to WTS, 13 October 1964, Scott Collection, John Hay Library; WTS to Frank Merchant, 17 February 1965.
50 WTS to Elizabeth Werner, 10 April 1967, Scott Collection, John Hay Library; WTS to Frank Merchant, 10 April 1967.

On 9 December 1967, Win measured the depth of his despair in "The Story," a poem which movingly treats of impotence and what it can do to a man—and to his wife:

> Snow fell slowly. The man and woman stood
> Like figures crowded by snow in one of those
> Glass paperweights rounded for earth and sky,
> Stood remote and sealed within a world;
> So locked in a lifetime as to be close, untouching;
> Uncertain what had impelled them out to storm.
> "Look," he said, "what I have left to give you:
> This brittle brush of chamisa sapped with cold,
> These dry husks of flowers, these urns of yucca
> Dead and the color of ashes, dead on this stalk
> As though they were moulds of flowers long forgotten
> Or, worse, remembered only as barren shapes
> Drained of their potency of flowering fragrance.
> "Look," he said, "all there is left to give you."
> Because its color—its dusted lavender color—
> Seemed to promise something would live again,
> She broke and held one wand of willow between them
> While still the snow fell slowly and her tears.
> "We are not so old?" she asked. "Is that not true?
> What reason could make you say that is not true?"[51]

Never had Win Scott so honestly and openly confronted himself in verse. "I have . . . at least begun to break through that sewer cover which so long defied me," he wrote to Sam Vaughan.[52] But he was hardly reassured by what he found underneath.

Visiting Santa Fe over the New Year's holidays, Webster Schott was alarmed by Win's apparent depression. He "talked about his psychiatrist, drank a lot, and, strangely, got angry in public at his wife. He said he had pretty well wasted a year." He spoke of his inability to write, and worried whether he should go back to Peterborough. He agonized "about Vietnam, his kids, life in general." El told Web privately that she was concerned about the possibility

---

[51] WTS, "The Story," *Hearse 10* (1969), unnumbered pages. The poem in manuscript is dated 9 December 1967.

[52] Webster Schott to Samuel S. Vaughan, 3 June 1968; WTS to Samuel S. Vaughan, 19 January 1968.

of suicide. During the last few years, Win had begun to talk increasingly of suicide: "I know how to do it," "I read in a book just how many to take," "You'll make an excellent widow—the best widow in town." On several occasions, following an outburst of anger, he had stomped off to the guest house carrying the deadly combination of a bottle of sleeping pills and a bottle of whiskey. El would wait until he slept, then check the contents of the bottles and remove them. To Schott, it looked as if Win were "systematically destroying his life with alcohol."[53] On Washington's Birthday, 22 February 1968, Win's letter about the war in Vietnam, seeing it as a national disaster which twinned his personal disintegration, ran in the *Santa Fe New Mexican*:

It is time—and more than time—that those of us who love our country should stand up and say to the President and to his fatuous secretary of state and to his inefficient general in command in Vietnam: No—you stop this. . . . Our hands are red with innocent blood, for which we can never forgive ourselves. Worse, perhaps, the rot in our minds and hearts —that we have failed so badly what we Americans [were] meant to be.[54]

As the nation had lost sight of its goals and purposes, Win began to question his own reason for existence. He lived, of course, for his poetry: "I have this life-long egocentricity, that this is important to do: at least, it is to me."[55] But almost no one else, he thought in darker moods, thought it important at all. In an alliterative poem he drew an implicit and bitter analogy to an old stone-cutter ignored and unappreciated while more facile, fashionable talents were honored:

> He works the way he chose to work.
> Out of fashion, he chisels stone
> Which hardly anybody loves
> Yet recognizes as his own.
> What has he got to show for it?
> Pairs of stink-stiffened socks.

[53] Interview, Webster Schott, Kansas City, 29 December 1969; EMS to SD, 7 September 1970.
[54] WTS, Letter to the Editor, *Santa Fe New Mexican*, 22 February 1968.
[55] Eulert, "Scott," p. 174.

Long since, the clever younger men
Have learned from him, have done so well
By molding into prettied curves
His harsh creations that theirs sell.
What has he got to show for it?
He sits in shit-stained shorts.

Occasional money, a trace of fame
He's glanced at as at crumbs of praise.
None of these seems to cling to him.
Alone he hammers out his days.
What has he got to show for it?
An armpit-rotted coat.[56]

In happier moments Win agreed with John Hall Wheelock that "the best of all happy things is to be allowed to go on, through a long lifetime, with one's work as a poet." Like Wheelock he wished, but dared hardly hope, that he might write poems, and better ones, as he grew older. But he realized, too, that "if they can't be better, it would perhaps be best not to have to go on."[57] And now Win's tendency to self-doubt was aggravated by the withering of his creative impulse and tentative signs of senility. In the last year "his forgetfulness was frightening." Ellie would tell him something about routine household matters, and a day or an hour later Win would ask, "Why didn't you tell me?" Such incidents made him terribly angry.[58] Furthermore, with his sexual powers gone, he became convinced, wrongly, that he could no longer create good poetry. The reassurance of impartial critics (Hayden Carruth, reviewing New and Selected Poems, had written: "Among the thirty-five new poems at the end of the book, all short, at least ten are—but why search for an adjective? All thirty-five make it") weighed little against his consuming doubt. It would be better for everyone, he would announce, if he were dead. El would be better off, and so would the children. So, possibly, would he, for though Win held no hope of an afterlife, dying offered a consolation: "What have I ever clung to except the conviction that life is all and that death gives life its significance?"[59]

[56] WTS, "Stone-Cutter," New and Selected Poems, p. 148.
[57] John Hall Wheelock to WTS, 10 August 1966. Scott thought Wheelock was writing better poems in his eighties than he had in his seventies.
[58] EMS to SD, 28 October 1969.
[59] Carruth, "Critic," p. 425; WTS, "a dirty hand," p. 136.

In March the Scotts—Win, Ellie, Jeannette, Dougie, and Jeannette's friend Kathy Adler—took a disastrous trip to Mexico. Win went in renewed anticipation that hotel bedrooms might solve ailments of the night, but it didn't work; there were some frighteningly unsuccessful sexual attempts. One night El awoke to see Win standing in shadow beside the open hotel window. Heart in her throat, she did not dare to say anything but watched until he returned, heavily, to his bed. As ever incompetent in arithmetic, Win could not manage the currency, and became furious with himself. On the next to last day of the trip, El took him to see the Rivera murals on the great square, the Zócalo. Crossing the long street, with four lanes of traffic circling around, he panicked, took El's arm and leaned on it hard in abject fear. On the day of departure, obsessed with time, he worried helplessly over lunch, apprehensive lest they miss their plane. Win returned from Mexico in a black mood. He and El drove at once to see the new roof on the opera house (which had burned down the previous year). Everyone was happy at their achievement in raising the new roof. "It's nice," Win said bitterly, "to spend an afternoon with people who are proud of themselves and happy in their work."[60] Three weeks later, he was dead. The lilacs had not yet bloomed.

The funeral of Winfield Townley Scott, at 1:30 P.M. on 30 April 1968, was surprisingly stereotyped, as conventional as if "a fairly prominent alderman had died." Lavish floral displays adorned the First Presbyterian Church, and the minister, Rev. Robert Boshen, hardly touched on Win's life. Instead, the poems stood for the man: Bob Kurth read three of them, "Come Green Again," "North Easter," and "I Held a Hummingbird in My Hand." His body was buried in the Memorial Gardens cemetery, out in the country, where hundreds of butterflies hovered over the grave. Then the mourners—two hundred of them, enough to fill the church and leave some standing at the rear—went home and, because they were not the one dead, once more about their business.[61]

For some, though, Win's death brought more than a pause in the day's occupation: to Richard Eberhart, about to give a reading at

---

[60] Interview, EMS, Santa Fe, 8 September 1969; interview, Jeannette Scott, Santa Fe, 5 February 1970.

[61] Interview, Ben and Betty Bagdikian, Washington, D.C., 15 March 1970; EMS to Paul and Frances Chadwick, 15 May 1968.

Syracuse; to James Purdy, who saw the news in the *New York Times* of the lady sitting next to him on a bench in Central Park; to Paul Horgan, at Wesleyan's Center for Advanced Studies, who told Eleanor: "I hate to believe it. Hate it."[62] If there were justice in the world, if people were rewarded on the basis of their sensitivity and knowledge, Tom Mayer wrote, "I think he would have lived to be a hundred and twenty."[63] These men loved Win, valued him as a man and as a poet. Speaking for them all, Webster Schott observed that Win was "considerate, delicate, modest, extremely sensitive to human need and its infinite expressions. He was willing to help, always. . . . I've wondered whether his work was as good as he was."[64]

Looking back on his collection of *15 Modern American Poets*, which includes Lowell, Roethke, Wilbur, and Jarrell, George Elliott still ranks Win Scott as high as or higher than any of the others. If Win escaped greatness, it was by the margin of his fears, his self-doubts, and his extraordinary modesty and gentleness. His poems treat of impotence, but not of its sources. They do not go into "the terrible bitterness that he showed sometimes in conversation—about reputation, about Ellie's supporting the family. If he *had* written the things he said when drunk, he could have been as good as Frost, as good as you can get. Frost was nasty, and he put all the nastiness into his poems. Win was too nice." He held something back, and carried it with him to his grave. But the final judgment lies decades off. In a poem written at Peterborough, Win Scott supplied his own unintended epitaph:

> We have spoken
> As best we can.
> Better maybe than you or we know
> So far.[65]

---

[62] Paul Horgan to EMS, 30 April 1968, Scott Collection, John Hay Library.
[63] Tom W. Mayer to SD, 19 December 1969.
[64] Webster Schott to Samuel S. Vaughan, 3 June 1968.
[65] Interview, George P. Elliott, New York, 3 September 1969; WTS, "Black Bean Soup with Hotdogs and Hard-Boiled Eggs," *New and Selected Poems*, pp. 135–136.

BIBLIOGRAPHY

Note: The following bibliography is intended as an aid to those interested in Winfield Townley Scott's work, and as a preliminary guide to the full bibliographical labor yet undone. Very few of Scott's hundreds of book reviews (for the *Providence Journal, Santa Fe New Mexican, New York Herald Tribune* and *New York Times* book sections, *Saturday Review, Poetry*, and others) are here itemized: only those which grew from a book review into a full-scale essay. An attempt has been made, however, to list all major writings, including poems and essays which have never been published in collections of Scott's work. (If those poems and essays were subsequently collected, their initial appearance in periodicals goes unremarked.) Unpublished work, including pieces written in high school and college, can be located among the Winfield Townley Scott papers in the John Hay Library, Brown University. Dates assigned to unpublished writings refer to the time of composition.

Books

1936 *Elegy for Robinson.* New York: Privately printed.
1937 *Biography for Traman.* New York: Covici Friede.
1941 *Wind the Clock.* Prairie City, Ill.: James Decker Press.
1942 *The Sword on the Table: Thomas Dorr's Rebellion.* Norfolk, Conn.: New Directions.
1945 *To Marry Strangers.* New York: Thomas Y. Crowell.
1948 *Mr. Whittier and Other Poems.* New York: Macmillan.
1958 *The Dark Sister.* New York: New York University Press.
1959 *Scrimshaw.* New York: Macmillan.
1961 *Exiles and Fabrications.* Garden City, N.Y.: Doubleday.
1962 *Collected Poems: 1937–1962.* New York: Macmillan.
1964 *Change of Weather.* Garden City, N.Y.: Doubleday.

1967 *New and Selected Poems.* Edited by George P. Elliott. Garden City, N.Y.: Doubleday.
1969 *"a dirty hand": The Literary Notebooks of Winfield Townley Scott.* Austin: University of Texas Press.
1971 *Alpha Omega.* Garden City, N.Y.: Doubleday.

POEMS ANTHOLOGIZED

(Although one or two of Scott's poems appear in many anthologies, substantial selections from his work are included only in the two anthologies noted below.)
1950 Selection of Poems, in *Mid-Century American Poets.* Edited by John Ciardi, pp. 110–118. New York: Twayne.
1956 Selection of Poems, in *15 Modern American Poets.* Edited by George P. Elliott, pp. 224–244. New York: Holt, Rinehart and Winston. Paperback.

RECORDINGS

1944 *Winfield Townley Scott Reading His Poems.* Harvard Vocarium Records, P-1090, H.F.S. 1806. Cambridge, Mass.
1944 *Winfield Townley Scott Reading His Poems.* Harvard Vocarium Records, P-1091, H.F.S. 1864. Cambridge, Mass.
1961 *Winfield Townley Scott Reads His Works.* Yale Series of Recorded Poets, Carillon YP321. New York.
1970 *The Poetry of Winfield Townley Scott.* McGraw-Hill Sound Seminar 75996. Taped transcription of reading at the YMHA Poetry Center, New York, 31 October 1965. New York.

JOURNALS

1944 Journal, 11 January–2 June. 434 pp.
1954 "The Country of a Cloud." In Journal, 1 January–22 February. 61 pp.
1965 Journal, 1 September–29 November. 50 pp.
1966 Journal, 31 August–13 October. 62 pp.

HIGH SCHOOL WRITINGS

1925–1926 Miscellaneous poems. Haverhill High *Chronicle,* and elsewhere, 9 October–4 June. Scrapbook 1, pp. 86–133.
1925–1926 Editorials. Haverhill High *Chronicle,* 9 October–18 June. Scrapbook 1, pp. 1–32.
1925–1926 "Book Corner." Haverhill High *Chronicle,* November–June. Scrapbook 1, pp. 39–82.
1926 "To Amy Lowell" (poem). Haverhill High *Chronicle,* 15 January.

1926 "Bootblack" (poem). *Scholastic*, 15 May, p. 10.

1926 "The Editor Says" (editorial). Haverhill High *Chronicle*, 3 December.

1926–1927 Poems. Haverhill High *Chronicle*, and elsewhere, February–May. Scrapbook 2, pp. 12–58.

1926–1929 "Barbara George" (poems).

1927 "And the Night Came Down" and "Dark Singing" (poems). *Gleam*, March, pp. 4–5.

1927 "Penance" and "Returning Moment" (poems). *Scholastic*, 30 April, p. 16.

1927 Sara Teasdale's *Dark of the Moon*, Joseph Auslander's *Cyclops' Eye*, and Amy Lowell's *East Wind* (book review). *Scholastic*, 30 April, p. 22.

1927 "Last Day by the Sea" (poem). 5 September.

1927 "Our Lady of Sorrows (A Painting by John Singer Sargent)" (poem). *Buffalo Arts Journal*, October.

COLLEGE WRITINGS

1928–1929 "The Book Corner," "The Bookstall," and "Speaking Off-hand" (book reviews and columns). *Brown Daily Herald*, 6 January–Spring. Scrapbook 6, pp. 1–141.

1928–1929 Parodies and humorous verse. *Brown Jug*, March–Fall. Scrapbook 5, pp. 15–77.

1928–1931 Poems and reviews. *Haverhill Gazette, Providence Journal*, and *Brown Daily Herald* (28 March 1928–2 June 1931). Scrapbook 2, pp. 79–129.

1928 "After Dreaming of One Dead (J.T.T.)" (poem). *Stratford Magazine*, February, p. 30.

1928 "Not Mauve, Not Lavender (for Sidney M. Chase's Picture: *Twilight*)" (poem). *Haverhill Gazette*, 6 April.

1928 "Hymning America" (book review). *Brown Literary Quarterly*, December, p. 11.

1928 (Arabab) "A Poet Lying Dead" (poem). *Brown Literary Quarterly*, December, pp. 12–13.

1929–1930 "The Bookstall," and "Speaking Offhand" (book reviews and columns). *Brown Daily Herald*, 22 October 1929–1930. Scrapbook 7, pp. 9–141.

1929 "Two Unusual Novels" (book review). *Brown Literary Quarterly*, February, p. 13.

1929 "Portrait of a Lady from Sweden (Greta Garbo)" (poem). *Brown Literary Quarterly*, April, p. 9.

1929 "Robert Frost" (essay). *Brown Literary Quarterly*, May, pp. 5–8.

1929 "Edwin Arlington Robinson" (essay). *Brown Literary Quarterly*, November, pp. 13–19.

1929 "To E. A. R. (At Peterborough, N.H., Aug. 22, 1929)" (poem). *Brown Literary Quarterly*, November, p. 12.

1930 "Footnote" and "To a Young Author" (poems). *Scholastic*, 4 January, p. 7.

1930 "The Last God" (poem). *Brown Literary Quarterly*, January, p. 27.

1930 "Amy Lowell" (essay). *Brown Literary Quarterly*, January, pp. 13–17.

1930 "Spring Came On Forever" (poem). *Brown Literary Quarterly*, March, pp. 11–16.

1930 "Edna St. Vincent Millay" (essay). *Brown Literary Quarterly*, May, pp. 17–22.

1930 "Evangelist" (poem). *Town and Gown: Arts and Letters in Rhode Island*. October, p. 11.

1931 "The Challenge to American Poetry" (essay). *Scholastic*, 3 January, pp. 4–5, 19.

1931 "King John" (poem). *Scholastic*, 3 January, p. 6.

1931 "Reluctant Interlude in a Dance Hall" (poem). *Folio*, December, p. 1.

Poems

1931 "Zion." *Smoke*, June.

1931 "The Living Corpse." *Smoke*, December.

1932 "The Searcher by the Way." *Stratford Magazine*, January, pp. 16–17.

1932 "This Was the Way." *Smoke*, March.

1932 "The Puppet-Master." *Smoke*, May.

1932 "The Enchanted Lady." *Poetry*, September, pp. 322–324.

1932 "The Agnostic before Stained Glass (to Charles J. Connick)." *Smoke*, October.

1933 "January Rain." *Scholastic*, 7 January, p. 6.

1933 "Nightmare," and "Where Ignorant Armies." *Scholastic*, 16 January, p. 11.

1933 "So You Will Remember." *Trend*, January–February–March, p. 135.

1933 "Pennies for an Old Cup." *Poetry*, April, pp. 11–13.

1934 "The Ultimate Bequest" and "Chant for the Grave." *Dust*, January.

1934 "The Necessity of Certainty" and "Low Sky." *Scholastic*, 24 February, pp. 3, 11.

1934 "Aztec Torso." *Tone*, March, p. 6.
1934 "Radio Broadcast: Hamlet (1934)." *Dust*, May.
1934 "Rockport Headland." *Provincetown*, May, p. 10.
1934 "King Canute's People." *Little Magazine*, May–June, p. 25.
1934 "Light of Morning." *Poetry*, June, pp. 131–133.
1934 "Vision before Midnight." *Provincetown*, June, p. 34.
1934 "Again toward Paradise." *American Poetry Journal*, August, pp. 18–19.
1934 "About Matter" and "Early Harvest." *Provincetown*, September, pp. 16–17.
1934 "Ten Miles Inland." *Little Magazine*, September–October, p. 2.
1934 "The Flowering Shadow." *Providence Journal*, 10 November, p. 10.
1935 "Balcony of Dust" and "Alternatives for My Clock." *Space*, January, p. 95.
1935 "The Way of Empire." *Scholastic*, 19 January, p. 11.
1935 "American Portrait." *Yankee Poetry Chapbook*, Winter, p. 5.
1935 "Biography for Traman," "Sunday Night," "He Remembers His Childhood (for Esther Wilbar)," "Paying: A Steeple," "Backdrop for this Particular Stage," and "Midway." *Poetry*, July, pp. 179–186.
1935 "Of Charity." *Smoke*, Summer.
1935 "For Certain Sectionalists." *New Republic*, 14 August, p. 15.
1936 "Finkelstein Faust." Unpublished. 14 pp.
1936 "Soliloquy." *Scholastic*, 18 January, p. 12.
1936 "Newburyport Gardenpiece." *Yankee*, July, pp. 24–25.
1936 "A Christmas Carol." *Signatures*, No. 2, Autumn, pp. 229–230.
1936 "See in the Dark." *Poems for a Dime*, 25 November.
1937 "Winter Arches." *Fantasy* 5, p. 10.
1937 "1620." *Smoke*, Winter.
1937 "The Mask of Nod." *Bozart-Westminster*, Spring, p. 18.
1937 "Newsreel." *New Masses*, 6 April, p. 14.
1937 "Now in Doom." *Prairie Schooner*, Summer, p. 120.
1937 "Blood and Seashell" and "At Least One Spring." *Poetry*, July, pp. 188–190.
1938 "Rory and the Snow" and "Rory Blaine's Return." *Fantasy* 6, pp. 15–16.
1938 "Those Autobiographical Blues." *Partisan Review*, February, pp. 16–17.
1938 "Tide Running" and "Letter." *Scholastic*, 26 February, p. 175.
1938 "Notes for a Future Ballet." *Poetry*, May, pp. 57–61.

1938 "Morning Song," "All Our Answers," "The Game," and "1925–1938." *Poetry*, December, pp. 124–126.
1939 "Glaze," "Piano," "Six Feet," and "Black Night Cone." *Fantasy* 6:2, pp. 3–4.
1939 "The Agate and the Shell." *Fantasy* 6:3, pp. 35–36.
1939 "Metal Shadow," "The Stake," and "The Menace." *Compass*, Summer, pp. 3–5.
194? "Prologue to a Portrait of an American City." Unpublished. 95 lines.
194? "Birth." Unpublished.
1940 "City Moon." *The New Yorker*, 20 January, p. 34.
1940 "Twenty-Ninth Winter," and "The House." *Compass*, February, pp. 17–18.
1942 "A 'Cave Sonnet' " and "A New Testament (See Henry Thoreau, Henry Beston, R. W. Emerson, and Frank Lloyd Wright)." *Fantasy* 7, p. 12.
1942 "Warehouse by Moonlight." *American Mercury*, September, p. 369.
1943 "Will the Stick that Props the Window Prop the House?" "Flight of Angels," and "Cold Hell." *Fantasy* 8, pp. 13–14.
1943 "The Dawn." Unpublished.
1944 "Ways of Looking at Death." *Contemporary Poetry*, Winter, p. 12.
1944 "What You Wanted to Ask." *Contemporary Poetry*, Autumn, p. 8.
1947 "A Letter to Schoolmates." *Brunonia*, February, p. 5.
1947 "Poem," and "Late Summer." *Contemporary Poetry*, Summer, p. 12.
1948 "Job Townsend and John Goddard." *Contemporary Poetry*, Winter, pp. 10–11.
1948 "Obit for Hart Crane." *Epoch*, Summer, p. 58.
1950 "Refusal of a Sort of Music," in *Contemporary Poetry* 10, p. 28. Ed. Mary Owings Miller.
1950 "The Point of View 1948–1920 (for G.Y.L.)." *Hopkins Review*, Spring, pp. 30–32.
1950 "Blue Sleigh," and "Numbered Summers." *Poetry*, April, pp. 16–17.
1951 "Pound Etc." *Experiment*, p. 5.
1951 "What I Assembled and Dissemble," and "Poem," *Epoch*, Summer, pp. 166–167.
1952 "The White Mask," "Requires Fresh Air," and "The Poet Becomes Meteorologist." *Experiment*, pp. 35–37.
1952 "All by Himself." *Epoch*, Summer, p. 249.
1953 "Biography at the Open Grave." Unpublished. 34 pp.

1953 "Postscript," and "Pencil Sketch." *Shenandoah*, Winter, pp. 56–57.

1954 "Old Pew Everywhere." *Interim*, p. 46.

1954 "The Man at Mid-Century," and "On Not Going to New Bedford." *California Quarterly*, pp. 10–11.

1954 "A Lick and a Promise" and "From Chirico to Charon." *Nucleus*, Winter, pp. 82, 108.

1954 "From A for Artist to Z for Zebra." Unpublished. 10 March.

1955 "Unsexed by the Cold Sea." *Discovery #5*, p. 84.

1955 "At Sea Remove." *Folio*, Spring, p. 16.

1955 "To Willa Cather." *Santa Fe New Mexican*, 10 April, p. 5.

1956 "Just Before the Hurricane." *New World Writing #9*, p. 110.

1956 "Questions for Us and Coronado," "Merrill's Brook," and "The Blue Tree." *Poetry*, February, pp. 268–270.

1956 "Celebrity," and "N.M." *Coastlines*, Spring, p. 22.

1956 "The Double Tree." *New Orleans Poetry Journal*, April, p. 19.

1956 "Alas!" *Saturday Review*, 7 July, p. 13.

1956 "Friday So Soon." *Saturday Review*, 4 August, p. 24.

1956 "Unfurnished Room." *New Republic*, 1 October, p. 18.

1956–1957 "Notes to a Gentleman I Once Met." *Colorado Review*, Winter, p. 41.

1957 "An Old Boy's Will (for Robert Frost)." *Beloit Poetry Journal Chapbook #5*, p. 43.

1957 "Two Contemporary Ways." *Arizona Quarterly*, Spring, p. 18.

1957 "The Owl in the Hall." Unpublished. 15 October.

1959 "The Fall." *Inscape No. 1*, pp. 12–13.

1959 "Traveling Weather," "The Room," and "Christmas Asparagus." *Fresco*, Spring, pp. 12–13.

1959 "N.Y. Summer Night." *Fresco*, Summer, p. 1.

1960 "Mum's the Word." *Chelsea Eight*, October, p. 31.

1962 "Amorous Out of Sleep," and "September." *Blue Grass*, p. 25.

1964 "My Wife Walking the Black Mesa." Unpublished. 25 March.

1965 "Questions Out of the Cellar." Unpublished. 22 September.

1966 "December Music." *Christmas Treasures* (Kansas City: Hallmark), pp. 78–79.

1966 "Into the Wind," "The Outcast," "Postscript," "Master of Arts," "To All Objectivists," "If All the Unplayed Pianos," and "Confidential." *Literary Cavalcade*, January, pp. 8–11.

1966 "Saint Lenin," "George and Emily and Others," and "Middle-Aged Poet." *University of Denver Quarterly*, Spring, pp. 107–109.

1966 "Marriage." Unpublished. 1 September.

1966 "Poem for a Birthday." Unpublished. 22 September.

1966–1967 "Black Bean Soup with Hotdogs and Hard-Boiled Eggs,"
"Ritual Dance," "There's Nobody Left . . . ," "In the Last Darkness," and "The Two-Faced Day." *Poetry Northwest*, Winter, pp.
3–7.
1967 "Ziggy, Our Squirrel Monkey." Unpublished. 30 January.
1967 "Incident in White and Green," "The Almost Perfect Lady,"
"Mistletoe," "On Going to Bed at the Same Time," "Year of
Drought," and "Film-Maker." *Poetry Bag*, Spring, pp. 21–23.
1967 "Radicals." Unpublished. 30 October.
1968 "Folly to the World," "Tender Star," and "Electric Silence (for
J.F.K.)." *Poems Southwest*. Ed. A. Wilbur Stevens (Prescott,
Ariz.: Prescott College Press), pp. 64–65.
1968 "There Was an English Poet" and "As I Took the Evening Air."
Religious Humanism, Spring, p. 52.

ESSAYS AND INTRODUCTIONS

1933 "Robinson Jeffers and the Theme of Failure." Unpublished. 12 pp.
1934 "Poetry in America": A New Consideration of Whittier's Verse."
New England Quarterly, June, pp. 258–275.
1935 "Amy Lowell after Ten Years." *New England Quarterly*, September, pp. 320–330.
1935 "Yankee Troubadour" (brief biographical portrait of Jonathan
Plummer). Unpublished. 15 pp.
1935 "Pianos in the Street." Unpublished.
1935 "Literature: North–North-East." Unpublished. 6 pp.
1937 "The Unaccredited Profession" (about E. A. Robinson). *Poetry*,
June, pp. 150–154.
1938 "A Frontispiece for Horace Gregory." *Direction*, May, pp. 4–7.
1939 "No Amusements of an Artificial Kind" (about trip to Scotland).
Unpublished. 14 pp.
1939 "The Brittle Street." Unfinished novel. 11 May–28 June, 88 pp.
1939 "The War Intellectualism: Two Views: I. The Dry Reaction."
Poetry, May, pp. 86–90.
1941 "Ernest Walsh: The Poet Against Despair." *Decision*, August, pp.
36–46.
1941 "Pegasus Hits the Street" (about "New Verse" column). *New
Republic*, 27 October, pp. 541–542.
1943 "New England's Newspaper World." *Saturday Review of Literature*, 22 May, pp. 19–21.
1944 "Jesse H. Metcalf" and "Something about Rhode Island." In
Jesse H. Metcalf, Citizen of Rhode Island, pp. 11–19. Providence.

1944 "The Haunter of the Dark: Some Notes on Howard Phillips Lovecraft." *Books at Brown*, March, pp. 1–4.

1944–1951 "Bookman's Galley." Columns in *Providence Sunday Journal*, 25 June–6 May.

1945 "Nationalism in Culture." In *The Challenge of the World Crisis*.
Middlebury, Vt.

1945 "Poetry . . . a Quarter Note." *Senior Scholastic*, 22 October, p. 25.

1946 "The Tower at Newport." *American-Scandinavian Review*, September, pp. 232–238.

1947 "In New England Can Be Found a Variety of Styles." *Chicago
Sun Book Week*, 20 July, p. 6.

1949 Foreword to "Howard Phillips Lovecraft as His Wife Remembers
Him," by Sonia Davis. *Books at Brown*, February, pp. 1–13.

1950 "Dear Jeff." In *Mid-Century American Poets*. (Precedes a selection of Scott's verse.) Edited by John Ciardi, pp. 107–109. New
York: Twayne.

1950 "Anne Parrish's Novels." *University of Kansas City Review*,
Autumn, pp. 52–58.

1950 "The Literary Summing-Up: A Personal Winnowing of 1950's
Books." *Saturday Review of Literature*, 30 December, pp. 6–8,
28–29.

1951 "Mr. Scott Looks Back Across 20 Years of Books." *Providence
Sunday Journal*, 6 May, pp. VI-1, VI-6.

1952 "Poet or Peasant?" *The American Writer*, December, pp. 5–7.

1953 "After a Certain Age One Wants to be Wary." (Precedes a selection of Scott's verse). *Beloit Poetry Journal Chapbook* #2, p. 25.

1953 "The Kings are Dead." *Saturday Review*, 21 March, pp. 19–20.

1953 "The Sitwells, a Three-Headed Basilisk." *Saturday Review*, 19
December, pp. 11–14.

1954 "The Death, and Some Dominions of It" (about Dylan Thomas).
Yale Literary Magazine, November, pp. 13–14.

1958 "Robert Hillyer: A Poet's First Forty Years." *Literary Review*,
Summer, pp. 431–440.

1959 "Has Anyone Seen a Trend?" *Saturday Review*, 3 January, pp.
12–14, 32.

1962 "Walden Pond in the Nuclear Age." *New York Times Magazine*,
6 May, pp. 34–35, 84, 86, 88, 90.

1964 "The Still Young Sunlight: Chimayo, New Mexico," in *A Vanish-
ing America: The Life and Times of the Small Town*. Edited by
Thomas C. Wheeler, pp. 122–135. New York: Holt, Rinehart, and
Winston.

1965 "Guaranteed Performance" (about Santa Fe Opera). *New Mexico Magazine*, April, pp. 14–18.

1965 Foreword to "15 Poems," by Lucile Adler. *Desert Review*, Spring, p. 1.

1966 Introduction to *The Man with the Calabash Pipe*, by Oliver H. P. La Farge. Edited by Winfield Townley Scott, pp. xi–xxi. Boston: Houghton Mifflin.

1966 Introduction to *Collected Stories*, by Jack Schaefer, pp. vii–xi. Boston: Houghton Mifflin.

1967 Preface to *Poems of Robert Herrick*. New York: Crowell. Pp. 1–11.

1967 "Dr. Williams: An Appreciation." St. John's College (Santa Fe) *Seven*, April–May, pp. 11–13.

1968 Afterword to *Judge Tenderly of Me: The Poems of Emily Dickinson*. Kansas City: Hallmark. Pp. 57–62.

1970 "A Pilgrimage to Amherst." *Emily Dickinson Bulletin*, December, pp. 88–91.

INDEX